FUNDAMENTALS of BUSINESS COMMUNICATION

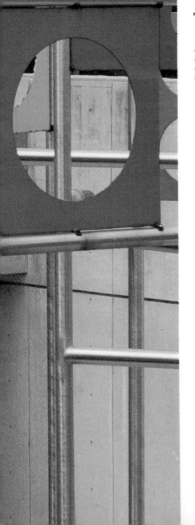

FUNDAMENTALS of BUSINESS COMMUNICATION

CAROL HENSON, Ed. D.
Clayton State College
Morrow, Georgia

THOMAS L. MEANS, Ed. D.
Louisiana Tech University
Ruston, Louisiana

E28
PUBLISHED BY
SOUTH-WESTERN PUBLISHING CO.
CINCINNATI   WEST CHICAGO, IL   CARROLLTON, TX   LIVERMORE, CA

Employers of our postsecondary graduates tell us that communication is one of the top skills they look for in a job applicant. Many students lack certain communication skills that will make them competitive in the job market. The goal of *Fundamentals of Business Communication* is to help students in one- and two-year postsecondary programs improve their skills so that they can communicate effectively in the workplace.

ORGANIZATION

Fundamentals of Business Communication contains 28 chapters organized into 7 parts: Part 1 introduces the importance and purposes of business communication and the role electronic communication plays in today's offices. Part 2 and Part 3 provide an intensive review of the rules governing written communication. This review is included to meet the needs of schools that find it difficult to offer a separate grammar course. Part 4 introduces students to the five C's of effective business writing: courtesy, consideration, conciseness, clarity, and completeness. Students then are shown how to plan, organize, and edit messages.

Part 5 presents specific methods for developing effective routine, good news, bad news, and persuasive letters and memos as well as reports. Students will plan, organize, and compose applying the simple concepts of direct and indirect structure to most of the documents they create.

Part 6 covers nonverbal communication, listening, and oral communication. Students will learn to apply the concepts of nonverbal communication and listening as they plan, organize, and deliver short oral presentations. Part 7 wraps up the text with comprehensive, up-to-date instructions on career communication, including the resume, letter of application, application form, job interview, and follow-up messages.

FEATURES

Fundamentals of Business Communication includes these features:

Chapter Objectives.   Each chapter begins with a list of objectives.

Visual Aids.   A variety of photographs, illustrations, examples, and documents are used to assist learning. Key terms are highlighted.

Checkpoints.   Throughout most chapters, checkpoints are provided so that students can determine whether they understand the material being presented; an appendix provides answers to the checkpoints.

Chapter Summary.   The main points within each chapter are summarized to reinforce the material presented.

End-of-Chapter Activities.   The following activities may be used in class or assigned as homework:

- *Discussion Questions* except for Parts 2 and 3.
- *Practical Applications* that reinforce the content and instruction presented within each chapter.
- *Editing Applications* that apply the grammar and English mechanics presented in Parts 2 and 3. A group of commonly misspelled and misused words are built into the business documents that students edit.

Appendices.   The text contains four appendices. Appendix A reviews the commonly misspelled and misused words applied in Parts 2 and 3. Appendix B illustrates the commonly used proofreaders' marks. Appendix C contains a glossary of terms that have been highlighted throughout the text, and Appendix D provides the solutions to the chapter checkpoints.

Instructional Supplements.   An instructor's manual and a computerized test bank are available to assist the instructor. The comprehensive in-

structor's manual contains the following items: chapter objectives; instructor's outline and teaching aids for each chapter; supplemental editing applications for Parts 2 and 3; pretests for Parts 2 and 3; chapter quizzes and unit tests on MicroSWAT II software; transparency masters; and solutions to all communication activities within the text and the supplemental editing applications, quizzes, and tests found in the manual.

MicroSWAT II is a computerized version of the unit tests found in the instructor's manual. It is available for the IBM computer. Instructors may generate tests from the test bank by selecting specific questions, adding their own questions, or letting the computer select questions randomly.

ACKNOWLEDGMENTS

We wish to extend our appreciation to all those who helped us create this book. We are particularly grateful to the following educators who reviewed the manuscript and offered helpful suggestions for improvement:

Dr. Vanessa Arnold, The University of Mississippi, University, Mississippi
Paige P. Baker, Trinity Valley Community College, Athens, Texas
Janice Brown, Athens Area Vocational-Technical College, Athens, Georgia
Richard R. Williams, Grayson County College, Denison, Texas
Dr. Andrea Wise, Georgia College, Milledgeville, Georgia

CAROL W. HENSON and THOMAS L. MEANS

CONTENTS

Contents

Contents

Contents

Communication Concepts

PART 1

Communication is an important part of a person's personal life and professional life. Communication takes place any time ideas are exchanged between people. Effective communication takes place when the person receiving the message understands what the person sending the message meant to convey.

Chapter 1 explores the nature of communication, the communication process, and the forms of business communication. People spend about two-thirds of any given day communicating with others. Communication skills, therefore, are important if we are to be effective communicators.

Chapter 2 introduces various technologies used in business to send messages efficiently and fast. During the five stages of the document cycle, electronic communication can both speed up the transmission of messages and reduce costs for business. Electronic communication includes a variety of equipment and technologies, such as computers, electronic mail, facsimile, and optical disk storage.

CHAPTER 1

Understanding Business Communication

Objectives

After studying this chapter and completing the chapter exercises, you should understand:

1. The nature of communication.
2. The communication process.
3. The forms of business communication.

When was the last time you communicated? Do you communicate frequently? When you watch the news on television, shake your head at something you disagree with, or talk with a friend, you are communicating. Each morning as you choose your clothes you are making choices that involve communication. Your posture, facial expressions, and tone of voice communicate your perception of yourself. Although you may not realize it, you are communicating your desire to improve your ability to write, read, listen, and speak as you read this text and participate in class.

Communication is part of both your personal life and your professional life. In this course, however, you will be primarily concerned with business communication. By understanding what business communication is and the different forms it takes, you will obtain better results from the messages you send.

WHAT IS BUSINESS COMMUNICATION?

Every day in the business environment information is shared, ideas are explored, and attitudes are revealed. The process used to send and interpret messages so that they are understood is called **communication**. When this process occurs within the business environment, it is called business communication.

The communication process is successful only to the extent that *meaning* has been conveyed from the sender to the receiver. Have you ever discussed a situation with another person in great detail only to realize that the other person has not understood what you were trying to say? Have you and a friend ever written many letters back and forth without expressing your real feelings? Although we may talk for hours or exchange many letters, communication does not occur unless the receiver attaches the same meaning to the message as the sender intended.

Communication is successful when:

1. The receiver interprets the message as the sender intended it.
2. It achieves the sender's purposes.

Communication that achieves these two objectives is referred to as **effective communication.** For example, if a supervisor outlines the steps for properly formatting correspondence to a document specialist and he or she follows those procedures, effective communication has occurred. To become an effective communicator, you must be aware of the importance and purposes of communication.

The Importance of Communication

Adults spend about two thirds of their day communicating. Responding to friends, maintaining relationships with co-workers and supervisors, interpreting messages, and persuading customers are all ways we interact with others. Studies indicate that managers spend over 50 percent of their time attending meetings, making phone calls, writing, and traveling. Every day we interact with other people in order to meet our personal and professional goals.

To meet our goals, we depend upon our communication skills. These skills include the ability to use language grammatically, with good word choice and correct spelling; they include the ability to speak, teach, counsel, debate, and listen. Our success within any organization will depend on our ability to use these communication skills.

A coach who can successfully communicate the importance of an upcoming game is more likely to have a winning team than a coach who cannot. A person who can tactfully reject a request is more likely to retain goodwill than a person who cannot. A manager whose instructions are accurate and timely will be successful at motivating employees to do their best. An executive who keeps the channels of communication open with subordinates is likely to have a loyal and contented staff.

The Purposes of Communication

Even though we spend a great deal of our time sending and receiving information, communication has only five basic purposes:

1. *To establish and build goodwill.* In order to work effectively with others, we must be able to recognize and understand their feelings, attitudes, and motives. Our ability to establish and build good relationships with co-workers, clients, and customers has a major effect on our professional development and advancement. Good relationships result in **goodwill**, or the favorable reputation that a business has with its customers. Goodwill must exist before the other purposes of communication can be achieved.

2. *To influence the actions of others.* The ability to motivate or persuade others to act in a certain way depends on our ability to convince them that they will benefit from such action.

3. *To obtain or share information.* Information is one of the most valuable resources of an organization. Obtaining, using, and sharing information in an appropriate manner is critical to the success of an organization.

4. *To establish personal effectiveness.* When we receive a communication that is accurate, easy to understand, and error free, we form a positive image of the person who sent it. We are likely to see the sender as attentive to detail, intelligent, and concerned about others—a good person to do business with. On the other hand, a message with numerous errors suggests carelessness, lack of intelligence, or thoughtlessness. As senders, we are constantly being evaluated based on our ability to communicate.

5. *To build self-esteem.* Positive comments and reactions from others that result from effective communication build our confidence. As a result, we feel good about ourselves and continue to be successful.

THE COMMUNICATION PROCESS

Before the communication process begins, an idea must be created or developed by the sender. Once the idea is developed, various components are involved in transferring that idea from one person to another in order for it to be acted upon. The communication process involves (1) the sender, (2) the message, (3) the receiver, (4) the feedback, and (5) a channel.

The following example illustrates how the components of the communication process function:

> Terri went to an automatic teller machine (ATC) to withdraw some money. She sent a message to the machine that enabled her to withdraw $20 from her checking account. The machine responded by sending her $20 and a receipt giving details of the transaction.

In this communication, Terri is the sender. The message is "Terri wants to withdraw $20 from her checking account." The receiver is the teller machine. The feedback is the $20 and the receipt, and the channel is the ATC.

The communication process is generally interpersonal (between persons). However, it may occur between a person and a machine such as a computer, or it may occur between two machines. Machines such as computers, printers, or facsimile devices, for example, can exchange information. Electronic communication will be discussed in Chapter 2. As you study the communication process, refer to the communication model, Figure 1-1, to learn how each element impacts on the communication process.

The Sender

The **sender** originates the message or initiates the communication process. The sender has the primary responsibility for conveying the message

FIGURE 1-1   **The main components of the communication process are included in the model.**

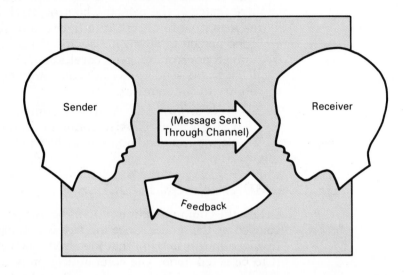

accurately, completely, and in a manner that can be easily understood. If the sender fulfills this responsibility, the receiver is likely to interpret the message as the sender intended. The better the sender understands how the receiver thinks and feels, the easier it will be to construct an effective message. By applying what is known about the receiver, the sender can anticipate the receiver's response.

The Message

The **message** is simply a set of symbols that represent meaning. The message can be composed of either verbal or nonverbal symbols or both. **Verbal symbols** are words used when speaking or writing. Letters, memos, reports, brochures, catalogs, manuals, and annual reports are composed of verbal symbols. Verbal symbols are also used when speaking face-to-face or on the telephone, participating in a conference or meeting, or delivering a speech.

Nonverbal symbols such as gestures, posture, facial expression, appearance, time, tone of voice, eye contact, and space usually accompany verbal symbols. Nonverbal symbols help to convey attitudes. An executive who stands and extends her hand when a visitor enters her office conveys a nonverbal message of respect for the visitor. If the visitor is dressed appropriately, the feeling of respect is confirmed. Similarly, the visitor will form an opinion of the executive's status based on the size, location, and furnishings of the executive's office. In this situation, the executive's environment is a nonverbal symbol.

Nonverbal symbols also help the receiver interpret the verbal symbols. For example, a salesperson's prompt response to a customer's complaint is a nonverbal indication that the customer is important to the business. If the verbal and nonverbal symbols conflict, receivers generally attach more importance to the nonverbal symbols than to the verbal symbols. For example, if the salesperson keeps the customer waiting too long or acts in a condescending manner, the customer may indeed decide not to do further business with the company, even though the complaint may have been settled satisfactorily.

The Receiver

The person or machine to whom the message is sent is the **receiver**. The responsibility of the receiver is to give meaning to the verbal and nonverbal symbols used by the sender. The meaning the receiver attaches to the message depends upon the receiver's education, experiences, interests, opinions, and emotional state. Miscommunication results if the receiver gives the message a different meaning from that intended by the sender.

Feedback

Feedback is the response the receiver gives to the message. Feedback may be nonverbal—a smile, a frown, a smirk, a glare, a calculated pause, a blank stare; or feedback may be verbal—a telephone call or a letter. Lack of response is also a form of feedback. For example, suppose someone greets you, but because you did not hear the person, you do not respond. Even though you did not return the greeting, you did communicate. Your message to the sender was that you were not going to respond. Miscommunication of this sort is common and illustrates how difficult accurate communication can be.

Feedback is a critical component of the communication process because it helps the sender determine if the receiver has understood the message. Feedback enables the receiver to clarify the message or to provide additional information to modify the message if necessary.

To be meaningful, feedback must accurately reflect the receiver's reaction to the message. This means that the receiver must respond honestly, even if that means providing negative feedback. For example, a member of a planning committee who strongly disagrees with a proposal made by another member must make his or her feelings known. Not to do so would hamper the effectiveness of the committee's work.

The Channel

The means the sender selects to send the message is known as a **channel**. Letters, memorandums, and reports are the most common channels for written messages. Face-to-face discussions, telephone conversations, and meetings are common oral channels of communication.

Sometimes the sender selects a channel almost automatically. For example, an employee who receives a promotion may want to share this good news immediately with a spouse or a good friend. Without hesitation, the employee would telephone the message.

Channel selection becomes increasingly significant as the importance or sensitivity of the message increases. When trying to resolve a sensitive issue with a customer, for example, a manager must carefully weigh the merits of communicating by phone or by letter. Using the telephone indicates a sense of urgency and allows immediate feedback; on the other hand, a letter enables the sender to explain a position and provides a record of the message for further review. Often using both channels is appropriate—the manager might discuss the situation over the telephone and then follow up with a letter.

Communication Barriers

Although one of the primary goals of communication is for the receiver to interpret the message as the sender intended, frequently this goal is not achieved. Differences within the sender or receiver and factors external to them interfere with or interrupt the communication process, as shown in Figure 1-2. These factors are called **communication barriers.** Learning to recognize these barriers will help you plan your messages and become a more effective communicator.

External Barriers

Conditions that exist outside the receiver and that detract from the communication process are called **external barriers.** Examples include environmental factors such as heat, humidity, lighting, comfort, and noise. Imagine that two of your friends are standing nearby talking while an associate is giving you instructions for your next task. The conversation

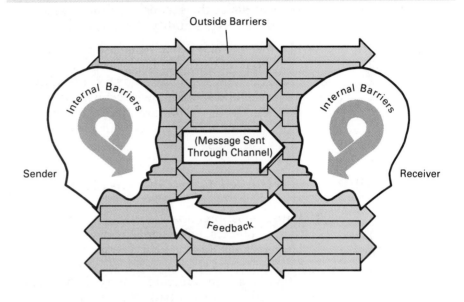

of your friends, an external barrier, would interfere with your receiving the instructions.

In a similar way, the appearance of a written document may be a barrier to communication. A document that is smudged, contains errors in content, spelling, or grammar, or is presented in an inappropriate format sends a nonverbal message that the sender didn't care enough about the communication to prepare it properly. As a result, the message is not likely to be successful.

Another barrier to communication within an organization is an autocratic climate in which policies are made and implemented by edict. Conversely, an open climate in which information flows easily and supervisors and managers are receptive to ideas from subordinates facilitates communication. Most managers in progressive organizations realize the importance of maintaining open communication. They know that being sensitive to employees' attitudes and ideas encourages creativity and growth.

Internal Barriers

No two persons are the same. We differ in our personalities, education, experiences, culture, status, and biases. These factors are **internal barriers** that affect the sender's willingness and ability to express messages and the receiver's ability to interpret messages.

In a meeting of a department's supervisors and vice president, a supervisor who is an extrovert is more apt to express ideas and feelings than an introvert. New employees may feel intimidated by employees who are experienced and more knowledgeable. On the other hand, employees with the same status (rank) are likely to find it easier to converse with each other than with someone of a higher or lower status.

FORMS OF COMMUNICATION WITHIN ORGANIZATIONS

Within most organizations there are various levels of employees: executives or officers, middle managers, professionals such as accountants and lawyers, and office support personnel who may have such titles as administrative assistant, secretary, receptionist, or document specialist. These employees communicate among themselves (internal communication) and with persons outside their organization (external communication) both informally and formally. Messages may be in written, oral, or electronic form.

External and Internal Communication

External communication originates within a company and is sent to receivers outside the company. Communication to clients, customers, sales representatives, governmental agencies, advertising agencies, and transportation agencies is external. The primary responsibility of the sales department, purchasing department, and advertising department is external communication.

Internal communication originates within a company and is sent to receivers within the company. For example, a memo from a supervisor to an employee is an internal communication. Human resources and accounting departments typically communicate internally.

Formal and Informal Communication

Formal communication within an organization is that which occurs through established lines of authority. As Figure 1-3 demonstrates, communication may travel down, across, or up those lines of authority.

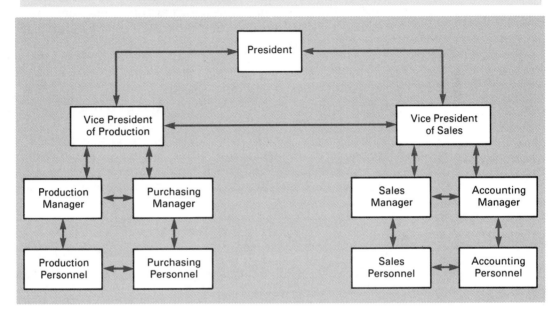

FIGURE 1-3 **Messages travel in various directions within the lines of formal communication.**

Communication that travels from a superior (supervisor, manager, executive) to subordinates is *downward communication.* Instructions from a supervisor to subordinates travel downward. Policies established by the board of directors and company officers are relayed downward to department managers and then to other employees. Communication between peers or persons of the same status level is called *lateral communication.* A memo from one department head to another is an example of lateral communication. If organizations are to succeed and be profitable, departments must work together and coordinate their activities; therefore, lateral communication is important.

Upward communication refers to communication from subordinates to superiors. When employees convey their suggestions for improving production, their attitudes and feelings toward their jobs, and their perception of the organization to their supervisors, they are communicating upward. Likewise, managers' recommendations to company officers are upward communication. The success of an organization is often determined by how well the formal lines of communication work.

Informal communication within an organization is unrelated to established lines of authority. Informal communication may be written or oral. Sharing interests over lunch or during breaks and socializing after work hours are examples of informal communication. Often referred to as the *grapevine*, informal communication can be a rapid channel of communication, but not always an accurate channel. Much misinformation travels through the grapevine. Nevertheless, use of the grapevine can be an effective management tool. For example, assume that an organization has improved its employee insurance package. Management, however, is concerned that employees will be skeptical of the new package because people are often suspicious of change. To help ensure a positive reception of the package, management could use the grapevine to leak the news of the package and some of its beneficial changes. Then when the new insurance package is formally announced, employees would already be somewhat familiar with it and more likely to be receptive to the change.

Written, Oral, and Electronic Communication

Business communication can also be classified as written, oral, or electronic. Each of these forms of messages has certain characteristics that make it appropriate in various situations.

Written Communication

Letters, memorandums, and reports are common forms of written business communication. Each form is used in specific situations. **Letters** are external documents that may be addressed to business associates, customers, and clients. As a form of external communication, letters act as ambassadors for the business. Thus they are printed on high-quality stationery and revised until their appearance and content are perfect.

Memorandums, often simply called memos, are internal documents used to communicate with one or more co-workers. Memos are less formal than letters. However, memos should be prepared with care because other associates or supervisors judge employees by the quality of their communication.

Reports are designed to provide meaningful information to a group of people. They may be formal documents such as research studies or proposals to top management or informal documents such as memo reports. Minutes of meetings, agendas, speeches, brochures, business directories, legal documents, office manuals, and announcements are other forms of written communication used in business.

Written communication is widely used in business for three reasons. First, it provides a record that information has been exchanged. For example, the price quoted in a written bid cannot be disputed at a later time. Agreements that are recorded in a letter are evidence that may be used in court. Second, written communication can be revised until the final message is logical and clear. This factor is especially important when complex information must be explained. Third, written messages enable the reader to analyze the communication and refer to it as many times as necessary. For example, procedures outlined in a memo from a manager to subordinates can be revised by the writer until they are complete and easy to understand. Conversely, subordinates can study these procedures and refer to them as needed.

Oral Communication

A great deal of communication within organizations is conducted in face-to-face meetings and over the telephone. Generally oral communication is quick to send and provides immediate feedback to the sender. Oral communication is advantageous when seeking opinions, explaining procedures, counseling, and building relationships. The nonverbal symbols that accompany the verbal messages may help to develop personal relationships and attitudes within the organization.

Electronic Communication

Both written and oral communication may originate by traditional methods. Letters and memos are dictated or handwritten and distributed by postal service or intracompany (within the company) mail. Business people communicate by telephone and travel to business meetings away from the office. Increasingly, however, both written and oral messages are originated and distributed by electronic means.

Written messages may be composed, edited, and transmitted on a computer, or an exact copy of a message may be transmitted by a facsimile receiver. Such written electronic messages are forms of **electronic mail.** Likewise, oral messages may be sent over the telephone but stored electronically in a computer for later playback. Such oral electronic messages are a form of **voice mail.** Electronic and voice mail will be discussed in greater detail in Chapter 2.

SUMMARY

Communication is the process used to exchange ideas. The components of the process include the sender, the message, the receiver, the feedback, and a channel. Though this process seems simple, barriers to effective communication complicate the process. Barriers that originate outside the sender or the receiver are external; those that originate within the sender or the receiver are internal.

Communication enables us to attain our personal and professional goals. These goals are as follows: (1) to establish and build goodwill, (2) to influence the actions of others, (3) to obtain or share information, (4) to establish personal effectiveness, and (5) to build self-esteem.

Communication within an organization is in various forms: external and internal; formal and informal; written, oral, or electronic. Each of these forms is appropriate in certain situations and critical to the successful operation of a business.

● ● ● ● ● ● ● ● ● Communication Activities

Discussion Questions

1. Do you agree with the statement "Everything we do results in communication"? Why or why not?
2. "Because we are always sending and receiving messages, we have a great deal of experience communicating. This experience makes it easy for us to communicate effectively." Do you agree or disagree with this reasoning? Why?
3. Why is it important for the business person to have good communication skills? What is the result if a person has poor communication skills?
4. Explain the function of each of the five parts of the communication process.
5. What types of symbols are used when communicating?
6. Referring to Figure 1-1, explain how the model works. Is one element of the model more important than the others? Why or why not?
7. Indicate whether each of the following symbols is verbal or nonverbal.
   a. A grunt accompanying a message
   b. The words that make up the message
   c. An icy stare
   d. A copy of the book *Seven Days in May*
   e. A cheer at a football game

8. What effect do barriers have on the communication process? Explain the differences between external and internal barriers.

9. Referring to the organization chart (Figure 1-3) as necessary, put each of the following messages into the appropriate categories:

>Downward, upward, or lateral
>Internal or external
>Oral or written

   a. Lunchtime conversation between an employee and the supervisor about opening day at the stadium.
   b. Memo from the vice president of sales of Company A to an executive officer of Company B.
   c. Presentation to employees by the vice president of production.
   d. Letter containing a proposal from the vice president of sales of Company A to the vice president of sales of Company B.
   e. Memo from an employee to the supervisor informing the supervisor that the employee will be taking a personal day next Wednesday.

10. Identify and describe the forms of communication present within an organization.

CHAPTER 2

Electronic Communication

Objectives

After studying this chapter and completing the chapter exercises, you should be able to:

1. Name and define the five stages of the document cycle.
2. Identify technologies, equipment, and software used in electronic communication.

Office technology has had a tremendous impact on the way messages are sent and received. You have probably heard of word processing, micro-computers, and electronic mail; these are just some of the technologies used in today's electronic office. Communication can now travel much faster and more efficiently because of these new technologies.

First, let's look at some terms commonly used in the automated office. **Information processing** is the broad term used to describe the movement of information from origination to storage. The information may be in the form of text (words) or numerical data, images such as photos or graphics, or voice. *Word processing* refers to equipment or software that automates the tasks related to the production of text documents. Because text can be integrated with numbers and images, the term *word/information processing* describes the process more accurately than word processing does.

THE DOCUMENT CYCLE

The **document cycle** is the flow of the document from the time it is created until it is distributed or stored. Whether processed in the traditional manner or with the latest technologies, all documents pass through five major stages in the document cycle. At each stage in the cycle, various technologies have improved the quality and speed of communication. Let's trace the path of a document such as a letter traveling through the traditional office.

To create a letter, the originator (author or writer) gathers ideas and information and probably writes a draft copy. This first stage of the document cycle, the point at which ideas are created, is called the **origination stage.** The second stage, known as the **production stage,** involves preparing the letter in final written form. The draft copy is keyed on a typewriter one or more times, depending on whether changes were required.

Once the letter is produced, copies for other people or for the files may need to be made—generally photocopies or perhaps carbon copies. Making copies is known as the **reproduction stage.** At the **distribution/ transmission stage,** the letter is sent to its destination, perhaps by mailing it to the intended receiver. Finally, a copy of the letter is filed so that it can be retrieved at a later time for reference or for further distribution. This last stage is known as **storage/retrieval.**

Whether a message is processed in the traditional way just described or using the latest tools of the automated office, the message would still move through these five stages. To be most effective in communicating your messages, you must take advantage of the new technologies discussed in this chapter. We will look at these technologies and discuss how they can benefit you at each stage of the document cycle.

ORIGINATION

Although documents originate in the sender's mind, many different tools are available to get thoughts into the document cycle. The traditional method, writing in longhand or shorthand, is still commonly used, but it is slow. Keyboarding, machine dictation, scanners, and voice recognition provide more efficient means for originating documents.

Keyboarding

Today most managers have access to a computer keyboard, and increasingly they are using it to create all or a portion of their documents. For example, managers or executives may use their computer to access information from various files, merge it, and compose a report. Sales representatives attending a business seminar may compose a report on their portable or laptop computer and transmit the document electronically to the office.

Documents can be created efficiently on a keyboard if the originator has basic keyboarding skills. Generally documents created by managers at the keyboard are edited and printed by document specialists who are experts at editing, formatting, and printing.

Machine Dictation

Machine dictation is an efficient means for originating letters, memos, and short reports, and it offers many advantages over longhand and shorthand. Compared to longhand, machine dictation is faster and therefore less costly. Unlike shorthand, machine dictation requires only one person's time—the originator's. While the originator is dictating, the secretary can be attending to other duties. In addition, the originator can dictate at a time and place that is convenient.

With machine dictation the originator speaks into a microphone or telephone, and the message is recorded onto a magnetic medium. The transcriber, wearing headphones, listens to the recording and keys the message to produce a final copy. Various types of dictation equipment can be purchased: desktop units, portable units, and centralized systems.

Each enables the originator to record the document, provide instructions to the transcriber, listen to what has been recorded, and make corrections.

Types of Equipment

Dictation equipment is often categorized by its location and the manner in which it is used. The typical classifications are desktop, portable, and centralized.

Desktop equipment, as its name implies, is placed on an individual's desk. It is ideal for persons who dictate frequently from one location. Generally the recorder includes a hand-held microphone and records onto cassette tapes. Tapes are available in four sizes: standard cassettes, minicassettes, microcassettes, and picocassettes.

Some desktop units, such as the one shown in Figure 2-2, are flexible communication tools that combine many features in one machine. These multifunctional devices consolidate the functions of a dictation machine,

telephone, conference recorder, answering machine, calculator, and clock.
Often these units offer helpful telephone features such as automatic
redial, an electronic telephone directory that stores about 100 numbers,
automatic speed dialing, and a speakerphone.

Portable units are hand-held devices ideal for the traveling executive.
They are small enough to carry in a pocket or briefcase and generally
include most of the features of desktop units. Portable units include
both a recorder and a microphone; most record on microcassettes or
picocassettes.

Centralized systems are used for heavy dictation requirements. The
recorders are grouped in a central location for the transcriber's use, and
the dictation units are placed on workstations throughout the organization for use by the dictators. The dictation unit may be either a hand-
held microphone that resembles a telephone receiver or an actual
telephone. The dictation units are connected by wire to the recorders. An
optional control console may be purchased for managing the work flow
in a centralized environment. The console identifies the status of each
job, those presently dictating, the backlog, and the turnaround time.

Many centralized systems record dictation on magnetic media such
as cassettes. The latest innovation in centralized systems, however, is

digital dictation. Sound is converted to binary digits (on/off signals) and stored on a hard disk similar to that of a computer. (See Figure 2-4.) Digital dictation offers many advantages. Instructions can be inserted easily. Deletions can be made without creating a long pause in the dictation. Locating documents on a hard disk is as quick and easy as it is on a computer.

Dictation Skills

Many people avoid machine dictation because they do not have dictation skills. These skills, however, can be developed through appropriate procedures and through practice.

When preparing to dictate, gather all reference materials, including previous correspondence relating to the document you are planning to dictate. Prepare an outline by marking the document you are responding to or by jotting thoughts down on a separate sheet of paper.

When you begin to dictate, identify yourself, your position, and your department or division, if necessary. Identify the format of the message (letter, memo, report) and indicate whether you need a draft or a final copy.

Specify the type of paper, number of copies, enclosures, priority, mailing procedures, and other needed information.

As you dictate, pronounce words clearly and distinctly. Avoid gum chewing, eating, smoking, or other distractions. Use a natural tone of voice. Spell out names, technical terms, and any words that might confuse the transcriber. Provide punctuation if there might be a question about it. Specify capitalization, underscoring, paragraphs, and columns or indentions. Through continued use, dictation skills will develop to the point that the dictator feels comfortable with this method.

Scanners

Scanners can convert typewritten text (and often typeset text) into digital form that can be read by another electronic workstation such as a computer or word processor. For example, updating a typewritten manual would be relatively easy using a scanner. The scanner would read the typed pages and record them in digital form on a disk. The word processing operator would then call the manual to the screen and key only the revisions.

Generally, scanners read documents and record their contents onto a magnetic medium. Some scanners, however, interact directly with various word processing programs; as text is scanned, it appears on the display in the correct format. Image scanners can read graphs, charts, or photographs. Once scanned, these images can be integrated into text documents. Images are, however, harder to edit than text. Desktop publishing, which is described later, is increasing the need for image scanners.

FIGURE 2-5 **Image scanners convert images as well as printed text into a form that can be read by computers.**

Voice Recognition

Voice recognition is a technology that enables the originator to speak into a microphone or headset and have the words reproduced on a computer screen. A processor converts the voice sounds into digital impulses that are then compared with sound patterns recorded in the computer's memory. If the two match, the spoken words will be displayed on the computer screen. Voice recognition technology is not yet able to record continuous speech because of the multitudes of different speech patterns that must be recognized by the equipment. Voice input is definitely a technology on the horizon.

PRODUCTION

Document production includes all of the steps necessary to convert the draft document into final form. Production generally includes keying, proofreading, printing, and often revising the document. In the traditional office, document production was done on an electric typewriter. Today's electronic workstations and software make the process much easier.

Electronic Workstations

An electronic workstation consists of a keyboard, a monitor or display screen, a printer, the logic or central processing unit, and a storage device. The **keyboard** contains the traditional alphabetic and numeric keys and additional keys that perform various functions such as formatting or editing. The **screen** or monitor displays the document as it is keyed, and the **printer** produces the final copy.

The **logic** or **central processing unit (CPU)** consists of electronic computer chips that control the operating functions of the workstation. These microprocessors work with the software (programmed instructions) to process text, perform mathematical calculations, sort information, and so forth. As information is keyed, it is recorded on a **storage device.** The storage device may either be internal (internal memory chips or hard disk) or external (floppy disks).

The arrangement and sophistication of these parts depend upon the workstation. Electronic typewriters, word processors, and computers are the electronic workstations most commonly used to produce documents in today's offices.

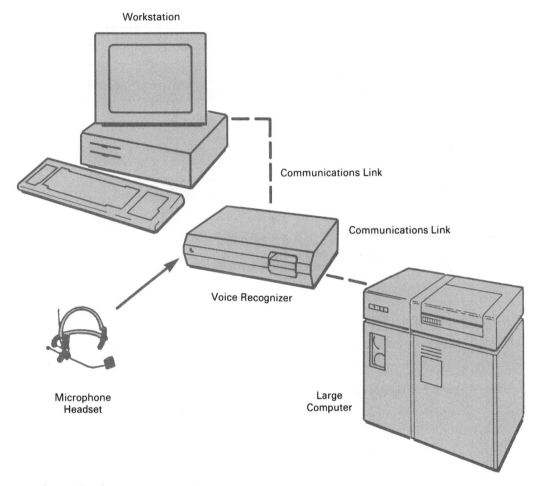

Workstation

Communications Link

Communications Link

Voice Recognizer

Microphone
Headset

Large
Computer

Electronic Typewriters

Electronic typewriters, often called ETs, look much like electric type-writers, but they have many more time-saving features. These features include automatic centering, simultaneous underscoring, and rapid error correction. ETs have an internal memory that may range from a few lines to over 100 pages. Most ETs have at least a one-line display for error correction.

The basic models of ETs may be upgraded to include a larger display screen and a disk drive that provides for removable storage. Some ETs

FIGURE 2-7 Electronic typewriters automate many formatting functions and often have the capability to store a limited number of documents.

may be connected to a computer to act as a printing device. Electronic typewriters produce print comparable to that of a typewriter. They are suitable for producing short documents such as letters and memos, forms, and envelopes.

Word Processors

Unlike ETs, word processors consist of separate units. They have a separate keyboard, display screen, printer, and processor. Word processors that perform only word processing functions are called dedicated word processors. Some word processors perform other functions through the use of software. Although dedicated word processors are still being used, the trend is toward using workstations that can handle more than one application.

Computers

Computers range in size and power from a large supercomputer to a small laptop computer that can fit in a briefcase. The most pervasive workstation in today's office, however, is the personal computer (PC) or microcomputer. The personal computer has made office technology more accessible to workers at all levels and less expensive. The personal com-

puter is popular because it can handle many different applications with a simple change in software.

The keyboard of a personal computer is designed with **function keys,** such as F1 and F2, which carry out different functions depending upon the software being used. In addition, the CTRL key, SHIFT key, and ALT key, when used with a function key or a regular key, enable additional commands to be given.

Applications Software

Applications software provides instruction to the computer on how to carry out particular functions. Applications software is purchased separately from the computer. It is stored on a disk and loaded into the computer's memory. Once the software is loaded, it interacts with the logic of the computer to perform the desired operations. Word processing is the most popular applications software. Spreadsheets, database management, graphics, and desktop publishing are examples of other leading applications software in wide use today.

Word Processing

Similar to word processing equipment, word processing software enables text to be entered, formatted, revised, and printed efficiently. Among the best-selling commercial software packages are WordPerfect, MicroSoft Word, MultiMate, and DisplayWrite.™ Table 2-1 lists many of the word processing features common to both word processing equipment and word processing software.

Spreadsheets

A spreadsheet is an electronic worksheet consisting of rows and columns. Rows are read across a spreadsheet and columns are read down. The point at which a column and row meet is called a cell. Spreadsheet software is used for tasks that were previously performed with pencil and paper and a calculator.

Words, figures, or formulas may be entered in a spreadsheet. Labels are assigned to each row and column to make the items meaningful. Figures are entered within cells to represent values for various items. Formulas are entered within cells to add, subtract, multiply, or divide the various figures. By using formulas, a user could change one figure in the spreadsheet and the rest of the figures would be updated automatically. For example, if you were preparing a budget on a spreadsheet and a figure such as the amount spent on supplies changed, use of formulas would update all figures affected by the change in the value of the supplies.

In addition to keeping records of expenses, inventories, and payrolls, spreadsheets are used for analyzing data and making predictions (forecasting). Testing "What if" assumptions used in forecasting is one of the most popular uses of spreadsheets. The user is asking, "If I change this amount, how will it affect the results?" Whether analyzing data or forecasting, the user is able to make better-informed decisions through the use of a spreadsheet. Popular spreadsheet packages are Lotus 1-2-3, MultiPlan, and SuperCalc.

Database Management

Database management software provides a way to store and retrieve information electronically on the computer. This information was previously stored on paper and retrieved from file cabinets or other paper sources.

Database software works very much like a commonly used database — the telephone directory. When you use a telephone directory, you look up

TABLE 2-1   Word Processing Features

Keying Features

Word Wrap	Enables a word that will not fit at the end of a line to automatically carry over ("wrap") to the next line without depressing the RETURN key.
Phrase Storage	Enables short phrases frequently used (date, closing lines in a letter) to be stored and recalled by using only one or two keystrokes.

Editing Features

Insert	Allows insertion of characters within existing text.
Delete	Removes characters and closes up the space automatically.
Move	Allows blocks of text to be moved to another location within the document or to another document.
Search and Replace	Allows automatic replacement of identified words or phrases.
Spelling Check	Locates misspelled words within a document. The operator has the option of correcting them.
Thesaurus	Provides a list of words with similar meanings to the one identified.

Formatting Features

Bold	Highlights text to be printed darker than regular text.
Center	Automatically centers document within established margins.
Headers and Footers	Automatically places page numbers, titles, or other specified information at top or bottom of the page.
Indent	Automatically skips space to indent a line or lines.
Underscoring	Automatically underlines words, phrases, or lines.

a name you know to find information you need to know, such as the address or phone number. With electronic databases, the known is also used to find the unknown. Many companies store client or customer information in a database. Specific information needed — date of last order, for example, or payment record — can be quickly retrieved by searching the database. Among the database software packages available are dBase III Plus, R:Base System V, and PC Oracle.

Graphics

Graphics software is used primarily for two purposes: analyzing data and making visual aids to support presentations. Analytical graphics software converts figures, which may originate from a spreadsheet or database, into meaningful charts and graphs. Typical business graphs include line charts, bar charts, and pie charts. Such visuals enable managers and other professionals to analyze data more easily. Presentation graphics software is used for creating visual aids such as transparency masters and slides. Such visuals enhance a speaker's presentation and make the meaning and relationships clearer. Using sophisticated equipment and software, users can produce high-quality color graphics.

Desktop Publishing

Desktop publishing software enables a personal computer and a high-quality printer to produce documents of almost typeset quality. Businesses use desktop publishing software to produce their newsletters,

FIGURE 2-9 Desktop publishing software enables a personal computer to produce documents of almost typeset quality.

brochures, advertisements, reports, and other shorter publications without having to use the services of a commercial typesetter.

Desktop publishing software enables text to be formatted in different type sizes and styles. Spacing between lines can be adjusted to add more or less white space to give the desired effect. Copy can be formatted in columns as in a newspaper, and graphics and scanned images can be combined with the text. Information appears on the screen as it will when it is printed so that the operator can see what the type sizes will look like and change them if desired.

Much of the new and sophisticated word processing software incorporates some desktop publishing features. Use of different type sizes and fonts, formatting copy in columns, and wrapping text around graphics or illustrations are examples.

✔ Checkpoint 1   ORIGINATION AND PRODUCTION

Match the following equipment and software with the correct function or definition:

1. Electronic typewriter

2. Desktop publishing

3. Personal computer

4. Word processing

5. Scanner

6. Dictation/transcription equipment

7. Spreadsheet software

8. Graphics software

a. Software that enables text to be keyed, stored, and revised easily

b. Reads paper documents and converts them into a form that can be read by computer

c. Records for transcriber to listen to and key into other equipment

d. Supports word processing and other applications

e. Enables a PC to produce documents of near typeset quality

f. An electronic worksheet

g. Software that designs illustrations or charts

h. Equipment that is more versatile than an electric typewriter

Check your answers in Appendix D.

REPRODUCTION

After documents are produced, copies are usually required. Most of the copies are made on paper. Today's reproduction equipment can produce high-quality copies of the original document. The process of reproducing copies using photocopiers or duplicating equipment is **reprographics**.

Photocopiers

The photocopier is the most common reprographic equipment in today's office. Most copiers use plain paper and are thus known as plain-paper copiers.

Copiers are frequently classified by the volume of copies they normally produce. Low-volume copiers, often referred to as convenience copiers, can produce up to 20 copies per minute; high-volume copiers can produce as many as 50 to 90 copies per minute.

Many photocopiers can reduce or enlarge images, copy on both sides of the sheet, and automatically feed originals into the machine one at a time. Copiers with a recirculating feature can automatically reproduce originals as collated sets. Some models will also staple each set. A feature that is becoming more popular is reproduction in full color.

Offset Duplicating

Offset duplicating is a reproduction method used to produce a high quality of print. The document may be prepared using desktop publishing or typesetting equipment that provides the professional typesetting quality of books. Once the original is prepared, a picture of the document is taken on a metal or paper plate called an offset master. The master is attached to the drum of the offset press, which transfers the image to paper. Offset printing can produce documents in various colors.

DISTRIBUTION/TRANSMISSION

After being produced—and reproduced—documents are sent to the receivers. The distribution step traditionally used physical means of sending documents, such as hand delivery, interoffice mail, the U.S. Postal Service, and private carriers such as Federal Express. Although these methods are still widely used, distribution by electronic methods provides delivery faster and more efficiently.

Communication that is sent electronically generally travels over local and wide area communication networks. These networks use telephone lines, microwave, and satellites. A **local area network (LAN)** is a popular way to connect various workstations within a building or nearby buildings.

A LAN consists of software and a direct cable link with other workstations. The means for connecting the workstations in a LAN may be copper wire, coaxial cable (as in transmission of television images), or the more recently developed fiber optic cable. **Fiber optic cable** consists of tiny glass threads that use light to carry information. They are much lighter and can carry more information than an equivalent thickness of wire cable. Several means of distributing information electronically are available.

Electronic Mail

Electronic mail sends and stores messages by means of a computer. To use an electronic mail system, the sender keys and edits the message at the workstation and then transmits the message to one or more workstations. The receiver views the message on the display and then either saves, deletes, or prints the message. Electronic mail allows the sender to transmit messages almost instantaneously and avoids the problem of "telephone tag" (repeatedly calling and missing the receiver). Messages may travel over a local area network (LAN), over telephone lines, or by a computer-based message system.

Using a **computer-based message system** (CBMS) to send a message can be convenient and relatively inexpensive. The sender keys the message at a PC or a terminal on a mainframe and sends it to one or more recipients. The message waits in the receiver's electronic "mailbox" (the computer) until the receiver picks up the message. Messages can also be "broadcast" to many mailboxes.

An electronic mail system (E-Mail) may be either an internal system that runs on a LAN or on a mainframe, or it may be a public system. For a subscription fee, E-mail services such as Western Union's EasyLink, MCI Mail, CompuServe, and US Sprint's Telenet enable users to send, receive, and store messages in these services' mailboxes.

Facsimile

Exact copies of documents can be sent electronically by means of a facsimile device. Although a facsimile device can transmit any form of printed information, it is particularly useful for sending graphics or im-

FIGURE 2-10 A facsimile device can transmit an exact copy of any printed image to another facsimile or, in some cases, to a personal computer.

ages such as blueprints, drawings, and photographs. Facsimile is a widely used and growing technology.

A facsimile device scans the image and converts it to digital form. The digitized document travels over the telephone lines and is converted back to its original form on the receiver's end. Sending messages by facsimile is almost as quick and cheap as making a telephone call.

Teletypewriters (Telex)

Teletypewriters send messages over communication lines. Telex I and Telex II are services offered by Western Union. Messages are keyed by the sender and forwarded to the receiver's teletypewriter, which may receive the message without an operator present. Almost every large metropolitan hotel has a telex.

FIGURE 2-11 Telex machines provide electronic communication worldwide.

Teleconferencing

Teleconferencing uses the telephone or other media to link two or more persons in two or more locations. Instead of traveling to a meeting, participants are able to communicate in one or more forms, depending upon the type of conference.

The simplest form of teleconference is an audioconference, which is simply a long-distance telephone conference call. If more than two persons are involved, speakerphones may be used. Participants could also exchange documents via facsimile or a computer during their conference.

Video conferences, a more sophisticated form of teleconferencing, allow members to see as well as hear each other. Voices, images, and data

FIGURE 2-12 Teleconferencing enables participants in various locations to communicate in one or more forms.

are transmitted over telephone lines. Video conferences may either be full-motion video or freeze frame. Full-motion video, in which every continuous movement is broadcast, is the most sophisticated form of video conference. With freeze frame, images change every few seconds.

Teleconferencing is appropriate for exchanging information. Appropriate uses of teleconferencing might be introducing new products to sales representatives or orienting new employees to certain procedures. Teleconferences are not, however, a substitute for face-to-face meetings that require negotiations, persuasion, or strong nonverbal communication skills.

Voice Mail

When telephone tag is a problem, voice mail may be a solution. To use a voice mail system, you simply dictate your message into an ordinary push-button telephone. The message is stored in a "voice mailbox" until the receiver can retrieve the message. The message is played back in speech form rather than in written form. Voice mail systems are expensive to set up, but they can save money on monthly telephone bills.

STORAGE/RETRIEVAL

Messages usually must be saved so that they may be retrieved later for reference or for distribution to others. The most common method of storing documents is on paper. The printed documents are stored in file cabinets, on shelf files, or in other containers such as trays or boxes. Because of the high cost of paper storage and the time it takes to find a document once it has been stored, companies are gradually moving toward other means of storage and retrieval.

Magnetic Disk Storage

Information keyed on a computer is generally saved onto a magnetic disk for later printing or editing. Disks are generally classified as either flexible diskettes or hard disks.

A **flexible diskette** is a removable storage medium that can store about 90 pages, which in paper form would require a large volume of file space. The newer diskettes are smaller and rigid. Most word processors and computers and some electronic typewriters use flexible diskettes.

Hard disks provide storage which is built right into the computer and is usually not removable. Since many pages of information can be stored on hard disk, the storage space is divided into manageable areas called **directories**. Each directory contains a number of documents. Usually directories can be accessed with a password, which is keyed into the terminal.

Microforms

Companies handling large numbers of documents that need to be stored for extended periods of time usually photograph them as microforms. A **microform** is a reduced image of a paper document stored on film, in forms such as roll film, microfiche, or ultrafiche. Figure 2-13 shows several varieties of microforms.

FIGURE 2-13 Microforms store documents in miniaturized form.

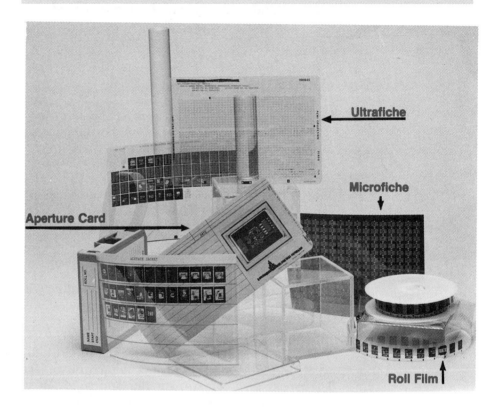

Since microfilming is a relatively expensive process, companies often use it for records that must be maintained over a lengthy period of time. Documents suitable for microfilming might be checks, customer records, or accounting records.

Optical Disks

A newer form of disk, the optical disk, is a product of laser technology. Information is recorded and read back by a laser beam or light. The storage capacity of an optical disk is massive—approximately 4 million pages of text. Optical disks can store all forms of information—text, data, voice, and images. They are more suitable for storing than for recording information.

Checkpoint 2 REPRODUCTION, DISTRIBUTION, AND STORAGE

Match the following equipment and technologies with the correct function or definition:

1. Electronic mail

2. Facsimile

3. Flexible diskette

4. Telex

5. Photocopier

6. Computer-based message system

7. Voice mail

8. Microform

9. Teleconferencing

10. Reprographics

a. Makes an exact copy of a document

b. Enables participants to communicate without travel

c. Reduced image of a paper document

d. Stores text messages in an electronic "mailbox"

e. Communication that is transmitted electronically over telephone lines, a LAN, or a computer system

f. Teletypewriter exchange system made available by Western Union

g. Stores information recorded in magnetic form

h. Transmits an exact copy of text or graphics electronically

i. Stores spoken messages in an electronic "mailbox"

j. The process of copying documents using photocopiers or offset duplicators or presses

Check your answers in Appendix D.

SUMMARY

Office automation has improved the speed and efficiency of sending messages. New equipment, software, and technologies have had a tremendous impact on communication and document production.

Documents travel through the document cycle in five stages: origination, production, reproduction, distribution/transmission, and storage/retrieval. In today's electronic office, each of these stages uses automated equipment.

Origination equipment and technology include dictation/transcription machines, keyboards, scanners, and voice input. Production equipment includes electronic typewriters, dedicated word processors, and computers with word processing software. Production software includes word processing, spreadsheets, database management, graphics, and desktop publishing.

Copies are usually produced on photocopiers or by offset duplicating during the reproduction stage. Documents are distributed by means of electronic mail, facsimile, and teletypewriter. Teleconferencing and voice mail are other means of electronic communication. Documents are stored on flexible diskettes, hard disks, microforms, and optical disks.

● ● ● ● ● ● ● ● ● **Communication Activities**

Discussion Questions

1. Define the following terms: information processing, word processing, word/information processing.
2. Name and describe the five stages of the document cycle.
3. What types of equipment are used in the origination stage?
4. Describe how production equipment is used in an organization you are familiar with.
5. What are the different types of applications software available and what are the uses of each?
6. Describe reproduction equipment in the automated office.

7. Define the technologies and equipment used in
   a. Electronic mail
   b. Facsimile
   c. Teletypewriters
   d. Voice mail
   e. Teleconferencing
8. How are documents stored and retrieved in automated offices?

Grammar Review

PART 2

• •

Using correct grammar is a prerequisite to effective business communication. People who use incorrect grammar in speaking and writing make a poor impression on the receivers of their messages, very likely hindering the process of communication.

Chapters 3 through 10 provide a comprehensive review of grammar. Chapter 3 reviews the correct use of singular and plural nouns in both the general and the possessive cases. Chapter 4 focuses on verb tenses, active and passive voice, and troublesome verbs. Chapter 5 reviews agreement of subject and verb.

Chapter 6 discusses using pronouns correctly in the nominative, possessive, and objective cases. Chapter 7 covers agreement of pronouns and nouns.

Chapter 8 discusses the choice and placement of adjectives and adverbs to add life to our writing. Prepositions, conjunctions, and interjections are covered in Chapter 9. Chapter 10 reviews the elements of effective sentences (including phrases and clauses), types of sentences, and sentence structures.

CHAPTER 3

Singular, Plural, and Possessive Nouns

Objectives

After studying this chapter and completing the chapter exercises, you should be able to:

1. Recognize general and possessive case nouns.
2. Form the plural of general case nouns.
3. Form the possessive case of nouns.
4. Spell and use a list of common business terms.

One or more nouns occur in almost every sentence you use. A noun is the name of a person, place, thing, or idea. Common nouns such as *student*, *city*, and *savings* do not refer to particular persons, places, things, or ideas. In contrast, proper nouns such as *Kathleen* and *Memphis* refer to specific persons, places, things, or ideas. Proper nouns are always capitalized. The common and proper nouns are italicized in the following examples:

> The *executives* must travel to *New York* for the *meeting.*

> *Mom* reminded me that *happiness* is not a *state* to arrive at but a *means* of *traveling.*

> *Economics* is the *study* of the *production, distribution,* and *consumption* of *goods* and *services.*

Nouns have two cases: general and possessive. Possessive case nouns are used to show ownership; general case nouns are used in all other relationships. Most nouns have a singular form that refers to one item and a plural form that refers to more than one item. Thus, there are four forms of nouns from which to choose. To communicate accurately, you must use the correct form. The four forms of a noun are shown in the following examples.

GENERAL CASE		POSSESSIVE CASE	
SINGULAR	PLURAL	SINGULAR	PLURAL
report	reports	report's	reports'
book	books	book's	books'
blueprint	blueprints	blueprint's	blueprints'
New York		New York's	

FORMING THE PLURAL OF NOUNS

The plurals of most nouns are formed by adding an *s* to the noun.

SINGULAR FORM	PLURAL FORM
computer	computers
office	offices
terminal	terminals

Some nouns, however, do not follow this general rule for forming plurals. The following rules—several of which have exceptions—will help you to spell nouns correctly. Whenever you are in doubt about the spelling of a noun, check a dictionary. As you study the rules for forming the plurals of nouns, remember that a few nouns, like *news* and *honesty*, have only a singular form; other nouns, such as *earnings* and *goods,* are generally considered plural. Nouns such as *deer, means,* and *series* are spelled the same in both their singular and plural forms.

Rule 1 Nouns ending in a hissing sound (*s x, z, ch,* or *sh*) form their plural by adding *es*. (Hint: When the plural creates an extra syllable, add *es* to form the plural noun.)

SINGULAR FORM	PLURAL FORM
glass	glasses
box	boxes
buzz	buzzes
church	churches
dish	dishes

Rule 2 Nouns ending in *y* form their plurals in one of two ways. Nouns ending in *y* preceded by a *vowel* form plurals by adding *s*.

SINGULAR FORM	PLURAL FORM
attorney	attorneys
delay	delays
joy	joys

Nouns ending in *y* preceded by a consonant form plurals by changing the *y* to *i* and adding *es*.

SINGULAR FORM	PLURAL FORM
ability	abilities
grocery	groceries
quality	qualities

Rule 3 Nouns ending in *o* form their plurals in one of two ways. Nouns ending in *o* preceded by a vowel sound form their plurals by adding *s*.

SINGULAR FORM	PLURAL FORM
ratio	ratios
video	videos
embryo	embryos
studio	studios

Nouns ending in *o* preceded by a consonant form their plurals by adding either *s* or *es*. Many musical terms ending in *o* form their plurals by simply adding *s*.

SINGULAR FORM	PLURAL FORM
Add *s*	
auto	autos
memo	memos
photo	photos
two	twos
Musical terms	
alto	altos
banjo	banjos
piano	pianos
soprano	sopranos
solo	solos
Add *es*	
hero	heroes
potato	potatoes
tomato	tomatoes
torpedo	torpedoes

Rule 4 Nouns that end in *f, fe,* or *ff* generally form their plurals by adding *s*.

SINGULAR FORM	PLURAL FORM
belief	beliefs
proof	proofs
safe	safes
cliff	cliffs
tariff	tariffs

However, some nouns ending in *f* or *fe* form their plurals by changing the *f* or *fe* to *ve* and adding *s*.

SINGULAR FORM	PLURAL FORM
leaf	leaves
half	halves
life	lives
wife	wives

A few nouns ending in *f* have two plural forms. Use the preferred form listed below:

PREFERRED FORM	SECOND CHOICE
dwarfs	dwarves
scarfs	scarves

Rule 5   Some nouns are irregular, and their spellings change to form their plurals.

SINGULAR FORM	PLURAL FORM
child	children
foot	feet
goose	geese
man	men
woman	women

Rule 6   Compound nouns (nouns consisting of more than one word) may be written as one word, as separate words, or as hyphenated words. Compound nouns written as one word form their plurals as explained in the previously listed rules. Compound nouns written as separate words or hyphenated words form their plurals by adding *s* to the *main* word.

SINGULAR FORM	PLURAL FORM
One word	
blueprint	blueprints
bookshelf	bookshelves
Separate words	
account payable	accounts payable
bill of lading	bills of lading
post office	post offices
Hyphenated words	
daughter-in-law	daughters-in-law
stock-in-trade	stocks-in-trade
runner-up	runners-up

Because the spellings of compound words change with time, check an up-to-date dictionary if you are in doubt of the spelling.

Rule 7   Some foreign words retain the plural spellings of their native language. Others have been given English spellings and thus have two spellings. Check a dictionary for the preferred spellings—those that are listed first in the dictionary. The preferred spellings are marked with an asterisk (*).

SINGULAR NOUN	ENGLISH PLURAL	FOREIGN PLURAL
analysis	analyses	
datum	datums	data*
criterion	criterions	criteria*
memorandum	memorandums	memoranda

Part 2   Grammar Review

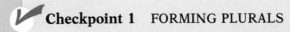

Checkpoint 1   FORMING PLURALS

Below is a list of singular nouns. To check your skills in changing nouns to their plural forms, write each of these in its plural form.

1. volume	13. business	25. hero
2. wish	14. raspberry	26. money
3. city	15. trio	27. tornado
4. commando	16. knife	28. wife
5. cafe	17. thief	29. calf
6. half	18. moose	30. child
7. criterion	19. datum	31. basis
8. trademark	20. iceberg	32. mother-in-law
9. son-in-law	21. father-in-law	33. post office
10. news	22. table	34. council
11. hive	23. class	35. mouse
12. audience	24. drama	

Check your answers in Appendix D.

FORMING THE POSSESSIVE CASE OF NOUNS

Nouns in the possessive case are used to show ownership. The apostrophe is used to indicate the possessive case. Like general case nouns, possessive case nouns have both singular and plural forms.

Singular Possessive Case

The singular possessive case indicates that something belongs to just one person, place, or thing. To form the possessive case of a singular noun, add an apostrophe and an *s* to the noun.

SINGULAR NOUN	POSSESSIVE SINGULAR NOUN
box	box's label
glass	glass's shine
man	man's tie
Chris	Chris's car
sister-in-law	sister-in-law's baby

There is an exception to this rule. If adding an additional *s* to a singular noun already ending in an *s* sound would make the noun difficult to pronounce, form the possessive case by adding only an apostrophe.

SINGULAR NOUN	POSSESSIVE SINGULAR NOUN
appearance	appearance' sake
species	species' characteristics
Los Angeles	Los Angeles' skyline
goodness	goodness' sake

Plural Possessive Case

The plural possessive case indicates that something belongs to more than one person, place, or thing. When forming possessive case plural nouns, write the noun in its plural form. If the plural form ends in an *s*, add only an apostrophe. If the plural form does not end in *s*, add an apostrophe and an *s*.

PLURAL NOUN ENDING IN *s*	POSSESSIVE PLURAL NOUN
boxes	boxes' labels
Davises	Davises' home
years	years' figures
post offices	post offices' windows

PLURAL NOUN NOT ENDING IN *s*	POSSESSIVE PLURAL NOUN
children	children's toys
fathers-in-law	fathers-in-law's businesses
chiefs-of-staff	chiefs-of-staff's offices
alumni	alumni's contributions
women	women's clothing

Now let's look at an example and see how a possessive case noun is used in a sentence:

My *brother's* favorite sport is soccer.

The italicized noun is in the possessive case. It shows possession because it tells the receiver whose favorite sport the sender is referring to. The sender is talking about only one brother. How many brothers are referred to in the following sentence?

My *brothers'* favorite sport is soccer.

The placement of the apostrophe indicates that the sender is referring to more than one brother.

To avoid confusion when forming the plural or possessive case of family names, remember that the possessive case is used to show possession. If a family named *Davidson* invites you to a party at their house, it is the *Davidsons* (plural form, no apostrophe) who are giving the party, but you are going to the *Davidsons'* (possessive form) house. Now let's check your ability to convert general case nouns into possessive case nouns.

✔ Checkpoint 2   FORMING POSSESSIVES

Below is a list of general case singular nouns. Write each of them in its singular and plural possessive case form.

1. Johnson
2. city
3. alto
4. datum
5. mouse
6. executive
7. brother-in-law
8. dictionary
9. deer
10. knife

Check your answers in Appendix D.

SUMMARY

A noun is the name of a person, place, thing, or idea. Unlike common nouns, proper nouns refer to specific persons, places, things, or ideas.

Common and proper nouns have two cases—general and possessive. Most general case nouns and possessive case nouns have both a singular and a plural form. Usually we use the general case noun. Check an up-to-date dictionary if you are not sure about the spelling of these nouns.

Possessive case nouns are used to show ownership. The majority of singular nouns form the possessive case by adding an apostrophe and an *s*. The possessive case of plural nouns is formed by adding an apostrophe or an apostrophe and an *s*. To decide the proper spelling, write the noun in its general case plural form. If the plural noun ends in *s*, simply add an apostrophe. If the plural noun does not end in an *s*, add an apostrophe and an *s*.

Spelling and Word Usage

Correct spelling and word usage are keys to effective communication. These skills are necessary to succeed in the business world. Exercises are included at the end of the chapters in Parts 2 and 3 to strengthen your ability to spell and use words that commonly cause confusion. Learn to spell and use the following words. Be alert for them in the Editing Applications at the end of the chapter.

accommodation	grievance	quantity
bankruptcy	knowledge	salary
calendar	miscellaneous	television
discussion	necessary	versus
efficient	pamphlet	

If necessary, refer to Appendix A for the correct usage of these words.

accept/except	forth/fourth	principal/principle

Practical Applications

Part A   Write these nouns in their plural forms:

accommodation	Dickerson's	jack-in-the-box
commodity	back order	bluff
potato	son-in-law	woman
dish	loaf	human
safe	bush	post office
password	announcement	pacemaker
dwarf	factory	player's
stratum	volcano	typewriter's

Part B   Correct the misspelled nouns in the following sentence. Write "C" if the sentence is correct.

1. While listening to the news last Wednesday, I heard about an accident in which the number of casualtys was in the nineties.

2. My mother-in-law said that the tenor's and bass's were weak but that the altoes and sopranoes sang beautifully.

3. They obtained the datum from boxs which were hidden in the backrooms closet, and they calculated the ratioes themselfes.

4. Good restaurant's are scarcitys in this part of the state.

5. John's typewriter has elite pitch, but the other typewriter's pitch is pica.

6. Some consider executives lifes as being stressful.

7. Although the safe was guaranteed for ten year's, the safes hinge has broken.

8. Many volcanoes are sleeping giants about to be awakened.

9. While setting the table, Tom accidentally broke three glass's.

10. Though wars create heros, history illustrates that wars are serious tragedys.

Editing Applications

Part A   Read the following paragraphs and correct all the misspelled words.

1. Even though New Orleans's cafes and restaurants are plentiful and their service is efficeint, Juanitas lunch time activities are much more diversified than eating. Sometime she attends an art class', watchs drama at the open theater, or simply sits at a picnic table observing people. These choices are available with no cost to Juanita at the cities' park located just three blocks from her office.

2. Because of Tonys' father's-in-law wishs, heir's to his estate must be in a certain social strata. This decision has caused several grievences in the family. Accept for Allens' and Jeffery's wifes, no one qualifies. Hence, some of the family members have filed miscelaneous bankruptcy suits. Discusion is calendered for September 5 to determine if such action enables them to meet the conditions of the will.

Part B   Correct all errors in the following memorandum.

> **TO:**   Randy Green, Supervisor of Legal Services
> **FROM:**   Kelly Hansen, Vice President
> **DATE:**   January 20, 19--
> **SUBJECT:**   Your Trip to Chicago

According to my calander, you are to be in Chicago on January 27. Accomodations have been made for you at the Lakeside Hotel — it has cable telivision, a spa, exclusive shops, and two good restaurants that you will enjoy.

Enclosed are the documents necesary for your consultation with Mr. Snipe concerning the bankrupcy case and the greivance.   In the case Jones versus Smith, everything was questioned accept Mrs. Smiths' salery.

Mr. Snipe is very efficeint and has a great quanity of knowledge about the case.   However, your discussion with him should focus on the basic principals.   Miscellaneous details should be omitted except for the greivance.   The case is scheduled for court on the forth of February.

By the way, John's and Terry's wifes will be going to Chicago in April. Would you please bring them some pamplets about Chicagoes museums, restaurants, and other tourist attractions.

xx

Enclosure

CHAPTER 4

Using Verbs Correctly

Objectives

After studying this chapter and completing the chapter exercises, you should be able to:

1. Avoid unnecessary shifts in tenses of verbs.
2. Use active- and passive-voice verbs correctly.
3. Use troublesome verbs correctly.
4. Spell and use a list of common business terms.

You will remember from previous studies of grammar that every sentence must have a verb as well as a subject. Verbs express action (*swim, talk, ride*) or a state of being (*am, feel, seem, have been*). Verbs express what the subject is doing or what is being done to the subject.

VERB FACTS

In order to know how to use verbs correctly, it is important to recognize the main types of verbs and the parts of verbs.

Types of Verbs

Verbs may be classified as main verbs, helping verbs, and linking verbs. Sentences may have only one verb, called a **main verb,** which expresses action or a state of being.

> Sally *spoke* in a soft voice. (*Spoke* expresses action.)
>
> Sally *is* a finalist. (*Is* refers to a state of being.)

Helping verbs indicate timing. The most common helping verbs are forms of *to be* (*is, are, was, were*) and *to have* (*has, have,* and *had*). Other helping verbs, which have only one form, are listed below:

can	ought
could	shall
may	should
might	will
must	would

Many sentences have a combination of a main verb and a helping verb. Together they form a verb phrase.

> Sally *has spoken* in a soft voice. (*Has spoken* is the verb phrase: *has* is the helping verb; *spoken* is the main verb.)

The last verb in a verb phrase is the main verb; all other verbs are helping verbs. Note the main action verbs and their helping verbs in the following examples.

	SUBJECT	ACTION VERB	
The	typist	completed	the task.
	Mr. Jones	was elected	president.
	He	answered	the questions.

Linking verbs join nouns, pronouns, or adjectives (words that describe nouns or pronouns) to the subject. Linking verbs are state-of-being verbs.

The most common linking verbs are forms of *to be* (*is, are, was, were*). Other linking verbs include *appear, become, feel, look, seem,* and *sound.* (Words following a linking verb that refer to the subject are sometimes called **subject complements** or **predicate nouns, predicate pronouns,** or **predicate adjectives.** An example of each is given below.)

	SUBJECT	LINKING VERB	
	It	was	she. (pronoun)
The new	president	is	Mr. Jones. (noun)
The old	programs	were	the most expensive. (adj.)
	Chris	appears	content. (adj.)

Parts of Verbs

Every verb (except the ten helping verbs on page 56) has three principal parts: present tense, past tense, and past participle. The parts of verbs are used to form different tenses in order to express the time of action.

PRESENT TENSE	PAST TENSE	PAST PARTICIPLE
talk	talked	talked
purchase	purchased	purchased
employ	employed	employed
go	went	gone
break	broke	broken
teach	taught	taught

Notice that the past tense and past participle of the first three verbs in the above list are spelled alike and are formed by adding *d* or *ed* to the present form. These are called **regular verbs.** Notice that the past tense and past participle in the last three verbs do not follow this pattern. These are called **irregular verbs.** Care must be taken when using irregular verbs to use the correct past tense and past participle.

VERB TENSES

Verbs express time as well as action. Time is expressed in **tense.** Using the correct tense is important if the receiver is to know when an action takes place. Helping verbs (forms of *to be* and *to have*) are often used with the main verb to indicate the verb tense.

The two groups of tenses are simple tenses and perfect tenses. In order to form the proper tense of verbs, it is important to understand the parts of verbs.

Simple Tenses

The three simple tenses are *present*, *past*, and *future*.

PRESENT   Edie *answers* the phone promptly.

PAST   Edie *answered* the phone promptly.

FUTURE   Edie *will answer* the phone promptly.

Present Tense

The **present tense** expresses what is happening now. It also expresses action in progress or a general statement of truth. The main verb and the helping verb appear in italics in the examples.

> Computer services *sell* information.   (happening now)
>
> I *am learning* to speak Italian.   (in progress)
>
> Joan *likes* her new personal computer.   (statement of truth)

The present tense of a regular verb adds an *s* when it is used with a third-person singular pronoun (*he, she, it*) or a singular noun. (Note the third example above and below.)

PERSON	SINGULAR	PLURAL
First	I help	we help
Second	you help	you help
Third	he, she, it helps	they help

Past Tense

The **past tense** expresses action that has been completed. Regular verbs add *ed* to form their past tense. Some irregular verbs change spelling to form their past tense (*see, saw; begin, began*), while a few verbs have only one form (*burst, cost*) for all three principal parts.

> Delwood *completed* the Hughes report yesterday.   (regular)
>
> She *ate* all the birthday cake.   (irregular)
>
> They *shut* the door.   (one form)

Be careful when expressing the past tense of irregular verbs. A common error is to use the past participle instead of the simple past tense.

INCORRECT   I *done* my work.

CORRECT   I *did* my work.

INCORRECT   I *seen* the photograph.

CORRECT   I *saw* the photograph.

Future Tense

The **future tense** expresses an action or condition yet to come. Verbs form their future tense by using the helping verb *will* before the verb. *Shall* is sometimes used to form the future tense in formal communication.

> Charlene *will buy* a new car in June.
>
> *Will* you *assist* me by chairing this committee?

Perfect Tenses

The perfect tenses describe the action of the verb in relation to a certain time, some other action, or a state of being. Form the perfect tenses by using a form of the helping verb *have* with the past participle form of the verb. The three perfect tenses are *present perfect, past perfect,* and *future perfect.*

Present Perfect

The **present perfect tense** expresses action that was begun in the past and is just completed or was begun in the past and is still continuing. Use *has* or *have* with the past participle to form the present perfect tense. Use *has* with third-person singular subjects and *have* with other subjects.

> I *have finished* my homework. (The action was begun in the past and has just been completed.)
>
> Phil *has worked* for this company for three years. (The action was begun in the past and is still continuing.)

Past Perfect Tense

The **past perfect tense** describes an action that was completed before some other past action or time. Use *had* with the past participle of the verb to form the past perfect tense.

> When I arrived at the movie, it *had* already *started.*
>
> They *had completed* the specifications before the notice was sent.

Future Perfect Tense

The **future perfect tense** indicates an action that will be finished before another future action or by a certain time in the future. Use *will have* with the past participle to form the future perfect tense.

> By noon tomorrow, I *will have written* the report. (The action will be completed by a certain time.)
>
> By the time the review gets here, I *will have given* my presentation. (The action will be completed before another future action.)

Unnecessary Change in Tenses

It is important not only to know the correct tense but also to know when to use it. Avoid changing tenses within a sentence unless there is an actual change in time. Consider the following examples:

WEAK   Successful people *handle* their finances wisely and *will make* their money work for them.

STRONG   Successful people *handle* their finances wisely and *make* their money work for them.

In the first sentence, there is an unnecessary change in tense from the present tense (*handle*) to the future tense (*will make*). The sentence is strengthened (see second example) by avoiding the shift in tense. Sometimes, however, there is a real difference in time, making it necessary to change verb tenses within a sentence.

Yesterday she *purchased* a new personal computer and *will begin* a training program soon.

✔ Checkpoint 1   VERB TENSES

Determine if the correct verb tenses have been used. Correct any errors. Write "C" if the sentence is correct.

1. She slammed down the receiver and then storms out of the office.
2. Don Wright was with Temp four years when he was promoted to office manager.
3. Simpson couldn't tell us where St. Paul is located on the map.
4. You will enjoy the play that will be presented by the Little Theatre next week.
5. By 5 p.m. Friday, Johnson will complete a full 40 hours of work.

Check your answers in Appendix D.

ACTIVE AND PASSIVE VOICE

Verbs may be written in either the active or the passive voice. Voice indicates whether the subject is doing the action or receiving the action of the verb. **Active voice** means that the subject is doing the action. **Passive voice** means that the subject is receiving the action.

ACTIVE   John *wrote* his book using a word processor.   (Subject *John* does the action.)

PASSIVE The book *was written* by John using a word processor.   (Subject *book* receives the action.)

ACTIVE I *caught* the ball.   (Subject *I* performs the action.)

PASSIVE The ball *was caught* by me.   (Subject *ball* receives the action.)

In general, use the active voice in business writing. The active voice creates a clear, sharp picture in the receiver's mind. It is more direct, more forceful, and more concise than the passive voice. The passive voice sends a fuzzy, less distinct image to the receiver.

The passive voice is formed with the past participle and a form of *to be*. Use the passive voice in the following cases:

● When the subject is unknown or better left unidentified

   Property taxes *will be increased* next year.

● To emphasize the action or the receiver of the action rather than the person who performed the action

   Our only son *was killed* in an automobile accident.

● To reduce the impact of a negative or unpleasant statement

   The report *was not sent* on time.   (Avoids saying: *You* did not send the report on time.)

As a rule, avoid shifts in voice when writing. Shifting from the active to the passive voice diminishes the strength of the statement. Both verbs should be in either the active or the passive voice. Since the active voice is stronger, it is preferred in business.

WEAK Mary *wrote* the book, and it *was edited* by John.

STRONG Mary *wrote* the book, and John *edited* it.

Checkpoint 2   ACTIVE AND PASSIVE VOICE

If appropriate, change the passive voice to the active voice in the following sentences. Write "C" if the sentence is effective as written.

1. To reduce stress, vacations should be taken by employees.
2. Unfortunately, incorrect information was given to Mr. Craig.
3. Mr. Carson was helped with his problem by the accountant.
4. Janice reported that sales were high this quarter.
5. The speech was given by Dr. Paulson.

Check your answers in Appendix D.

MOOD

The mood of a verb indicates whether the sender considers the message to be a fact or a question, a request or a condition. There are three verb moods. The **indicative mood** is used to make statements or ask questions.

STATEMENT   Jerry works for a brokerage firm.

QUESTION   Will you be flying to New York?

The **imperative mood** is used to give orders or make requests.

> Close the door when you leave.
>
> Please send me a catalog by May 15.

(Since the indicative and imperative moods give few problems in writing verbs, they will not be covered in the chapter exercises.)

The **subjunctive mood** is used in the following situations and may prove more difficult to master.

- Use the subjunctive mood to express ideas contrary to fact. Substitute *were* for *was*.

INCORRECT   If I *was* going on vacation, I would visit Hawaii.

CORRECT   If I *were* going on vacation, I would visit Hawaii.

- Use the subjunctive mood to express a desire, demand, or recommendation. Substitute the verb *be* for *am*, *are*, and *is* or drop the *s* ending from third-person singular present tense verbs.

INCORRECT   I request that an adjustment *is* made to my bill.

CORRECT   I request that an adjustment *be* made to my bill.

INCORRECT   It is important that all members *are* present.

CORRECT   It is important that all members *be* present.

INCORRECT   We suggest that Betty *drives* her car to the conference.

CORRECT   We suggest that Betty *drive* her car to the conference.

MISUSED VERBS

Certain verbs cause a great deal of confusion because they have similar meanings. Some of these verbs are easier to use if you understand the difference between transitive and intransitive verbs. **A transitive verb** passes its action along to an object. The object may be a noun, a pronoun, or a group of words serving as a noun. To determine the object, ask *what*?

or *whom*? after the verb. The transitive verbs are italicized in the following sentences:

Sabrina *repaired* the computer.   (repaired *what*? the computer)

David *met* him at the mall.   (met *whom*? him)

Phillip *said* that he would be late.   (said *what*? that he would be late)

An **intransitive verb** does not need an object to complete its meaning. Although words may follow an intransitive verb, they do not answer the questions *what*? or *whom*? about the verb. The intransitive verbs are italicized in the following sentences:

She *walked* into the room.   (walked *what*? *whom*? no object)

John *worked* with me for two years.   (worked *what*? *whom*? no object)

Linking verbs are always intransitive and never take objects. The most common linking verb is *to be* (*am, is, are, was, were*) and verb phrases ending in *be, being,* or *been. Feel, seem, look,* and *become* are also often used as linking verbs.

I *feel* good today.   (feel *what*? *whom*? intransitive)

He *was* late to work.   (was *what*? *whom*? intransitive)

Lay, Lie; Raise, Rise; Set, Sit

Apply what you have learned about transitive and intransitive verbs to these three pairs of common verbs. Confusion between *lie* and *lay* often arises because the past tense of *to lie* (*lay*) is the same as the present tense of *to lay.*

TRANSITIVE VERBS (object)	INTRANSITIVE VERBS (no object)
lay/laid/laid (place an object)	lie/lay/lain (recline)
raise, raised, raised (lift an object)	rise/rose/risen (ascend; go up)
set, set, set (place an object)	sit, sat, sat (be seated)

Study Table 4-1, which gives examples of the correct use of these verbs. The object is italicized in the sentences containing transitive verbs.

Note: Be careful never to use *set* when you mean *sit* or *lay* when you mean *lie.* People never *set* down in a chair or *lay* down for a rest.

The transitive verbs *lay, set,* and *raise* always take an object when used in the active voice. However, transitive verbs do not take an object when they are used in the passive voice. Note how the word used as the object

TABLE 4-1 Commonly Confused Verbs

Verb Form	Transitive Verbs (object)	Intransitive Verbs (no object)
Present	I lay (am laying) the *book* down today.	I lie (am lying) down today.
Past	I laid (was laying) the *book* down yesterday.	I lay (was lying) down yesterday.
Past Participle	I have laid the *book* down on the table.	I have lain here for an hour.
Present	He raises the *flag*.	The sun rises in the east.
Past	He raised the *flag*.	They rose to greet the speaker.
Past Participle	He has raised the *flag*.	The sun has risen already.
Present	Please set the *table*.	John, please sit down.
Past	I set the *dishes* on the table.	John sat down.
Past Participle	I have set the *dishes* on the table.	John has sat down.

in an active-voice sentence becomes the subject when the sentence is rewritten in the passive voice.

ACTIVE I laid the book on the shelf.

PASSIVE The book was laid on the shelf.

ACTIVE I set the dishes on the table.

PASSIVE The dishes were set on the table.

ACTIVE I raised the flag.

PASSIVE The flag was raised.

Should Versus *Would*

Some business writers prefer to use *should* with first-person subjects in formal contexts. The majority of business writers, however, recommend using *would* because *should* implies obligation.

FORMAL I *should* like to attend the seminar.

INFORMAL I *would* like to attend the seminar.

Can Versus *May*

In choosing whether to use *may* or *can*, use *may* to express permission or possibility; use *can* to express the ability or power to do something.

You *may* attend the business luncheon with us.

Can you fill the customer's order by August 13?

✔ Checkpoint 3 MISUSED VERBS

Select the correct or recommended verb in each of the following sentences.

1. When you arrive at the meeting, (sit/set) your materials on the conference table.
2. Did Shelley (lie/lay) down for a short nap?
3. The ceiling on the national debt was (risen/raised).
4. (Can/May) I leave the office early today?
5. If you (should/would) like to attend the seminar, please see me by Monday.

Check your answers in Appendix D.

SUMMARY

Verbs may be used in different tenses to express time. Unless there is an actual difference in time, avoid changing tenses unnecessarily. Business writers usually use the active voice, in which the subject is doing the action. However, the passive voice may be effective when an indirect approach is useful. Care should be taken to use troublesome verbs correctly. Don't confuse the present tense of *lie* with the past tense of *lay.* Use *can* when you want to express the power to do something; use *may* to express permission. Generally, business writers use *would* rather than *should* unless they need to express the idea of an obligation or condition.

● ● ● ● ● ● ● ● ● ● **Communication Activities**

Spelling and Word Usage

Learn to spell and use the following words. Be alert for them in the Editing Applications at the end of this chapter.

analyze	familiar	planning
changeable	incidentally	recommendation
client	librarian	similar
envelope	obvious	usable
equipment		

If necessary, refer to Appendix A for the correct usage of the following words.

already/all ready   past/passed

Practical Applications

Part A   Select the correct verb in each of the following sentences.

1. Since joining the firm six years ago, Lucy (has worked/worked) as an intern in every department.
2. It is difficult to (sit/set) for several hours during a corporate board meeting.
3. Yesterday's article in the *Herald* stated that the new Sonar electronic typewriter (is/was) one of the best on the market.
4. The delegates should (rise/raise) from their seats when the national anthem is played.
5. (May/Can) I contact you about our new product for hair care?
6. As soon as everyone is ready, we (start/will start) the training program.
7. Jonathan (will give/will have given) his speech over 25 times by the end of this year.
8. You can become very refreshed by (lying/laying) down for a few minutes.
9. If you (should/would) like to see the Broadway play, you must make reservations early.
10. By taking many workshops, she learned the business and (begins/began) to develop sales skills.

11. After returning from your meeting, please (lie/lay) your report on my desk.

12. By the end of the summer, I (painted/had painted) all the rooms in the house.

13. We have (set/sat) the meeting time for 2 p.m.

14. She purchases personal computers so that employees (have/will have) the opportunity to maintain their own files.

Part B Rewrite the following sentences using the appropriate voice (active or passive). Write "C" if the sentence does not need to be changed.

1. A new office automation project was set up by my supervisor.

2. The shipping company advertises, "We run the tightest ship in the shipping business."

3. The restaurant served beef stroganoff on Monday and on Wednesday chicken cacciatore was served.

4. The new electronic typewriters are built for reliability.

5. The warehouse staff filled the orders incorrectly.

6. Early-morning hours are often used by executives to complete yesterday's unfinished tasks.

Editing Applications

Part A Rewrite the following paragraphs in the active voice. Correct any errors in spelling and usage.

Studies are being conducted by our company to determine if the new electronic typewriters shall be useable for tasks we need to perform. After these studies are completed by our Research Department, we should not allow them to lay around unused.

Questions about the new equipment can be raised by many secretaries who did not know about the obvious ways others have benefited from them. Standard electric typewriters have been used by our office staff for the past 20 years. Hopefully, the studies shall help us decide whether we are buying new equipment.

In the meantime, information about this new equipment should be gathered by all office personnel so that you may make reccommendations to the Research Department.

Part B   Correct all errors in spelling and word usage in the following memo.

TO:	E. T. Barnes
FROM:	Valerie McCartney
DATE:	New Electronic Typewriters
SUBJECT:	January 14, 19--

As you requested this passed Monday, I have researched the new electronic typewriters, concentrating on the features most useable in our company.

Having analysed the data, I find that electronic typewriters are user-friendly in many obvous ways.   They combine the familar features of typewriters with additional features that made it easier to create and edit documents.

The following features should assist us when planing correspondence with clientes:

1. The paper may be loaded automatically.   (This feature will also apply to envelops.)

2. Errors can be corrected with a single keystroke.   Information that is changable can be dealt with easily by the secretary.

3. Pages may be stored and recalled as needed.

My reccomendation is to replace existing electric typewriters with electronic typewriters.

CHAPTER 5

Agreement of Subject and Verb

Objectives

After studying this chapter and completing the chapter exercises, you should be able to:

1. Identify the subject of a sentence.
2. Identify the verb(s) of a sentence.
3. Use verbs that agree with their subjects.
4. Spell and use a list of common business terms.

Sentences are the heart of our communication because they are the form in which we usually communicate. To be complete and correct, a sentence must have a subject and a verb and express a complete thought. A **subject** is a word or group of words that names the person, place, thing, or idea about which something is said. The subject may be a noun or a **personal pronoun** (*I, you, he, she, it, we, they*) which takes the place of the noun. The verb may be either an action verb or a linking verb that joins other words to the subject.

SINGULAR AND PLURAL SUBJECTS

To be correct, the subject and the verb must agree in number (singular or plural) and in person (first, second, or third). Although this general rule is understood by most writers, errors are frequently made in agreement because writers are uncertain of the subject or the number of the subject.

Singular Subjects

A singular subject requires a singular verb. The following examples contain singular action verbs and singular linking verbs:

	SUBJECT	VERB	
The	man	saw	the secret document.
	Mr. Bowman	has finished	the task.
The	report	is	accurate.
The	student	seems	happy.

Most present tense verbs add *s* or *es* in the third-person singular form. (Third person refers to *he, she, it,* or a noun.) A verb ending in *s*, therefore, is singular.

PERSON	VERB
First	I hold
Second	you hold
Third	he, she, it holds; the boy holds

SUBJECT	VERB	
He	sees	his friend.
Maria	writes	well.
It	looks	beautiful.

Plural Subjects

Sentences with plural subjects require plural verbs. The following examples contain plural action verbs and plural linking verbs.

	SUBJECT	VERB	
The	movers	unloaded	the furniture.
The	sentences	are written	in the past tense.
The	employees	look	upset.
	All	appear	satisfied.

To Be and *To Have*

The verbs *to be* and *to have* can cause problems in agreement because their forms are irregular. The following chart shows the singular and plural forms and the present and past tenses of *to be* and *to have*.

TO BE

Present Tense

Person	Singular	Plural
First	I am	we are
Second	you are	you are
Third	he, she, it is	they are

Past Tense

Person	Singular	Plural
First	I was	we were
Second	you were	you were
Third	he, she, it was	they were

TO HAVE

Present Tense

Person	Singular	Plural
First	I have	we have
Second	you have	you have
Third	he, she, it has	they have

Past Tense

Person	Singular	Plural
First	I had	we had
Second	you had	you had
Third	he, she, it had	they had

The verbs *to be* and *to have* may be used alone as main verbs or as helping verbs. A helping verb indicates the timing of the main verb.

SUBJECT	VERB	
He	is	an excellent employee.
She	has	the opportunity.
We	are filling	orders immediately.
They	have completed	the assignment.

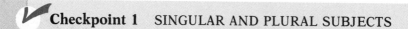

Checkpoint 1 SINGULAR AND PLURAL SUBJECTS

Examine each of the following subjects and select the verb that agrees with the subject in number (singular or plural). If both of the verb choices could be correct, select *either* as your answer. If neither of the verb choices is correct, select *neither* as your answer.

Subject	**Verb Choices**
1. memorandum	indicate, indicates, either, neither
2. cafes	is, are, either, neither
3. fathers-in-law	has seen, sees, either, neither
4. class	is watching, watches, either, neither
5. moose	graze, grazes, either, neither
6. criterion	restricts, restrict, either, neither
7. tenor	has sung, have sung, either, neither
8. wishes	comes, come, either, neither
9. executive	works, work, either, neither
10. knife	is, have, either, neither

Check your answers in Appendix D. If you answered two or more incorrectly, review the sections entitled (1) Singular Subjects, (2) Plural Subjects, and (3) *To Be* and *To Have.*

COMPOUND SUBJECTS

Sentences with compound subjects contain more than one subject. Apply the following rules for agreement of the verb with a compound subject. The subjects are underlined once and the verbs are underlined twice.

Rule 1   A compound subject joined by *and* is usually plural.

President Stephen Hunter and his secretary are in agreement.

The electrician and the plumber are scheduled to be here on Monday.

There are only two exceptions to this rule. When the compound subject joined by *and* is considered to be one unit, use a singular verb.

The CEO and president, Mrs. Flannigan, has resigned.

If *each, every, many a,* or *many an* precedes the compound subject, always use a singular verb.

Each staff person and **each** manager is covered under the new benefits program.

Many an investor and homeowner has supported the tax levy.

Rule 2   When a compound subject is joined by *or, nor, either/or,* or *neither/nor,* the verb agrees with the subject closest to the verb.

Either Mr. Jones **or** his employees are responsible for the error.

Neither his employees **nor** Mr. Jones was satisfied.

✔ **Checkpoint 2**   COMPOUND SUBJECTS

Correct the errors in subject-verb agreement in the following sentences. Write "C" if the sentence is correct.

1. Alisa and William is to be at the sales meeting.
2. Each sales representative and each store manager hopes to sell at least $150,000 this month.
3. Every executive and secretary are to attend the conference.
4. Neither Jean nor the other managers is happy about the decision.
5. My instructor and advisor, Dr. Tiger, has given me a great deal of help.
6. When they was asking for the data, Juan and Neil was checking the content of the report.
7. Either the men or Margaret were to complete the form.
8. The cook and the waiter were having an argument.

Check your answers in Appendix D. If you missed more than two items, review the section entitled Compound Subjects.

COLLECTIVE NOUNS

Collective nouns identify groups. Examples include such nouns as *audience, board, class, club, committee, department, faculty, family, jury, majority, school,* and *team.* In the following examples, the subject is underlined once and the verb is underlined twice.

Rule 1   A collective noun uses a singular verb when the group acts as one unit.

> The jury has reached its decision.

> The board of directors meets quarterly.

Rule 2   A collective noun uses a plural verb when members of the group act separately.

> The jury do not agree on the defendant's motive.

> The board of directors are voting on the proposal.

To emphasize that the group is acting separately, you may wish to rewrite the sentence.

> The members of the jury do not agree on the defendant's motive.

> The members of the board of directors are voting on the proposal.

INTERVENING MODIFIERS

Modifiers (words that describe) occurring between the subject and the verb are called **intervening modifiers.** Intervening modifiers may be single words, but often they are a group of words containing nouns that differ in number from the subject. Disregard intervening modifiers when determining the subject and the verb of the sentence. The intervening modifiers are italicized in the following examples.

>   S   V
> The manager *of the musical group* is going to New York.

>   S   V
> The members *of the audience* have different reactions to the play.

In the first example, the singular subject *manager* requires the singular verb *is.* In the second example, the plural subject requires a plural verb. In both cases, the intervening modifiers are ignored.

Select the correct verb in the following sentences. If both of the verb
choices could be correct, select *either* as your answer; if neither of the
verb choices is correct, select *neither*.

1. The audience _____ the play. (like, likes, either, neither)
2. The representative of the Committee for New Policies _____ to
   attend the January 5 meeting. (are going, were going, either, neither)
3. The members of Congress _____ voting on bill #11978-a. (is,
   are, either, neither)
4. The news _____ important enough to put on the front page.
   (was, were, either, neither)
5. The deer _____ standing in the middle of the road. (is, was, either, neither)

Check your answers in Appendix D.

SUMMARY

To be an effective business communicator, follow these rules to assure
that the subjects and the verbs of your sentences are in agreement:

1. Use a singular subject with a singular verb and a plural subject with
   a plural verb.
2. Generally use a plural verb when *and* is used to connect the items in
   a compound subject. When *or, nor, either/or,* or *neither/nor* is used to
   connect the items in a compound subject, however, the verb could
   be singular or plural, depending on the subject that is closest to the
   verb. If the subject nearest the verb is singular, use a singular verb;
   if it is plural, use a plural verb.
3. The verbs *to be* and *to have* are used both as main verbs and as helping verbs. Because they are very irregular, exercise care when using
   them.
4. If a collective noun acts as a unit, use a singular verb. If members of
   the group act separately, use a plural verb.
5. Disregard intervening modifiers that separate subjects from their
   verbs.

Spelling and Word Usage

Your ability to spell and to use words correctly is an essential skill in the business world. Learn to spell and use the following words. Be alert for them in the Editing Applications at the end of the chapter.

acknowledgment	guarantee	questionnaire
basically	leisure	schedule
cannot	misspell	temperament
deficiency	ninety	visibility
eligible	parallel	

If necessary, refer to Appendix A for the correct usage of the following words:

addition/edition	hear/here	stationary/stationery

Some of the misspelled words and misused words presented in previous chapters are also applied in the Editing Applications.

Practical Applications

Part A   Select the verb that agrees with the subject. If both of the verb choices could be correct, select *either* as your answer; if neither of the verb choices is correct, select *neither*.

Subject	Verb Choices
1. car	run, runs, either, neither
2. students	study, studies, either, neither
3. walls	are, were, either, neither
4. daughter	were telling, are telling, either, neither
5. trees	are, were, either, neither
6. employees	has listened, had listened, either, neither
7. players	have run, ran, either, neither
8. child	stands, stand, either, neither
9. datum	is, are, either, neither
10. deer	was, are, either, neither

Part B   Correct the errors in subject-verb agreement in the following sentences. Write "C" if the sentence is correct.

1. All executives are to attend the sales meeting.
2. The goods was obtained from donations made by the neighbors.
3. The papers on the desk is not to be filed; they is to be given to Ms. Taylor, the new vice president.
4. Though they believes that he is responsible for the loss, no one thinks he will lose his position.
5. Donnie, while searching for the missing documents, have found several items which had been misplaced.
6. While transferring the data to the disks, Juanita and Quincy was distracted by the noise.
7. Effective listening, one of the major means of communication, takes a great deal of concentration.
8. Neither Mr. Welch nor his students is going to the school's reunion.
9. Matt or Derek are going to represent us at the meeting.
10. The committee was unified in its decision.

Editing Applications

Part A   Correct all errors in spelling and subject-verb agreement in the following paragraphs.

1. The results of the questionnaire sent to ninety-five organizations reveals that the visibility of information processing workstations within the office environment are unparalelled. Managers and executives basically use their workstations to create documents and make decisions. Support personnel produce final documents on letterhead stationary and performs other supportive work.

   Users, regardless of their level, acknowlege their lack of expertise in utilizing much of the applications software and report they can not perform the infrequently used functions. Some users complain that they do not have the time or temperment to learn new applications.

2. Professional people such as yourself who travel frequently realize the importance of scheduling liesure time during business trips. For your enjoyment, the Sundowner has added ninty rooms or suites. Each have luxury accomodations, including a big screen telavision.

The expansive grounds surrounding the Sundowner features tennis courts, an Olympic-sized swimming pool, and a championship golf course. As a preferred corporate customer, you is elgible for a 20 percent discount. We gaurantee your satisfaction.

Part B   Read the following memo carefully; correct all errors.

October 3, 19--

All Employees

NEW COMPANY INVESTMENT PLAN

To provide you with an additional means of building financial security and overcome any retirement fund deficeincy you may have, the Board of Directors have voted to institute a stock purchase plan effective immediately.   This voluntary plan provides you with another opportunity to acquire stock.   Here's how it works:

1. Through payroll deductions, you elects to make contributions. In a year's time, you may contribute as little as the price of ten shares or as much as 15 percent of your salary.

2. The amount you contribute is applied toward the purchase price of the stock.   You receive a 5 percent discount on the market price, and the company pay the brokerage fee.

3. Upon receiving a stock certificate, you may earn dividends and vote as a stockholder.

Every company employee, including marketers, are eligible. Just fill out the enclosed questionaire and return it within ninety days.   Check to be sure that your social security number is correct and that none of the information is mispelled.

Louise D. Claybourne

CHAPTER 6

Pronoun Selection

Objectives

After studying this chapter and completing the chapter exercises, you should be able to:

1. Identify and use nominative case pronouns correctly.
2. Identify and use possessive case pronouns correctly.
3. Identify and use objective case pronouns correctly.
4. Spell and use a list of common business terms.

Pronouns take the place of nouns. The personal pronoun is one of the few parts of speech that has different cases (or forms). For example, the pronouns *I, me, my,* and *mine* all refer to the person who is writing or speaking. A personal pronoun changes its case depending upon its relationship to other words in the sentence. The three main cases of personal pronouns are nominative, possessive, and objective.

THE NOMINATIVE CASE

Pronouns that act as the subject of the verb or a complement of a linking verb are referred to as **nominative case** (or *subjective case*) **pronouns.** The pronoun *who* and the personal pronouns that follow are in the nominative case.

PERSON	SINGULAR	PLURAL
First	I	we
Second	you	you
Third	he, she, it	they

Rule 1   Use a nominative case pronoun when it is the subject of a verb.

Carla and *I* were pleased with the results.

He is happy that *she* received the promotion.

They would like to see the movie again.

Rule 2   When the pronoun appears after a form of the verb *to be* (*am, is, are, was, were*) or a verb phrase ending in *be, being,* or *been,* use a nominative case pronoun. (A pronoun that renames the subject and follows the verb *to be* is called a **predicate nominative**.)

It is *she* who received the award.

It must have been *he* who called.

If I were *he,* I would have finished the report today.

Was it *she* who received the award?   (Mentally rearrange the sentence: It was *she* who received the award.)

THE POSSESSIVE CASE

Pronouns that show ownership or possession are referred to as **possessive case pronouns.** Unlike nouns, however, pronouns never include an apostrophe when indicating possessive case. The pronoun *whose* and the personal pronouns in the following list are in the possessive case.

PERSON	SINGULAR	PLURAL
First	my, mine	our, ours
Second	your, yours	your, yours
Third	his, her, hers, its	their, theirs

Rule 1 Use a possessive case pronoun to show ownership.

Use *my, your, his, her, its, their,* or *our* when the possessive case pronoun comes immediately before the noun it modifies.

>Those are *my* books.

>The animal cannot climb because *its* claws have been removed.

>*Their* favorite flavor is strawberry.

Use *mine, yours, his, hers, ours,* and *theirs* when the possessive pronoun is separated from the noun it modifies or when the noun being modified is not stated.

>Those are *mine.*

>The idea was not *hers.*

Note: Do not confuse the possessive pronouns *whose, its, your,* and *their* with the contractions *who's, it's, you're,* and *they're.*

Rule 2 Use possessive case pronouns immediately before a gerund. A **gerund** is a verb form with an *-ing* suffix (*singing, buying, selling*) that is used as a noun.

>*His* transferring into the department caused problems.

>The insurance company was aided by *your* witnessing the accident.

THE OBJECTIVE CASE

Pronouns that act as objects to complete the thought expressed by the subject and verb are referred to as **objective case pronouns.** The pronoun *whom* and the pronouns that follow are in the objective case.

PERSON	SINGULAR	PLURAL
First	me	us
Second	you	you
Third	her, him, it	them

Rule   Use objective case pronouns for all objects.

Use an objective case pronoun when the pronoun follows a transitive verb or receives the action of the verb.

> Please send *them* by express mail.   (Send what? Send *them*.)
>
> He bought *her* a necklace.   (Bought a necklace for whom? For *her*.)
>
> The manager gave *us* his tickets for the game.   (Gave his tickets to whom? To *us*.)

Note: If the pronoun answers the questions "what" or "whom" about the action verb, it is a **direct object.** If the pronoun states "to whom" or "for whom" something is done, it is an **indirect object.**

Use an objective case pronoun when the pronoun follows a preposition. (Prepositions are words like *as, on, to, for,* or *about.* See page 114 for a list of prepositions.) A pronoun following a preposition is called the **object of the preposition.** The object answers the question "what" or "whom."

> Dennis gave a copy of the printout to *me*.   (To whom? To *me*.)
>
> I made it available for *her* to analyze on Monday.   (For whom? For *her*.)

✔ **Checkpoint 1**   SELECTING PRONOUN CASES

Select the correct form in the sentences below.

1. Bob and (I/me) will be able to attend the meeting.
2. Jan and (he/him) were able to finish the book on schedule.
3. Ling said that (you/your) singing was the hit of the show.
4. (Its, It's) up to the group; the choice is (their's/theirs).
5. He responded, "It was not (I/me); Alexia and (he/him) assisted the man who was injured."
6. (You/Your) working overtime enabled us to meet (our/ours) deadline.
7. It was (he/him) who discovered the mistake.
8. Nick arrived at the concert hall with (she/her) and (my/mine) aunt.
9. Please give Ted and (she/her) a copy of the proposal and ask for (they're/their) suggestions.
10. (It's/Its) Senator Bagwell (whose/who's) policies have been criticized by the press.

Check your answers in Appendix D.

WHO AND *WHOM*

Although the pronouns *who* and *whom* cause many problems, they can be mastered quite easily. Simply apply the same rules that you would for another nominative or objective case pronoun.

Who is a nominative case pronoun. It functions as a subject or as a **predicate pronoun** (a pronoun that refers to the subject and follows a form of *to be*). *Whom* is an objective case pronoun. It functions as an object — either an object of the verb or the object of a preposition.

Who and *whom* are used to ask questions and to introduce clauses.

Who/Whom in Questions

Whenever *who* and *whom* ask questions, mentally rearrange the sentence and substitute *he/she/they* or *him/her/them* as shown in parentheses after the following examples:

> *Who* should attend?   (*She* should attend. *Who* is the subject of the interrogative sentence.)
>
> *Who* is she?   (She is *she. Who* is a predicate pronoun.)
>
> To *whom* do you wish to speak?   (I wish to speak to *him. Whom* is the object of the preposition *to.*)
>
> *Whom* did Tom select?   (Tom did select *him. Whom* is the object of the verb *did select.*)

Who/Whom in Clauses

Who and *whom* frequently introduce a dependent clause. **A clause** is a group of words that contains a subject and a verb. A **dependent clause** does not form a complete thought and cannot stand alone as a sentence. The dependent clauses are italicized in the following sentences:

> A man *who was standing on the corner* saw the accident.
>
> The woman *whom we trust* will attend the meeting.

Whenever *who* or *whom* appear in a dependent clause, determine how the pronoun is used within the clause. Ignore the rest of the sentence. As you analyze the sentence, follow these steps:

1. Identify the dependent clause beginning with *who* or *whom*.
2. If necessary, rearrange the clause in its natural order — subject, verb, complement or object. Ignore expressions such as *I know, in my judgment, you say,* or *we believe* that may occur within the clause.
3. Substitute *he/she/they* or *him/her/them* for *who* or *whom*.

Now apply these steps to understand why *who* or *whom* is selected in the following examples. The dependent clauses are italicized.

- Remember, use *who* or *whoever* if the pronoun is the subject of the clause.

    A man *who* I believe *was standing on the corner* saw the accident.   (*He* was standing on the corner. *Who* is used because it is the subject of the dependent clause.)

    I will speak to *whoever is available.*   (*She* or *he* is available. *Whoever* is the subject of the clause.)

- Use *whom* or *whomever* if the pronoun acts as an object of the clause. Note that each of the clauses already contains a subject and a verb.

    Brian is a friend *whom I can trust.*   (I can trust *him*. *Whom* acts as the object of the verb *can trust.*)

    Is the man *to whom we gave the letter* in the room?   (We gave the letter to *him*. *Whom* acts as the object of the preposition *to.*)

    The agent *to whom the award was given* sold over $8 million of real estate. (The award was given to *her*. *Whom* is the object of the preposition *to.*)

COMPOUND PERSONAL PRONOUNS

Compound personal pronouns are formed by adding *self* or *selves* to personal pronouns.

SINGULAR	PLURAL
myself	ourselves
yourself	yourselves
himself, herself	themselves

Rule 1   Use a compound personal pronoun to emphasize preceding nouns or pronouns in the sentence.

    I *myself* corrected the compositions.   (*Myself* emphasizes the action of *I.*)

    Terri did the work *herself.*   (Using *herself* emphasizes that Terri did the work.)

Rule 2   Use a compound personal pronoun to direct the action of the verb back to the subject.

    They satisfied *themselves.*

    Stephen excused *himself.*

Note: The correct third person pronouns are *himself*, not *hisself*, and *themselves*, not *theirselves*. *Hisself* and *theirselves* are never correct. Be careful when using compound personal pronouns. Frequently these "self" pronouns are incorrectly used as substitutes for nominative or objective case pronouns.

INCORRECT   Victor and *myself* went to the clothing market.   (There is no preceding noun or pronoun for *myself* to emphasize or refer to.)

CORRECT   Victor and *I* went to the clothing market.

✔ Checkpoint 2   SELECTING CORRECT PRONOUNS

Select the correct pronoun in each of the following sentences.

1. I will complete the forms for (him/himself/hisself).
2. Judy finished the memorandum and gave the graphs to Robert and (me/myself).
3. Tom (him/himself/hisself) gave Dee Dee the final draft of the play.
4. To (who/whom) did you give the book?
5. Wayne Smith, (who/whom) we believe caused the accident, drives a red convertible.
6. Where is the man (who/whom) we saw last night?
7. She delivered the plans to Andrea and (me/myself).
8. Give the message to (whoever/whomever) answers the telephone.
9. Michele provided the information for Joshua and (him/himself).
10. The woman (who/whom) we worked for is now working at Selby and Smith's.

Check your answers in Appendix D.

SUMMARY

Pronouns can cause problems because they take different forms depending on their relationship to other words in a sentence. The forms of pronouns that we can use are the nominative case, the possessive case, the objective case, and compound personal pronouns.

Nominative case pronouns have two uses: (1) as subjects of sentences or clauses and (2) as predicate pronouns. Possessive case pronouns are used (1) when showing possession and (2) when a pronoun immediately precedes a gerund. Objective case pronouns are used (1) when a pronoun is an object and (2) when a preposition immediately precedes a pronoun. Compound personal pronouns also have two uses: (1) to emphasize preceding nouns or pronouns and (2) to direct the action of the verb back to the subject.

● ● ● ● ● ● ● ● ● Communication Activities

Spelling and Word Usage

Learn to spell and use the following words. Be alert for them in the Editing Applications at the end of the chapter.

allocate	illegible	receipt
beginning	liaison	scissors
career	morale	tragedy
definitely	noticeable	volume
enthusiasm	partial	

If necessary, refer to Appendix A for the correct usage of these words.

advise/advice	its/it's	your/you're

Some of the frequently misspelled and misused words presented in previous chapters are also applied in this chapter's Editing Applications.

Practical Applications

Part A   Select the correct pronoun in each sentence.

1. The trainer will work with (whoever/whomever) has completed the first module.
2. If I were (he/him), I would not attend tonight's meeting.
3. She gave Mary and (he/him) the copy of the document.
4. Did June see Greg and (he/him) at the conference this weekend?
5. The supervisors had no objections to (him/his) moving to the new location.
6. She indicated that those boxes belonged to you and (she/her).

7. The teacher administered the test (himself/hisself).

8. Joe and (I/myself) are going to the opera tonight.

9. The man (who/whom) is wearing a conservative blue suit will pass the message on to our co-workers in his department.

10. From (who/whom) did the package come?

Part B Underline each pronoun in the following sentences. Then determine if each pronoun is in the correct form. Correct sentences containing pronoun errors by rewriting the sentences using the appropriate pronoun. Write "C" if the sentence is correct.

1. By them assisting the officer and me, he and I were able to keep the traffic moving in spite of the accident.

2. Jenny and Brian corrected the test theirselves.

3. Scott, the man who you recommended, wrote the report hisself.

4. Me and him are pleased that we were selected for the team.

5. If I were him, I would not respond to the memorandum that was sent by Alice and he.

6. Randy and him asked Debbie to return the shoes to the locker.

7. Did May ask for the operator who assisted her when making the collect call?

8. Him working on the report hisself helped to persuade John to accept the results of the study.

9. Go to the kitchen and get your food yourself.

10. Mark hisself was able to complete the project for Terra and I.

Editing Applications

Part A Read the following paragraphs carefully. Correct all errors in spelling and pronoun usage.

1. Your definately correct! The clerk whom I believe calculated your bill did make an error. Because of you noticing the error and returning your reciept, Jan and myself were able to correct you're account and our inventory records. The correction will be reflected in your statement, which will be sent on the forth of next month.

Thank you for calling the error to our attention. By your helping us to hold down the number of errors made by my staff and I, we are able to help in maintaining employee enthusiasm and moral.

2. Thank you for you're inquiry regarding the position of marketing representative for our firm. A marketing representative's primary role is that of liason between our sales and advertising departments. The enclosed job description explains this potential carear choice in detail, including a general range of salaries alocated for entry-level marketers. I advice you to follow these procedures when submitting the application provided: (1) attach a cover letter—printed on high-quality stationary—to (2) your completed application. Although we prefer typewritten responses, a handwritten application *is* acceptable, provided that your writing is not ellegible.

Part B   Read the memo carefully and correct all errors.

TO: Leigh Ann Royal, Supervisor
FROM: John Arenis, Auditing Department Head
DATE: February 10, 19--
SUBJECT: Training for Income Tax Laws

Because of the changes in income tax law, we will need to train our auditors.   Because your schedale at the beginning of the new fiscal year is not as demanding as during the begining of the calendar year, the training sessions are schedaled for July 6–8.   Both Bob Johansen and myself will attend the sessions as well.

Leigh Ann, thank you for your immediate response to the 19-- budget request.   You're enthusasm is a credit to our department; I can see why the moral is high among your co-workers.

CHAPTER 7

Agreement of Pronouns and Nouns

Objectives

After studying this chapter and completing the chapter exercises, you should be able to:

1. Identify the antecedents of pronouns.
2. Use pronouns that agree with their antecedents in person, number, and gender.
3. Provide pronouns with clear antecedents.
4. Spell and use a list of common business terms.

As you have learned, a pronoun is a word that takes the place of a noun. Pronouns are used in a sentence so that the nouns do not have to be repeated. The word the pronoun replaces is its **antecedent**. Generally the antecedent is a noun, but it may be a pronoun. In the examples in this chapter, the antecedents are italicized and the pronouns are in bold print.

> *Eric* asked if **his** requisition had been processed. (**His** refers to the antecedent *Eric.*)

> *She* is anxious to learn if **her** request has been approved. (**Her** refers to the antecedent *she.*)

When selecting pronouns to act as substitutes for nouns, you will want to be sure that the appropriate pronoun is selected and that the reference to the antecedent is clear.

AGREEMENT OF PERSONAL PRONOUNS AND ANTECEDENTS

To communicate accurately, personal pronouns must agree with their antecedents in three ways:

1. *Gender.* Use feminine pronouns to refer to feminine antecedents and masculine pronouns to refer to masculine antecedents. Use neuter pronouns when gender is unimportant.
2. *Person.* A first-person pronoun is used to refer to the person speaking. Use a second-person pronoun to refer to the person spoken to; use a third-person pronoun to refer to the person or thing spoken about.
3. *Number.* Use a singular pronoun to refer to a singular noun. Use a plural pronoun to refer to a plural noun.

The sentences that follow apply pronoun-antecedent agreement in gender, person, and number. The pronouns are in bold and the antecedents are italicized.

FIRST PERSON   Hi! My name is *Suzanne.* **I** am a new student.

SECOND PERSON   *Mary,* the tickets are **yours** if **you** would like to attend.

In the first example, *Suzanne* is speaking about herself; therefore, Suzanne refers to herself as **I**. In the second example, the speaker is addressing *Mary;* **you** and **yours** refer to the antecedent *Mary.*

Third-Person Pronoun Agreement

Although the rule for pronoun-antecedent agreement is not difficult, third-person pronouns often cause problems in either gender or number.

Problems arise in gender when a singular antecedent could be either male or female. For example, nouns such as *manager, nurse, plumber, president, secretary,* or *worker* could apply to either gender. It is no longer appropriate to use *his* to refer to both genders, nor should jobs or positions be classified as "men's" work or "women's" work. When replacing a singular noun with a pronoun, therefore, use both the male and the female pronouns or rewrite the sentence to avoid language stereotyping. The pronouns are in bold and the antecedents are italicized in the following examples.

OUTDATED	A good *manager* encourages **his** staff.
MALE AND FEMALE PRONOUNS	A good *manager* encourages **his** or **her** staff.
REWRITTEN IN PLURAL	Good *managers* encourage **their** staff.
REWRITTEN IN SECOND PERSON	Encourage your staff.
ELIMINATE THE PRONOUN	Good managers provide encouragement.

Third-person pronouns must also agree with their antecedents in number. A singular antecedent requires a singular pronoun; a plural antecedent requires a plural pronoun. When applying this rule to a collective noun, you must determine whether the group is acting as a unit or individually. In the following examples, the pronouns are in bold and the antecedents are italicized.

SINGULAR	*Dick* completed **his** report at **his** workstation.
PLURAL	The *students* completed **their** reports at **their** workstations.
SINGULAR	The *jury* reached **its** decision. (The jury is acting as one unit.)
PLURAL	The *police* were issued **their** assignments. (Each person has an individual assignment.)

Indefinite Pronoun Agreement

Agreement in number may also be a problem when the antecedent is an **indefinite pronoun**—a word that does not refer to a specific noun. The following indefinite pronouns are always singular:

anyone	anybody	anything
each	every	everything
everyone	everybody	something
one	no one	
someone	somebody	

- When a singular indefinite pronoun is used as an antecedent, the pronoun that refers to the antecedent must be singular.

    Each horse must have **its** tail braided.   (*Each* refers to *horse,* which is singular.)

    Everyone is to state **his** or **her** opinion.   (*Everyone* is singular.)

- The pronouns *both, few, many, others,* and *several* are always plural. Use a plural pronoun to refer to each of these words.

    Several students have **their** own computers.

    Both of the managers brought **their** golf clubs.

- *All, none, any, some, more,* and *most* may be either singular or plural, depending upon their use in the sentence.

    Most of the men left **their** notes at home.   (*Most* refers to *men,* which is plural.)

    Some of the merchandise has arrived, but **it** has not been displayed yet. (*Some* refers to *merchandise,* which is singular.)

Compound Antecedents

Agreement in number is sometimes a problem with compound antecedents, which consist of more than one element. When two elements are joined by *and,* generally use a plural pronoun to refer to the compound antecedent. In the following examples, the pronouns are in bold and the antecedents to which they refer are italicized.

    When *David* and *I* drafted the proposal, **we** remembered **our** memo to Mr. Albert.

- Compound antecedents joined by *or/nor, either/or,* and *neither/nor* require special attention. If the two antecedents are singular, use a singular pronoun.

    Either *Steven* or *Sara* has to share **his** or **her** printer.

    Neither *Michael* nor *James* has done **his** homework.

If the two antecedents are plural, use a plural pronoun.

    Neither the *men* nor the *women* are willing to share **their** profits.

- When one antecedent is singular and the other is plural, the pronoun must agree in person, number, and gender with the antecedent nearest the pronoun.

    Neither the man nor the *students* expressed **their** opinion.

    Neither the students nor the *man* expressed **his** opinion.

Complete each statement by supplying the correct pronoun(s). Then underline the appropriate antecedent(s).

1. The executive herself indicated that _____ felt the new policy was needed.

2. William Wilson and Mrs. Phillips implied that _____ were not satisfied with the procedure used when making exchanges.

3. Did the managers indicate that _____ were going to Dallas next week?

4. My name is Jeff Clark. _____ have just moved into the neighborhood.

5. Once hired, the new electrical engineer will be given _____ assignment.

6. The workers were happy with _____ new equipment.

7. Each of the auditors in the department received _____ bonus.

8. Others who work for the company will also receive _____ bonuses.

9. Some of the players were happy with _____ new shoes.

10. Neither the school board nor the faculty presented _____ case clearly.

Check your answers in Appendix D.

PRONOUNS WITH SPECIAL USES

The pronouns *who, which,* and *that* are **relative pronouns** used to introduce a dependent clause. (*Who* includes the forms *whose* and *whom.*) Use *who* to refer to persons, *which* to refer to animals and inanimate objects, and *that* to refer to persons, animals, and inanimate objects. To assure that the meaning is clear, the dependent clause should immediately follow the noun it describes. In the following examples, the clauses are underlined and the antecedents they describe are italicized; relative pronouns are in bold.

The *man* **who** did the work is standing next to Bob.

Emily is the *type* of student **that** anyone would love to hire.

The *man* **whom** we hired is in the Accounting Department.

The *boy* **whose** touchdown won last Saturday's game cannot play this week.

Where are the *pets* **that** won the blue ribbons?

The pronouns *this, that, these,* and *those* are often called **demonstrative pronouns** because they point out (or demonstrate) specific nouns. Use *this* and *that* to refer to a singular noun; use *these* and *those* to refer to plural nouns.

SINGULAR **This** is my *decision* to make.

PLURAL **These** *chips* taste better than **those.**

Sometimes *them* is incorrectly substituted for *these* or *those*.

INCORRECT Give me them shoes.

CORRECT Give me those shoes.

Note: When *this, that, these,* and *those* immediately precede the noun they modify (*these chips, those shoes*), they are called **demonstrative adjectives.**

CLEAR PRONOUN REFERENCE

Pronouns depend upon a noun or another pronoun for their meaning. The meaning will be ambiguous if the relationship between the pronoun and its antecedent is not clear. To assure that your message can be interpreted accurately and easily, make the pronoun-antecedent relationship obvious. Repeat the noun or use a direct quotation if the sentence contains two possible antecedents for a pronoun. If the antecedent cannot easily be determined, revise the sentence.

AMBIGUOUS John told Bob that it was his fault.   (Whose fault was it?)

CLEAR John told Bob, "It was my fault."

AMBIGUOUS She told her sister that she dances well.   (Which sister dances well?)

CLEAR She said to her sister, "You dance well."

AMBIGUOUS The advisors studied the proposals for hours before submitting their decisions. They were well written.   (Were the decisions or the proposals well written?)

CLEAR The advisors studied the proposals for hours before submitting their decisions. All of the proposals were well written.

Avoid using pronouns such as *this, which,* and *that* to refer to the idea expressed in the preceding clause or sentence. Remember, a pronoun can only refer to a noun or another pronoun. To correct a vague reference of a pronoun, insert a specific antecedent after the pronoun or rewrite the sentence to eliminate the pronoun.

VAGUE   We sang a song. This made everyone feel good.   (**This** cannot refer to *sang a song.*)

CLEAR   We sang a song. Singing made everyone feel good.

VAGUE   The teacher was pleased that they had all read the assignment. This made for a lively class discussion.   (**This** cannot refer to the clause *that they had all read the assignment.*)

CLEAR   The teacher was pleased that they had all read the assignment. This preparation made for a lively class discussion.

Be consistent in your use of pronouns within a sentence or a series of related sentences. Once you have made a choice, use the same person (first, second, or third) consistently throughout.

INCONSISTENT   Before planting *your* garden, **one** should take time to prepare the soil.   (Shifts from the second person to the third person.)

INCONSISTENT   Before planting *one's* garden, **you** should take time to prepare the soil.   (Shifts from the third person to the second person.)

CONSISTENT   Before planting *one's* garden, **one** should take time to prepare the soil.

✔ Checkpoint 2 PRONOUN REFERENCE

Rewrite the following sentences to correct any errors in pronoun-antecedent agreement. Write "C" if the sentence is correct.

1. Mary and WynnDee played in the game last night. The coach was pleased with the way they played.

2. Listening to Mr. Callens speak was inspiring. That made everyone feel much better.

3. Tanya told Clarise that she should attend class.

4. The statement was issued last week. This satisfied everyone.

5. Mrs. Ruiz told Miss Gray that she would be able to travel to Europe this summer.

6. Because of the lack of equipment, neither John nor the men will have his jobs completed on schedule.

7. Neither the engineers nor the technical writers have made their position clear.

8. Even though you may not approve of the time set for the presentation, one has to be happy with the opportunity to give it.

9. When one has to do a job, seldom are they happy about it.

10. The administrator which presided over the meeting was an eloquent speaker.

Check your answers in Appendix D.

SUMMARY

The word that a pronoun refers to is called an antecedent. For accurate communication, antecedents and pronouns must agree in person, number, and gender; and the relationship between the antecedent and the pronoun must be clear. The relative pronoun *who* is used to refer to persons, *which* to refer to animals and inanimate objects, and *that* to refer to persons, animals, and inanimate objects.

Determining whether an indefinite pronoun such as *each, one, both,* and *most* is singular or plural can be difficult. Some indefinite pronouns are always singular, some are always plural, and others can be either singular or plural. Sentences containing compound antecedents joined by *and* require a plural pronoun. If the compound antecedents are joined by *or/nor, either/or,* or *neither/nor,* the pronoun should agree with the nearest antecedent. Sometimes you must repeat the noun or revise the sentence if the relationship between the pronoun and its antecedent is not clear.

● ● ● ● ● ● ● ● ● Communication Activities

Spelling and Word Usage

Learn to spell and use the following words. Be alert for them in the Editing Applications at the end of this chapter.

believe	immediately	receive
census	libel	separate
dependent	mortgage	unique
enthusiastic	personnel	waive
facilities		

If necessary, refer to Appendix A for the correct usage of these words.

affect/effect   all ready/already   allot/a lot   lay/lie

Some of the misspelled and misused words presented in previous chapters are also applied in the Editing Applications.

Practical Applications

Part A   For each sentence, identify the antecedent of the italicized pronoun.

1. Athough the teacher was late for class, *he* still gave the test.
2. The test was very difficult, and *it* required a great deal of concentration.
3. Both Frank and Mike, *who* work for a furniture manufacturer, were able to complete the course.
4. Ling Mae and Chou Mai have had *their* visas cancelled.
5. The chairperson said, "I believe everyone will be able to finish *his or her* work on schedule."

Part B   Correct the errors in pronoun-antecedent agreement. Write "C" if the sentence is correct.

1. The accountant who keeps the books for my companies said that he respects their privacy.
2. The man which was standing near the entrance reported that the child had run into the cave.
3. Jones Brothers, Inc., submitted their bid of $5,000 a house.
4. Neither Jane nor Karen had their assignment.
5. Alton indicated that the books belong to them children.
6. Either Miss McGee or Miss Donaldson is going to present their view about Proposal #159-a.
7. After one works so hard to complete the project, we cannot help but be disappointed when it was cancelled.
8. Dr. Ramirez will be busy grading exams; she has to give her class its final scores by Monday.

Part C   Select the correct pronouns in the sentences below.

1. Where are (them/those) reports?

2. Each soldier and the sailors received (its/their) orders for the new military facility.
3. The family said that (its/their) new house is beautiful.
4. Had one known the woman whom you nominated, (one/you/we/they) would have voted for her.
5. The cats (who/that) won the awards were beautiful.
6. The team is supportive of every one of (its/their) members.
7. Either Matt or his peers will give (his/their) report.
8. Either his peers or Matt will give (his/their) report.

Editing Applications

Part A   Read this paragraph carefully. Correct all errors in pronoun agreement, spelling, and word usage.

The census has all ready been completed. The survey on the IRS revealed several findings.

a. Most households have more than one dependant.
b. Many of the forms that were returned contained illegible handwriting.
c. Only a few forms were recieved at the beginning of the tax season. Most of them required a refund.
d. The principle of one dependant—one deduction was carefully followed.
e. The IRS employees were among the first to apply for its refunds.
f. Most taxpayers will receive his or her refund within six weeks of their filing date.
g. Few people are enthusiastic about the system.

These findings confirm earlier studies. The volume of work each form requires is overwhelming due to the forms' complexity.

Part B   Copy the paragraph below on a separate sheet of paper, correcting all errors.

Ms. Andrews, who is in charge of all advertising pamphlets, has developed new procedures for ordering advertising pamphlets. Beginning next Monday, all pamphlets will be distributed only from the corporate office. This will eliminate stocking seperate inventories of pamphlets at each branch office as well as the corporate office. Should a salesperson require pamphlets, he should request them by its stock number so that the order can be filled easily and quickly. All regional branch managers are encouraged to implement this procedure with his or her customer support staff as well.

Part C   Correct all errors in pronouns, spelling, and word usage in the memo.

TO: Sabrina Irwin
FROM: Danny Montgomery
DATE: December 15, 19--
SUBJECT: Townshed versus Bell

Sabrina, because we have allot of experience with cases similar to Townshed versus Bell, I recommend we accept this case.   I believe that you and me are the most qualified to accept the case.   We will, of course, request a support staff.

We should expect the plaintiffs lawyers to seek a lien on the building and stationary equipment.   This will enable the defendent to file for bankruptcy.   If bankruptcy is unacceptable to the plaintiff, we will then be in a position for bargaining.

CHAPTER 8

General Direction for Writing a B__
I Items to Include in Review
  A Title and Name of Author
  B Central Theme of Book
  C Some of the Important People
  D Setting for the Story
  E Brief Summary of Some Incidents
  F Comments and Opinion of th__
II General ___ Followed
  A Sho___ s Intere___

Misplaced and Misused Modifiers

Objectives

After studying this chapter and completing the chapter exercises, you should be able to:

1. Use appropriate adjectives and adverbs to add variety to your communication.
2. Avoid using misplaced and dangling modifiers.
3. Use the comparative and superlative forms of modifiers correctly.
4. Use confusing modifiers correctly.
5. Spell and use a list of common business terms.

MODIFIERS: ADJECTIVES AND ADVERBS

So far we have reviewed nouns, pronouns, and verbs, which tell us what is happening in a sentence. In this chapter we will review **modifiers**, words that bring color and variety to our writing style. Consider the following two sentences:

> That Christmas tree is decorated.
>
> That tall Christmas tree is decorated with Mary's sparkling garland and over forty colorful glass ornaments.

Notice how the use of modifiers in the second sentence creates a vivid image in your mind. Using modifiers effectively can help you to write precisely and forcefully. Modifiers are classified as either adjectives or adverbs.

Identifying Adjectives

Adjectives describe or modify nouns and pronouns. The adjectives are italicized in the following examples.

> *That tall Christmas* tree is decorated with *Mary's sparkling* garland and over *forty colorful glass* ornaments.

Adjectives generally answer the questions *what kind? which one?* and *how many?*

What Kind? Descriptive adjectives describe the characteristics and qualities of a noun or pronoun.

> She is an *ambitious, creative* leader.
>
> The automobile features *tinted glass* windows and an *automatic* transmission.

Which One? Demonstrative pronouns (*this, that, these,* and *those*) can be used as adjectives to indicate specific nouns or pronouns.

> Please complete *these* assignments by Friday.
>
> *This* Italian restaurant is my favorite.

Possessive nouns and pronouns (*my, your, his, her, its, our,* and *their*) may be used as adjectives to identify nouns.

> It is *my* job to sell *their* house.
>
> *Your* uncle visited me on *his* vacation.

How Many?   Articles (*a, an,* and *the*) are limiting adjectives that introduce general (*a* or *an*) or specific (*the*) nouns or pronouns. Use *a* if the word following the article begins with a consonant sound; if the word begins with a vowel sound, use *an.*

> *A* dealer purchased *an* antique clock at *an* auction.
>
> *The* dealer purchased *a* unique clock at *the* auction.

Identifying Adverbs

Adverbs modify verbs, adjectives, or other adverbs:

> Sean worked *happily.*   (The adverb *happily* modifies the <u>verb</u> *worked.*)
>
> Marge is *extremely* tired.   (The adverb *extremely* modifies the <u>adjective</u> *tired.*)
>
> She spoke *very* softly.   (The adverb *very* modifies the <u>adverb</u> *softly.*)

Many adverbs are formed by adding *ly* to the adjective form; however, not all adverbs end in *ly.*

ADJECTIVES	ADVERBS
formal invitation	*formally* invite
quick decision	*quickly* decide
sure victory	*surely* win
good report	played *well*
	will *not* go
	leave it *here*

Adverbs answer the questions *how? when? where?* and *to what extent?* about the verb or other word they modify. The adverbs are italicized in the following examples.

HOW?	The house is decorated *beautifully.* (It is decorated how? Beautifully. The adverb *beautifully* modifies the verb *is decorated.*)
WHEN?	John will leave *soon.* (He will leave when? Soon. The adverb *soon* modifies the verb *will leave.*)
WHERE?	The cat is sleeping *there.* (It is sleeping where? There. The adverb *there* modifies the verb *is sleeping.*)
TO WHAT EXTENT?	She was *exceedingly* worried about the test. (To what extent was she worried? Exceedingly. The adverb *exceedingly* modifies the adjective *worried.*)

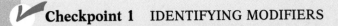

Checkpoint 1   IDENTIFYING MODIFIERS

Identify each of the modifiers in the following sentences as either an adjective (*adj.*) or an adverb (*adv.*)

1. The secretarial field presents a tremendously complex challenge for the 21st century.
2. If a word is mistakenly keyed, the spelling checker will highlight the error.
3. It is extremely rare to find two individuals in any office who are exactly the same height, weight, and proportion.
4. We recently bought a new computer system for our office.
5. Place the 30 ergonomic chairs there.

Check your answers in Appendix D.

Selecting Modifiers

When using adjectives and adverbs, select words that precisely describe or identify other words. In this way, you will provide specific information to the person receiving your message. Identify the better choice of modifiers in the following examples:

Our company has just built a (tall/20-story) office building.

The better choice is *20-story*, since it is more specific than *tall*.

She always does her work (nicely/efficiently).

Efficiently is the preferable modifier, since it is more descriptive than *nicely*.

Checkpoint 2   SELECTING MODIFIERS

Select the preferable modifier in each of the following sentences.

1. A (cheerful/nice) voice answers the call with your company's name.
2. Your success as a manager depends upon how (well/quickly) you respond to change.
3. (Several/Five) people will be coming for job interviews.
4. The changeover from electric to electronic typewriters was (very/surprisingly) easy.
5. She is (efficient/great) at filing.

Check your answers in Appendix D.

MISPLACED AND DANGLING MODIFIERS

Position modifiers within a sentence as close to the words they modify as possible. Proper placement of modifiers assures that the intended meaning is clear to the reader. Compare the following sentences:

INCORRECT   The company bought new ergonomic chairs for all receptionists with padded seats.

CORRECT   The company bought new ergonomic chairs with padded seats for all receptionists.

With padded seats is an adjective phrase modifying the noun *chairs*. Because of the misplaced modifier, the first sentence is confusing (and somewhat humorous!). To improve the sentence and avoid confusion, the adjective phrase *with padded seats* should be positioned closer to the noun it modifies.

Words and phrases that cause special problems in placement are *only*, *merely*, and *at least*. Writers frequently overlook the importance of placing these words nearest the word or words being modified. Notice how the placement of *only* changes the meaning of each of the following sentences.

Only Sandy rented the microcomputer.   (No one else rented the computer.)

Sandy *only* rented the microcomputer.   (She did not purchase the computer.)

Sandy rented *only* the microcomputer.   (She did not rent anything else.)

Sandy rented the *only* microcomputer.   (There was just one microcomputer available to rent.)

A dangling modifier is usually a phrase or clause that doesn't modify the subject of the sentence. Introductory phrases or clauses should refer to and immediately precede the subject of the sentence. Correct dangling modifiers by rewriting the sentence to make the meaning clear. The adjective phrases or clauses are italicized in the examples. The word being modified is in bold.

INCORRECT   *Driving fast on a country road,* a **deer** narrowly missed hitting Jeff. (The *deer* was not driving the car!)

CORRECTED   *Driving fast on a country road,* **Jeff** narrowly missed hitting a deer. (The sentence is corrected by making *Jeff* the subject.)

If you will keep in mind *who* or *what* is doing the action, you will avoid dangling modifiers. Consider the following sentence:

INCORRECT   *If bought on sale,* **I** will pay $30 for the pocketbook. (*I* am not being bought on sale.)

CORRECTED   *If bought on sale,* the **pocketbook** will cost me $30. (The sentence is corrected by making *pocketbook* the subject.)

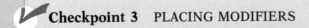

Checkpoint 3   PLACING MODIFIERS

Rewrite any sentences that contain misplaced or dangling modifiers. Write "C" if the sentence is correct.

1. Any business package shipped during the normal business hours under 70 pounds will arrive the same day.
2. The new Syntax 500 office copier only gives you the same features as a more expensive copier.
3. Made of a special water-resistant fiber, these new envelopes are stronger than paper envelopes.
4. This open plan offers you an inexpensive, flexible space management system.
5. Stepping into the new office, 50 electronic typewriters are seen.

Check your answers in Appendix D.

COMPARISON OF MODIFIERS

Both adjectives and adverbs are used to make comparisons. There are three forms or degrees of comparison: positive, comparative, and superlative.

The **positive degree** of an adjective or adverb is the simple form with no comparison intended.

ADJECTIVES   *long* speech, *cold* weather, *excellent* report

ADVERBS   arrived *late,* spoke *softly,* ran *fast*

The **comparative degree** of an adjective or adverb is used to compare two things. The comparative degree of most one- and two-syllable adjectives and some short adverbs is formed by adding *er* to the positive degree.

ADJECTIVES   His speech was *longer* than mine. Winter weather is *colder* than summer weather.

ADVERBS   She arrived *later* than her friend. Doug ran *faster* than John.

The **superlative degree** of an adjective or adverb is used to compare three or more things. The superlative degree of most simple adjectives and some short adverbs is formed by adding *est* to the positive degree.

ADJECTIVES   His speech was the *longest.* That was the *coldest* weather we've had.

ADVERB   Of the five couples, we arrived *latest.* Our team ran *fastest* in the race.

Longer adjectives and most adverbs do not use *er* or *est* to form the comparative and superlative degrees because they would be awkward to pronounce. For these words, add *more* or *less* for the comparative and *most* or *least* for the superlative.

ADJECTIVES	more cooperative	most cooperative
	less expensive	least expensive
ADVERBS	more softly	most softly
	more accurately	most accurately

Some adjectives and adverbs are irregular and must be memorized.

POSITIVE	COMPARATIVE	SUPERLATIVE
bad, badly	worse	worst
good, well	better	best
many, much	more	most
far	farther, further	farthest, furthest
little	less	least
late	later, latter	latest, last

✔ **Checkpoint 4** COMPARING MODIFIERS

For each of the following sentences, supply the appropriate degree of the modifier in parentheses.

> **Ex.** *finest* This company makes the (fine) cheese sauce available.

1. Our long distance service is (good) than theirs.
2. Because typeset information uses less space than typewritten information, typesetting is (economical) than typewriting.
3. The employee who works the (fast) sometimes makes careless mistakes.
4. According to test scores, she is the (intelligent) student in the class.
5. Of all the accounting systems surveyed, this one worked (efficiently).

Check your answers in Appendix D.

MISUSED MODIFIERS

Modifiers often cause confusion. For example, some modifiers can be used as both adjectives and adverbs.

ADVERB	He ran *fast.* (*Fast* is an adverb describing the verb *ran.*)
ADJECTIVE	She drives a *fast* car. (*Fast* is an adjective describing the noun *car.*)
ADVERB	Birds fly *high* in the sky. (*High* is an adverb modifying the verb *fly.*)
ADJECTIVE	This mountain is *high.* (*High* is an adjective describing the noun *mountain.*)

Note: Linking verbs (forms of the verb *to be*) and verbs of the senses (*feel, hear, taste*) are usually followed by adjectives.

| **INCORRECT** | I feel badly/differently/happily. |
| **CORRECT** | I feel bad/different/happy. |

If you are uncertain of which modifier to use, determine whether you need an adjective or an adverb. For proper usage and spelling, you may need to consult a dictionary.

Other modifiers cause problems because their forms are irregular. Some of the real troublemakers are highlighted in the following section.

Almost/Most

Almost is an adverb meaning *nearly.*

It is *almost* time for the meeting.

Most is an adjective or noun meaning *the greatest number or amount (of).*

Most fans cheered for the home team. (adjective)

Most of the fans cheered for the home team. (noun)

Most can also be used as an adverb meaning *to a high degree.*

We were *most* happy to receive your proposal. (Adverb modifying the adjective *happy.*)

Bad/Badly

Bad is an adjective and is often used after the verb *feel* or *look. Badly* is an adverb which tells how something is done.

Don't feel *bad* [not *badly*] about the mistake. (Adjective modifying the understood pronoun *you.*)

Kim wrecked her car *badly* [not *bad*]. (Adverb modifying the verb *wrecked.*)

Good/Well

Good is always an adjective. *Well* may be used as an adjective when refer- ring to health or as an adverb telling how something is done. *Well* usually modifies a verb and answers the question *how?*

> We received a *good* response from our ad.   (Adjective modifying the noun *response.*)
>
> Mollie doesn't feel *well* today.   (Adjective modifying the noun *Mollie.*)
>
> She looked *good* after her makeover.   (Adjective modifying the pronoun *she.*)
>
> He communicates *well* with others.   (Adverb modifying the verb *commu- nicates.*)

Note: *To feel well* means "to be in good health." *To feel good* means "to be in a good mood" or "to be contented or satisfied."

Less/Fewer

Both words are adjectives. *Less* refers to amounts and is used with singu- lar nouns; *fewer* refers to number and is used with plural nouns.

> John makes *less* money at his new job.
>
> They published *fewer* [not *less*] copies of his new book.

Real/Really/Very

Real is an adjective; *really* and *very* are adverbs. To test whether you are using the correct modifier, substitute *genuine* for *real, actually* for *really,* and *extremely* for *very.*

> He receives *real* [genuine] joy from gift-giving.   (Adjective modifying the noun *joy.*)
>
> He *really* [actually] receives joy from gift-giving.   (Adverb modifying the verb *receives.*)
>
> I was *very* [extremely] pleased to receive the gift.   (Adverb modifying the verb *was pleased.*)

Sure/Surely

Sure is an adjective meaning *certain. Surely* is an adverb meaning *cer- tainly.*

> We were *sure* [certain] to get on the mailing list.   (Adjective modifying the pronoun *we.*)
>
> We were *surely* [certainly] sorry to see him leave.   (Adverb modifying the verb *were sorry.*)

This/That, These/Those

Demonstrative pronouns frequently function as adjectives in sentences. The plural of *this* is *these;* the plural of *that* is *those.* Be careful to match the adjective in number to the noun it modifies.

> *this* book; *these* books
> *this* kind; *these* kinds   [not *these kind*]
>
> *that* book; *those* books
> *that* sort; *those* sorts   [not *those sort*]

Them

Them is an objective case pronoun, not an adjective, and should never be used to modify a noun or another pronoun.

> these books   [not *them books*]
> that kind   [not *them kind*]

Checkpoint 5   USING MODIFIERS

Select the correct modifier in each of the following sentences.

1. The investigation will (sure/surely) determine how (good/well) the airlines are maintaining their fleets.
2. (Them/Those) shoes felt good on my feet although I usually can't wear (those kind/those kinds).
3. Although it is (almost/most) time for Christmas, I have received (less/fewer) Christmas cards this year than last year.
4. He felt (bad/badly) because he performed (bad/badly) in the play.
5. I feel (real/really) (good/well) that you are feeling so (good/well) since your surgery.

Check your answers in Appendix D. If all items were correct, continue with the end-of-chapter exercises. If not, review this section.

SUMMARY

Adjectives and adverbs are modifiers that add variety to our writing. Adjectives modify nouns and pronouns; adverbs modify verbs, adjectives, or other adverbs.

To avoid confusion, adjectives and adverbs should be placed close to the words they modify. Dangling modifiers result when a phrase or clause doesn't modify the subject of the sentence.

Modifiers may be written in different degrees for comparison: the positive, the comparative, and the superlative. The positive degree is the simple form with no comparison intended; the comparative form is used for comparing two items; the superlative form is used for comparing three or more items. Most simple adjectives add *er* for the comparative degree and *est* for the superlative degree. Longer adjectives and most adverbs use *more/less* for the comparative and *most/least* for the superlative. Some modifiers are irregular and must be memorized.

Many modifiers can be used as both adjectives and adverbs. Caution should be taken to use these confusing modifiers correctly: *good/well, real/really/very, bad/badly, sure/surely, almost/most, less/fewer,* and *this/that/these/those.*

● ● ● ● ● ● ● ● ● Communication Activities

Spelling and Word Usage

Learn to spell and use the following words. Be alert for them in the Editing Applications at the end of the chapter.

announcement	environment	occasionally
bookkeeping	February	precede
clientele	innovation	proceed
commitment	library	reference

Practical Applications

Part A   Select the appropriate modifier in each sentence.

1. Files can be accessed (faster/fastest) by using the Arrow System rather than your present system.

2. The keyboard is built for an (incredible/incredibly) smooth touch.

3. (Better/Best) of all, the 2210 and 2215 electronic typewriters come with optional disk drives.

4. For a secretary, a full-size typewriter with memory means (fewer/less) hours retyping.

5. Possibly the (stronger/strongest) advantage of the Entertel phone system is the ability to allow billing to clients.

6. (This kind/These kinds) of copiers allow you to change colors with a flick of the switch.

7. Make your plans early for a (real/really) successful business trip.

8. Did you feel (bad/badly) about the drop in the stock market yesterday?

9. The new shuttle service can fly you from the airport to Wall Street in (eight/several) minutes.

10. Send off for a guide to the world's (more/most) enchanting vacation spots.

Part B   Rewrite any of the following sentences that contain misplaced or dangling modifiers. Write "C" if the sentence is correct.

1. Knocking over a cup of coffee, the report was ruined by Fred.

2. She spent her vacation in Florida on the beach with her dog and cat wearing a new bikini.

3. When I start my new business, please send your orders to our sales department through the mail.

4. We designed the new office with flexible furniture in Atlanta.

5. Working in the electronic office, people work at computer pace.

6. Papers are piled up in all of the offices that haven't been filed.

7. Printing ten pages a minute, we have a sophisticated laser printer in Mr. Romei's office.

8. Your new telephone system cost over $10,000 from Western Satellite Corporation.

9. Our company added shelf files in the records management center in order to save valuable space.

10. We plan to go to the mountains driving along Route 202.

Editing Applications

Part A   Correct the italicized modifiers in the following paragraphs. Some modifiers may be misplaced.

Innovation is taking place in the *modernest* offices of today. The office environment has been greatly affected by "office landscaping," often known as the open plan. *Real* eager to proceed with *later* technology, *newer* offices are designed to aid information flow.

These kind of offices have *less* fixed walls than the *most* traditional offices, although there is still a need for separately walled offices *occasionally*. Open plan offices have movable partitions, which can be *easier* rearranged to meet changing needs of equipment and personnel.

With the office growing increasingly *noisier*, however, there is more demand for enclosed space. Today's planners *sure* must design offices to meet the needs of personnel *with more flexibility*.

Part B   The following document contains grammar and spelling errors discussed in this chapter and previous chapters. Correct each error.

February 14, 19--

Dr. Samuel O'Kelley, Director
Learning Resources Center
Westboro Junior College
Westboro, MA 01581-4100

Dear Doctor O'Kelley:

I recently seen an anouncement about your new remodeled liberry at Westboro Junior College.   We at Wright Community College are planning a similiar remodeling of our library, which was needed real bad.

Could you share with me them changes which has beneffited your clientel?   After reviewing your plans, our building will be studied to see if the idea seems well enough to go ahead with the neccessary changes.

We would sure be interested in receiving a floor plan in the near future of your building.

Sincerely,

Margaret Bayne
Staff Assistant

hm

CHAPTER 9

Prepositions, Conjunctions, and Interjections

Objectives

After studying this chapter and completing the chapter exercises, you should be able to:

1. Identify prepositions and prepositional phrases.
2. Use prepositional phrases as adjectives or adverbs.
3. Use appropriate "problem" prepositions.
4. Place prepositions correctly within a sentence.
5. Use coordinate, correlative, and subordinate conjunctions correctly.
6. Recognize interjections.
7. Spell and use a list of common business terms.

In this chapter we will study the use of prepositions, conjunctions, and interjections. Using these parts of speech correctly will increase your writing effectiveness.

PREPOSITIONS

A **preposition** is a word used to show the relationship between a noun, a pronoun, or a phrase or clause used as a noun and another word in the sentence. Prepositions usually indicate direction, position, or time. The prepositions are italicized in the following examples.

DIRECTION   We walked *into* the room.   (*Into* indicates the relationship between *room* and *walked*.)

POSITION   Jane is *behind* the door.   (*Behind* indicates the relationship between *Jane* and *door*.)

TIME   My supervisor will be transferred *after* Christmas.   (*After* shows a relationship between *transferred* and *Christmas*.)

COMMON PREPOSITIONS

about	behind	for	through
above	below	from	to
across	beneath	in	toward
after	beside	into	under
against	between	like	until
along	beyond	of	up
among	by	off	upon
around	concerning	on	with
at	during	out	within
before	except	over	without

The noun or pronoun following a preposition is called the **object of the preposition.** The object answers the question *what?* or *whom?* The objects of the prepositions are italicized in the following examples.

We walked along the *path.*   (Along *what?* Along the *path. Path* is the object of the preposition *along.*)

Mario gave the book to *Jane.*   (To *whom?* To *Jane. Jane* is the object of the preposition *to.*)

The preposition, its object, and any modifiers form a **prepositional phrase.** Prepositional phrases are italicized in the following examples.

> I don't like to travel *without traveler's checks.* (*Without* is the preposition; *checks* is the object of the preposition.)

> Please don't vote *against my candidate.* (*Against* is the preposition; *candidate* is the object.)

Placement and Use of Prepositional Phrases

Now that we have reviewed the makeup of prepositional phrases, let's look at how they are used as modifiers in sentences. Prepositional phrases, like other modifiers we have studied, can be used as adjectives or adverbs. As you recall, adjectives modify nouns and pronouns while adverbs modify verbs, adjectives, and other adverbs.

As Adjectives

Prepositional phrases may be used as adjectives to modify nouns and pronouns. As adjectives, prepositional phrases will answer the question *what kind?* or *which one?* about the noun or pronoun they modify. When using prepositional phrases as adjectives, generally place the phrase immediately after the noun or pronoun modified or after a linking verb. The prepositional phrases are italicized in the following examples, and the words modified appear in bold.

> **Employees** *of our temporary service* get the job done. (*Of our temporary service* describes the noun *employees,* telling *which* employees.)

> **They** are *among the fortunate few* who made A's. (*Among the fortunate few* modifies the pronoun *they.*)

As Adverbs

Prepositional phrases may also modify verbs, adjectives, or other adverbs. As adverbs, prepositional phrases answer the question *when, where, why, how,* or *to what extent* about the words they modify. When using prepositional phrases as *adverbs,* follow the placement guides below. The prepositional phrases are italicized in the following examples, and the words modified are in bold.

● To achieve the desired emphasis, vary the placement when using prepositional phrases to modify verbs. Beginning a sentence with a prepositional phrase avoids having to begin with *I.*

> I **must finish** the article *before one o'clock.*

> *Before one o'clock* I **must finish** the article. (*Before one o'clock* modifies the verb *must finish,* answering the question *when?*)

- Generally place prepositional phrases immediately after the adjectives or adverbs they modify.

> Ms. Wang was **experienced** *on three word processors.*   (*On three word processors* modifies the adjective *experienced.*)

> She ran **rapidly** *past the finish line.*   (*Past the finish line* modifies the adverb *rapidly.*)

Special Considerations When Using Prepositions

We have seen how prepositions provide links between ideas in a sentence. In some cases, however, prepositions may be used when they are not needed — or omitted when they *are* needed. When deciding whether or not a preposition is needed, follow these guidelines:

Rule 1   Avoid using unnecessary prepositions.

INCORRECT   Where are you going *to?*

CORRECT   Where are you going?

INCORRECT   Please take the book off *of* the table.

CORRECT   Please take the book off the table.

INCORRECT   I don't know where my keys are *at.*

CORRECT   I don't know where my keys are.

Rule 2   Don't omit necessary prepositions.

INCORRECT   This type mixer is old-fashioned.

CORRECT   This type *of* mixer is old-fashioned.

INCORRECT   She has an enjoyment and an interest in gourmet cooking.

CORRECT   She has an enjoyment *of* and an interest in gourmet cooking.

- Often a sentence ends naturally with a preposition. Such sentences are informal in tone.

INFORMAL   Whom did you give the book *to?*

FORMAL   *To* whom did you give the book?

INFORMAL   I need a loan to purchase a computer *with.*

FORMAL   I need a loan *with* which to purchase a computer.

If moving the preposition to another part of the sentence makes the sentence sound stilted or awkward, leave the preposition at the end of the sentence.

AWKWARD   *For* what are you looking?

IMPROVED   What are you looking *for?*

In the following sentences underline each prepositional phrase and draw an arrow from the phrase to the word(s) modified.

Ex. Your contribution to United Way goes to important charities.

1. The phone is ringing with that important call and you have just gone on break.
2. Select a planning calendar from our catalog located in the stock room.
3. Happily for our stockholders, we made a profit this quarter.
4. One of my favorite cartoons shows a secretary suggesting to her boss that they throw out old files.
5. Write for the free booklet "How to Maintain Records for Government Offices."

Check your answers in Appendix D.

Problem Prepositions

Some prepositions are frequently misused. Use the following prepositions with care:

Beside/Besides.   *Beside* means *by the side of; besides* means *in addition to.*

She set the vase *beside* the paperweight on her desk.

Besides potatoes, we are having rice and pasta on the menu.

Between/Among.   Use *between* to refer to two people or things; use *among* to refer to three or more.

Estelle sat *between* Mr. and Mrs. Serafini.

Yours was *among* the largest of all the orders we received.

From/Than.   Use *different from* rather than *different than.*

My recipe for apple pie is different *from* yours.

In/Into.   Use *in* to indicate position or location (no motion); use *into* to indicate movement or change.

Ralph is *in* the classroom.

Ralph walked *into* the classroom from the lab.   (Saying "Ralph walked *in* the classroom" would mean that Ralph was walking around inside the room.)

Like/As. *Like* is a preposition and requires an object; *as* is a conjunction used to introduce clauses of comparison. Avoid mixing up their uses.

> I want to buy a new typewriter just *like* my old one.

> She doesn't write letters *as* she once did.

✔ **Checkpoint 2**   PROBLEM PREPOSITIONS

Select the appropriate preposition in each of the following sentences.

1. (Like/As) a flame in the darkness, Acutone telephone equipment sheds light (like/as) no other company can.
2. When you enter (in/into) an agreement with our firm, we provide service (in/into) all your branches.
3. (Beside/Besides) French and German, I want to study Spanish at the liberal arts college (beside/besides) the lake.
4. All tournaments (between/among) top tennis pros end up in a battle (between/among) the two finalists.
5. My approach to the problem may be different (from/than) yours.

Check your answers in Appendix D.

CONJUNCTIONS

Conjunctions are words that join two or more sentence parts (words, phrases, or clauses). **Coordinate conjunctions** connect sentence elements that are grammatically and logically equal. Some coordinate conjunctions are *and, but, or, nor, for,* and *yet*. The conjunctions are italicized in the following examples.

> Mr. Platt *and* Ms. Bayne worked on the project together.   (Joining two nouns.)

> You may travel by car *or* by train.   (Joining two prepositional phrases.)

> Have you decided to write *or* type the letter?   (Joining two verbs.)

> Joan arrived early this morning, *but* she still did not finish her work. (Joining two clauses.)

Correlative conjunctions are used in pairs to join two or more elements (words, phrases, or clauses) of equal rank. Some correlative conjunctions are *both/and, either/or, neither/nor,* and *not only/but also*.

> I plan to visit *either* Russia *or* China on my next trip.

> *Neither* snow *nor* sleet will keep me away from my job.

Not only young men *but also* young women are enrolled in electronics courses.

Be careful to use **parallel construction** with coordinate and correlative conjunctions. Parallel construction requires each part of a sentence joined by the conjunction to be of the same grammatical construction.

INCORRECT   Customers want not only good *service* but also *to be treated with courtesy.*   (Not parallel: joining a noun and an infinitive.)

CORRECT   Customers want not only good *service* but also *courtesy.* (Parallel: two nouns.)

CORRECT   Customers want not only *to receive* good service but also *to be treated* with courtesy.   (Parallel: two infinitives.)

Subordinate conjunctions join dependent clauses to independent clauses.

COMMON SUBORDINATE CONJUNCTIONS

after	if	unless
although	provided	until
as	since	when
as if	so that	whenever
as though	than	where
because	that	while
before	though	why

We will plant our garden *when* spring arrives.   (*When* introduces the dependent clause.)

If you are to succeed in business, you usually have to work at it.   (*If* introduces the dependent clause.)

✔ **Checkpoint 3**   CONJUNCTIONS

Supply an appropriate conjunction for each of the following sentences.

1. We have a wide variety of word processors _____ computers in our organization.

2. I will not be able to go to the circus _____ I have to work late.

3. We plan _____ to go out to dinner _____ to see a movie.

4. _____ the paint dries, we will move the furniture back into the office.

5. Dr. Cortez plans to attend the conference, _____ Dr. James will not be able to attend.

Check your answers in Appendix D.

INTERJECTIONS

Interjections are exclamatory words or phrases used to express emotion. Interjections are not related grammatically to other words in sentences. Any word or phrase may be used as an interjection. Mild interjections are usually followed by a comma, and stronger interjections are followed by an exclamation point.

Oh, where did you find that beautiful dress?

Gosh! What will we do about the broken copier?

Well, I plan to get my report in early.

✔ Checkpoint 4   INTERJECTIONS

Identify each interjection in the following sentences.

1. Help! The bathtub is running over!
2. Well, we won't know the answer until the mail arrives.
3. He sighed, "Gee, it must be nice to get a raise."
4. Yes, I'll be able to go to the party with you.
5. Ouch! I caught my finger in the door.

Check your answers in Appendix D.

SUMMARY

In this chapter you have learned how to use prepositions, conjunctions, and interjections.

Prepositions are used to show the relationship between a noun, a pronoun, or a phrase or clause used as a noun and another word in the sentence. A prepositional phrase, consisting of the preposition, its object, and any modifiers, may be used as an adjective or adverb. Generally place prepositional phrases as close as possible to the words being modified. Use problem prepositions with care.

Conjunctions are of three types: coordinate, correlative, and subordinate. *Coordinate* conjunctions connect sentence elements of equal rank. *Correlative* conjunctions are used in pairs to join two or more elements of equal rank. Use *parallel* construction with coordinate and correlative conjunctions. *Subordinate* conjunctions join dependent clauses to independent clauses.

Interjections are words or phrases used to express emotion or reaction and are not grammatically related to other words in a sentence.

● ● ● ● ● ● ● ● ● **Communication Activities**

Spelling and Word Usage

Learn to spell and use the following words. Be alert for them in the Editing Applications at the end of the chapter.

anxiety	financial	preferred
brochure	interference	referred
committee	maintenance	succeed
congratulations	occurrence	using
evaluate		

If necessary, refer to Appendix A for the correct usage of these words.

assure/ensure/insure   quite/quiet/quit

Practical Applications

Part A   In the following sentences, underline each prepositional phrase and draw an arrow from the phrase to the word(s) modified.

1. New technology in the office affects everyone.
2. A well-phrased question can open doors to new information.
3. Keep your boss aware of your assignments.
4. Many office workers think that the backless chairs relieve stress on the back.
5. The office grapevine rumbles behind office doors and wanders down corridors.
6. You should deposit a check promptly for three reasons.
7. A good communicator looks people in the eye.
8. You should avoid contractions in formal business writing.

Part B   Identify the conjunctions in each of the following sentences and then indicate whether the conjunction is a coordinate conjunction, a correlative conjunction, or a subordinate conjunction.

1. Since filing systems vary from company to company, it is difficult to make general statements about them.
2. Walking is a great form of exercise and is good for your heart.
3. If you know which questions to ask, you can find answers to almost any problem.
4. You not only should thank him in person for the interview but also should write a thank-you letter.
5. He will attend the banquet but will not stay for the awards program.
6. Making decisions is a routine part of life when you go about it the right way.
7. As Sally returns to her word processor, she decides to back up all her work.
8. I would like to work in either accounting or real estate.

Part C   Identify the interjections in the following sentences.

1. No, you can't go with us.
2. Sure, we can help you with your filing.
3. After the class she said, "Wow! The test was hard!"
4. Gosh, the new office layout looks great.

Editing Applications

Part A   Correct all errors in spelling and word usage, including misused prepositions.

Do you have anziety when you work besides your boss on financiel matters? Between all the people I work with, I ensure you that it makes me quiet nervous when my boss walks in my office to evaluate me. However, I just read a broshure which refered to ways to suceed not only with your boss but also how to work with committees.

Now, when there is an occurence in which I will be working with the boss, my anxiaty will not cause interferrence. I will be useing those good human relations techniques which I have been looking for.

Part B   Correct any errors in the following memo.

TO:	Eileen Ricciardi
FROM:	Dan McAteer
DATE:	March 25, 19--
SUBJECT:	Taking Meeting Minutes

Congradulations, Eileen!   You are doing an excellent job in Main-teinance.   Although I would have prefered to have had you in the Finnancial Department, you will succede very well into your new job.

Thank you for getting the necesary training to precede with taking minutes at board meetings, which are different than committe meetings.   Beside usually being longer than comittee meetings, board meetings are quit complicated because of legal jargon.   Try to obtain a copy of either a legal dictionary or buy a legal word book just as the one on Martha's desk.   After studying the legal terms, you will find you can write minutes just like you used to.

CHAPTER 10

Sentence Structure

Objectives

After studying this chapter and completing the chapter exercises, you should be able to:

1. Identify and use different types of phrases.
2. Identify and use dependent and independent clauses.
3. Identify sentence types.
4. Recognize sentence fragments.
5. Apply end punctuation correctly.
6. Identify sentence styles.
7. Write coherent sentences.
8. Spell and use a list of common business terms.

As you know, a sentence is a group of words that expresses a complete thought. To express a complete thought, the sentence must contain at least one subject and one verb and must be able to stand alone. To communicate effectively in your business writing, you must be able to construct sentences that express the message you are trying to send. In this chapter, we will look at some common elements of sentences and learn how to combine these elements to construct effective sentences.

PHRASES

Phrases are groups of related words that do *not* contain both a subject and a verb but are sometimes important when constructing effective sentences. A phrase functions as a part of speech within a sentence, a clause, or another phrase. The different types of phrases are identified by the parts of speech they represent.

Noun phrases function as nouns.

> *Reading the paper* is his favorite pastime.   (This noun phrase is used as the subject of the sentence.)

> The basketball player hopes *to score the winning points.*   (Hopes what? *To score the winning points* is a noun phrase acting as a direct object.)

Verb phrases include the main verb plus any helping verbs.

> Leo *has not taken* his lunch break.

> The car *will be sold* next week.

Adjective phrases are used like adjectives to modify nouns and pronouns.

> We must keep the office *running smoothly.*   (This adjective phrase modifies the noun *office.*)

> The boxes *on the floor* should be moved.   (This adjective phrase, which is also a prepositional phrase, modifies the noun *boxes.*)

Adverb phrases are used like adverbs to modify verbs, adjectives, and other adverbs.

> Company headquarters have been moved *to our Denver location.*   (This adverb phrase, which is also a prepositional phrase, modifies the verb *have been moved.*)

> She was late *arriving home.*   (This adverb phrase modifies the adjective *late.*)

> Tania worked diligently *to finish the speech.*   (This adverb phrase modifies the adverb *diligently.*)

CLAUSES

Clauses are groups of related words that contain both a subject and a verb. Clauses are either independent or dependent.

Independent Clauses

An **independent** (or *main*) **clause** can stand alone as a complete sentence. In the following examples, each subject is underlined once and each verb is underlined twice.

Harry resigned.

Office space costs a fortune.

We all caught bad colds this winter.

The San Diego Zoo has a variety of exotic animals.

Dependent Clauses

A **dependent clause** cannot stand alone as a sentence. Although a dependent clause contains both a subject and a verb, it must be combined with an independent clause to form a complete sentence. Dependent clauses usually begin with subordinate words like *that, because,* or *if* and function as nouns, adjectives, or adverbs. (Note that clauses may also contain phrases.) In the following clauses, each subject is underlined once and each verb is underlined twice.

> When you buy products from us ...

> ... if you decide to sell your car

> ... that diamonds are a girl's best friend

In the following sentences, the independent clauses are underlined and the dependent clauses are italicized.

> Mr. Leister arrived in town *after his wife had left.*

> *If you mail the form today,* you will receive a free sample.

> The brochure contains information *that can save us thousands of dollars.*
> (*That* is a relative pronoun referring to *information.* It is used as the subject of the dependent clause. Other relative pronouns frequently used to introduce dependent clauses are *which, who, whom,* and *whose.*)

✔ **Checkpoint 2**   PHRASES AND CLAUSES

For each of the following sentences, indicate whether the italicized group of words is a phrase, an independent clause, or a dependent clause.

1. *Your computer could be damaged* by the electricity that makes it run.
2. Your computer could be damaged *by the electricity* that makes it run.
3. Your computer could be damaged by the electricity *that makes it run.*
4. *If you are looking for a bargain,* you might consider shopping at the flea market.
5. They enjoyed *sailing their Sunfish.*

Check your answers in Appendix D.

Noun Clauses

Noun clauses, although generally used as direct objects, are sometimes used as subjects or subject complements. Noun clauses are frequently introduced by subordinate words such as *whether, that, what, why,* or *which.* In the following sentences, the noun clauses are italicized.

> I don't remember *why I bought that dress.*   (Noun clause used as a direct object.)

> *Whether we should drive or fly* makes no difference.   (Noun clause used as a subject.)

> A formal bound report is *what we expect to receive.*   (Noun clause used as a subject complement.)

Adjective Clauses

Adjective clauses are dependent clauses that modify nouns or pronouns. The relative pronouns *who, whom, whose, that,* and *which* usually introduce adjective clauses. They may be restrictive or nonrestrictive.

Restrictive Clauses.   Restrictive clauses are needed to identify the person or thing being described. Because a restrictive clause is necessary to the meaning of the sentence, a restrictive clause is *not* set off by commas. The restrictive clauses are italicized in the following examples.

> I returned the shoes *that I bought yesterday.*   (The clause identifies which shoes are being described.)

> The doctor *who delivered her baby* is retiring.   (This clause identifies which doctor is being discussed.)

Nonrestrictive Clauses.   Nonrestrictive clauses provide additional information about persons or things being described but are *not* needed to identify them. Since a nonrestrictive clause could be omitted without changing the meaning of the sentence, a nonrestrictive clause is set off by commas. The nonrestrictive clauses are italicized in the following examples.

> Dr. Peter Abrams, *who delivered her baby,* is retiring.   (This clause is nonrestrictive because it provides additional information about the doctor but is not needed to identify him.)

> Miss Polinski, *who was my teacher,* moved to Maine.   (This clause provides additional information about Miss Polinski but is not needed to identify her.)

> Bill's Talkfone Service, *which installed my telephone system,* is going out of business.   (This clause is not needed to identify the company.)

Adverb Clauses

Adverb clauses are dependent clauses used as adverbs to modify verbs, adjectives, and other adverbs. Adverb clauses are introduced by subordinate conjunctions such as *while, when, since, if, where,* and *because* (see page 119, Subordinate Conjunctions) and answer such questions as *why, where, when,* and *how.* In the following examples, the adverb clauses are italicized.

Let's plant immediately *because it will be dark soon.*   (This adverb clause modifies the adverb *immediately* and answers the question *why.*)

Please meet me *where the two roads intersect.*   (This adverb clause modifies the verb *meet* and answers the question *where.*)

We saw the Broadway play *when we went to New York.*   (This adverb clause modifies the verb *saw* and answers the question *when.*)

Sally appeared as sorry *as we were* to lose the ball game.   (This adverb clause modifies the adjective *sorry* and answers the question *how* or *to what extent.*)

✔ Checkpoint 3   DEPENDENT CLAUSES

Identify dependent clauses in the following sentences and indicate whether the clause is a noun, adjective, or adverb clause. For each adjective clause, write "R" if it is restrictive and "N" if it is nonrestrictive. Remember: A dependent clause contains a subject and verb but cannot stand alone as a sentence.

1. When you use the new Alpha filing system, you reduce misfiles.
2. Tough performance is what you demand from office copiers.
3. Eisen's Office Supply provides business forms that meet our needs.
4. Everyone knows that inflation is decreasing.
5. My Siamese cat, which is three years old, likes to chase birds.

Check your answers in Appendix D.

SENTENCES

Let's analyze different types of sentences and the end punctuation needed with each type. Remember, a sentence is an independent group of words which contains at least one subject and one verb. Independent clauses can stand alone as complete sentences. (Dependent clauses, however, contain a subject and a verb but cannot stand alone as sentences.) In each of the following sentences, the subject is underlined once and the verb is underlined twice.

Jeffrey and his brothers went fishing last Tuesday.

Before going to the play, I would like to eat dinner.

Please join me for dessert at the Ice Cream Shoppe.   (*You* is understood to be the subject.)

Types of Sentences

Sentences always begin with a capital letter; however, they end with different punctuation marks according to sentence type. There are four basic types of sentences: the statement, the question, the command/request, and the exclamation.

Statement

A sentence which states a fact is a **statement** and should be followed by a period.

Lucy is in terrific shape since she began exercising.

Thousands of secretaries use Infotype typewriters.

Question

A sentence which asks a **direct question** should be followed by a question mark.

When did you apply for a new credit card?

Is your copier smart enough to choose paper size?

An **indirect question** is a statement that includes someone else's question but does not use the person's exact words. This type of sentence is a statement and should be followed by a period.

Captain Chen asked whether the toll road had been paved.

The show director wants to know how much we spent.

Command/Request

A sentence which makes a command or a request should be followed by a period. The subject *you* is implied in a command or courteous request.

Leave the report on my desk by noon.

Please join me for lunch on Tuesday.

A polite request often sounds like a question. To distinguish between the two, determine what type of response a sentence requires. If you expect someone to answer in words, the sentence is a question and should be followed by a question mark. However, if you expect someone to respond with an action, the sentence is a request and should be followed by a period.

QUESTION   Will you leave the report on my desk by noon?

REQUEST   Would you send me your shoe size by return mail.

Exclamation

A sentence which shows strong emotion is an **exclamation** and should be followed by an exclamation point. Whenever an expression (whether or not it is a complete sentence) shows excitement, urgency, or other strong emotion, it should be followed by an exclamation point.

Don't miss this opportunity to make money!

With our new invention, possibilities are endless!

Congratulations on winning first place!

Help! Marvelous! Stop the presses!

Use exclamation points sparingly. Because exclamation points show emphasis, they lose their impact if overused.

✔**Checkpoint 4**   SENTENCES AND PUNCTUATION

Place correct end punctuation after each of the following sentences and identify the type of sentence (statement, question, command/request, or exclamation).

1. Mail the coupon or call our toll-free number
2. You can print one document while you work on another
3. The first plain paper copier that doesn't come at a premium is sold by Excel
4. Wonderful news — Pat won first place in the state Phi Beta Lambda competition
5. Will you please order supplies for our department
6. What supplies did you order for our department

Check your answers in Appendix D.

Sentence Structures

When writing, you need to be familiar with the four basic structures of sentences in order to make your writing style interesting. Skilled writers use a variety of sentence structures, such as simple, compound, and complex, to communicate their ideas forcefully and clearly. Avoid a series of short, choppy simple sentences just as you would avoid a series of long, compound-complex sentences. Both types of writing are equally dull.

Simple Sentences

Simple sentences contain only one independent clause. They may also include phrases, and they may have compound subjects or verbs. In the following simple sentences, simple subjects are underlined once and main verbs are underlined twice.

> We arrived at the ball park by 7 p.m.

> Please get me a glass of water.   (*You* is the implied subject.)

> Ginny, Susie, and Bill grew up in the country.

> The golfer entered the tournament and won.

> The pen and paper are lying on the desk and waiting for me to use them.

Compound Sentences

Compound sentences contain two or more related independent clauses. In the following examples, the subject of each independent clause is underlined once and the verb is underlined twice.

> The ergonomic chair was expensive, but it provides good back support.

> Miss Smith came to my wedding; Miss Jones did not come.

> I am going on vacation in July; however, I plan to be home for the Fourth of July celebrations.

Note that the independent clauses in a compound sentence could be written as separate sentences.

Complex Sentences

Complex sentences contain one independent clause and one or more dependent clauses. In the following sentences, the dependent clauses are italicized.

> Your house is probably the largest purchase *that you will ever make.*

> Everyone rises *when the judge enters the courtroom.*

> *Which restaurant you choose* is unimportant to me.

> *If you travel first class,* you will be more comfortable on a long trip.

Compound-Complex Sentences

Compound-complex sentences contain two or more independent clauses and at least one dependent clause. In the following sentences, the dependent clauses are italicized.

The opera season gets under way this month *when the National Opera Company performs,* and I plan to buy season tickets.

You may see a jogger on every corner, but 80 percent of Americans are still *what one fitness professional calls "marshmallow people"* and *what federal health officials, in a recent report on the state of the nation's physical activity, more politely termed "sedentary."*

Avoid using too many compound-complex sentences because they are usually very long and complicated. Instead, break them down into simple, compound, and complex sentences.

✔ Checkpoint 5 SENTENCE STRUCTURE

Identify each of the following sentences as simple, compound, complex, or compound-complex. Underline the dependent clauses.

1. Her approach is colorful, and she has made all of us think about the importance of organization.
2. Combining a number of special conveniences, these grills are designed to cook steaks, chops, and burgers.
3. Since companies try to put their best foot forward in their annual reports, you have to search through the glossy photos to find important information.
4. When she started her flower-importing business, she had no marketing strategy, but she quickly put one together.
5. Hawaii has many treasures, but its greatest one is its beaches.

Check your answers in Appendix D.

COHERENT CONSTRUCTION

We are now ready to construct coherent sentences — that is, sentences which flow smoothly and fit together logically. To do this, write complete sentences with proper punctuation and parallel construction.

Complete Sentences

Write complete sentences, not sentence fragments. Sentence fragments are not sentences. Avoid using sentence fragments in business writing. To communicate effectively in business, you should express your thoughts in complete sentences. Make sure your sentences contain a subject (either expressed or understood) and a main verb that together can stand alone. In the following examples, note how the sentence fragments are corrected.

FRAGMENT   The baby sleeping in his crib.

COMPLETE SENTENCES   The baby sleeps in his crib.
The baby is sleeping in his crib.
The baby, sleeping in his crib, looks angelic.

FRAGMENT   How you can make money in the stock market.

COMPLETE SENTENCES   I will tell you how you can make money in the stock market.
You can make money in the stock market.

Proper Punctuation

Avoid run-on sentences. **Run-on sentences** result when two or more independent clauses are joined without the correct punctuation or without the appropriate conjunction. Notice the following run-on sentence:

Mr. Schwartz bought a new car, he sold his old one.

Never separate two independent clauses with a comma only. Part 3 of this text covers the use of punctuation within sentences. This chapter will illustrate some uses of internal punctuation to help you avoid run-on sentences.

Correct the run-on sentence above in one of the following ways:

● Separate the two independent clauses into two sentences.

Mr. Schwartz bought a new car. He sold his old one.

● Place a semicolon between the two independent clauses, forming a compound sentence. You may also add a transitional word or phrase between the two clauses.

Mr. Schwartz bought a new car; he sold his old one.

Mr. Schwartz bought a new car; in the meantime, he sold his old one.

● Add a coordinate conjunction, such as *or*, *but*, or *and*, between the two clauses.

Mr. Schwartz bought a new car, and he sold his old one.

Parallel Construction

When combining two or more similar sentence elements, be sure to use parallelism. **Parallelism** is using the same structure for words, phrases, or clauses that are related in meaning. The use of parallel construction helps you to achieve coherence and clarity in your writing.

NOT PARALLEL	The new house was elegant, large, and cost a great deal.
PARALLEL	The new house was elegant, large, and expensive. (Turn the third element into an adjective to match the other two elements.)
NOT PARALLEL	The sales representatives like demonstrating new products and to meet new customers.
PARALLEL	The sales representatives like demonstrating new products and meeting new customers. (Change the second element to a gerund phrase to make construction parallel.)

✔ **Checkpoint 6**   COHERENT CONSTRUCTION

Correct the following sentences to make them more coherent. Rewrite sentence fragments as complete sentences.

1. If you're dissatisfied with the lower rates currently available on many investments.
2. At 26, she's already exactly where she wants to be, professionally and in her personal life.
3. This performance made possible by Autolife.
4. Kazuko spent most of his vacation in England, he returned to the United States for a family reunion on July 4.
5. Appleby says many companies are requesting these names and they use them to send invitations to the annual meeting.

Check your answers in Appendix D.

SUMMARY

Sentence structure is extremely important for effective business communication. To be able to construct complete, coherent sentences, you must be able to identify and use different sentence components. Phrases are groups of words that do not contain both a subject and a verb. They can be used as nouns, verbs, adjectives, and adverbs.

Clauses are groups of related words that contain both a subject and a verb. An independent (or *main*) clause can stand alone as a complete sentence. A dependent clause contains a subject and a verb but must be combined with an independent clause to form a sentence. Dependent clauses may be either restrictive or nonrestrictive. Restrictive clauses are essential to the meaning of the sentence. Nonrestrictive clauses are not essential to the identification of the word modified and are thus set off with commas.

There are four types of sentences: the statement, the question, the command/request, and the exclamation. Each requires appropriate end punctuation. (Sentence fragments should be avoided in business communication.) The four sentence styles are simple, compound, complex, and compound-complex.

To write coherently, follow these guidelines: (a) write sentences, not sentence fragments; (b) avoid run-on sentences; and (c) use parallel construction.

● ● ● ● ● ● ● ● ● ● Communication Activities

Spelling and Word Usage

Learn to spell and use the following words. Be alert for them in the Editing Applications at the end of this chapter.

apologize	forcible	prejudice
bulletin	interrupt	relevant
conscientious	manageable	successful
conscious	occurring	warranty
excellent		

If necessary, refer to Appendix A for the correct usage of the following words.

choose/chose	cite/sight/site	than/then

Practical Applications

Part A   For each of the following sentences, indicate sentence type and add the correct end punctuation.

statement
question
command/request
exclamation

1. Are you planning to remodel your home, or would you consider building

2. Start a moderate exercise program, and then progress to a more vigorous program

3. Glare from video display terminals causes eye problems and stress

4. I won $5000 and a trip to Hawaii

5. Will you please make reservations for eight at the new Italian restaurant

Part B   Circle each phrase and underline each dependent clause in the sentences below. Then indicate the sentence structure as one of the following:

simple
compound
complex
compound-complex

Ex. Complex   Knowledgeable workers may select (from an array) (of features) that will increase their productivity.

1. Executives in the storage industry have the best outlook on changing technology in that field.

2. He ended his 20-year career in labor negotiations and formed his own company.

3. Some companies are launching a new line of cosmetics, but we have something that is just as good and much less expensive.

4. At last he has received a promotion!

5. What workers really want and need to be satisfied with their jobs is the knowledge of what to do to improve their own health, comfort, and well-being.

6. Are you interested in ways to finance your capital improvements?

7. There are too few accountants who know how to operate microcomputers, and this is creating a problem for placement agencies.

8. If you use temporary personnel, are you familiar with our agency?

9. The issue of restricting smoking is becoming a problem in the workplace; however, companies are seeking solutions.

Part C   If needed, rewrite each of the following sentences and sentence fragments to make them more coherent.

1. Reward new employees on their efforts rather than on what they achieve.
2. The Bank of Atlanta willingly provides loans to individuals, they do require business references.
3. How to maintain the people who manage your business.
4. I will go to the office for a few hours to answer phone messages and for working on the new sales project.
5. With postage by phone, no trips to the post office to refill your postage meter.
6. Today's new electronic typewriters provide expanded features, they cannot replace microcomputers.

Editing Applications

Part A   Correct errors in grammar, spelling, and usage in the following paragraphs.

The revelant issue of smoking restrictions in the workplace occuring more frequently then ever before. Conscientous employees, both smokers and those who do not smoke, have not been too sucessful in resolving the issue? Those persons conscious of the dangers of smoking naturally have some predjudice about the issue, their arguments against smoking have become more forsible.

Since non-smokers do not apologize for asking that no-smoking areas be set aside. Companies responding by providing sights, such as lunchrooms and bathrooms, off limits for smoking!

If your company choses to implement a no-smoking policy, be sure it is one that is both managable and which will provide education. You should be conscience of the effect upon employees because of the excellant production records of many employees?

Part B   Correct all errors in the following document.

TO: Olivia Mullikan, Coordinator
Office Automation
FROM: Jacob Jenssen, President
DATE: May 14, 19--
SUBJECT: Planning Microcomputer Implementation

As we move toward the successfull automation of our offices.   I have some relavent concerns about the changes that will take place.

Office automation is ocurring faster than we might chose, we must be conscius that employees may become nervous and have fear because of rapid change.   I can sight numerous instances of companies in which automation caused a sudden reduction in productivity and absenteeism rose sharply.

Since I don't want us to have to apoligize to customers or employees. I ask that you put together a set of office automation guidelines which can be distributed to employees and you will also need to post them on bulettin boards.   Would you please make sure this is a managable plan which will overcome employee prejudise toward microcomputers?

Mechanics of Writing

PART 3

• •

"My goodness! Look at this memo. This person does not know how to use a comma. And look at that! 'English' is not capitalized." Have you ever heard a similar comment? Have you ever made such a comment?

In addition to grammar, the mechanics of punctuation, abbreviation, capitalization, and number expression must be correct. To the receiver, these mechanical aspects of written communication reveal the sender's capabilities and reflect the importance that the sender attaches to the receiver. In effect, correctness communicates nonverbally that the sender is a good person with whom to do business.

Part 3 is designed to help you develop the necessary knowledge of the mechanical aspects of communication. Having good mechanical skills will not ensure your success, but lacking them may be devastating to your career.

CHAPTER 11

The Comma

Objectives

After studying this chapter and completing the chapter exercises, you should be able to:

1. Use commas with items in a series.
2. Use commas to set off introductory elements.
3. Use commas to set off nonessential elements.
4. Use commas with parallel consecutive adjectives.
5. Use commas with independent clauses.
6. Use commas with titles, dates, and addresses.
7. Spell and use a list of common business terms.

Just as the punctuation that ends a sentence indicates whether the sender intends the message to be interpreted as a statement, a question, or an expression of emotion, internal punctuation helps to make the meaning of a sentence clear and precise. The most common internal punctuation mark is the comma. Its main purpose is to aid the reader in interpreting the sentence as the writer intended. The comma is used to separate, to join, and to set off elements within a sentence. Proper use of the comma clarifies the importance of the relationships between elements within the sentence.

WITH ITEMS IN A SERIES

Use a comma to separate three or more items in a series. The series may consist of words, phrases, or clauses. To avoid confusion, always use a comma before the conjunction preceding the last item.

The flag is *red, white,* and *blue.*

The book is *on my desk, in the out-basket,* or *in the file cabinet.*

He told us *where he was going, when he was going, why he was going,* and *how he was going.*

Remember, the series must have at least three items. In a series of only two, the items are not separated by commas.

The report was *precise* and *accurate.*

Travel arrangements and *hotel accommodations* are part of the tour package.

WITH INTRODUCTORY ELEMENTS

Use commas to set off most introductory words, phrases, and clauses from the main clause. Introductory clauses are often dependent clauses.

Nevertheless, I think we could attend the meeting.

In the long run, the cutback will be beneficial.

Although he was not present, his influence was evident.

When applying this rule, be alert for what may seem, at first glance, to be an introductory phrase but is actually the subject of the sentence. Do not use a comma after a phrase that functions as the subject of the sentence.

If you do, you will be separating the subject from the verb. In the following examples, the subjects of the sentences are italicized.

Folding a letter correctly is important to me.

You're Never Walking Alone is the theme of the conference.

To prepare for the meeting will require several hours.

Commas are usually omitted after ordinary introductory adverbs (*frequently, now, recently, tomorrow, often*) and short introductory adverbial phrases.

Tomorrow I will begin a new job.

Occasionally we have an opportunity to attend a national conference.

In the morning I will call for an appointment.

During February the prices will be reduced.

✔ Checkpoint 1   SERIES AND INTRODUCTORY ELEMENTS

Read each sentence and insert commas to separate items in a series and to set off appropriate introductory elements. Write "C" if the sentence is correct.

1. Stocks bonds and T-bills were among the investment options discussed at the financial planning seminar.
2. While waiting for the bus she spoke with Kelli about the vacant position.
3. To obtain the information it was necessary to recall the document file.
4. Listening effectively is a critical personal skill.
5. Incidentally there will be a large Christmas bonus this year.
6. Working every Saturday is a bore.
7. Frequently the group rehearses on Friday night.
8. Applications software will be made available for word processing desktop publishing spreadsheets and database management.

Check your answers in Appendix D.

WITH NONESSENTIAL ELEMENTS

Nonessential elements include information that is not necessary to the meaning or the structure of a sentence. Nonessential words, phrases, or clauses are set off with commas. Essential elements, on the other hand, include information that is necessary to the meaning or for correct sentence structure. To determine whether a word, phrase, or clause is nonessential, omit it from the sentence. If the element can be omitted without changing the meaning of the sentence, the element is set off with commas. Nonessential elements include interrupting expressions, nonrestrictive elements, and appositives.

Interrupting Expressions

Set off with commas nonessential words or phrases that interrupt or change the flow of the sentence. Such expressions can be omitted without changing the meaning of the sentence. They are often used to indicate the writer's feelings about the sentence (*by all means, fortunately, unfortunately, most important*) or to provide a transition between ideas or sentences (*in addition, furthermore, however, for example, therefore, in conclusion*). The interrupting expressions are italicized in the following examples.

I think, *however,* that he will accept the proposal.

He should, *on the other hand,* separate the items in a series with commas.

Next summer, *regardless of my schedule,* we will go camping.

Nonrestrictive Elements

Phrases or clauses that provide explanatory or descriptive information about the noun or pronoun they modify may be restrictive or nonrestrictive. Nonrestrictive elements provide additional information, but they are not required to identify the word they modify. Because nonrestrictive elements could be omitted without changing the meaning of the sentence, they are set off with commas. Nonrestrictive clauses often begin with *who* or *which*. In the following sentences, the nonrestrictive expressions appear in italics.

Monte Hook, *who is the brother of Jared Hook,* is sitting next to the window. (The nonrestrictive clause is not necessary to identify Monte Hook.)

Tomorrow we will order part No. 763-ts, *which is a replacement part.* (The nonrestrictive clause is not needed to identify the part.)

Ms. Taylor, *who is the supervisor of the Accounting Department,* will be our guest speaker. (The nonrestrictive clause is not needed to identify Ms. Taylor.)

Phrases or clauses that are essential to the meaning of the sentence (restrictive) are not set off with commas. In the following sentences the restrictive clauses are in italics.

The woman *who is the supervisor of the Purchasing Department* will be promoted.   (The restrictive clause is needed to identify which woman is being described.)

The door *that is solid oak* is very valuable.   (The restrictive clause is needed to identify which door is being described.)

Appositives

Appositives are words or phrases that describe preceding nouns or pronouns by renaming them. Generally appositives are nonrestrictive and are set off with commas. If the appositive is needed to identify the noun being described, however, the appositive is not set off with commas. The nonrestrictive appositives in the sentences below are italicized.

Tom Kellogg, *my best friend,* will go to the camp with me.   (The appositive provides additional information but is not needed to identify Tom Kellogg.)

I will be traveling to Madison, *the state capital.*   (The appositive provides additional information but is not needed to identify Madison.)

My daughter Julie received a scholarship to the university.   (Julie is needed to identify which daughter.)

Checkpoint 2   NONESSENTIAL ELEMENTS

Read each sentence carefully and insert or delete commas as needed to set off nonessential elements. Write "C" if the sentence is correct.

1. Jeanne indicated, nevertheless that she will run in the track meet.

2. The bill as you can well imagine is now overdue.

3. When visiting the Information Management Department, see Ms. Hopkins the department's supervisor.

4. Mr. Eli Johnson the new secretary/treasurer will attend the meeting and represent us.

5. Dale Murphy who plays for the Atlanta Braves was the National League's Most Valuable Player in 1983.

6. The woman who is entering the room is one of the nicest people I know.

7. Your co-worker Janet Benson is to receive the award.

8. Postage prices are being driven up by the Postal Service's labor costs which account for 85 percent of its expenditures.

Check your answers in Appendix D.

WITH PARALLEL ADJECTIVES

Separate consecutive adjectives with commas if they are parallel. **Parallel adjectives** are of equal rank; they modify the same noun to the same degree.

To determine whether consecutive adjectives are parallel and should be separated by a comma, reverse the order of the adjectives and insert the word *and*. If the sentence still makes sense, separate the adjectives with a comma. If the sentence doesn't work with these changes, omit the comma. The consecutive adjectives are italicized in the following examples:

> The *short, stocky* man stood under the tree.   (The stocky and short man stood under the tree. Still makes sense—use a comma.)

> The *tired, hungry* student went to his apartment.   (The hungry and tired student went to his apartment. Still makes sense—use a comma.)

> The *enormous brown* dog jumped the fence.   (The brown and enormous dog jumped the fence. Doesn't work—omit the comma.)

WITH INDEPENDENT CLAUSES

When the independent clauses of a compound sentence are joined by a coordinating conjunction (*and, but, or,* or *nor*), separate the clauses with a comma. The coordinating conjunctions are italicized in the following examples, and the subject and verb of each independent clause are labeled.

> S   V   S   V
> The new order forms are on standard size paper, *and* they cost $7.50 per thousand.

> V   V
> Please send a letter to the addresses marked, *and* prepare ten address labels for each person.   (Subject *you* is understood.)

When the subject is understood to be *you,* as in the second example above, the sentence is treated as a compound sentence. Simple sentences containing compound verbs do not require a comma.

> S   V   V
> The supervisor understands the system's limitations *and* has requested additional equipment.

> S   V   V
> The supervisor is referred to as a systems administrator *and* performs such functions as assigning passwords and trouble-shooting equipment problems.

If both clauses of the compound sentence are short and closely related, a comma is not required.

Tom will do the research and Ellen will write the report.

WITH TITLES, DATES, AND ADDRESSES

Use commas to set off the following:
- Titles which follow personal names
- The year when given as part of a date; the day of the week when it precedes the month and day's date
- Individual items in an address

Dr. John A. Campbell, executive director, will speak to us this Thursday night.

The July 25, 1988, meeting was the beginning of his term as president.

The pool will close for repairs Monday, June 30.

Karen's new address is Apartment #45, 4090 Clay Avenue, Tolar, FL 34219-0092.

Checkpoint 3   ADDITIONAL COMMAS

Read the following sentences carefully and insert the necessary commas. Write "C" if the sentence is correct.

1. The hard-working, contented subordinate complimented her supervisor by telling him that he was competent.
2. The bank gives low-cost, low-interest loans.
3. We went to the movies last night and we saw an outstanding film.
4. The sales representative indicates that the used car is in good condition and costs $3,400.
5. Jim is on salary and he receives no overtime pay.
6. Julie Johnson M.D., is the floor supervisor on the fifth floor of the hospital.
7. Please review my analysis by Monday, August 10; send your revisions directly to me.
8. Turk now lives at 4592 Yearly Drive, Visalia, California, a garden spot in the state.

Check your answers in Appendix D.

SUMMARY

Commas add clarity to sentences by indicating the importance of sentence elements and the relationships between them. The comma is used to separate the following elements in a sentence: three or more items in a series; introductory words, phrases, and clauses from the independent clause; parallel consecutive adjectives; names from titles; and parts of dates and addresses. Commas are used to set off nonessential elements such as interrupting expressions, nonrestrictive clauses, and nonrestrictive appositives. Commas join independent clauses within compound sentences.

Communication Activities

Spelling and Word Usage

Learn to spell and use the following words. Be alert for them in the Editing Applications at the end of the chapter.

approximately	foreign	responsible
argument	institution	sufficient
business	material	weather
consistent	offered	whether
existence	privilege	

If necessary, refer to Appendix A for the correct usage of these words:

allude/elude   council/counsel/consul   there/their/they're

Although these are the frequently misspelled and misused words emphasized at the end of this chapter, remember that other words from previous chapters may also be applied in the editing exercises.

Practical Applications

Part A   Read these sentences carefully and insert the necessary commas. Indicate the reason for adding the commas. Write "C" if the sentence is correct.

1. When I was a boy I attended Stauton Junior High.
2. Over the past decade the high-yield bond market has become large diverse and dynamic.
3. Shannon and Eric walked to the mall and purchased some of the things needed for their science project.
4. The store's manager Sheila Johnson has changed several credit procedures.
5. The cost for the freight has of course been paid.
6. The water passes through several filters before it is used again.
7. When visiting Clifton Laboratories ask for Miss Darla Stephenson supervisor of Word Processing Services.
8. No the blueprints were examined by Morgan Schmidt.
9. Dick Garrison who just turned 27 yesterday is an ambitious assertive salesperson.
10. Without a doubt, the majority of bonds are issued to fund expansion innovation and growth.

Part B   Read this paragraph carefully and correct all comma errors.

While Tim and Tina were watching the parade Toby their independent four-year old son wandered away. As soon as they realized he was gone, they looked, called and shouted for him. They were very scared, and concerned for his safety. After the parade ended and the sidewalks cleared they found Toby lying on the edge of the sidewalk fast asleep. Both parents were needless to say very relieved.

Part C   Write a series of sentences showing each of the uses of the comma. For each sentence, explain the usage being employed.

Editing Applications

Part A   Read the following paragraphs carefully. Correct all errors in comma usage, spelling, and word usage.

1. The business world is an interesting complex institution, especially when it includes the foriegn sector. Because the institutions that govern foreign markets are not consistent arguements arise about not only the role of national business but also international business. Should local or national firms be responsable for quality and quantity while competing with international firms? A lot of informa-

tion has been gathered and many employers are enthusiastic about the results. However, there are no practical obvious conclusions.

2. Recently our librarian Charles LaBlanc submitted a recomendation that shelving be moved to the second floor. His proposal is similar to your counsel's and to the proposal submitted by Ronnie Gomez last February. Getting the necessary material to make the shelves stationery could be a problem and we must make sure that the changes are consistant with the other decor on the second floor.

Part B   Read this memo carefully and correct all errors in grammar, word usage, spelling, and punctuation.

TO:	Alex Hestor
FROM:	Janie Steinman
DATE:	January 25, 19--
SUBJECT:	Zoning of Proposed Business Office Property

As you are aware the city counsel met last night to discuss the zoning classification for the property, on which we want to build our offices.

Sufficient information supporting our proposal was given.   Because the proposal was consistant with the classifications already in existence their was no arguements about the zoning classification.

The counsel was neither concerned that the property is owned by foreign developers, nor that nearby property has been zoned for condominiums.   In addition no other rezoning proposals were offered.

My council to you therefore is to proceed with the plans as quickly as possible. We need them offices.

CHAPTER 12

Other Internal Punctuation

Objectives

After studying this chapter and completing the chapter exercises, you should be able to:

1. Use the semicolon and colon correctly.
2. Use the underscore and quotation marks correctly.
3. Use the apostrophe and hyphen correctly.
4. Use the dash and parentheses correctly.
5. Spell and use a list of common business terms.

In this chapter we will learn to use eight internal punctuation marks correctly. Like the comma, these internal punctuation marks help us to write more effectively by guiding the reader through our writing. Punctuation marks add clarity to our writing.

THE SEMICOLON

The semicolon provides a stronger break than the comma but a weaker break than the period. Semicolons are frequently used to join independent clauses in compound sentences or to separate items that contain internal commas.

Rule 1   Use a semicolon to connect main (independent) clauses closely related in thought. The semicolon is used instead of a comma and coordinate conjunction.

> Derek attended a convention in Las Vegas last month; he will vacation in Panama City in July.

> We had strawberry shortcake for dessert tonight; tomorrow night we will have apple pie; on Thursday we will have chocolate cake.

Rule 2   Use a semicolon to join the main clauses in a compound sentence when one of the clauses contains a transitional expression.

TRANSITIONAL EXPRESSIONS

accordingly	furthermore	moreover
also	however	nevertheless
as a result	indeed	on the other hand
besides	in fact	otherwise
consequently	in other words	that is (i.e.)
for example (e.g.)	instead	then
for instance	meanwhile	therefore

> The computer industry's growth has slowed down; however, both voice mail and electronic mail are enjoying remarkable growth.

> This summer's drought is the worst in years; farmers, for instance, are having to import hay from other states.

Rule 3   To prevent misreading or for the sake of clarity, use a semicolon to separate items in a series when the items contain internal commas.

> Our sales offices are located in Akron, Ohio; Stamford, Connecticut; Chicago, Illinois; and Atlanta, Georgia.

> We designed our own home, a two-story colonial; drew the blueprints; and built most of it ourselves.

Rule 4   Use a semicolon before expressions such as *for example (e.g.)*, *that is (i.e.)*, and *for instance* when they introduce a list of examples that are incidental to the meaning of the sentence. Use a comma after the expression.

> Choose basic core colors for your working wardrobe; for example, beige, brown, navy, taupe, or gray.

> You should practice wise money management; i.e., save a portion of your income, invest wisely, and avoid impulse spending.

THE COLON

The colon generally directs the reader's attention to what is to follow. Usually what follows the colon completes or explains the clause before the colon.

Rule 1   Use a colon before enumerations, lists, and explanations which provide more information about what came before the colon. The items are often introduced by words such as *the following* or *as follows*. (You may capitalize the first word of a main clause following a colon.) Enumerations that are run into the text are not capitalized.

> I have one reason for purchasing a microwave oven: to cut down on time spent in the kitchen.

> His new electronic typewriter has the following features: automatic centering, electronic storage, and automatic return.

If the items appear in a vertical list, capitalize the first word in each item. Omit periods after the items unless one or more of them are complete sentences.

> Managers should follow these steps in working with their unit's budget:
>
> 1. Set goals.
> 2. Tally resources.
> 3. Enhance resources.
> 4. Make requests.
> 5. Prepare for next year.

> Our conference has it all:
>
> PC workshops
> Expert presentations
> Vendor exhibits
> Excellent accommodations

Rule 2   Use a colon between main clauses of a compound sentence when the second clause explains or illustrates the first clause. In such cases, the colon replaces the semicolon. For emphasis, you may capitalize the first word after the colon.

> Remember this rule: Time Is Money.

> Here is one way you can improve your sense of humor: Recall events in your life that seemed serious at the time but that you now appreciate as funny.

Rule 3   Use a colon to introduce a long quotation or to formally introduce a quotation.

> In his review of the classic film *The Bridge on the River Kwai,* the critic stated: "This magnificent film about British soldiers in a Japanese prison camp richly deserved its Best Picture Oscar. Alec Guinness (who won an Oscar) is perfect as the driven officer who has his men build a bridge for the Japanese."

> The article on stress concluded: "Learning to delegate jobs and responsibilities to others is another key step toward lowering stress."

Rule 4   Use a colon in the following situations:

Between hours and minutes when expressing time in figures.

> We caught the 7:30 p.m. train to Washington.

After the salutation of a business letter.

> Dear Ms. Loux:

Between Bible chapter and verse.

> During Sunday's service, the minister quoted John 3:16.

In ratios and proportions when figures are used.

> The mixture of chemicals is 10:2:5.

✔ Checkpoint 1   SEMICOLONS AND COLONS

Insert semicolons and colons as needed in the following examples.

1. Art collectors might rejoice at this news A computer data bank now lists all major works.
2. We have scheduled regional meetings on the following dates October 8, 1988, in Charleston, South Carolina October 15, 1988, in Atlanta, Georgia and October 20, 1988, in Knoxville, Tennessee.
3. She gets up at 5 30 a.m. she has to be at work by 7 00.
4. Everyone who drives should have automobile insurance furthermore, every driver should have adequate liability coverage.

5. Our office now has a great deal of automated equipment for instance, electronic typewriters, microcomputers, and word processors.

6. In the article on real estate, the author stated "Middle-class single-family homes are the best investment."

Check your answers in Appendix D.

THE UNDERSCORE

Underscoring (or underlining) indicates that words are being used in a special way. In print, italics are used instead of the underscore. Many computer printers also have the italics feature. The following examples show the use of the underscore when italics are not available.

Rule 1   Use the underscore to set off titles of complete, separate works, such as books, magazines, newspapers, pamphlets, movies, plays, television and radio programs, paintings, and similar items.

> While in the waiting room, I browsed through The Wall Street Journal, Newsweek, and The One-Minute Manager.

> Two of my all-time favorite productions are Gone with the Wind and A Chorus Line.

Rule 2   Use an underscore when defining, emphasizing, or referring to specific words and examples.

> A compound document contains information in at least two forms, such as text and graphics.

> The verbs lie and lay are often misused.

> When choosing a shoe, look for one that gives support and comfort. (Emphasis)

QUOTATION MARKS

The main use of quotation marks is to enclose quotations. However, quotation marks also enclose certain titles and words used in an unusual way.

Rule 1   Use quotation marks to set off direct quotations (the exact words of a speaker or writer).

"We each have our own bank account," Peggy explained. "I take care of the mortgage and Jerry makes the car payment."

In his article on white-water rafting, Miller wrote, "This is a sport for people who demand something different."

The ad for Flakies cereal emphasized its "whole-grain goodness."

Do not use quotation marks around indirect quotations.

She said that she believes walking is the best exercise.

The defendant answered no to all of the prosecutor's questions.

Use single quotation marks to enclose a quotation within a quotation.

Amanda said, "The police officer shouted, 'Don't get in the line of fire!' "

Note: Place punctuation with quotation marks in the following manner:

- Periods and commas always go inside quotation marks.
- Colons and semicolons always go outside quotation marks.
- A question mark and an exclamation point go inside the closing quotation mark if only the quotation is a question or an exclamation. They go outside the closing quotation mark if they apply to the entire sentence.

She shouted, "Watch out!"

Did he say, "I'm tired"?

Rule 2   Use quotation marks to set off parts of whole works, such as articles in magazines or chapters in books. Also enclose titles of songs, essays, lectures, and complete but unpublished works such as reports.

I read the article "Buying Yourself a Business" in this month's <u>Changing Times</u>.

Study Chapter 10, "Developing Visual Aids," for homework tonight.

Rule 3   Use quotation marks around words used in an unconventional manner.

By adopting a "can-do" attitude, the area blossomed from dusty cotton fields into a bustling business mecca.

✔ **Checkpoint 2**   THE UNDERSCORE AND QUOTATION MARKS

Underline or place quotation marks where appropriate in the following sentences.

1. Some of the respondents answered no to several questions in the survey entitled Computer Skills for the Future.

2. The July issue of Changing Times described new kinds of mortgages, including stripped mortgages.

3. Writers sometimes confuse the words accept and except.

4. When buying a new house, she said, be sure to shop around for a mortgage.

5. Chapter 28, Job Interview and Follow-up Messages, from the text Fundamentals of Business Communication, helped prepare me for job interviews.

Check your answers in Appendix D.

THE APOSTROPHE

The apostrophe is used to form possessives, contractions, and—in some cases—plurals.

Rule 1   Use an apostrophe to show possession and to express time spans. For a complete discussion of forming possessives, refer to pages 49–51.

We took Jane's cat to the vet.

This project represents two years' work.

Rule 2   Use an apostrophe to indicate omitted letters in a contraction.

cannot ⟶ can't	will not ⟶ won't
did not ⟶ didn't	do not ⟶ don't
you are ⟶ you're	it is ⟶ it's

Rule 3   Use an apostrophe to form the plural of letters, figures, symbols, and abbreviations if the apostrophe is needed to avoid misreading the expression.

APOSTROPHE NEEDED	APOSTROPHE NOT NEEDED
i's	YMCAs
a's	$s
M's	9s
u's	1990s

THE HYPHEN

The hyphen is commonly used to form compound words or separate parts of a single unit. Compound words, however, are sometimes hyphenated, sometimes open, and sometimes solid. Because the expression of compound words is a matter of current practice, always consult an up-to-date dictionary for the current usage.

HYPHENATED COMPOUNDS	OPEN COMPOUNDS	SOLID COMPOUNDS
air-condition (verb)	air conditioning (noun)	carsick
attorney-at-law	face value	foghorn
double-space (verb)	double space (noun)	getaway
on-line	high school	noisemaker
president-elect	ice cream	notebook
trade-in (noun)	post office	typesetting

Rule 1   Use a hyphen between words in a compound adjective when the adjective comes before the word modified. When the compound adjective follows the word modified, do not use a hyphen unless a current dictionary shows the expression hyphenated.

HYPHENS NEEDED	HYPHENS NOT NEEDED
user-friendly equipment	Our equipment is user friendly.
four-year-old child	The child is four years old.
40-story building	The building is 40 stories high.

Rule 2   Use a hyphen after prefixes in some words. Check an up-to-date dictionary for current usage.

self-contained	ex-president
semi-invalid	pro-American
co-worker	de-escalation

Rule 3   Use a hyphen between numbers from twenty-one to ninety-nine and fractions used as modifiers.

forty-five	two-thirds majority
sixty-seven	one-half of the members

Rule 4   Use a hyphen between syllables of a word to show word division at the end of a line.

founda-tion	free-dom
situ-ated	trans-late

Note: Divide a hyphenated word only at the hyphen.

self- important	co- leader

Insert apostrophes and hyphens as needed in the following sentences.

1. Our companys mailroom staff uses up to date equipment.
2. One third of the executives dont need to attend seminars on self motivation.
3. Twenty five students plan to run for student council offices.
4. His application letter shouldnt contain so many Is.
5. Chris has applied for a high level position with the firm.

Check your answers in Appendix D.

THE DASH

The dash, a somewhat informal but lively and emphatic punctuation mark, is formed by keying two unspaced hyphens. The dash is used instead of a comma, semicolon, or colon to join a group of words to the main sentence or to set off interrupting words. The dash shows emphasis and should be used infrequently in business communication so that it does not lose its effectiveness.

Rule 1   Use a dash to set off parenthetical expressions or appositives to be emphasized (especially when the material contains commas).

> Our new office--the best-equipped, most spacious one on this floor--will be ready in May.

> Kites rise against the wind--not with it!

Rule 2   Use a dash instead of a colon or semicolon to set off a listing or an explanation that provides details or an example.

> Hawaiian ice comes in several exotic flavors--strawberry, coconut, bubble gum, and orange.

> Three students--Mary, June, and Sue--will attend the convention.

> Turn your typists into typesetters--that is, buy them the new Docutype typesetting system.

Rule 3   Use a dash after a listing at the beginning of a sentence that is followed by a summarizing word such as *all* or *these*.

> Correct grammar, correct punctuation, and precise wording--these are important factors when writing business letters.

Rule 4   Use a dash to indicate an abrupt change in thought.

I feel so bogged down with work--wouldn't it be nice to escape to the mountains this weekend?

PARENTHESES

Parentheses are used to set off explanatory material which is not necessary to the meaning of the sentence.

Rule 1   Use parentheses to set off nonessential information such as references and explanatory details. By using parentheses, you are deemphasizing the information.

In his article on home gardening (April issue of *Home and Garden*), the writer provided a list of peak growing times (see page 6).

Note: Since *see page 6* is part of the sentence, it needs no end punctuation (i.e., no period) within the parentheses. Also, note that the comma separating the introductory phrase from the main clause is placed *after* the first end parenthesis.

We are submitting a large purchase order for new computers.   (A smaller order is being submitted for computer supplies.)

Note: The information in parentheses is a separate sentence and requires end punctuation within the parentheses.

A high percentage (73.4 percent) of secretaries believe that computer skills will increase their career mobility.

Use the dollar symbol ($) only with the first figure in a column.

Rule 2   Use parentheses to enclose a name following an abbreviation or figures of spelled-out amounts of money.

This conveyance is intended to secure the payment of a debt in the principal sum of Fifty Thousand Dollars ($50,000).

The SEC (Securities and Exchange Commission) requires annual reports from corporations.

Rule 3   Use parentheses to enclose figures or letters within an enumeration.

To answer the phone like a pro, (1) be prepared, (2) screen calls courteously, and (3) offer to help the caller.

Several shorthand systems are available: (a) Century 21, (b) Gregg, (c) Pitman, and (d) Speed-writing.

✔ Checkpoint 4 DASHES AND PARENTHESES

Insert dashes and parentheses as needed in the following sentences.

1. One of the first and often the only contacts the public has with an organization is by telephone.

2. Results of the survey indicate that more than half 67 percent of the people interviewed and that is a large percentage favored Lynn for school superintendent.

3. Frequent overtime is one of the drawbacks to this job but you would rather talk about benefits, I'm sure.

4. Be sure you know the components of a computer system the monitor, keyboard, CPU central processing unit, and disk drives.

5. In the telephone directory the white pages you can locate information by 1 company names, 2 government listings, and 3 individuals' names.

Check your answers in Appendix D.

SUMMARY

As guideposts to the reader, internal punctuation marks make our writing more interesting and understandable. Coherent business communications employ the following internal punctuation:

The semicolon connects main clauses in a sentence or separates items in a series that already contains commas. The colon usually directs the reader's attention to what follows. Underscoring (or italics in print) indicates that words are being used in specific ways or are being emphasized. Quotation marks enclose exact quotations and certain titles or indicate that words are being used in an unusual way. The apostrophe is used to form the possessive case of nouns, some plurals, and contractions.

The hyphen is used to form some compound words, to join prefixes, and to indicate division of words. Dashes are informal punctuation marks used to show emphasis or indicate an abrupt change in thought. Parentheses set off material not necessary to the meaning of a sentence.

• • • • • • • • • Communication Activities

Spelling and Word Usage

Learn to spell and use the following words. Be alert for them in the Editing Applications at the end of the chapter.

attorneys	fulfill	restaurant
automation	judgment	supersede
controlling	mathematics	vacancies
convenience	omitted	variable
extension	procedure	

If necessary, refer to Appendix A for the correct usage of these words.

cooperation/corporation   envelope/envelop   to/too/two

Practical Applications

Part A   Correct the internal punctuation in each of the following sentences. Write "C" if the sentence is correct.

1. There are advantages and rewards to having computer skills e.g., mental challenge and stimulation.

2. You can plug in printers almost any model, your video recorder, or a modem.

3. Carl's Steakhouses launched a major expansion, opening 20 new restaurants in three states--all with a heavy emphasis on a traditional steaks and chops menu.

4. The dance ended with the strains of Goodnight Ladies (a tradition at our club), but no one wanted to leave.

5. The writer said, "After I wrote my book, my children told me 'Dad, we are proud of you.'"

6. I read the article, "Buy Your Own Business," in Decembers issue of Changing Times.

7. Some banks offer "junior" accounts, these accounts require a lower minimum deposit but have fewer services.

8. Vehicles with records of high thefts, Porsche, BMW, and Mercedes, to name a few, now have to carry vehicle identification numbers (VINs).

9. The following positions will switch from part time to full time status: sales clerk, janitor, and receptionist.
10. To avoid jargonese (a formal and boring writing style), use simple words such as "use" instead of "utilize."

Part B   Insert the correct internal punctuation in each of the following sentences. (Commas have already been provided.) Write "C" if the sentence is correct.

1. The consultant gave the following advice Act on it or throw it away.
2. The title of secretary was held by more respondents 31 percent than any other however, there were nearly as many executive secretaries 26 percent.
3. The article stated Manufacturers are working on sophisticated techniques to fingerprint their merchandise.
4. Adjustable-rate mortgages recently accounted for about one fifth of conventional and government backed loans.
5. There is one thing you cant do without a will name a guardian for your minor children.
6. She didnt use the you attitude in her letters I counted ten Is in three short paragraphs.
7. Concerts have been scheduled in Cincinnati, Ohio, on June 10 in Chicago, Illinois, on July 2 and in Detroit, Michigan, on August 4.
8. The meeting is scheduled for 2 30 p.m. try not to be late.
9. Josef served as vice president of the Data Processing Management Association DPMA.
10. Unlike automakers, electronics companies dont classify their VCRs by model year.

Editing Applications

Part A   Insert internal punctuation and correct all misspelled or misused words in the following paragraphs.

Giant cooperations Coca Cola, Johnson & Johnson, and Du Pont, to name a few spend large amounts of money on advertising two make sure we recognize hundred's of products. These corporations must protect their product names therefore, many companies hire trademark examiners who fulfil the responsibility of looking for trademark violators retailers and writers who improperly use trademark names. Companies often have too hire attornies moreover, lawsuits must often be filed.

Autamation has resulted in trademark problems for some companies. Xerox Corperation is trying to gain the coperation of the public they ask us to use Xerox as an adjective, as in Please make a Xerox copy of this letter. Then, to, it's convenient to use terms like Dictaphone actually a brand name instead of the correct term transcribing machine.

The courts have made judgements over the years that have removed trademark protection from many products. The following products are now so familiar that controling of trademarks is no longer legal in fact, its hard to believe these generic names were once trademarks 1 aspirin, 2 escalator, 3 kerosene, 4 linoleum, 5 thermos, and 6 yo-yo.

Part B   Insert appropriate internal punctuation and correct all misspelled words in the following letter. (Commas have already been inserted.)

October 5, 19--

Mr. Jeffrey Yacinski
Dorsey Personnel Services
3829 H Street NW
Washington, D.C. 20006

Dear Mr. Yacinski:

Here is the information you requested on proceedures for training office personnel to handle the telephone.   This report supercedes all previous reports from our firm.

HANDLING THE TELEPHONE

One of the most important tasks in any office whether you have office autamation or not is handling the telephone.   One of the first and sometimes only contacts the public has with a business is by telephone consequently, a lasting impression can be made.

Here are some helpful telephone techniques that your staff can use to enhance your companys image.

1. Always be prepared with a message pad--and a pencil, to---by the telephone.

2. Screen calls courteously by saying, May I ask whose calling, please?   rather than Whose calling?

3. Take complete phone messages, including the callers name, phone number including extention, company, and a brief message.   None of this important information should be omited.

4. Ask if someone else can help if your supervisor is 1 out of the office or 2 not available for calls.   If possible, explain her absence by indicating whether shes out of town, in a meeting, or on vacation however, dont tell where she is.

5. Finally, dont automatically put someone on hold many people prefer to leave a message.   If they do decide too hold, its important two check back with them every 15 seconds.

Mr. Yacinski, please complete the enclosed survey regarding telephone automaton in your office, and return it by October 15 in the envelop provided.   If you desire further information about telephone techniques, may I suggest that you read the article Business Telephone Techniques in the April issue of Telephone Talk.   Let me know if you or your vice presidents decide to go ahead with the telephone seminar.

Sincerely,

Carla Kagan, President

er

Enclosure

CHAPTER 13

Abbreviations, Capitalization, and Number Expression

Objectives

After studying this chapter and completing the chapter exercises, you should be able to:

1. Use abbreviations appropriately in business communications.
2. Capitalize words and abbreviations correctly.
3. Express numbers correctly in figures and in words.
4. Spell and use a list of common business terms.

Using abbreviations, capitalization, and number expression correctly will impress the reader with your business communication skills. This chapter will present guidelines to help you use the appropriate rules. For more specific information, you may need to consult a current reference manual.

ABBREVIATIONS

An **abbreviation** is a shortened form of a word or phrase generally used to save space. Abbreviations are not suitable for all types of business communication, but they are frequently used in statistical and technical documents.

General Style

The following general rules will cover most situations in which abbreviating is acceptable in business correspondence. For more detailed information on the rules of abbreviation, refer to a reliable style manual. If in doubt about the correctness of an abbreviation, consult an up-to-date dictionary.

Addresses. Don't abbreviate such words as *Street, Avenue, Boulevard,* or *Lane* in street addresses.

> She lives at 58 Maple Street.

Compass point designations after the street names may be abbreviated.

> 16 Robin Avenue, NW   20 First Street, SE

Use the two-letter state abbreviations only with ZIP Codes. These two-letter abbreviations, preferred by the U.S. Postal Service, appear without periods and in all capitals. Within the main text of a business letter, spell out state names. In tables, lists, notes, and similar matter, use the standard state abbreviations. (In the following listing, a blank indicates that the name is not abbreviated.)

	TWO-LETTER ABBREVIATION	STANDARD ABBREVIATION
Alabama	AL	Ala.
Alaska	AK	—
Arizona	AZ	Ariz.
Arkansas	AR	Ark.
California	CA	Calif.
Colorado	CO	Colo.
Connecticut	CT	Conn.

Delaware	DE	Del.
District of Columbia	DC	D.C.
Florida	FL	Fla.
Georgia	GA	Ga.
Hawaii	HI	—
Idaho	ID	—
Illinois	IL	Ill.
Indiana	IN	Ind.
Iowa	IA	—
Kansas	KS	Kans.
Kentucky	KY	Ky.
Louisiana	LA	La.
Maine	ME	—
Maryland	MD	Md.
Massachusetts	MA	Mass.
Michigan	MI	Mich.
Minnesota	MN	Minn.
Mississippi	MS	Miss.
Missouri	MO	Mo.
Montana	MT	Mont.
Nebraska	NE	Nebr.
Nevada	NV	Nev.
New Hampshire	NH	N.H.
New Jersey	NJ	N.J.
New Mexico	NM	N.Mex.
New York	NY	N.Y.
North Carolina	NC	N.C.
North Dakota	ND	N.Dak.
Ohio	OH	—
Oklahoma	OK	Okla.
Oregon	OR	Oreg.
Pennsylvania	PA	Pa.
Rhode Island	RI	R.I.
South Carolina	SC	S.C.
South Dakota	SD	S.Dak.
Tennessee	TN	Tenn.
Texas	TX	Tex.
Utah	UT	—
Vermont	VT	Vt.
Virginia	VA	Va.
Washington	WA	Wash.
West Virginia	WV	W.Va.
Wisconsin	WI	Wis.
Wyoming	WY	Wyo.

Company Names. Official names of businesses often contain abbreviations. Check the letterhead for proper style.

Nelson Office Equipment Co.
Clifton James & Associates, Inc.
Classic Roadsters, Ltd.

Organizations. Abbreviate names of many organizations, associations, unions, government agencies, and other groups. Write these abbreviations in all capitals with no periods or spaces.

FBI	Federal Bureau of Investigation
YWCA	Young Women's Christian Association
AMA	American Management Association *or*
	American Medical Association
SBA	Small Business Administration
UAW	United Automobile Workers
IRS	Internal Revenue Service

Titles. Abbreviate personal titles (such as *Mr.* or *Messrs., Mrs.* or *Mme., Dr.*) that come before names.

Dr. Nancy Goodwin   Messrs. Steinbrecher and Nead
Mrs. Caruso   Ms. Jan Greenberg

Note: *Ms.* is appropriate when the marital status is unknown or irrelevant or when the woman prefers *Ms.* Titles such as *President, Senator,* or *Professor* may be abbreviated unless they appear with only a surname (last name).

Sen. John H. Glenn   Professor Stockwell

Abbreviate titles that come after personal names. The comma between the name and titles such as *Jr., Sr., III, IV,* and ordinals (*3d, 4th*) is optional. Academic degrees following a name are set off with commas.

Nancy Goodwin, M.D.   [but *not* Dr. Nancy Goodwin, M.D.]
J. Steven Byrd Sr.   Phil Smith III
Edward Brown, D.D.S.   Ellen Carino, Ph.D.

Technical Style

Technical material (tables, charts, and so forth) generally makes use of abbreviations that would not be used in general material.

Business Expressions. Abbreviate expressions commonly used in business forms, tables, and statistical documents. (Notice the difference in punctuation, capitalization, and spacing in the following abbreviations.)

mph	miles per hour
vs.	versus
FYI	for your information
No. (when followed by figure)	number

CPA	certified public accountant
FY	fiscal year
acct.	account
bal.	balance
mdse.	merchandise
mfg.	manufacturing
pd.	paid
in.	inch(es)

Country Names. Don't abbreviate country names except in technical material, such as business forms and tables. Exception: A long name such as Union of Soviet Socialist Republics is usually abbreviated U.S.S.R.

Germany   Mexico

Abbreviate the name United States when it is part of the name of a government agency or used as an adjective. Otherwise, spell it out.

U.S. Army   U.S. government

Days and Months. Don't abbreviate days of the week and months of the year except when keying statistical documents such as lists and business forms.

Mon.	Jan.	Aug.
Tues.	Feb.	Sept.
Wed.	Mar.	Oct.
Thurs.	Apr.	Nov.
Fri.	May	Dec.
Sat.	June	
Sun.	July	

✔ **Checkpoint 1**   ABBREVIATIONS

Correct abbreviation errors in the following sentences.

1. Doctor Stanley White visits his patients on Tues. and Wed. mornings beginning at 8 a.m.
2. The meeting was held at the Dexter St. Y.M.C.A. on Nov. 4.
3. Send my mail to the following address:
   Mister Fred Blum Junior
   Blum & Smith, Inc.
   522 State St. NW
   Boulder, Colo. 80322-3621
4. He was driving 80 mph when stopped by the st. patrol last Friday in Cleveland, OH.

Check your answers in Appendix D.

CAPITALIZATION

Capitalization draws attention to words we wish to emphasize. As a rule, it is better to avoid over-capitalizing, which only makes our communication look cluttered and busy.

When to Capitalize

If in doubt about capitalization, consult an up-to-date office reference manual or dictionary. Here are some do's and don'ts for using capitalization.

Academic Degrees. Capitalize academic degrees following a name and abbreviations used alone, but do not capitalize degrees used in general terms.

David Evans, M.D.   M.A. in English
bachelor of arts degree   master's degree

Family Relations. Capitalize words indicating family relationships when used before a proper name or used alone.

Mother [but *my mother*]

Aunt Elsie

First Words. Capitalize the first word of every sentence and, for emphasis, the first word in a sentence following a colon.

You are ready for your next job.

Here is the solution: Use a spreadsheet for your budget.

Capitalize the first word of a direct quotation. However, do not capitalize the first word of an interrupted quote.

Celina asked, "Are we having beef for lunch?"

The article stated: "Taxes will be lowered."

"The time has arrived," Mr. Ross said, "for us to get to work."

Geographic Terms. Capitalize compass points referring to a geographical area or a definite region, but do not capitalize words indicating direction.

Middle East		the West Coast
the South	*but*	travel south
Northern Ireland	*but*	northern part of Ireland

Hyphenated Words. Capitalize elements of hyphenated words if they are proper nouns or proper adjectives. Do not capitalize prefixes or suffixes added to such words.

Atlanta-Chicago flight   mid-Atlantic states
Spanish-American students   President-elect Pierce

Letter Parts. Capitalize the first word and all titles and proper nouns in the salutation and complimentary close of a business letter.

Dear Mr. Sawyer   Sincerely yours

Nouns Followed by Numbers or Letters. Capitalize nouns and abbreviations followed by numbers or letters that indicate sequence. Exceptions: page, paragraph, sentence, line, verse, and size.

No. 504	Chap. 8	Appendix A
Flight 315	Check 52	Act II
page 15	line 6	size 10

Pronoun *I*. Capitalize the pronoun *I*.

You and I should visit Jane in the hospital.

Proper Nouns. Capitalize a *proper* noun (the name of a *particular* person, place, or thing) and any adjective derived from a specific name. Do not capitalize *common* nouns, which refer to a general classification.

DO NOT CAPITALIZE	DO CAPITALIZE
course in shorthand	Shorthand I (specific course)
marketing	Marketing 100 (specific course)
U.S. history	History 211 (specific course)
person	Yoko Tanaka
department in a firm	Accounting Department
computers in our school	IBM, Burroughs, Apple
a famous river	Mississippi River
my favorite uncle	Uncle Ernest
the church I attend	First Methodist Church
automobile she drives	Chrysler LeBaron
street he lives on	Riverside Drive
a former U.S. president	President John F. Kennedy
particular countries	Japan, Great Britain, Italy
nationalities	Japanese, British, Italian
product types: soaps, candy, cars	Tide, Hershey, Oldsmobile (specific brands)
states	Florida, Texas, New York
people from states	Floridian, Texan, New Yorker
cities	Boston, Atlanta
people from cities	Bostonian, Atlantan
month	April
day	Wednesday
holiday	Yom Kippur
building	Empire State Building
university	Ohio State University
ethnic groups	Hispanics, Indians
religious groups	Catholics, Jews, Buddhists
athletic teams	Chicago Bears
businesses	General Electric Company
organizations	the Girl Scouts
historic event	Civil War

DO NOT CAPITALIZE	DO CAPITALIZE
parks	Yellowstone National Park
an award	the Nobel Peace Prize
a governmental agency	the Department of Labor
a school	Hampton High School

Supreme Being.   Capitalize words that refer to a supreme being.

God   the Lord   His word   Yahweh   Allah

Titles of Persons.   Capitalize titles that come before a name.

Dr. Nancy Miller   Mr. Larry Spatola
Governor Sarah Cox   Rev. Clement Beckford

Capitalize titles that follow a name in an address or typed signature.

Thomas Blum, Marketing Manager
Linda Jordan, County Commissioner
Jack Abrams, President

Generally do *not* capitalize titles when they follow a name or are used in place of a name. (An exception may be made for high-ranking officials when the title follows or is used in place of a specific name.)

Thomas Blum is *marketing manager* for our firm.

The new *county commissioner* arrived late.

Bill Bates, *governor* of New Hampshire, will be the after-dinner speaker.

The *President* of the United States spoke tonight.

Titles of Written Works.   Capitalize the first and last words and all other important words in the titles of written works (books, magazines, newspapers) and their contents (articles, chapters). Also capitalize the first word after a colon in a title. Do not capitalize coordinate conjunctions, articles, and prepositions unless they are the first or last words of the title or subtitle. (Exception: Capitalize prepositions if they are more than four letters long.)

The Far Pavilions

U.S. News and World Report

Yeager: An Autobiography

How to Succeed in Business Without Really Trying   (Capitalize *without* because it is more than four letters long.)

When Not to Capitalize

Avoid capitalizing in the following situations:

Common Nouns with Proper Nouns.   Don't capitalize common nouns that refer to, but are not a part of, a proper noun.

>   Atlantic and Pacific oceans *but* Pacific Ocean
>
>   Marriott or Sheraton hotels *but* Marriott Hotel

Seasons.   Don't capitalize the names of seasons (unless they are personified).

>   in the summer   *but*   Old Man Winter

✔ Checkpoint 2   CAPITALIZATION

Correct all capitalization errors in each of the following sentences.

1. sam, dr. parker, and i drove south to reach cape cod, located in eastern massachusetts.
2. the office administration department of bridgeport junior college purchased ten new brother typewriters, model no. em-811.
3. as a member of the association of information systems professionals, gwen clark (president of the miami chapter) receives *words* magazine.
4. during fall quarter governor andrews will visit the north campus of our school; he was unable to visit last spring.
5. both of my parents believe in god; however, my father is a baptist, while mother is a member of the presbyterian church.
6. the author of *traveling through america* stated: "the arkansas and missouri rivers both flow into the mississippi river."

Check your answers in Appendix D.

NUMBER EXPRESSION

Numbers are frequently used in business writing. The major decision you will have to make about numbers is whether to write them as figures or as words. The guidelines presented will help you solve most of your number problems. For more comprehensive information about the writing of numbers, consult a reference manual.

General Guidelines

Follow these general guidelines for writing numbers.

Small and Large Numbers. Generally express the numbers one through ten in words and express numbers above ten as figures.

> Mail three copies of the report.
>
> We live in a seven-room house.
>
> We bought 50 acres of pasture land.

Use figures for a series of numbers applying to the same category in a sentence if any one of the numbers is generally written in figures.

> Our word processing lab contains 25 microcomputers and 8 word processors and is open nine hours a day.
>
> She has written five books, nine short stories, and ten plays during the past 12 years.

Approximate Numbers. Use words for indefinite (round) or approximate numbers.

> She spent thousands of dollars on medical bills.
>
> John received around twenty requests for his speech on time management.

Express round numbers such as 1,200 as twelve hundred, not as one thousand two hundred. Express very large numbers in combinations of figures and words.

> 1 billion   15 million

At Beginning of Sentence. Spell out a number beginning a sentence. (If the number is long, rewrite the sentence so that it doesn't begin with a number.)

> Fifty people attended the office picnic.
>
> Two hundred companies participated in the Christmas Stocking program.
>
> There are 6,546 employees working in our company. (*Avoid:* Six thousand five hundred forty-six employees work for our company.)

Consecutive Numbers. Use words for the *shorter* (not necessarily smaller) of two consecutive numbers.

> Pat mailed 148 twenty-page reports.
>
> Last week we sold fifteen $5,000 computers.

Formal Style. Use words to express numbers in formal writing (social invitations, many legal documents, and proclamations). In legal documents, follow written numbers with figures in parentheses.

> You are cordially invited to a reception for President Gates on June sixteenth, nineteen hundred eighty-nine.
>
> The price of land is six thousand five hundred dollars ($6,500) an acre.

Ordinals. Use words to express ordinal numbers (*first, second*) that can be written in one or two words.

> The couple recently celebrated their fiftieth wedding anniversary.
>
> I work on the twenty-first floor of the Equitable Building.

> *but*

> This is their 350th day in captivity.

Specific Guidelines

The following guidelines address specific instances of number expression.

Addresses. Spell out numbered street names *First* through *Tenth* using ordinals.

> Yesterday we drove down Fifth Avenue.
>
> She lives next door to me on Second Street.

Use figures for numbered street names above *Tenth*.

> Our sales office is located on 14th Avenue.

Use figures for house and building numbers unless the building's name serves as its address.

> My uncle lives at 132 Oakridge Drive.
>
> Send her mail to 1450 Bryant Road, Apartment 4D.
>
> We recently moved to One Park Place.

Use figures for ZIP Codes, post office box numbers, and suite and room numbers.

> The law offices are in Suite 21, Yorktown Office Center.
>
> Write me at P.O. Box 32977, Madison, WI 53794-1701.

Decimals, Percentages, and Fractions. Use figures to express decimals and percentages. (Substitute the symbol % for the word *percent* only in a technical or statistical context.)

> Class enrollment was up 5 percent over last year.
>
> The average class size was 22.4 students.

Use words to express fractions in general business writing.

> Our manager sent three-fourths of the staff to the workshop.
>
> The rock star received one-third of the gross earnings from the concert.

Use figures to express combinations of whole numbers and fractions.

> 5 1/2   45 3/4

Measurements.   Use figures for measurements, weights, and dimensions.

> Mr. Lance travels 35 miles to his office.
>
> The cake recipe calls for 2 cups of flour.
>
> He lost 7 pounds last month.
>
> Sally is 5 feet 6 inches tall.

Money.   Express amounts of money in figures. Dollar amounts that are even are written without decimals ($15) unless another amount in the same context includes a fractional dollar amount requiring the use of a decimal ($15.00 and $12.50). If the amount is less than a dollar, spell out the word *cents*.

> Our new car cost $15,000, not including the tax.
>
> Sean earned $420.50 in his part-time job last month, and I earned $410.00.

Use a combination of words and figures for very large sums of money that would otherwise be awkward to express.

> The company is building a $2 million factory.

Time and Dates.   Express time in figures unless used alone or with the more formal *o'clock*).

> My class meets at 7:30 p.m. on Tuesday and 8:00 a.m. on Saturdays.
>
> Please join me for lunch at one o'clock.
>
> Could we schedule the meeting for ten?

Express the date in figures when it follows the month.

> Tom was born on May 29, 1965.
>
> The conference will begin on October 5.

When the day precedes the month or the month is omitted, use ordinal figures. In formal style, use ordinal words.

> The 10th of April is on a Tuesday.
>
> The tenth of April is on a Tuesday.
>
> Patrick arrives on the 2d and departs on the 4th.

✔ **Checkpoint 3**   NUMBER EXPRESSION

Correct each incorrectly written number in the following sentences.

1. The new 5-story building, which houses 120 thousand square feet of office space, was first planned twenty years ago.

2. In our 7th Avenue office, approximately 30 dictation machines are available for work groups of two to 15 managers.

3. 17 people from our office, located at sixty-two Mason Street, caught the 5:50 p.m. train to Washington.

4. Over 2/3 of the staff will attend the luncheon on April 3rd at a cost of three hundred fifty dollars to the company.

5. According to page six of the annual report, in our 12th year of operation, profits are down by four percent in the second quarter.

6. Anna Powers, 42, will move sixty miles to her new job, which begins on the 5th of November.

7. At our Forty-first Street office, our staff is housed in 14 12-room suites.

Check your answers in Appendix D.

SUMMARY

In this chapter you have learned some important mechanics of business communication: using correct abbreviations, capitalization, and number expression.

Abbreviations are shortened forms of words or phrases and should be used cautiously in general business communications. However, you will find that abbreviating will make technical and statistical communications easier to read.

Capitalization is used to emphasize words. A general guide to good capitalization skills is to capitalize proper names but not common names.

Numbers may be expressed in words or figures. In general, spell out numbers one through ten and write numbers above ten in figures. Figures are usually used in technical writing.

● ● ● ● ● ● ● ● ● Communication Activities

Spelling and Word Usage

Learn to spell and use the following words. Be alert for them in the Editing Applications at the end of the chapter.

awkward   fundamental   ridiculous
corporation   justifiable   synonymous
courteous   memorandum   vein
discrepancy   opportunity   withheld
extraordinary   proprietor

If necessary, refer to Appendix A for the correct usage of these words.

complement/compliment   farther/further   loose/lose

Practical Applications

Correct all errors in abbreviation, capitalization, and number expression in the following sentences.

1. the 12 annual office automation conference will convene in san francisco, Calif., on june 6th.

2. If you order between now and Aug. 10th, you will receive a sixty dollar factory rebate on our 3 top-rated Typewriters.

3. Offset Duplicating has been around for over 40 years; the new models measure less than 50 in. high and thirty in. wide.

4. More than thirteen million computer terminals are switched on daily throughout the u.s.

5. write to dr. romei at fifteen west 42d Street, saint paul, mn 55164-0418.

6. We purchased twenty-one word processors from berne equipment company last mo.

7. at 10 am you will find me answering 3 10-line telephones when the sec. goes on break.

8. After a 7-yr. study of one thousand two hundred eighty patients in 16 Medical Centers, doctor miller, M.D., wrote his report.

9. members of the legislature voted to provide two million dollars for aid to victims of hurricane anne.

10. Over eighty percent of the respondents revealed that the at&t breakup had increased communication costs.

11. the office manual "automating the office of today" covers over 500 office automation terms — in plain english.

12. john davis, Executive Vice President of marketing at novak systems corp. in brooklyn, NY, attended the Conference in philadelphia.

13. Jane robbins, sixty-five, and paula Domino, sixty, filed an Age Discrimination suit against the navy.

14. if you send three dollars for your spiegel catalog, you will receive a $3 certificate toward your first purchase.

15. New Mail room equipment can now sort ZIP Codes by the first 3 digits.

16. Management Consultant sarah seymour has trained 1000's of mgrs. for the new york city-based american management association (a.m.a.).

17. Legislators have introduced vdt (visual display terminal) bills in 10 states, including Calif. and N.J.

18. For over 40 years, h&r block has employed Temporary Employees during tax season (jan.–apr.).

19. The information for the Study comes from 14 female and eight male managers from three major industries.

20. In the two-and-half years since our last report on edp (electronic data processing), pc's have overtaken the market.

Editing Applications

Part A   Correct all errors in abbreviations, capitalization, number expression, spelling, and word usage in the following paragraphs.

The bureau of labor statistics (bls) projects that there will be two hundred sixty-eight thousand more secretaries in the united states in 1995 than in 1984 — a ten percent increase over the eleven-year period. Will there be a descrepancy between the No. of secretarial openings and the No. of secs. available to fill the openings?

In the united states, based on the number of 1982–83 graduates of Secretarial Programs, there will be an extrordinary shortage of students to fill the four hundred seventy-eight thousand secretarial job openings. Fewer than twenty percent of these openings will be filled by students completing some type of Postsecondary Program, such as the program at fullerton technical college in kansas city, MO. A farther thirty percent of the openings can be filled by High School graduates of secretarial programs, such as the program at East Point high school in Union, n.j.

50 percent of the job openings will have to be filled by people with minimal training or from within coperations. This shortage of secretaries is an akward situation for our schools, which have the oppertunity to prepare people for 1000s of these openings. It is almost a ridicoulous situation that so many openings exist and people are not choosing this career field. As Office Automation continues to expand the scope and the image of the secretary, however, secretaries are saying that *professional* and *secretary* are synonymus terms.

Part B   Correct all errors in abbreviations, capitalization, number expression, spelling, and word usage in the following letter.

January 14th, 19--

ms. Joanne Dzubeck
supervisor, word processing
Adler Mfg. Co.
54 adams st.
braintree, mass. 02184-4128

dear ms. dzubeck:

the new Digital Dictation Systems on the market today are making fundemental changes in dictation and transcription.   Our new voicephone dictating machine can compliment your present word processing equipment by making transcription easier for your WP Operators. According to Alison Rubin, Word Processing Supervisor for franklin national bank in austin, Texas, "the new Voicephone System 2 has cut turnaround time in half.   Now, 1/4 of our bank's approximately eight hundred employees use Dictation Equipment."

After seeing the voicephone system 2, ms. Dzubeck, we think you will easily find justifyable reasons for purchasing this remarkable equipment.   The Dictation Unit, called the execuphone, measures a small four in. high and two in. wide.   It weighs only 5.9 ounces & costs three hundred ninety-five dollars.   System 2, designed for fourteen or fewer mgrs., will allow dictators in your corporation to dictate into 1 system located at the transcriber's desk.

we know that you don't want to loose any of your present mgrs. to longhand, which takes 6 times longer than voice dictation.   Call us at 1-800-453-2296 for farther information about system 2.

sincerely yours,

don wise, marketing manager

Fundamentals of Business Writing

PART 4

● ●

In order to have a 50-page booklet prepared on time, your administrative assistant worked four hours overtime last night. Today when you walked into the office, your assistant handed you a copy and said, "Finishing this report was a difficult task, but here it is." Unthinkingly, you casually said "Thanks" and walked into your office. A few minutes later your assistant came in and said, "Is the report all right?" Now you realize your neglect. You stammer out, "Gee, it is fine. Thank you for staying late last night to finish the report. I really appreciate your efforts." Your initial failure to show appreciation, however, sent an offensive message.

All of us have unintentionally sent offensive messages. Generally, such messages are offensive because the content is insensitive to the receiver. Research shows that tone—the part of the message that reflects attitude—is just as important as the actual words of the message.

Effective messages are courteous, clear, considerate, concise, and complete. Such messages require careful planning, organizing, and editing.

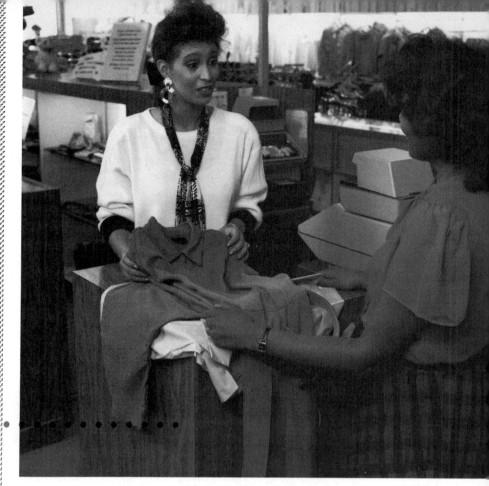

CHAPTER 14

Developing Courteous and Considerate Communication

Objectives

After studying this chapter and completing the chapter exercises, you should be able to:

1. Use words and phrases that convey courtesy to the reader.
2. Develop the "you" approach in your messages.
3. Understand the importance of being positive and prompt in your business messages and using gender-free words to convey consideration.

In this chapter, we begin the study of the characteristics of effective communication and techniques for implementing them. Incorporating these techniques will help your messages achieve positive results. Being courteous and considerate are the characteristics discussed in this chapter.

COURTESY

Courtesy is being polite, kind, and respectful to others. Just as we expect our family and friends to speak and act in a courteous manner, we expect business people to demonstrate courtesy at all times. To show courtesy, find a reason to say "please" or "thank you" in each letter you send:

Thank you for inquiring about...

Please send me...

I appreciate your willingness to...

Please let me know if I can be of further service to you.

CONSIDERATION

Although courtesy and consideration are closely related, consideration goes beyond courtesy. Whereas courtesy may involve a mere "please" or "thank you," consideration means having **empathy**—being sensitive to the receiver's probable attitudes, feelings, or emotional state. To show consideration as well as courtesy, send messages that are "you" oriented, that are positive, that treat males and females equally, and that are prompt.

Be "You" Oriented

"You" oriented messages focus on what the receiver wants to know and needs to do rather than on what the sender has done or needs to know. In contrast, "I" or "company" oriented messages are more concerned about the needs of the sender than about those of the receiver. Is the message below "I" or "you" oriented?

We have received your request for permission to use our computers during the next session of summer school. We are pleased to inform you that you may use all 35 of the microcomputers you requested. Would you please come in and fill out the necessary paperwork any time before April 1.

Compare the preceding message with the "you" approach message that follows:

> Good news, Jessica! All 35 of the microcomputers you requested will be available to use during the next session of summer school. Please come by the office before April 1 to fill out the necessary forms.

Use the following techniques to employ the "you" approach:

Personalize the Message

To emphasize the receiver, use *you* and *your* rather than *I* or *we,* and personalize the message by occasionally addressing the receiver by name. These devices make the receiver feel important — a necessary factor in view of the many impersonal computer letters that are sent out daily. Addressing the receiver by name is especially appropriate when you know the receiver. The first and last paragraphs of a letter or memo are ideal places to use the receiver's name. Compare the following "I" or "company" oriented messages with the "you" oriented messages.

"I" OR "COMPANY" ORIENTED	"YOU" ORIENTED
I think your report was well written.	You wrote an excellent report.
I am pleased to inform you that your request to use the conference room on May 15 has been granted.	You may use the conference room on May 15 as requested.
Enclosed is a copy of our new policy.	It is a pleasure to inform you, Mrs. Wilson, about our new policy.
We cannot send you your order until you send us the information we requested.	For immediate delivery, please complete the enclosed order form and return it.

Be Helpful

A helpful communicator tries to anticipate questions or concerns the receiver may have and respond to them before a problem develops. Adopting a problem-solving attitude and being sensitive to the receiver's interests builds goodwill. Which of the following closing paragraphs indicates a sender who is willing to be helpful?

> Thank you for considering us when looking for employment. Unfortunately, we do not have any openings at this time. Your application will be kept on file for six months and will be considered should an opening become available. Good luck in your job search.

> Thank you for considering us for employment. Unfortunately we do not have any openings in our Eastgate store at this time. You may be interested in knowing, however, that applications are being taken at our Northside store. If you would be interested in applying there, contact Edward Jones, personnel director, 555-7785.

While the first paragraph is polite and courteous, it essentially closes the door. The second paragraph takes an extra step, sending the positive message that the sender wants to be of help in the receiver's job search. The receiver will have positive feelings about the sender and the store.

Be Sincere

Sincere communications are genuine—without pretense or deceit. Messages that are too complimentary or too self-congratulatory make the receiver question the sincerity of the sender.

INSINCERE	SINCERE
Because the ABC company is so far superior to any other company in its field, I would like to work for you.	ABC Company's #1 ranking by the *Wall Street Journal* convinces me that I would like to work for your company.
Buy your high-quality, beautiful Yamamoto lamp today. Its unbelievably low price is just $19.95, which is only 25 percent of the normal retail price. It is also the lowest price ever.	Buy your Yamamoto lamp today for just $19.95—just 25 percent of its normal retail price. This may be its lowest price ever.

Be Tactful

Tact is a keen sense of what to do or say in order to build goodwill or avoid being offensive. How would you feel if your instructor said to you, "Well, as usual, you're late again for class"?

Such a statement would probably put you on the defensive. Even if the statement were justified, you would probably reject the message and the receiver. Chances of your accepting the criticism would be greater if the instructor had said, "Being late for class or missing class will probably result in minimum learning and low test scores."

To be tactful, avoid these expressions:

I do not agree with you	surely you don't expect
I find it impossible to believe	you claim that
if you care	you did not tell us
I'm sure you must realize	surely you realize
inexcusable	you say that
irresponsible	your stubbornness
obnoxious	your neglect
simply nonsense	your defense
I can't believe	your complaint
we are confused	you forgot
we must insist	your claim
we are unable to grant	your insinuation
why in the world	everybody knows

When dealing with touchy issues, the sender must be sensitive to the receiver's viewpoint. Expressions of concern and understanding as illustrated in the following example will keep the lines of communication open and help the receiver feel good about the reply.

> Your feelings of frustration are understandable. You have made many good points that deserve consideration. I have given a great deal of thought to your suggestions in addition to discussing them at great length with other members of our Marketing Department.

Be tactful when using humor. If a sales manager began a monthly meeting by stating in jest, "A penny saved is a penny earned, and we saved the company a lot of pennies last month because of low commissions," the statement might not be well received. Make sure that what is said and how it is said will not be offensive to the receiver. Ill humor can be interpreted by the receiver as belittling, as insensitive, or as overly familiar.

Avoid Condescension

When fulfilling a business request, such as providing a customer with a replacement or refund, be aware of the tone you use in your message. **Tone** is the manner of expression. Do not imply that you are granting a favor. Note the tone in the following example:

CONDESCENDING We were surprised to learn that the Pacific water hose you purchased from us burst. Because of your fine purchase record with us, however, we are pleased to grant your request for another hose.

Even though the sender is fulfilling the customer's request, the tone of the message suggests that the customer does not really deserve a replacement and that another hose is being sent *only* because of the receiver's purchase record—an unrelated fact—and the generosity of management. The customer might well be offended by such a message. Note the constructive tone the sender has used in the following message. It conveys the message in a positive tone and provides a helpful reminder about proper care.

POSITIVE Another Pacific hose is being sent to you today. To ensure maximum usage of the hose, protect it from freezing temperatures and avoid extremely high water pressure.

Use Titles Appropriately

Using correct titles is an indication of respect. Follow these general rules when using titles:

- Use the personal (Mr., Mrs., Miss, Ms.) or professional (Dr., Reverend) title preferred by the receiver.
- If you do not know the preferred title of a woman, use Ms.

- In addresses on envelopes and letters, use the official titles of company officers after or below their names. Such titles may be Chief Executive Officer, President, Vice President, Director, Department Head, etc.

- Use first names of people cautiously. The use of someone's first name implies a personal relationship with that person. If the receiver believes that you do not have that kind of relationship, using the first name may be offensive to him or her.

✔ Checkpoint 1   "YOU" ORIENTED

Read the following memo and identify the elements that give it a poor tone.

> **TO:** Mrs. Jackie Powell
> **FROM:** George Wessels, Supervisor
> **DATE:** March 9, 19--
> **SUBJECT:** Permission to Purchase a New Chair
>
> Sorry to have been so slow in responding to your memo of January 26, but I have been busy with other things.   Yes, I give you my permission to purchase a new chair for your desk.   The one you have is quite worn, and I am sure your claim that it is uncomfortable is true.   Please buy one that is as cheap as possible because our budget is very tight.
>
> Speaking of budgets, I'll bet your household budget is very tight. Didn't you just have your sixth boy?   What a family!

Check your answers in Appendix D.

Be Positive

People enjoy and react favorably to positive messages. A positive tone builds the receiver's confidence in the sender's ability to solve problems and strengthens personal and business relationships. Even negative messages can be stated in a positive way. If you were the receiver, which of the following messages would you prefer?

> We will not be able to send you the three dozen file cabinets you ordered until March 31 when the next shipment comes in.

> Your order for the three dozen file cabinets will be shipped when the next shipment arrives on March 31.

The second example is better than the first because it indicates what the sender *can* do, not what the sender cannot do. Compare the following examples:

NEGATIVE TONE	POSITIVE TONE
We have decided not to offer you employment at this time.	Your application will be kept on file for six months should other openings occur.
I am sorry that we are unable to reimburse you until October 10.	Your check will be mailed October 10.
I am not interested in buying a VUDAC computer.	I am interested in buying an EZ-DO computer.

Use of the subjunctive mood can also help to soften a negative response.

NEGATIVE TONE	SUBJUNCTIVE MOOD
I am not going to buy a used computer and printer.	If I were interested in buying a used computer and printer, I would consider these.
Sid is not going to the picnic.	I wish Sid were going to the picnic.
I cannot answer your question because my textbook is not here.	If my textbook were here, I could answer your question.

Should the receiver be at fault or fail to supply sufficient information, never scold or make the receiver feel guilty. Maintain a positive tone by concentrating on ways the receiver can improve the situation. Apply the "you" approach by emphasizing the benefits the improvement will bring the receiver. Compare the following negative and positive messages; will the receiver feel scolded in the positive messages? Probably not.

NEGATIVE You did not format this letter in the proper style.

POSITIVE Please format this letter in the block style shown in the Office Procedures Manual.

NEGATIVE You missed the December meeting.

POSITIVE Did I forget to send you a notice of the December meeting?

NEGATIVE Thank you for returning the personal inquiry form. However, you failed to send me your spouse's social security number. Please do so immediately.

POSITIVE Thank you for returning the personal inquiry form. So that you and your dependents can start receiving the new employee benefits promptly, please send me your spouse's social security number today.

The negative tone may be necessary when your patience is running out. Apply the negative tone carefully, however. Make sure the negative tone conveys the message you want to send. If used carelessly, a negative tone can destroy your relationships with others.

Be Prompt

How do you feel when you receive a reply to an inquiry, to a complaint, or to a request within a few days? Do you feel important? good about the person or organization that is responding? that your needs are important to the sender? Prompt messages convey positive feelings. On the other hand, even the most courteous, considerate, tactful, "you" oriented message in the world may be ineffective at building goodwill if the receiver has had to wait too long for it. To be prompt in business communication, follow these guidelines:

- Answer letters and memorandums within two or three days or low-priority mail within two weeks.
- Return telephone calls the same day if possible.
- Inform the receiver if a matter requires research and you cannot give a complete answer at this time.

Use Gender-Free Language

Today, men and women are employed in a wide variety of occupations. Women are pilots, police officers, engineers, doctors, and lawyers. Men are nurses, secretaries, elementary school teachers, and the principal caretakers of small children. Therefore, do not make any assumptions when you do not know the gender of the person about whom you are communicating. Note the assumption in the following example:

> If a *nurse* wants to become a supervisor, tell *her* to see Mr. Tobias, the floor manager.

To avoid assumptions about gender in your communications, follow these guidelines:

- Use plural nouns that require plural pronouns.

GENDER-SPECIFIC If a *manager* wants to buy floppy disks, *he* must order the 3½″ size.

NEUTRAL If *managers* want to buy floppy disks, *they* must order the 3½″ size.

- Replace the pronoun with an article (*the, a,* or *an*).

GENDER-SPECIFIC A good *writer* identifies with *his* reader.

NEUTRAL A good *writer* identifies with *the* reader.

- Reword the sentence.

GENDER-SPECIFIC   A *secretary* needs to call immediately if *she* wants to order some of these floppy disks.

NEUTRAL   To order these floppy disks, a secretary should call immediately.

- Use neutral nouns that do not imply the sex of a person.

GENDER-SPECIFIC   Please give this to the *foreman* of the night shift.

NEUTRAL   Please give this to the *supervisor* of the night shift.

GENDER-SPECIFIC	NEUTRAL
congressman	member of congress
businessman	business person or business people
foreman	supervisor
maid	houseworker
mailman	mail carrier
male nurse	nurse
policeman	police officer
repairman	repairer
salesman	salesperson
spokesman	spokesperson
stewardess	flight attendant
stockboy	store clerk
usherette	usher
waitress or waiter	server
workmen	workers

✔ **Checkpoint 2**   POSITIVE, PROMPT, AND GENDER-FREE LANGUAGE

Rewrite the following sentences using a positive tone and gender-free language.

1. Of the 75 items on the test, Marian missed 10 of them.

2. Because you were late with your payment, we are unable to renew your policy.

3. Because our supply of item #3895-A is depleted, we cannot send you the two dozen ribbons you ordered.

4. The salesmen meet at the home office next week.

5. We cannot send you your jeans and shirt because you did not indicate what sizes you need.

Check your answers in Appendix D.

SUMMARY

Messages that have a courteous and considerate tone reflect the needs, feelings, and viewpoints of the receiver. To convey the receiver's viewpoint, use *you* and *your* rather than *I* or *we*; occasionally personalize messages by using the receiver's name; and extend whatever help you can. Be careful to use a sincere, tactful tone. Avoid condescension and attempts at humor that might offend the receiver, and use personal titles appropriately. Courtesy and consideration are also extended by being positive, responding promptly, and using gender-free language.

● ● ● ● ● ● ● ● ● **Communication Activities**

Discussion Questions

1. How does a sender show courtesy to a receiver?
2. What is the difference between courtesy and consideration?
3. How does a sender show consideration to a receiver?
4. What is the difference between a "you" oriented message and an "I" oriented message? Which of these orientations illustrates consideration for the receiver? Why?
5. Explain six ways of expressing the "you" approach in messages.
6. Why should senders use the positive tone? Why should senders use the negative tone carefully?
7. Why is being prompt important?
8. Gender-specific language shows lack of consideration for the receiver. What are the techniques used to avoid gender-specific language? Explain how each technique eliminates the gender-specific language.

Practical Applications

1. Rewrite the following sentences using a positive tone.
   a. Because the scissors were dull, the edges you cut are ragged.
   b. I can't enjoy my new job because there is too much paperwork.
   c. We didn't finish the report on schedule because you did not give us the information on time.

d. Sales increased only 2 percent last month.

e. We won't be able to keep up with demand until you get us five more power saws.

2. Rewrite these statements using neutral language.

a. The leader of the walkout is the foreman.

b. A good communicator always considers her audience.

c. She called a repairman to fix her dishwasher.

d. The workmen were able to restore power to our home in less than 20 minutes.

e. Each of Colorado's congressmen voted "yes" on bill #493-a.

3. Rewrite the following sentences making them "you" oriented.

a. Mr. Jones has scheduled an interview with you for tomorrow at 1:30 p.m.

b. We have not received our supplies because you forgot to send in the order.

c. You haven't made a payment in six months.

d. We reviewed your suggestions and found they have merit.

e. I want to congratulate you on a job well done.

f. I believe your paintings are quite good.

g. Until the shipment of cherries comes in next Tuesday, we won't have pie.

h. I examined the sound system about which you complained.

4. Rewrite the following sentences so they have a courteous, considerate tone.

a. I can't believe that you are requesting another change of rooms.

b. If you had told us that he was late every day this week, we would have dismissed him.

c. We are confused by your instructions.

d. You claim the report was turned in on schedule.

e. Though you do not qualify for it, I will give you the raise you requested.

f. You say that the replacement won't work because it is too large.

g. Kathleen Alzedo was our best salesman in the month of October.

h. When preparing the report on the Overland Project, you made three minor errors.

i. Though there were only three cars in the race, you came in next to last.

j. Sandi, though I have never met you, I am most pleased that you have your doctoral degree and will be the chairman of our department.

k. Mrs. Marge Clemson, the congressman from the 5th district, will speak at the fund-raising activity.

l. I won't send that information through the mail because it is classified.

5. Rewrite the following paragraphs so that they are as courteous and considerate as possible.
   a. The six dozen Diablo Electronic Games you ordered, Mr. James, will be sent just as soon as we receive them. As our salesman told you, you will not be able to take the 7 percent trade discount as that sale went off last week.
   b. As you know, you were nominated for the office of president of Club QBK. I am to inform you that you were elected. Congratulations. The installation dinner is scheduled for May 15 at 7:00 p.m. at the Quality Hotel in Queensburg.

CHAPTER 15

Developing Concise, Clear, and Complete Communication

Objectives

After studying this chapter and completing the chapter exercises, you should be able to:

1. Apply techniques for developing concise messages.
2. Select words that are concise and clear.
3. Apply correct grammar and parallel structure so that sentences are clear.
4. Apply techniques that assure complete messages.

"How can I make the receiver understand what I mean?" Have you ever asked yourself this question? Regardless of whether the communication is oral or written, a letter or a report, formal or informal, the sender has the main responsibility for conveying meaning. The sender must be concise and organize thoughts in a way that will make the message complete and easy to understand. Being concise, clear, and complete requires planning and practice.

In this chapter you will learn basic techniques for developing messages that are concise, clear, and complete. These techniques will help the receiver interpret your message as you intended.

CONCISE MESSAGES

Concise messages make each word count. They contain only necessary information. Unimportant words, phrases, clauses, and ideas are omitted. Concise messages have impact because they capture and hold the receiver's attention, and they save time. As a result, the sender is better able to achieve the objective of the message.

The key to being concise is to be as brief as possible without sacrificing clarity or completeness. To achieve conciseness, (1) use short sentences and (2) eliminate unnecessary information.

Use Short Sentences

Short, concise sentences are more effective than long sentences because their meaning can be grasped more quickly. Although sentences may of course vary in length, a good average is 16 to 17 words. To make your sentences less wordy, follow these suggestions.

- Delete unnecessary words and phrases. Note how omitting the italicized phrase in the following examples makes the sentences more direct:

WORDY   *As a general rule,* Dr. Ellis usually does not arrive until 9:30 a.m.

CONCISE   Dr. Ellis usually does not arrive until 9:30 a.m.

WORDY   *Because Rod and June are getting married,* Anita gave them a wedding gift.

CONCISE   Anita gave Rod and June a wedding gift.

- Substitute a concise word for an entire phrase or clause. When appropriate, condense a clause to a phrase or to a word.

WORDY   The suit jacket, *which is completely lined,* will keep its shape.

CONCISE   The lined suit jacket will keep its shape.

Chapter 15   Developing Concise, Clear, and Complete Communication   199

WORDY   When you convey complex information, *you need to ask yourself if a graphic illustration would make it easier to understand your message.*

CONCISE   To convey complex information, consider using a graphic illustration to clarify your message.

● Omit phrases such as *I believe* and *in my opinion.* Generally what is stated is the writer's opinion. In addition, avoid beginning sentences with *there is, there are, here is,* or *here are.* Sentences can usually be stated more concisely if these phrases are omitted.

WORDY   *In my opinion,* we should not compromise on document appearance.

CONCISE   We should not compromise on document appearance.

WORDY   *There are* several alternatives that we can implement.

CONCISE   We can implement several alternatives.

● Eliminate expressions that state the same idea twice. Such expressions are redundant.

WORDY   The consensus *of opinion* is that he is innocent.

CONCISE   The consensus is that he is innocent.

WORDY   In his example, he presented only *basic* fundamentals.

CONCISE   In his example, he presented only fundamentals.

Redundant expressions are given and then revised for conciseness in the following examples:

REDUNDANT EXPRESSION	CONCISE USAGE
basic fundamental	fundamental
but nevertheless	but
consensus of opinion	consensus
continue on	continue
end result	result
exact same	same
exactly identical	identical
free gift	gift
full and complete	complete
modern, up-to-date	modern
other alternative	alternative
past history	history
personal opinion	opinion
refer back	refer
true fact	fact
whether or not	whether

Eliminate phrases that repeat themselves. **Circular phrasing** often occurs in a complex sentence; the same idea is expressed in slightly different words in both the dependent and the independent clauses. Such redundancy should be avoided.

CIRCULAR PHRASING	CONCISE
Because Matt is a studious person, he studies a lot.	Matt is a studious person.
Marge, who is always working, is a busy person.	Marge is a busy person.
Marge is always working and is a busy person.	Marge is a busy person.

Eliminate Unnecessary Information

Unlike fiction writing, which generally relies on many details to help the reader visualize a situation, business writing should include only information that relates directly to the main idea. Meaningful information adds concreteness to a message. Providing excessive details, however, causes the receiver to lose sight of the objective of the message.

Generally in business writing, each paragraph has a main idea. Each sentence in that paragraph supports that one idea. To develop a concise writing style, eliminate ideas that do not relate to the main idea. Note how the elimination of unrelated ideas in the concise message makes it more precise and forceful.

CONTAINS UNNECESSARY INFORMATION	CONCISE
Yesterday, I changed the oil in my car and used my ratchet wrench, which is fifteen years old. While using the wrench, the ratchet dial popped out. Would you please send me your Model 32-B ratchet wrench. A check for $19.95 is enclosed. Send it to Shannon Harrison at Route 4, Box 589, in Tulela, LA 79021.	Please send me a Model 32-B ratchet wrench. A check for $19.95 is enclosed. Send it to Shannon Harrison Route 4, Box 589 Tulela, LA 79021

Conciseness, however, does not mean sacrificing a courteous tone for the sake of brevity. Messages that are too brief have a curt tone. For example, suppose Jason has written Bruce requesting references on how to write unfavorable messages. Bruce does not know any such references. The briefest answer possible is "Dear Jason: I don't have any. Sincerely, Bruce." If Bruce's objective is to offend Jason and to tell him "No," Bruce has made his point concisely. If, however, Bruce's objective is to maintain a good relationship with Jason, his message has not achieved its purpose.

CLEAR MESSAGES

Clear messages do not confuse the receiver. Although this sounds obvious, forming clear communication is sometimes difficult. If the sender is careless when selecting words and nonverbal symbols, miscommunication may occur. Likewise, if the sender overlooks mentioning a point that is not obvious to the receiver, miscommunication will occur. Clear words and logical organization are characteristics of clear communication.

Assume that Brett does not feel well this morning. As he enters the kitchen, he says to his roommate, "I don't feel very well this morning." His roommate replies, "Well, you used my car last night and you still must wash it." Even though Brett was simply sending the message that he did not feel well, his roommate interpreted the message to mean that Brett was trying to get out of washing the car. Though Brett thought his message was clear, he may have been careless in his presentation. As a result, his message was not clear and miscommunication occurred.

Select Clear Symbols

In written communication, words are the primary symbols for expressing ideas. Interpretation and understanding are within people, however, not within words. Because our backgrounds, experiences, and education vary, we interpret words and nonverbal symbols somewhat differently. It is the sender's responsibility, however, to use words and symbols that convey the intended message. Clear symbols result from (1) using appropriate words, (2) using words precisely, and (3) avoiding overused words or expressions.

Appropriate Words

Skillful communicators select words that will be understood by the receiver. Often this means using short, simple words that do not draw attention to the sender's motive for using them. Simple words enable the receiver to concentrate on the message rather than on the way it is presented. On the other hand, use of complex language may distract or annoy the receiver and create a barrier to good communication. The receiver may wonder why the sender is using such language. Is it to make the sender appear highly educated? impressive? superior? Complex language sometimes makes the receiver suspicious of the sender's motives. Compare the complex words and their simple substitutes in the following list:

COMPLEX	SIMPLE
anterior	front
ascertain	find out
faux pas	blunder
germane	appropriate
inapplicable	not suitable
inaugurate	begin
interrogate	ask
inoperative	not working
optimum	best
predisposition	tendency
proximity	nearness
recapitulate	sum up
substantiate	prove

Sometimes the experience and education of the receiver justify using technical language. For example, if the sender is writing to a college professor who teaches grammar, such words as "phonology," "syntax," and "semasiology" would be appropriate. Technical language and jargon, just like simple language, has its appropriate uses.

Precise Words

Choosing precise words enables the sender to convey just the right meaning. The sender must decide whether to use the general term *concerned* or the precise term *anxious*; the general term *store* or the precise term *jewelry store* or *McDonald's Jewelry Store*; the general phrase *appropriate time* or the specific phrase *within ten days*. Note the difference that using a general or a precise word makes in the following sentences:

GENERAL   Did you *contact* Tom yesterday?

PRECISE   Did you *telephone* Tom?

GENERAL   Sales have increased *substantially* this year.

PRECISE   Sales have increased *75 percent* this year.

Whether a word is appropriate can only be judged by the context in which it is used. It is up to the sender to decide whether a specific or a general term should be used.

Likewise, when selecting words, the sender must be aware of how they may be interpreted (the connotation of words). The receiver might attach a meaning that was not intended by the sender. **Connotation** is what is suggested in addition to the literal meaning. For example, assume that the sender, who types at 60 words a minute (WAM), says, "I type rapidly." What does *rapidly* mean? The meaning depends upon the experience of the receiver. If the receiver can type at only 30 WAM, the receiver would probably agree. To a person who types at 80 WAM, however, the statement could be misleading. Other examples of words that have different connotations include the following:

WORD	SENDER'S MEANING	RECEIVER'S CONNOTATION
average	normal	mediocre
cheap	inexpensive	poorly made
conservative	moderate	radical
determined	committed	stubborn
flashy	striking	gaudy
intelligent	smart	conceited
liberal	fair	radical
slender	lean	skinny
traditional	old-fashioned	dated

Communicators attach various connotations to words based on their experiences, backgrounds, education, and so forth. To avoid miscommunication, a sender should take these factors into account.

Overused Words and Expressions

Some words and expressions are outdated or overused and should be avoided. An easy way to identify most of these "business expressions" is simply to ask yourself, "Would I say this if I were talking with my receiver?" If the answer is "No," then don't use it in your writing. For example, if you were writing a letter to someone who had ordered supplies, would you start your letter with "As per your request"? Apply the test. Would you use this expression in conversation? Hopefully not! Avoid these obsolete expressions:

OBSOLETE	MODERN
acknowledge receipt of	received
are in receipt of	received
as per your request	as you requested
at your earliest convenience	as soon as possible
at your convenience	when convenient
due to the fact that	because
I have your letter of	I received your letter
I remain—sincerely yours	sincerely yours
in due course	eventually
in the event that	should
kindly	please
meet with your approval	approve
permit me to say	———
please be advised that	———
pursuant to your request	as you requested
take the liberty	———
thanking you in advance	thank you
trusting you will find	you will find
under separate cover	in another package, in another letter
we regret to inform you	unfortunately
would like to recommend	recommend
would like to say	———

✔ **Checkpoint 2** CLEAR SYMBOLS

Rewrite these sentences using clear symbols.

1. Topek motor scooters get good gas mileage.
2. Even though it has several new lights on it, the anterior of the old building has disintegrated badly.
3. As per your request, I was able to complete the report on the microcomputer.
4. The diskette will be sent to you under separate cover.
5. He is skinny but strong.

Check your answers in Appendix D.

Use Correct Grammar

If the relationship between the words within a sentence (for example, subject and verb) is incorrect or inconsistent, the message will not be clear. To send clear messages, be sure the following important rules of grammatical construction have been applied:

● Ideas are expressed in complete sentences, not in fragments.

FRAGMENT   Because I was listening to the officer's presentation.

COMPLETE   Because I was listening to the officer's presentation, I knew the goals and objectives of the company.

● Pronouns and their antecedents agree in number, gender, and person.

DO NOT AGREE   Each of the officers was to bring their five-year plan to the meeting.

AGREE   Each of the officers was to bring his or her five-year plan to the meeting.

● Introductory phrases and clauses modify the subject of the sentence.

WRONG   Being determined early to succeed, his success came as no surprise.

RIGHT   Being determined early to succeed, he succeeded and no one was surprised.

Apply Parallel Structure

When words, phrases, or clauses have something in common, they should be joined in a way that makes their relationship clear. To achieve clarity, express related sentence elements in parallel grammatical form. Compare the examples below. Note that the parallel sentences are strong, clear, and concise.

NOT PARALLEL   *Who, which,* and the pronoun *that* are relative pronouns.

PARALLEL   *Who, which,* and *that* are relative pronouns.

NOT PARALLEL   The company will move its head offices to Dallas, and San Antonio will be its production center.

PARALLEL   The company will move its head offices to Dallas and will centralize its production in San Antonio.

NOT PARALLEL   When starting to write a report, evaluate your audience, know your objective, and you should plan its structure.

PARALLEL   When starting to write a report, evaluate your audience, know your objective, and plan its structure.

✔ Checkpoint 3   CORRECT GRAMMAR AND PARALLEL STRUCTURE

Rewrite the following sentences so they are clear.

1. To get a good job, a crisp, well-polished image is important.
2. Anyone can enter their paintings in the contest.
3. Because he was out of town last week.
4. The new employee is efficient, accurate, and works hard.
5. The meeting will be held in the first floor conference room, the company library, or in Mr. Fletcher's office.

Check your answers in Appendix D.

COMPLETE MESSAGES

Nothing is more frustrating than to receive only a partial reply to an inquiry or to be unable to make a decision because important information has been omitted. Incomplete information can cause delays, loss of goodwill, or loss of business. Incomplete messages also send a negative, nonverbal message: The sender is careless. Complete messages include all of the information necessary to meet the sender's objective. Completeness sends a nonverbal message that the sender is a competent, efficient person.

To assure completeness, always reread your message. Check to be sure that items to be enclosed are actually enclosed. Other techniques that help to assure completeness are given in the following sections.

Enumerate Items

Before responding to a communication that requests information, reread it and highlight or number the items that need a response. Listings not only help us to achieve clarity, but they also help us to be complete. As you read the following request, note the items that need a response.

> I need some information on the Glenn Avenue Bridge Project. Please tell me what type of construction we are using, how many square feet of cement we are expecting to use, and what type of road covering will be used.

Note how use of enumerations makes the response clear.

> John, here is the information you requested about the Glenn Avenue Bridge Project.
> 1. The type of construction being used on the bridge is reinforced steel.
> 2. We anticipate using 150,000 square feet of cement in the construction of the bridge.
> 3. The state stipulated in the specifications that the bridge have an asphalt covering.

Check for the Five W's

To assure that all major points have been included in a message, test for the five W's.

- **Who:** Who is the receiver? Does the content consider the receiver's viewpoint, background, and experience?
- **What:** Has it been explained to the receiver what action is required?
- **When:** When must conditions be met? Are necessary times and dates included?
- **Where:** Where should conditions be met? Does the receiver know the sender's address?
- **Why:** Has it been explained to the receiver why certain action must be taken?

Check the following memorandum for the five W's. Are they all covered?

> **TO:** All Staff Members
> **FROM:** Frank Langford
> **DATE:** March 19, 19--
> **SUBJECT:** Monthly Departmental Meeting
>
> This month's departmental meeting will be held on March 26 in Conference Room 15 at 9 a.m.
>
> Two topics will be discussed: (1) the new employee insurance program; (2) procedures for using electronic mail.

Does the memorandum contain answers to all five W's?

Who is to attend?	All members of the staff
What is the occasion?	The monthly departmental meeting
When is the meeting?	March 26 at 9 a.m.
Where is the meeting	Conference Room 15
Why is the meeting being held?	To discuss the new insurance program and electronic mail procedures

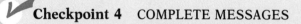

Checkpoint 4 COMPLETE MESSAGES

Revise the following memo so that it is complete. Explain why you made the changes.

> **TO:** Matthew Avenel
> **FROM:** Project Team
> **DATE:** March 29, 19--
> **SUBJECT:** System Selection Meeting
>
> On Tuesday we will have a meeting to refine policies for selecting our new computer system and software for text processing and electronic mail. Be sure to have everyone in your department complete the survey forms prior to the meeting.

SUMMARY

Effective messages are neither too long nor too short. They are as brief as possible yet attain their objectives. To communicate concisely, (1) use short sentences and (2) eliminate unnecessary information. Clear messages are free of confusion. To make messages clear, (1) select symbols that are appropriate to the receiver, (2) use correct grammar, and (3) maintain parallel structure.

Complete messages include all the necessary information to meet the sender's objective. To make communications complete, use enumerations when responding to many items and check for the five W's — who, what, when, where, and why.

● ● ● ● ● ● ● ● ● **Communication Activities**

Discussion Questions

1. Describe two ways of developing concise messages.
2. What are redundant phrases and circular phrasing? Give an example of each and explain how they differ.

3. Why do receivers prefer concise messages to messages which contain unnecessary information?

4. What are the three techniques which help in selecting clear symbols? Define each of them.

5. Some writers use such expressions as "pursuant to your request," "trusting you will find," and "as per your request." What impact do these expressions have upon the receiver?

6. What impact does incorrect grammar have upon a message? What effect does incorrect grammar have on the receiver's attitude toward the sender?

7. Why is it important to be complete? How can senders help to ensure completeness?

Practical Applications

1. Revise these statements to make them concise.
   a. It is my belief that most homes in this area cost about $85,000.
   b. The picture was hung in the gallery by the artist, Lydia Norris.
   c. Tom is tired because he was very weary.
   d. The basic fundamentals are given in the book.
   e. Past history teaches us that the people of certain societies are generally and usually trustworthy.
   f. The cabinets were made of oak and were made by Sam.
   g. The printer should be checked before employees arrive.
   h. There are several alternatives that could be applied.

2. Read the following sentences. Correct them so that they are clear. Add any details necessary.
   a. Tony interrogated Suzanne by asking how long it would take her to accomplish the task.
   b. Please be advised that we substituted a similar product in your order.
   c. We regret to inform you that we won't be able to complete your order until next month.
   d. As the result of your entry into the contest, we are pleased to inform you that you will not only receive a free gift of a bottle of ZKT perfume but also $5,000.
   e. A pound of that candy costs a lot of money.
   f. After dieting for only a month, she lost a great deal of weight.
   g. It was a good match.
   h. Stock in that company is very expensive.

3. Indicate the information that is missing in each of the sentences.
   a. Please reserve a room for me on Friday. I'll be arriving after 6 p.m.
   b. Please plan to meet my flight on Central Airlines, Tuesday, March 12.
   c. To obtain the $50 discount, return your registration early.
   d. Send the shipment to Fitness Craze, P.O. Box 399, Little Rock, AR.
   e. Please send me a pair of Comfort Racquetball shoes, No. R106, in white.
   f. Please mark your calendar for the Tenth Annual Sales Conference to be held at the home office.
   g. The following people will chair the committee:
      Darlene Habl – Exhibits
      Marilyn Balog – Registration
      Denis Deemling – Entertainment
      Jim Powell –
   h. Please reserve a large meeting room for the conference.
4. Rewrite the following paragraph, making it as concise as possible.

   The utilities in our town are inexpensively cheap. In my opinion, here are some good, typical examples: My water, which is from fresh-water wells just outside the city, averages about $10 a month. My electricity, which is produced by hydroelectric generators at Hoover Dam, averages about $85 a month. My gas, which comes by pipeline from Louisiana, has been averaging about $45 a month. Though these figures are not large in amount, conserving our resources is still an important essential to me.

5. Make all corrections necessary to make the following letter concise, clear, and complete. Add information if necessary.

   February 13, 19--

   Ms. Lillie Williams
   2049 Treceturn Avenue
   Atlanta, GA 46391

   Dear Ms. Williams

   Thank you for the invitation to speak at the dinner in honor of Frederick D. Coral.

   I am happy to inform you that I will be able to attend the dinner in his honor. Kindly accept my thanks.

Your willingness to pick me up at the airport is appreciated. My plane will be arriving in Atlanta at 3:30 p.m. Saturday afternoon.

In the event that my circumstances should change, I will take the liberty of letting you know so that you can adjust the arrangements.

Thanking you in advance.

I remain
Yours truly

Paul Jacobson

6. Write a paragraph informing a customer that he or she can have the credit requested. A $2,500 limit has been placed on the account — a normal procedure for a new account.

7. Write a paragraph telling a friend that you won't be able to attend your friend's graduation (Saturday, May 20). Your summer job requires you to be at home as soon as you finish your finals (Wednesday, May 17).

CHAPTER 16

Planning and Organizing the Message

Objectives

After studying this chapter and completing the chapter exercises, you should be able to:

1. Plan a message by determining its objective, main idea, and supporting information and adjusting the content to the receiver.
2. Organize a message using the direct order, the indirect order, or a combination of the two.
3. Form sentences, paragraphs, and messages that have unity, coherence, and proper emphasis.

Have you ever sent a message that you wished you had not sent? Have you ever wished you had stated your message differently? As senders we all face two major challenges: to say what we really mean and to make the meaning clear to the receiver. Successful communicators aren't effective by chance. They are effective because they take the time to plan and organize their messages. The more complex a message, the more important these steps become.

PLANNING THE MESSAGE

Planning a message involves identifying the objective, the main idea, and the supporting information and adjusting the content to the receiver.

Identify the Objective

The first step in planning a message is to determine its objective. The **objective** is what you hope to accomplish. It may be to establish goodwill, to request information, to provide information, or to persuade someone. To determine the objective of your message, ask these questions:

1. Why am I sending this message?
2. What do I hope to accomplish?

Generally a communication has one primary objective. It may also have a secondary objective. For example, suppose the sender must respond to a customer's complaint. The primary objective may be to tell the customer what action the sender is able to take, and the secondary objective may be to maintain goodwill with the customer. Conversely, if the customer is an extremely important one, the primary objective may be to maintain goodwill. The tone and emphasis of the message will depend upon the sender's primary objective.

Identify the Main Idea

The **main idea** is the focal point or focus of the message. Generally the main idea corresponds to the primary objective. For example, suppose that the manager of Eagles Auto Repair Center needs to order a fuel pump for a minivan, a water pump for a pickup truck, and a carburetor for a sedan. The sender's primary objective or purpose for writing is to order the parts for the three vehicles. The order will be the focus of the letter.

Sometimes the main idea is obvious, but expressing it in a way that will be acceptable to the receiver is difficult. Let's suppose that your objective is to persuade a client to accept a decision that he or she does not really favor and yet still maintain good relations with the client. Although there may be many reasons why the client should accept the decision, you must decide which is the most important reason.

To identify this main idea, brainstorm to determine every possible reason why the client should accept the decision. List all of the possible benefits to the client. Don't worry if some of the ideas seem unimportant. During this process, you will discover alternative approaches. Once all of the ideas are listed, select the best approach and let it become the focus of your message.

Determine the Supporting Information

Having determined the objective and the main idea of the message, you must now determine the **supporting details**—the facts, examples, or reasons—that reinforce or relate to the main idea. These details make the message forceful and convince the receiver that the message is valid or worthwhile. To provide supporting information, ask yourself these questions:

1. What does the receiver need to know in order to respond in the desired way?
2. How will the message benefit the receiver?
3. How do I want the receiver to respond?
4. Can I make it easier for the receiver to respond?

If you have already analyzed the main idea, some of the supporting information may already be apparent. Thoroughly planning the main idea and the supporting ideas will help to assure that the receiver has complete information.

Adjust the Content to the Receiver

Which is more important when dining out—top-quality food or a pleasing atmosphere and courteous service? Which is a more important aspect of sales—having a top-quality product or marketing it well? Which is more important in an instructor—knowledge of subject matter or classroom presentation?

In each of these situations, both aspects are important. One quality by itself is not enough. The same is true when sending a message. The content of the message and the presentation are equally important. For the main idea to be accepted by the receiver, the message must be presented in a way that takes the receiver's needs into account.

In order to apply the "you" approach, successful communicators analyze their receivers in terms of the receiver's level of interest in the topic, knowledge of the topic, and opinions or even biases. The more the sender knows about the receiver, the better the sender will be able to adjust the message to the receiver's needs.

The following example is a message that has been adjusted to the knowledge level of the receiver. The first message was written to the manager of a small business; the second, to an advertising executive. Although the objective of both messages is to promote television advertising, the sender realizes that the advertising executive is well aware of how advertising is justified.

Message to a Business Manager

Television advertising may be justified in three ways: (1) by the number of prospective buyers who view an ad, (2) by the number of times prospective buyers view an ad, and (3) by the cost per thousand of viewers. Regardless of how the cost is justified, small businesses cannot afford to eliminate television as an advertising medium.

Message to an Advertising Executive

Whether the cost is justified on the basis of reach, frequency, or CPT, small businesses should not eliminate television as an advertising medium.

Figure 16-1 provides a checklist for adjusting the message in content and tone. By answering these questions about the receiver, the sender will be

---

FIGURE 16-1   Checklist for Adjusting the Message

To adjust the content of a message:

1. To whom am I sending the message?
2. How much knowledge (experience, background, education) does the receiver have about the subject?
3. What does the receiver need to know about the subject?
4. What are the receiver's opinions of or interests in the subject?
5. How does the receiver feel about me, my department, and my company?

To adjust the tone of a message:

1. What is the relationship between the sender and the receiver? a personal friend? a business associate? a social acquaintance?
2. What is the mood of the receiver—satisfied, dissatisfied, angry, happy, neutral?
3. Does the receiver trust the sender?
4. What kinds of previous communication have occurred—face-to-face? written? formal? informal? favorable? unfavorable?

---

able to create a message that reflects the receiver's motivation, attitudes, and knowledge.

✓ Checkpoint 1   PLANNING THE MESSAGE

Identify the sentence that contains the main idea in each of the following items.

1. Yes, I am available to speak at your meeting on the 23rd; thank you for the invitation. The title of my presentation will be "Surviving Office Politics." My presentation will include slides; will a screen be available?

2. In order to synchronize our local advertising campaign with the release of the new cosmetic line, we will need additional information. For each new item, please provide the release date, the packaging requirements, and the units available. May I expect to receive this information within three weeks?

3. Friday was a very pleasant day for me. It was the day I learned that you are coming to stay with us. I will be most happy to pick you up at the airport at 5:30 on the 16th.

Check your answers in Appendix D.

ORGANIZING THE MESSAGE

After identifying the content of the message, the next step is to determine the order in which to present the information so that the message will achieve its objective. The order depends upon how you expect the receiver to react (favorably or unfavorably) to the message. Most business messages are organized using either direct, indirect, or direct-indirect order.

Direct Order

The **direct order** presents the main message first, follows it with the supporting information, and closes with an extension of goodwill. Favorable (good news) and neutral (routine) messages are organized in the direct order. Beginning with the good news enables the sender to immediately establish a positive tone. Routine messages are also organized in the direct order. The assumption is that the receiver will respond in a positive or neutral manner.

Main Message	Enclosed are the brochures you requested on the educational version of WordMagic. Thank you for your interest.
Supporting Information	WordMagic incorporates many of the desktop publishing features users have been requesting. For example, WordMagic will format columns that extend beyond a page and produce documents in different type sizes and fonts.
Goodwill Closing	Information on ordering your copies of WordMagic is included in the brochures. Use the coupons to receive your 20 percent discount.

Look what happens if the message is written with the main message after the supporting data.

Neutral Beginning	Thank you for your interest in WordMagic.
Supporting Information	WordMagic incorporates many of the desktop publishing features users have been requesting. For example, WordMagic will format columns that extend beyond a page and produce documents in different type sizes and fonts.
Main Message and Goodwill Closing	Enclosed are the brochures you requested on the educational version of WordMagic. Information on ordering copies is included in the brochures.

The tone of the message has changed. The sender seems to be more interested in selling the product than in responding to the request.

Indirect Order

The **indirect order** presents the supporting information before the main message. Unfavorable (bad news) messages and persuasive messages are organized using the indirect order. Because receivers are usually disappointed by bad news messages or suspicious of persuasive messages, it is better to provide an explanation before presenting the main message itself. In the following bad news message, the receiver is being told that the request for two computers cannot be filled by the manufacturer.

Neutral Beginning	Thank you for your order for two Fastwriter computers.
Supporting Information Main Message	We at Fastwriter are manufacturers only. Our products are sold directly through authorized dealers. The authorized Fastwriter dealer in your area is Jewel's Business Equipment. They will be able to provide you with excellent service and training support.
Goodwill Closing	Your order has been forwarded to Jewel's Business Equipment for fast processing. A representative of Jewel's will be calling you soon.

Even though this letter conveys a negative message, it is not unpleasant or insulting to the receiver. By first explaining why a sale cannot be made, the sender has prepared the receiver for the bad news. Therefore, the receiver will probably not lose his or her interest in buying the product.

Direct-Indirect Order

The direct-indirect order is used when the sender has both good news and bad news for the receiver. In these situations, present the good news first using the direct order. Second, follow the indirect order by providing the reasons for the bad news and then stating the bad news itself. The following example illustrates the direct-indirect order.

Good News– **Main Message**	Enclosed are the brochures and supporting information which you requested. Fastwriter International, Inc., is most pleased to be able to provide this information for you.
Supporting **Information**	Because we are manufacturers only, we sell our products directly through authorized dealers. The Fastwriter dealer in your area is Jewel's Business Equipment. They will be able to provide you with excellent service and training support.
Bad News– **Main Message** **Goodwill Closing**	Your order for the two Fastwriter computers has been forwarded to Jewel's Business Equipment for fast processing. A representative will be calling on you soon.

Use of the direct-indirect approach increases the chance that the receiver will understand the message and accept its outcome. Table 16-1 shows a comparison of each of the ways to organize a message.

TABLE 16-1　Organizing Messages

Direct Order	Indirect Order	Direct-Indirect Order
1. Main Message	1. Supporting Information	1. Good News–Main Message
2. Supporting Information	2. Main Message	2. Supporting Information
3. Goodwill Closing	3. Goodwill Closing	3. Bad News–Main Message
		4. Goodwill Closing

Checkpoint 2 ORGANIZING THE MESSAGE

Indicate whether each of the following paragraphs is organized in the direct order or the indirect order.

1. The difference between the boys shows up in many situations. Bob approaches new situations with eagerness. Tony usually refuses to participate, displaying his negative perspective.

2. A new roof will have to be added. The wood in the walls is deteriorating and will need to be replaced. The tower has to be painted, the floors refinished, and the walls repainted. Unfortunately, making the building usable will cost just over 30 percent of the asking price.

3. The president's duties seem endless. They include being the company's representative to the media, welcoming visiting dignitaries, working with the board of directors to develop policies and procedures, etc.

4. Tom was sure his W-2 form was incorrect. The amount of income reported was too high. Moreover, the amounts withheld for federal and state income tax were too low.

Check your answers in Appendix D.

USING ORGANIZATIONAL TECHNIQUES

Learning to form sentences and paragraphs that convey what you really mean is critical. In order for a sentence, paragraph, or message to be clear, it must have unity, coherence, and proper emphasis.

Unity

Unity means singleness—oneness. Like a jigsaw puzzle, sentences, paragraphs, and messages have unity when their parts fit together smoothly to form a cohesive whole. A message is unified when the main idea supports the objective of the message and all supporting ideas contribute to a single, clear main idea. Unity must be reflected in each paragraph and sentence within the message.

Paragraph Unity

Generally each paragraph within a letter, memo, or report has a single purpose. It may be to get the attention of the reader, to build goodwill, or to summarize actions that must be taken. In other cases, a paragraph may serve to complement another paragraph. For example, the first paragraph may introduce a problem and the second paragraph may offer a solution; one paragraph may introduce an idea and the following paragraph may give an example; one paragraph may compare while another contrasts. It is the sender's responsibility to make the purpose of the paragraph clear to the receiver.

For the sake of clarity, sometimes it is helpful to state the main idea of the paragraph in a single **topic sentence.** A topic sentence will guide the sender in developing a paragraph that holds to its central idea. The topic sentence in the following paragraph is italicized.

> *When sending a message, always adjust it to your receiver.* Consider the occupation, education, experiences, and personality of the receiver. Use technical words and jargon only if you know your receiver will understand them.

In other cases, the sender may not think in terms of the topic sentence and sentences that support it. Instead, the main idea may be expressed in several related sentences that communicate one central idea.

> When decorating her bedroom, Sara picked the wallpaper and the carpet. She and her mother chose the material for curtains and other accessories. Dad paid the bills.

Suppose the first paragraph had read as follows:

> When sending a message, always adjust it to your receiver. Consider the occupation, education, experience, and personality of your receiver. Use technical words or jargon only if you know the person will understand them. *However, long sentences may make your message hard to understand.*

Note the new idea that is expressed in the last sentence of the previous paragraph. Not only is it unrelated to the rest of the paragraph, but it disrupts the unity established in the paragraph. Therefore, it should be omitted.

Sentence Unity

For a sentence to be clear and easy to understand, it should usually contain only one main idea. Use the following techniques to develop unity within sentences.

● Eliminate phrases and clauses that do not relate to the main idea.

UNRELATED FACTS	Asumoto Akindo has been promoted to vice president of communication, and he was born in Stanislaus, Nevada.
UNIFIED	Asumoto Akindo has been promoted to vice president of communication.

- Express supporting ideas in a dependent clause to convey the proper relationship.

UNCLEAR RELATIONSHIP	The art scholarship has project requirements, and Suzanne needed to complete ten projects by February 15.
UNIFIED	Because the art scholarship has project requirements, Suzanne needed to complete ten projects by February 15.

Coherence

Coherence means that a clear and logical relationship exists within sentences and paragraphs. The relationships of words, phrases, and clauses to each other and to the main objective of the message are obvious. If a communication is coherent, the receiver can move easily from one part of a sentence to the next or from one sentence to another without losing the central idea. To convey clear, strong relationships among ideas, (1) maintain a consistent point of view, (2) repeat key words, and (3) use transitional devices.

Consistent Point of View

To maintain a consistent point of view within a communication, avoid shifts in person, voice, and tense. For example, once you establish that the subject is in the third person, don't switch to the second person, *you*.

INCONSISTENT PERSON	When planning sales, management must consider its inventories; and you should also consider the timeliness of the sale.
CONSISTENT PERSON	When planning sales, management must consider its inventories and the timeliness of the sale.
INCONSISTENT TENSE	While he was driving to work, he sees the accident.
CONSISTENT TENSE	While he was driving to work, he saw the accident.
INCONSISTENT VOICE	The assistant made the reservation, but it was erroneously canceled by the manager.
CONSISTENT VOICE	The assistant made the reservation, but the manager canceled it by mistake.

Repetition of Key Words

Another way to achieve coherence and carry the meaning clearly from sentence to sentence is to repeat key words. Notice how key words are reinforced in the following examples.

A dependent clause cannot stand alone. It depends upon another clause. Dependent clauses are usually introduced by relative pronouns or subordinating conjunctions. Some of these relative pronouns are *who, which,* and *that.* Some of the subordinating conjunctions are *because* and *when.*

Part 4   Fundamentals of Business Writing

Coordinating conjunctions are used to join items of equal importance. Some of these connectors are *and, but, or, so,* and *yet.*

Transitional Devices

Transitional words and phrases connect thoughts logically, add coherence, and indicate relationships. Such words help the receiver move from

TABLE 16-2   Transitional Words and Phrases

Relationship	*Word or Phrase*
Contrast	but however in contrast in spite of on the contrary on the other hand nevertheless
Cause-Result	because of consequently for this reason hence therefore thus
Explanation	also for example for instance to illustrate too
Likeness	in a like manner likewise similarly
Listing	besides first, second, third, etc. in addition moreover
Time	since first, second, third, . . . last finally

one idea to the next. In the following sentence, *however* indicates that a shift in meaning is coming.

> Tom was thoroughly satisfied with the new product; *however,* Toni was unhappy with it.

A transitional word or phrase is often placed at or near the beginning of a sentence to indicate the relationship to preceding or following elements. The word *Because* in the following example indicates the relationship of the introductory dependent clause to the main clause. The phrase *For this reason* in the second sentence indicates the relationship between the sentences.

> *Because* Dad felt it was important to read books, we were encouraged to read for at least 20 minutes each day. *For this reason,* we belonged to a book club and subscribed to several magazines.

Table 16-2 provides a list of transitional words and phrases that show various relationships.

✔ **Checkpoint 3**   COHERENCE

Rewrite these sentences so that they are coherent.

1. He saw the information in an article in *America Today;* so as soon as he got to work, he calls his supervisor.
2. Upon seeing the opportunity, the investor sold her 500 shares of common stock and $50,000 was made.
3. Dick was unhappy with his sales for the month and his supervisor thought Dick had done well.
4. Alex's sales totaled 300 percent of his monthly sales quota; he received the Salesperson of the Month award.
5. The university has an excellent academic reputation, but thousands of dollars of private funds must be raised by us each year to support it.

Emphasis

Emphasis adds clarity to the message by helping the receiver distinguish between important and incidental ideas. Emphasis can be achieved most easily by applying the techniques for developing concise, clear statements discussed earlier. Ideas can also be emphasized through length, placement, and formatting techniques.

Length

In order to provide sufficient details or explanation, generally give more space to important ideas than to less important ideas. Care must be taken, however, so that paragraphs do not become too lengthy. Short, concise paragraphs emphasize content.

To achieve emphasis in letters and memos, introduce important points in a short paragraph (one or two sentences). Introductory and concluding paragraphs should not exceed four typewritten lines, and no paragraph should exceed eight lines. In reports and memos, maximum paragraph length is ten lines.

Placement

Placement of ideas within a sentence or paragraph can serve to either emphasize or de-emphasize them. Position thoughts to be emphasized at the beginning or end of a sentence or as the first or last sentence in a paragraph. In the following examples, notice how placement affects the emphasis:

Office automation lets you take on new jobs and see old jobs in new ways.

To see old jobs in new ways, try office automation.

The whole point is that office automation lets you take on new jobs and see old jobs in new ways.

In the first and second examples, *office automation* is emphasized by being placed at the beginning or at the end of the sentence. In the third example, however, *office automation* is de-emphasized by appearing in the middle of the sentence—in this case within a subordinate clause.

Other ways to gain emphasis are to place parenthetic elements within the sentence:

The decision, as you can well imagine, was unpopular with the committee.

or to put words out of their usual order:

This he failed to do.

Sentence Structure

Sentence structure can also serve to provide emphasis. Generally, simple sentences containing one main idea provide the greatest emphasis.

Your order has been shipped.

Paul will begin work immediately upon graduation.

Sometimes, however, you may want to emphasize one idea and de-emphasize a related idea. If this is the case, use a complex sentence. As you remember, a complex sentence contains a subordinate clause (a clause that cannot stand by itself as a complete sentence) and a main clause. Position the idea that you want to emphasize in the main clause of a complex sentence. Position the idea that you want to de-emphasize in the subordinate clause of the complex sentence.

> **As soon as you have returned the questionnaire, we will enter your name in the drawing.**
>
> **When he graduates in October, Paul will begin work immediately.**

Unlike the clauses in a complex sentence, the clauses in a compound sentence are both main clauses and receive equal attention. Neither idea is emphasized—each idea is as important as the other.

> **Please return the questionnaire, and we will then enter your name in the drawing.**
>
> **Paul will graduate in October, and he will begin work immediately.**

Visuals and Formats

Visuals such as tables, images (for example, photographs), and graphics such as charts and graphs not only add interest within a document but also serve to emphasize the information. Receivers are better able to make comparisons, understand relationships, analyze figures, and make decisions through these aids.

Formatting techniques such as the use of headings, margin notations, enumerations, and distinctive type also add emphasis. Compare the following message with the same information presented in Figure 16-2. Which communicates more effectively?

> Follow this procedure to determine the net profit for LKM Company. Subtract the value of goods returned from the gross income. The gross income for the company is $150,000; the value of goods returned is $13,500. The difference between these two is called gross profit. To determine the net profit, subtract the expenses. The expenses were rent, $19,000; travel expense, $1,400; salaries, $90,000; depreciation of equipment, $3,450; taxes, $550; and interest paid on loans, $250. The net profit is the difference between total expenses and gross profit, $22,850.

Variety

Variety provides interest and should be a planned part of your writing. To add variety to your writing, apply these techniques:

- Vary word selection by using synonyms—too much repetition is monotonous.
- Use a combination of sentence types—simple, complex, compound, and compound-complex.

Follow these steps to determine the net profit for LKM Company:

1. Subtract the value of goods returned from the gross income; the difference is gross profit.
2. Total the expenses.
3. Subtract the total expenses from gross profit; the difference is the net profit for the last six months.

Gross Income		$150,000
− Value of Goods Returned		−13,500
Gross Profit		$136,500
Expenses		
Rent	$19,000	
Travel Expense	1,400	
Salaries	90,000	
Depreciation of Equipment	3,450	
Taxes	550	
Interest on Loans	250	
Total Expenses		114,650
Net Profit for Last Six Months		$ 21,850

The following pie chart shows these figures as percentages.

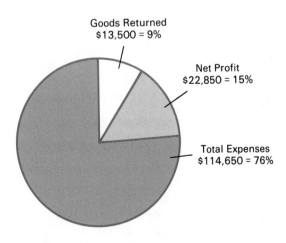

Goods Returned
$13,500 = 9%

Net Profit
$22,850 = 15%

Total Expenses
$114,650 = 76%

- Begin sentences in a variety of ways, including participial phrases, prepositional phrases, infinitive phrases, and adverbial clauses.
- Vary paragraph length and use a variety of formatting features.

✔Checkpoint 4 EMPHASIS AND VARIETY

Rewrite the following paragraph using a variety of sentence types and emphasizing the main idea.

Our spring sale illustrates a problem we often have during sales. We get behind in our alterations during large sales. Our suits were on sale 40 to 60 percent off. The demand during this sale increased greatly. Customers still needed their suits altered. The customers also wanted them altered within two days. Two days is the normal turnaround time for alterations. The solution is to hire additional help in the Alterations Department during sales and to charge for alterations to help pay the additional people.

Check your answers in Appendix D.

SUMMARY

Effective communication is carefully planned and organized. Planning the message involves identifying the objective, the main idea, and the supporting information and adjusting the content to the receiver.

Organizing the message involves determining the order in which the parts of the message will be presented. The direct order is used for messages which contain good news or neutral news. The indirect order is used for unfavorable messages or persuasive messages. When messages contain both good news and bad news, the direct-indirect order is used. The good news is presented first followed by the supporting information and the main idea.

Techniques that enhance communication are unity, coherence, emphasis, and variety. Unity requires that all ideas contribute to the main idea, forming a single, clear message. Both sentences and paragraphs need unity. Coherent messages are linked in a clear, logical manner. Coherence helps the receiver understand the relationship among ideas. Emphasis indicates what is important and what is incidental. Variety helps to maintain interest.

• • • • • • • • • Communication Activities

Discussion Questions

1. Explain whether the following statement is true or false: "Because we know what we want to say, we do not need to plan our messages."
2. How does the sender determine what supporting information to include in the message?
3. What are some of the considerations when adjusting the content and tone of the message to the receiver?
4. Messages can be organized in three ways: (1) the direct order, (2) the indirect order, and (3) the direct-indirect order. Define each of these plans and explain when they should be used.
5. How do topic sentences help to provide unity within a paragraph? Where is a topic sentence usually positioned within a paragraph?
6. What techniques can be applied to provide coherence? How do these techniques provide coherence?
7. What techniques can be applied to provide emphasis? What happens if sentences are consistently too long? (See Chapter 15, "Use Short Sentences.")
8. Do the concepts "repeat key words to provide coherence" and "vary word selection" contradict each other? Justify your answer.

Practical Applications

1. Which of the following sentences provides supporting information for the main idea?

   MAIN IDEA: Hire me as your new administrative assistant.
   a. In May I will graduate from Ultra University with my bachelor of science degree in Management Information Systems.
   b. I read your advertisement in the local paper.
   c. Two years of experience managing the department have helped me to understand a manager's role and challenges.
   d. I know that your benefits package is excellent.
   e. When I saw your advertisement, I was most excited.

2. Indicate the structure that is generally used for the message types listed. The message structures include direct order, indirect order, and direct-indirect order.
   a. Bad news message
   b. Routine message

c. Good news message

d. Persuasive message

e. Mixture of favorable and unfavorable news

3. Indicate whether each statement is direct or indirect.

a. The letter indicated that housing was unavailable because all vacancies had been filled.

b. Because the thermostat was set too high, the flowers have died.

c. Though the analysis was weak, we decided the plan derived from the analysis would be effective.

d. Because the parking lot is still vacant, resurfacing will begin today.

e. The workers found the Unser file while looking for the March balance sheet.

4. Write a sentence that provides the main idea for the following supporting information.

In 1986 sales increased 15 percent. Sales were static in 1987; but in 1987, sales increased 18 percent. Moreover, over the past five years, sales have doubled.

5. Rewrite this message so that it is unified and coherent.

As athletes, hikers are generally a laid-back group. You don't see them in front of mirrors flexing their muscles or discussing times for their latest 5K race, and they don't ever run in 10K races. Instead, they'll be talking about favorite trails or their next outing. To stay up-to-date with conservation issues, they frequently sit around and read recent editions of the appropriate magazines. As great as they believe it is, you won't hear them raving that hiking is the greatest or that it will change your life.

By definition, hiking is walking in the outdoors, usually up or down mountains. The mountains that you choose don't really matter. Yet it also includes walking across deserts and through woods. Hikers claim that hiking improves breathing capabilities, develops stronger calves and quadriceps, lowers resting pulses, and increases aerobic capacities. Doctors and psychologists agree that hiking provides these benefits and can be great recreation for the idle mind. To attain these benefits, I choose a Monday, Wednesday, and Friday format. Some of my friends, however, choose a Tuesday, Thursday, Friday format. They must also hike frequently, stretch their muscles, and use challenging terrains.

6. Write a paragraph on a topic that you enjoy using transitional words and phrases. The paragraph must contain three types of transitional words and phrases. Underline each transitional device and

indicate whether it shows contrast, cause-result, explanation, likeness, listing, or time.

7. Rewrite the following paragraph so that it has variety.

   Today, electronically prepared letters are becoming more common than in the past. Electronically prepared communications are an expected part of today's society. A major challenge for communicators will be to make these electronically prepared communications successful. They can make them effective by using the same skills as those needed for preparing communications in the traditional manner.

8. Rewrite this memo so that it has coherency, proper emphasis, and variety.

TO:	Jim Thompson
FROM:	Blaire Sicklemore, Advertising
DATE:	April 16, 19--
SUBJECT:	Promotional Idea for Breakfast Foods

   It is the opinion of researchers that children should eat breakfast every day. Recent studies show that children have better problem-solving abilities on mornings when they have eaten breakfast. On mornings when they do not have breakfast, children have lower test scores. They also have lower levels of insulin and glucose on those mornings. It is the opinion of researchers that glucose and insulin may have a direct effect on cognitive functioning of the brain. To put it another way, eating breakfast increases the child's brain power.

CHAPTER 17

Formatting and Editing the Message

Objectives

After studying this chapter and completing the chapter exercises, you should be able to:

1. Prepare memos in traditional and simplified format.
2. Prepare business letters in block, modified block, and simplified block formats.
3. Format minutes.
4. Format news releases.
5. Edit your messages effectively.

After writing your business message, you will want it to look as business-like as possible. Preparing a document with a professional appearance requires formatting and editing skills. **Formatting** is the technique of arranging a business message in an acceptable style. **Editing** involves making necessary corrections and revisions in the message.

FORMATTING MESSAGES

Although you may write a very well-composed message, if it looks sloppy it will make a poor impression. Consider the following message:

Mar. 8, --

Mr. Charles Fountain
232 W. Tenth St.
Mount Vernon
NY 10553-4126

Dear Mr. Fountain
If you enjoy gardening, then you will want a copy of *Growing Favorite Vegetables and Fruits.* This basic reference guide provides sound advice on planting, caring for, and harvesting vegetables and fruits.

By sending in the enclosed card, you can receive this new guide free for 30 days. If you aren't completely satisfied with this book at the end of 30 days, return it at no charge. We believe, Mr. Fountain, that you will find *Growing Favorite Vegetables and Fruits* to be one of your best gardening reference guides.
Sincerely,

Thomas R. Morton, Marketing
Manager

ep

Enc.

What kind of impression did this message make on you? Do you think Mr. Fountain will be interested in doing business with Mr. Morton? Even though the message is technically correct, it is not formatted in an easy-to-read style. Now look at the same message correctly formatted.

March 8, 19--

Mr. Charles Fountain
232 West Tenth Street
Mount Vernon, NY 10553-4126

Dear Mr. Fountain

If you enjoy gardening, then you will want a copy of *Growing Favorite Vegetables and Fruits*. This basic reference guide provides sound advice on planting, caring for, and harvesting vegetables and fruits.

By sending in the enclosed card, you can receive this new guide free for 30 days. If you aren't completely satisfied with this book at the end of 30 days, return it at no charge. We believe, Mr. Fountain, that you will find *Growing Favorite Vegetables and Fruits* to be one of your best gardening reference guides.

Sincerely

Thomas R. Morton
Marketing Manager

ep

Enclosure

Doesn't formatting make a difference? The message is easier to read, and it is more businesslike. People are likely to want to conduct business with an organization that uses good formatting techniques.

Formatting Memos

Interoffice memorandums (*memos* for short) are informal messages sent to persons within an organization. A memo includes only the basic parts needed to communicate the message in a clear, concise way: whom it is being sent to, whom it is from, the date the memo is written, the subject of the memo, the message itself, and any special notations (such as the initials of the typist and enclosure notations). The originator of a memo usually writes his or her initials below the printed name.

Memorandums are often formatted in the *traditional* style, either on a printed form or on plain paper. The *simplified* memo, however, is produced more easily on a computer or word processor because of its uncomplicated format.

Traditional Memo

Refer to Figures 17-1 and 17-2 as you review the following guidelines for preparing a memo in traditional format:

1. Use a 1 1/2-inch top margin on a full sheet and a 1-inch top margin on a half sheet.
2. Use 1-inch side margins. (If a printed form is used, align the left margin as shown in Figure 17-1.)
3. Use the headings TO, FROM, DATE, and SUBJECT in capital letters (followed by a colon) running vertically down the left margin. (Printed forms have these headings on them.)
4. Double-space after the headings and between paragraphs in the body of the memo.
5. Place the typist's initials a double space below the body of the memo and any additional notations below them.
6. Try to limit a memo to one page.

Simplified Memo

Because of the wide use of word processing in today's offices, the simplified format is becoming increasingly popular. This format is easily produced on automated equipment, which uses standard-size, continuous-feed memohead or plain paper. Time and effort are saved because the printed message does not have to be aligned with the printed callouts.

Refer to Figure 17-3 as you review the guidelines for preparing a memo in simplified format.

1. Use block format (all lines begin at the left margin) with 1-inch side margins.
2. Omit the headings TO, FROM, DATE, and SUBJECT.
3. Place the date a double space below the letterhead or on line 10 of a plain sheet.
4. Place the name of the recipient four lines below the date.
5. Place the subject line in all capital letters a double space below the receiver's name.
6. Begin the body of the memo a double space below the subject line.
7. Place the name of the originator four lines below the body of the memo.
8. Place the operator's initials below the printed signature line.

Interoffice Memo

TO: All Georgia Electric Personnel

FROM: Monica Flores, Accounting Department

DATE: October 13, 19--

SUBJECT: Chili Cookoff

Our first annual chili cookoff will be held on Friday, October 24,
on the tenth floor parking deck. Cooking will begin at 1 p.m.
Bring your favorite recipe and all ingredients; cooking facilities
will be provided. Judging will be held at 6 p.m.

This event will be great fun. I know we have some gourmet chili
chefs out there; here is your chance to prove it!

ch

FIGURE 17-1   Traditional Memo on Printed Stationery

TO: All Georgia Electric Personnel

FROM: Monica Flores, Accounting Department

SUBJECT: Chili Cookoff

DATE: October 13, 19--

Our first annual chili cookoff will be held on Friday, October 24,
on the tenth floor parking deck. Cooking will begin at 1 p.m.
Bring your favorite recipe and all ingredients; cooking facilities
will be provided. Judging will be held at 6 p.m.

This event will be great fun. I know we have some gourmet chili
chefs out there; here is your chance to prove it!

ch

FIGURE 17-2   Traditional Memo on Plain Paper

Interoffice Memo

October 13, 19--

All Georgia Electric Personnel

CHILI COOKOFF

Our first annual chili cookoff will be held on Friday, October 24, on the tenth floor parking deck. Cooking will begin at 1 p.m. Bring your favorite recipe and all ingredients; cooking facilities will be provided. Judging will be held at 6 p.m.

This event will be great fun. I know we have some gourmet chili chefs out there; here is your chance to prove it!

Monica Flores, Accounting Department

ch

FIGURE 17-3 Simplified Memo Format

Formatting Letters

The basic written communication sent from one organization to another is the business *letter*. Business letters are prepared on letterhead stationery, which includes the printed company name, address, telephone number, the company logo, and sometimes the names of officials and departments. Because the letter is addressed to persons outside the organization, the letter is a more formal document than the memo.

Letter Parts

Business letters generally include such parts as the dateline, letter address, salutation (or greeting), body, complimentary close, and reference initials.

Dateline.   Position the current date about 2 1/2 inches from the top of the page or at least two lines below the letterhead. The horizontal placement of the dateline depends upon the letter format being used.

Letter Address.   The letter address includes the complete name and address of the addressee. Place each part of the letter address on a separate line, beginning at the left margin. The addressee's personal or professional title (*Mr., Ms., Dr., Mrs.*) is included; often the job title is included either on the same line with the name or on the line below, whichever gives better balance. Allow two spaces between the state abbreviation and the ZIP Code.

> Ms. Stacy Green, President
> Seymour and Associates
> 396 Stewart Avenue
> Franklin, TN 37064-7109

The envelope address should match the letter address with the exception that all capital letters (ALL CAP) and no punctuation are used (U.S. Postal Service format). The ALL CAP format may be used for the letter address if the letter is to be sent in a window envelope or if form letters are merged with mailing addresses.

> MS STACY GREEN PRESIDENT
> SEYMOUR AND ASSOCIATES
> 396 STEWART AVENUE
> FRANKLIN TN 37064-7109

Sometimes an attention line is included in the letter address. An **attention line** directs correspondence to a particular individual when the letter is addressed to an organization. Beginning at the left margin, position the attention line on the second line of the letter address or mailing address on an envelope.

> Seymour and Associates
> Attention Ms. Stacy Green
> 396 Stewart Avenue
> Franklin, TN 37064-7109

Subject Line.   The subject line informs the reader of the topic of the letter. Place the subject line in all capital letters a double space below the salutation at the left margin. Omit the word SUBJECT.

> Mr. Mario Fasano
> 5700 Orchard Road
> Northbrook, IL 60062-4110
>
> Dear Mr. Fasano:
>
> STATE TRAVEL REGULATIONS

Salutation.   The salutation acts as the greeting. Position it a double space below the letter address in most business letters. (Note: The simplified letter format omits the salutation.) The salutation should agree with the first line of the letter address. If the first line does not have a person's name, use *Ladies and Gentlemen*. If the letter is addressed to a job title, use *Dear Sir or Madam*. A colon follows the salutation if the letter is prepared with **mixed punctuation.** No punctuation is used after the salutation with **open punctuation.**

Brennan's Supermarket
1018 Eighth Street
Monroe, WI 53566-0011

Ladies and Gentlemen

Produce Manager
Brennan's Supermarket
1018 Eighth Street
Monroe, WI 53566-0011

Dear Sir or Madam

Body.   The body is the message of the letter. Single-space the body of the letter and double-space between paragraphs. Place the letter attractively on the page using side margins of 1, 1 1/2, or 2 inches, depending upon the length of the letter.

Complimentary Close.   The complimentary close is the formal closing or "goodbye." Place the complimentary close a double space below the body of the letter. Capitalize only the first word of the complimentary close. A comma follows the complimentary close if mixed punctuation is used; the comma is omitted if open punctuation is used.

Writer's Name and Title.   Position the writer's name four lines (a quadruple space) below the complimentary close. Omit the title *Mr.* before a man's name; *Miss, Mrs.,* or *Ms.* may be used before a woman's name, depending on the writer's preference. The writer's official title may be positioned on the same line as the name or on the line below it, whichever provides better balance.

Reference Initials.   The operator's initials are keyed in lowercase and positioned at the left margin a double space below the printed signature line. If the dictator's or writer's initials are also used, key them in all capital letters, but use lowercase for the operator's initials (GK:er).

Enclosure Notation.   If items are enclosed with the letter, key an enclosure notation a double space below the reference initials. Either spell out the word *Enclosure* or abbreviate *Enc.*

Copy Notation.   If others are receiving copies of the letter, include the copy notation a double space below the reference initials or enclosure notation. Where appropriate, use the following abbreviations followed by the name of the recipient: *pc* or *c* for photocopy and *bc* for blind copy. A blind copy notation is added on the copies but not on the original. A blind copy notation is used when you do not want the person receiving the document to know that you are sending a copy to someone else.

Postscript.   For emphasis, a postscript may be added at the end of a letter. Position it a double space below the last item. The letters *P.S.* may be omitted.

Letter Formats

Business letters may be prepared in different letter formats. Three formats are recommended: block, modified block, and simplified block.

Block Format.   The block format is popular and easy to prepare because all lines, including the date, begin at the left margin. Refer to Figure 17-4 for an example of the block format; the letter parts are identified.

Modified Block Format.   Traditionally, the modified block format has been popular because of its balanced appearance. As illustrated in Figure 17-5, all lines begin at the left margin except for the date, the complimentary close, and the typed signature lines, which begin at the center of the page. This format is still fairly efficient since it requires only one tab setting at center. Paragraphs may begin at the left margin or be indented five spaces. The indention is optional since paragraphs are separated by double spacing.

Simplified Block Format.   Designed for efficient processing, the simplified block format is compatible with window envelopes or with letters that are prepared by merging addresses from a database with a form letter. As in the block format, all lines begin at the left margin; the spacing between letter parts is the same as that in block or modified block format. As the following description shows, the originator may vary the format in several ways. Refer to Figure 17-6 as you read these guidelines.

1. The date is placed on line 12 so that the letter address is positioned for use within a window envelope. Standard margins are used for all letters regardless of their length.
2. The letter address is keyed in ALL CAP format without punctuation to comply with the U.S. Postal Service guidelines. The traditional format, however, is also permitted.
3. The salutation and complimentary close are omitted. (Omitting the salutation eliminates making errors in titles such as *Mr., Mrs., Miss.*)
4. A subject line is placed a double space below the letter address. It may be keyed in either ALL CAP letters or uppercase and lowercase letters.
5. The writer's name and title are positioned four lines below the body in either ALL CAPS or uppercase and lowercase, depending upon the writer's preference.
6. As in any format, the letter may be personalized by incorporating the receiver's name within the body of the letter.

Greenery, Inc.

Telephone: (317) 478-3438

1212 Hillside Drive
Cambridge City, IN 47327-2311

Dateline **March 8, 19--**

Letter **Mr. Charles Fountain**
Address **232 West Tenth Street**
Mount Vernon, NY 10553-4126

Salutation **Dear Mr. Fountain**

Body of **If you enjoy gardening, then you will want a copy of**
Letter **Growing Favorite Vegetables and Fruits. This basic ref-**
erence guide provides sound advice on planting, caring
for, and harvesting vegetables and fruits.

By sending in the enclosed card, you can receive this new
guide free for 30 days. If at the end of 30 days you are
not completely satisfied with this book, return it at no
charge. We believe, Mr. Fountain, that you will find
Growing Favorite Vegetables and Fruits to be one of your
best gardening reference guides.

Complimentary **Sincerely**
Close

Name and Title **Thomas R. Morton**
Marketing Manager
Reference
Initials **ep**

Enclosure **Enclosure**

Copy **c Mario Perez**
Notation

FIGURE 17-4 Block Format, Open Punctuation

Plainview Institute of Technology
University Circle
Urbandale, Iowa 50322

January 31, 19--

Ms. Sarah Fleming
343 Southview Drive
Des Moines, IA 50349-3213

Dear Ms. Fleming:

Today I received your request for a copy of our college catalog. We are pleased that you are interested in attending Plainview Institute of Technology.

Enclosed are our current catalog and an application for admission. If you have questions about any of our programs, please call me at 555-1832.

Best wishes to you in pursuing your plans for a career in office administration.

Sincerely yours,

James W. Brooks

James W. Brooks
Admissions Counselor

aw

Enclosures

FIGURE 17-5 Modified Block Format, Mixed Punctuation

Chapter 17   Formatting and Editing the Message

Plainview Institute of Technology
University Circle
Urbandale, Iowa 50322

January 31, 19--

MS. SARAH FLEMING
343 SOUTHVIEW DRIVE
DES MOINES IA 50349-3213

REQUEST FOR CATALOG

Today I received your request for a copy of our college
catalog. We are pleased that you are interested in attending Plainview Institute of Technology.

Enclosed are the current catalog and an application for
admission. If you have questions about any of our programs, please call me at 555-1832.

Best wishes to you, Ms. Fleming, as you pursue your plans
for a career in office administration.

James W. Brooks

James W. Brooks
Admissions Counselor

aw

Enclosures

FIGURE 17-6 Simplified Block Format

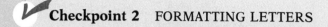

Checkpoint 2 FORMATTING LETTERS

1. Identify each of the following letter parts.
   a. Yours truly
   b. February 14, 19--
   c. Enc.
   d. Dear Mrs. Webster
   e. c Jean Wright
2. Name one feature of the block format.
3. Name two features of the modified block format.
4. Name four features of the simplified block format.

Check your answers in Appendix D.

Formatting Minutes

Minutes are the official report of a meeting. Refer to Figure 17-7 as you review the guidelines for formatting minutes of a meeting:

1. Use 1-inch side margins, a 1 1/2-inch top margin, and single spacing.
2. Center the name of the meeting and/or organization in **ALL CAPS.**
3. Center a subheading (optional) such as *Minutes of the Executive Board* and the date a double space below the heading in uppercase and lowercase letters.
4. Begin the body a quadruple space below the subheading.
5. Double-space between paragraphs.
6. Headings may be used within the minutes to identify the various parts. Key the headings in **ALL CAPS** or use the underscore as shown in Figure 17-7.
7. At the end of the minutes, key the name of the person taking the minutes and provide a signature line. (Sometimes the presider's name is also keyed.)

Formatting News Releases

News releases are brief announcements prepared for distribution to newspapers and magazines. Refer to Figure 17-8 as you review the guidelines for formatting news releases.

1. Use 1-inch side margins, a 1 1/2-inch top margin, and double spacing (indent paragraphs 5 spaces).

```
              MINUTES OF OFFICE ADMINISTRATION ADVISORY COMMITTEE
                            October 19, 19--


Call to Order

The meeting was called to order by Chairperson Lillie Brooks at
3:35 p.m. in Room C-47.

Members present were Ada Blanco, Wanda Daniels, Nila Geiger,
Eddie Hartley, Phyllis Jacks, Rich Marsh, Carol Monteith, Patsy
Smith, and Kathy Tripp.  Ex-officio memebers present were Carlos
Schmitt, Carol Henson, Marty Beliveau, and Benita Moore.

Minutes of the April 30, 19--, meeting were approved.

Report from OADT Department

Dr. Carlos Schmitt, Chairperson of the Vocational-Technical
Education Division, welcomed all new and returning committee
members.  He briefly discussed the new vo-tech building proposal
(near construction stage) and the college's four-year status.

Dr. Henson gave an update of the Office Administration Depart-
ment.  She provided an equipment inventory of the department and
noted that all the course guides have been updated and are avail-
able for preview.

Program of Work/Goals

Dr. Henson distributed the suggested program of Work/Goals for
(1) Curriculum (2) Facilities and Equipment, and (3) College and
Community.  A sign-up sheet was provided for members to select
the committee on which they would prefer to serve.

Unfinished Business

none

Meeting Dates

The Winter Quarter meeting will be January 28, 19--; the Spring
Quarter meeting will be April 29, 19--.

The meeting was adjourned at 4:55 p.m.
```

Marty Beliveau
_____
Marty Beliveau, Secretary

FIGURE 17-7 Format for Minutes of a Meeting

News Release

November 18, 19--

FOR IMMEDIATE RELEASE

STUDENT-FACULTY REUNION AT GEORGIA ELECTRIC

MORROW, Ga. Several members of Clayton State College's
faculty recently visited with Clayton State alumni employed at
Georgia Electric Corporation.

Office Administration faculty members, Mrs. Marty Oates,
Mrs. Ada Blanco, Dr. Yang Jen, and Dr. Benita Harris and Job
Placement Counselor, Mrs. Pat Gardner, were guests of Georgia
Electric for lunch, for a meeting with former students, and for a
tour of the corporate headquarters building.

Georgia Electric actively recruits Office Administration and
Technology majors from the College. In addition, Georgia Electric employment representatives provide valuable services to the
students and faculty. Ms. Frances Dunn, personnel services manager at Georgia Electric, serves on the Office Administration and
Technology Advisory Committee. Ms. Judy Horton, program manager
of Georgia TEMP, and Ms. Dorothy Ward, employment representative,
regularly visit the campus to assist students with job-seeking
skills by conducting simulated interviews.

James Peters

2760 Industrial Parkway · Morrow, GA 31754-2028 · Public Relations Office · (912) 555-3996, Extension 408

FIGURE 17-8 **Format for a News Release**

2. Use company letterhead (or a special letterhead for news releases) or key the company name and address at the top of the page.

3. Position the date and the release date (or *For Immediate Release*) at the top of the page.

4. Center the heading of the announcement in ALL CAPS a quadruple space below the release date information. Double-space after the heading.

5. Place the writer's name (or contact person) on the fourth line below the message at the left margin.

6. Try to limit news releases to one page. If the release is longer than one page, type *–more–* at the end of all pages except the last.

EDITING THE MESSAGE

After writing your message (memo, letter, minutes, news release), always reread it carefully to make sure you have written effectively. This process is called editing. Editing may involve changing words or sentences, correcting errors, or even rewriting the entire message. To edit your message, follow these guidelines:

- Wait for a day or two (if possible) to edit your message. You will be able to edit more objectively.

- Read the message as though you were reading it for the first time. Make sure all the information is complete and clear.

- Check for continuity in your message. Make sure that one idea flows into another and that the reader will be able to follow the message easily.

- Delete unnecessary words so that your message is as concise as possible without being curt or leaving out important information.

- Check the accuracy of your message. Make sure all facts and figures are correct.

- Check the format of your message. Make sure it is appropriate.

- Check the length. Don't give readers more than they need to know or omit information that is needed to make the message complete.

- Check for correctness. Make sure you have no spelling, punctuation, grammatical, or word usage errors.

- Make sure your message is organized logically. Every message should have a beginning, a middle, and an ending.

Editing is one of the most important procedures in writing. By editing effectively, you will write messages that are easily understood by others.

SUMMARY

By formatting your business communications effectively, you give them a professional appearance and make them easier to read. Memos, which may be formatted in either traditional or simplified style, include only the basic parts of a message: the names of the sender and receiver, the date, the subject, and the message itself. Letters may be prepared in several formats, including block, modified block, and simplified block. Basic letter parts include the dateline, letter address, salutation, body, complimentary close, writer's keyed name, and reference initials. Letters may also have an attention line, subject line, enclosure notation, copy notation, and postscript. Follow the suggested guidelines to format other business communications, including minutes of meetings and news releases.

Edit your business messages after writing them, checking for continuity, length, accuracy, format, style, grammar, and organization.

 Communication Activities

Discussion Questions

1. How are memos prepared in the traditional format?
2. How is the simplified memo formatted? When is the simplified memo used?
3. List and describe the parts of a business letter.
4. How does the block letter format differ from the modified block letter format?
5. How is the simplified block letter formatted?
6. What are the format guidelines for minutes?
7. How are news releases formatted?
8. What steps should be taken in editing a message?

Practical Applications

1. Edit and format the following memo first in (a) traditional and then in (b) simplified style. Your instructor may direct you to use a typewriter or computer/word processor.

Chapter 17   Formatting and Editing the Message

TO: Office Administration Faculty   FROM: Dean Georgia Rainwater
DATE: November 6, 19--   SUBJECT: Moving to New Offices

(¶1) You have been scheduled to move to your new office locations the dates of December 10, 11, and 12. Please begin boxing all instructional materials you are not currently using. On the inclosed form, indicate whether or not you would like the maintanance staff to assist you and the appropriate date December 10, 11, or 13) that you would like to move into your new office as soon as possible

(¶2) All new offices will be furnished with the following items; desk, desk chair side chair, two drawer file and five-shelf bookcase. Furniture will not be moved from your present office unless it is your own furniture.

(¶3) Please let me know if you have any questions about the move. Many of you have commented that you are looking forward to our all being together in the new School of Business office suit.

jm/Enclosure

2. Edit and prepare the following business letter in three different formats: (a) block, (b) modified block, and (c) simplified block. Use open punctuation. Your instructor may direct you to use a typewriter or computer/word processor.

[Current date] Ms. Charlene Redwine / 89 Barfield Road / Atlanta, GA 30328-5187 / Dear Ms. Redwine

(¶1) Welcome to Acme Mortgage Company. For your information and knowledge, we have enclosed herewith a brochure which should answer any questions you can have about your new mortgage loan.

(¶2) Your loan number is located in the upper left corner of the payment coupon. Payment coupons will be mailed to you under separate cover and must accompany all payments. Please write this number on your check in the event that the check is separated from the coupon. In addition always indicate your loan number when making any inquires about your account.

(¶3) Your first pament is due on or before February 1, 19-- and on the first of each month thereafter until your loan is paid in full. Payments received in our office more than fifteen (16) days after the due date are subject to a late charge of 4 percent of the payment amount, as specified in your mortgage.

(¶4) If you have any questions concerning your account, please be advised that you may contact our Customer Relations Department, Acme Mortgage Company. P.O. Box 3971, Atlanta, Ga 30303-5013.

Sincerely yours / Neil Tyler / Customer Relations Representative / xx / Enclosure

3. Edit and prepare the following news release, using the appropriate format.

CONTACT Gayle Smith 555-1295 / [Current date] / For Immediate Release

OFFICE DESIGN CONFERENCE

Atlanta, Ga. People space and technology will come together at the annual Office Design Conference, to be held May 15–17 at San Franciscos Moscone Convention Center.

This year's conference will feature more than 40 seminars, all designed to enhance the professional skills of office managers, space planners, facilities managers, interior designers, and other design professionals. In addition, more than two hundred exhibitors will feature their office equipment and products.

Special features of the show include a photo gallery which will illustrate the latest office design projects from all across the country. In addition, a video theater will offer daily presentations introduced by Robert Byars, a design consultant.

Janice Ruffini, managing director of the Design Group, New York City, will deliver the keynote address on Wednesday, May 15, at 9 a.m. In her talk, "Designing for the Workspace of the 90s," Ms. Ruffini will describe how technology will effect office design and the nature of work itself, as related to the office space environment.

Development of Messages

PART 5

A ssume that your boss has said to you, "We need to review our benefits package and be sure that it is competitive with others in our region and in the industry. Would you please review our benefits package and see if it needs to be updated. After you investigate the situation, send me a memo reporting your findings." Would you know how to proceed with this assignment?

A college graduate in an entry-level position may write several letters and memos within a week. Thus it is critical to your career that you know how to construct effective messages. In Part 5 you will learn to plan, organize, and write effective routine, goodwill, bad news, and persuasive messages.

CHAPTER 18

Routine, Good News, and Goodwill Messages

Objectives

After studying this chapter and completing the chapter exercises, you should be able to:

1. Plan routine, good news, and goodwill messages.
2. Organize routine, good news, and goodwill messages.
3. Compose routine, good news, and goodwill messages.

Routine messages communicate neutral news. Such messages might be written to make an inquiry, to promote goodwill, or to acknowledge an inquiry. Good news messages convey favorable information to the receiver. Letters and memorandums that order goods, issue credit, or grant requests are examples of good news messages. Routine and good news messages can be used to fill any of the five basic purposes of communication. Care should be given to planning, organizing, and writing good news and routine messages. They provide an excellent opportunity for the sender to build or strengthen a relationship with the receiver.

PLANNING THE MESSAGE

As you learned in Chapter 16, planning is the first step in composing a message. Let's apply these steps as we plan a good news letter offering an applicant a position as a training director in the Office Services Department. The applicant should give us a decision within one week.

Identify the Objective	To make an offer of employment
Identify the Main Idea	Offer applicant position as training director in the Office Services Department
Determine the Supporting Information	Impressed with knowledge of company Good work attitude Annual salary of $28,000; paid semimonthly Starting date is two weeks from today Conditions of employment Decision needed within one week
Adjust the Content to the Receiver	Applicant is knowledgeable about the job requirements and the company Applicant will be eager to hear from us
Select Channel	Letter

ORGANIZING THE MESSAGE

Because everyone likes to receive favorable news, routine and good news messages are organized in the direct order. The main idea is, therefore, presented immediately; it is followed by the supporting information. Follow these steps to organize messages in the direct order:

1. Begin by stating the main idea.
2. Include relevant supporting details.
3. End with a friendly goodwill closing which also specifies action to be taken by the receiver.

Main Idea

The key to an effective routine or good news message is to reveal clearly the main idea in the first or second sentence. Don't make the receiver search for the good news. Present the good news using the "you" approach in a clear, concise manner. Emphasize the good news by keeping the introductory paragraphs short—about one or two sentences. Do not let this paragraph exceed four printed lines.

Either of the following could be used as the first paragraph for the letter to be written to offer employment.

> You have been selected for the position of training director in the Office Services Department.

> We are delighted to offer you the position of training director in the Office Services Department.

✔ Checkpoint 1   MAIN IDEA

Read the following situation. Indicate which of the sentences would be *good* openings and which would be *poor* openings in your response to Mr. Orr.

The Situation: Mr. Jack Orr has written to request that you send him some credit information on Mrs. Cleo Zimmerman. You are now writing him and providing the requested information.

1. We appreciate your confidence in our credit information.
2. Thank you for your request for credit information on Mrs. Cleo Zimmerman.
3. The credit information on Mrs. Cleo Zimmerman is enclosed.
4. We receive many requests for credit information each day.
5. You can rate Mrs. Cleo Zimmerman as an excellent credit risk.

Check your answers in Appendix D.

Supporting Information

After conveying the good news or main idea in the first paragraph, the next step is to provide information that will clarify the main idea and be helpful to the receiver. The supporting information should furnish necessary explanations, state conditions of the good news, or answer questions.

This section of the message may contain one or more paragraphs depending upon the nature of the message. Each paragraph should have a central idea and be no longer than eight lines. For clarity, repeat key words and enumerate important points.

The following three paragraphs could be used to respond to an applicant when offering employment. The first paragraph explains why the applicant was chosen, the second provides details the receiver will want to know, and the third provides the conditions of the good news.

> During your visit we were impressed with your knowledge of our company and of the management techniques that we use. Your positive attitude is very apparent.

> Your starting date is July 1. If this date is inconvenient, please let us know—there is some flexibility. Your annual salary will be $28,000, and you will be paid semimonthly.

> Please let us know your decision in a letter by Wednesday, June 8.

Goodwill Closing

The closing provides the sender with an excellent opportunity to build goodwill. It should be friendly and courteous and leave a favorable impression with the sender. Should action be required, it is identified in the closing. Using the receiver's name in the closing adds a personal touch.

> Elizabeth, we sincerely hope that you will accept our offer. If you have any questions, please call me at (318) 299-5800.

If you work for a company which sells products or services, the closing may also include a **soft sale.** A soft sale is an attempt to sell a product or service. That attempt, however, should not be strong or pushy, nor should it be the obvious message in the closing. The following is a good example of a goodwill closing which contains a soft sale.

> Thank you, Mr. Ruiz, for your order. By the way, you may want to visit our store between the 15th and 29th of May—the days of our Anniversary Sale. All personal computers and word processors will be reduced 25 percent.

Now let's put together the entire good news letter to the applicant.

> Dear Elizabeth:

Main Idea You have been selected for the position of training director in the Office Services Department.

Supporting Information During your visit we were impressed with your knowledge of our company and of the management techniques that we use. Your positive attitude is very apparent.

Your starting date is July 1. If this date is inconvenient, please let us know—there is some flexibility. Your annual salary will be $28,000, and you will be paid $1,250 semimonthly.

Please let us know your decision in a letter by Wednesday, June 8. We are eager to hear from you.

Goodwill Closing
Elizabeth, we sincerely hope that you will accept our offer. If you have any questions, please call me at (318) 299-5800.

 Checkpoint 2   GOODWILL CLOSING

Using the same situation as in Checkpoint 1, indicate which of the sentences would be *good* endings and which would be *poor* endings.

The Situation: Mr. Jack Orr has written to request that you send him some credit information on Mrs. Cleo Zimmerman.

1. The next time I need credit information from your agency, you'll certainly hear from us.
2. Should you need additional information, please ask.
3. Please ask if you need more information on Mrs. Zimmerman.
4. Your request is most appreciated.
5. I am sure you'll find Mrs. Zimmerman to be an excellent credit customer.

Check your answers in Appendix D.

ROUTINE MESSAGES

Letters and memos are commonly used to order merchandise or services or to make requests or inquiries. The request may be for information, for someone's services (e.g., as a speaker), or for a favor. Requests are considered to be neutral messages; the assumption is that the receiver will not have to be persuaded to respond positively to the request.

Requests

"Will you please..." is the main idea of requests or inquiries. A successful letter of request motivates the receiver to respond. To aid the receiver, the writer must provide sufficient detail so that the receiver understands the request and can respond easily. Providing sufficient detail means anticipating questions the receiver may have and responding to them in the request. For example, if you were asking someone to be a speaker, you would need to provide the sender with answers to the following:

What is the topic?
What is the background, knowledge, and expected size of the audience?
What is the date, time, and location of the presentation?
Will there be remuneration?
If travel is involved, who will arrange for accommodations?

A letter of request should reveal its main idea quickly; provide the necessary data concisely; and close in a polite, helpful manner. The basic organizational plan for messages of request is the direct order.

- *Main Idea:* State the request politely and directly. If appropriate, provide a reason for the request.

- *Supporting Information:* Specify information required to obtain a complete response (such as times, dates, benefits to the receiver, terms of payment, and so forth).

- *Goodwill Closing:* End pleasantly and indicate the action to be taken by the receiver.

The following message uses the direct order to ask an associate to make a presentation.

Main Idea	On March 3 our sales representatives will be attending a seminar on improving oral presentations. Would you give a 45-minute presentation on the effective use of visual aids?
Supporting Information	Our representatives are receiving an increasing number of requests for presentations. Any techniques and hints that you could give them would be greatly appreciated.
	The seminar is to be held on the 15th floor in the Conference Room. Your presentation would be scheduled from 10:00 a.m. to 10:45 a.m. It is anticipated that you would be speaking to about 15 representatives.
Goodwill Closing	Your speaking at the seminar would be greatly appreciated. So that plans for the seminar can be finalized, please let me know your decision by February 20.

Next is a message requesting a leave of absence. Note that the supporting details emphasize the benefits to the receiver as well as to the sender.

Main Idea	May I take a year's leave of absence and work with Arthur P. Young, the Big Eight firm?
Supporting Information	As you know, I have been doing some consulting with this firm. Because of my work and of our company's interest in electronic

data processing at accounting firms, they have offered me a position for the 19-- academic year.

This experience would benefit both me and the department: (1) I would be updated in the field and have a feel for what accounting firms are doing in the area of electronic data processing; (2) I could better advise our department on curriculum matters; and (3) I would be a better prepared classroom teacher.

Goodwill Closing   Hank, this is an excellent opportunity. May I have your response by March 17? Arthur P. Young needs a reply from me by March 24.

Claims

Claims are a special type of request. They are written when customers or clients believe they have a right to ask for a refund, an exchange, or a discount on merchandise or services. When writing a claim letter, use the direct order to communicate to the receiver that you expect an **adjustment**—an adjustment is a positive settlement to a claim. The tone of a claim letter should be positive but firm; do not show anger or blame the receiver.

- *Main Idea:* Ask for an adjustment.
- *Supporting Information:* Explain the problem or the reason for the request. Identify the damage (if damage occurred).
- *Goodwill Closing:* End with a positive statement. Indicate how the situation can be corrected.

The following is a request to adjust an account.

Main Idea   Please adjust my account for $16.

Supporting Information   Last month I placed an order with Lehi and Alma's. As usual, you filled the order quickly and completely. Upon checking my invoice against my purchase order, however, I realized I was charged $6.95 per copy for *The Tunnel and the Pathway* instead of the list price of $4.95. Because I received the eight copies requested, I am asking that my account be adjusted for $16.

Goodwill Information   Please either credit my account for $16 or send me a refund. I look forward to receiving the adjustment.

GOOD NEWS MESSAGES

A good news message is the message the receiver wanted; therefore the direct order is used. Examples of good news messages are orders and "yes" responses to requests. Such replies may be given to requests, to orders for merchandise, to claims, and to credit applications. The basic structure of these messages is as follows:

- *Main Idea:* Say "yes" to the receiver.
- *Supporting Information:* Provide any details the receiver needs to carry out specific instructions.
- *Goodwill Closing:* End with a helpful, positive closing. If the sender sells goods or services, the closing should contain a soft sale.

Orders

Usually companies place orders by using a form called a purchase order similar to the one shown in Figure 18-1. These forms provide space for the name and address of the purchaser and vendor and the detailed information necessary to make the purchase.

Occasionally a small company or an individual will use a letter to place an order. "Please send me..." is the main idea when placing orders. To have your order filled correctly, you must provide complete supporting information. Failing to do so will waste time and money. Formatting the middle paragraph as a table will help to assure clarity and completeness.

- *Main Idea:* Request that the order be filled.
- *Supporting Information:* Supply specific details needed by the receiver. For each item ordered, indicate the stock number or catalog number; a description including the size and/or color where applicable; quantity ordered; unit cost; total cost; method of shipment and shipping address; and method of payment.
- *Goodwill Closing:* End with a statement indicating action to be taken by the receiver.

The following order letter is organized on this plan.

Main Idea	Please send the following items by Quick Express to the address shown above.				
Supporting Information	Item No.	Description	Quantity Ordered	Unit Cost	Total Cost
	#2986-A	Puffed-sleeve blouses (3 each of sizes 5–10, 12, and 14)	24	$9.99	$239.76
	#9041-M	Wool scarves	36	5.99	215.64
	#8695	Winter socks (6 each of sizes 7–10 and 11–13)	12	3.49	41.88
		TOTAL			$497.28
Goodwill Closing	Should you need additional information about this order, please call our toll-free number 1-800-254-8950.				

FIGURE 18-1 Purchase Order Form

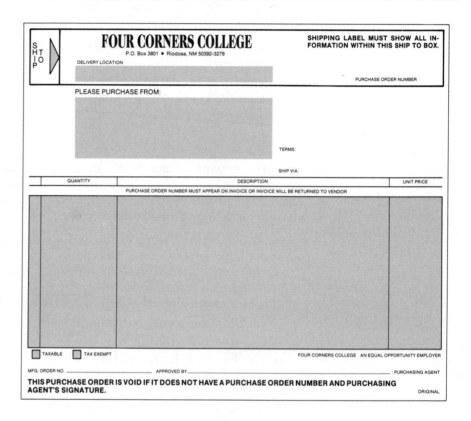

"Yes" Responses

A "yes" response also provides good news for the receiver. Following is an example of a "yes" response to a request for a speaker. Note that the supporting information confirms such details as the date, time, and place and provides additional information needed by the receiver.

Main Idea — I will be very pleased to speak in Seattle at the National Conference for Personnel Directors.

Supporting Information — The honorarium you offer is fine, as are the time and date of the presentation—November 6 from 11:00 to 11:45 a.m. Thank you for arranging my accommodations and picking me up at the airport.

I will be arriving on Delta Flight #1363 at 4 p.m. on November 5.

Goodwill Closing — Thank you for the opportunity to speak at this conference. I look forward to meeting you and visiting your beautiful city.

A "yes" response to a credit request is good news to the receiver. Note that the supporting information in the following response includes a description of the restrictions on the account and how the account should be paid. The closing includes a soft sale.

Main Idea	We are most pleased to open a charge account for you. Thank you for your interest in our products.
Supporting Information	For your new account, the terms are 2/10, net/30. Because your credit rating and references are excellent, the ceiling for your account is $15,000.
Goodwill Closing	Enclosed are catalogues of our products. Should you have questions about our products, our trained salespersons will be most happy to help you.

GOODWILL MESSAGES

Goodwill messages are friendship messages designed to build relationships. Goodwill messages may express congratulations, sympathy, welcome, appreciation, or invitations. This expression is the main idea of the message.

Supporting details may or may not be needed. For example, when expressing sympathy, details would be inappropriate. Yet detail in an invitation is critical because the receiver needs to know who is invited, when and where the celebration is to be held, and how to dress. Plan and organize each goodwill message thoughtfully.

The following congratulatory message needs no detailed information:

> **TO:** Mark Mortonsen, Supervisor of Office Services
> **FROM:** Jeff Peshov, Supervisor of Accounts Receivable
> **DATE:** August 19, 19--
> **SUBJECT:** Congratulations

Main Idea and Goodwill Closing	Congratulations on your recent promotion to Supervisor of Office Services. You are most deserving, and those who work with you are most fortunate to have you as their supervisor.

The following goodwill message includes necessary supporting information:

> **TO:** Jeff Peshov
> **FROM:** Tom Lambert
> **DATE:** August 20, 19--
> **SUBJECT:** It's a Party

Main Idea and Supporting Information	You are invited to a small surprise party to congratulate Mark Mortonsen on his recent promotion. It will be held on the third floor in the cafeteria at 4:15 p.m. on Wednesday, August 25.

| **Goodwill Closing** | Please come and help us congratulate Mark. RSVP to me by Monday, August 23, at ext. 5068. |

Acknowledgments are goodwill messages because their main purpose is to maintain or build goodwill with their receivers. They tell the receiver that his or her message has been received; however, they are sometimes sent to inform the receiver that a request cannot be filled right away. Common acknowledgments are those acknowledging orders and credit applications. In these messages the supporting information usually reveals the reasons for the delay, and the goodwill closing contains a soft sale.

Main Idea	Thank you for your order. We are pleased to have you as one of our customers.
Supporting Information	The demand for the earthenware plant holders has far exceeded our supply. Your order will be shipped next Tuesday, the day we expect our shipment.
Goodwill Closing	In the meantime, look over the enclosed flier announcing our "Spring Fling Sale." Place your order now to enjoy a 50 percent savings on several items.

Figure 18-2 provides a checklist to help you compose effective routine, good news, and goodwill messages. The questions listed under the planning stage will help you to determine the content of the message and adjust it to your receiver. Items listed in the writing stage will help you to organize and to present the message in a complete, considerate manner. The items in the editing stage will help you to be correct and concise.

SUMMARY

Though rather easy to compose, routine, good news, and goodwill messages should be planned and organized carefully. Their objectives and supporting details should be identified even before the writing process begins. These types of messages have three components, which are always presented in the direct order: first the main idea, then the supporting details, and then a helpful, courteous ending.

FIGURE 18-2 Checklist for Routine, Good News, and Goodwill Messages

		Yes	No
Planning Stage			
1.	Have I identified the objective of the message?	____	____
2.	Have I identified the main idea of the message?	____	____
3.	Have I identified the supporting details needed by the receiver?	____	____
4.	Have I adjusted the main idea and supporting details to the needs and background of my receiver?	____	____
Writing Stage			
5.	Have I presented the main idea in the first or second sentence of the first paragraph?	____	____
6.	Have I presented all the supporting details the receiver will need in order to do what I want?	____	____
7.	Have I presented the supporting details after the main idea?	____	____
8.	Is the ending friendly, courteous and personable?	____	____
Editing Stage			
9.	Is the language clear and concise, and is the message in the appropriate tone?	____	____
10.	Are the format, grammar, punctuation, and spelling correct?	____	____
11.	Are the first and last paragraphs no longer than four lines each?	____	____
12.	Are other paragraphs no longer than eight lines?	____	____

Discussion Questions

1. Why should routine, good news, and goodwill messages be planned and organized carefully?
2. Why is the direct order used in these types of messages?
3. What should make up the supporting information in
   a. an order?
   b. a request?
   c. a "yes" response?
   d. a goodwill message?
4. What types of closings are appropriate for "yes" responses?
5. Which is more commonly used, a form usually entitled "Purchase Order" or an order in the form of a letter or memo? How are these messages similar? How do they differ?
6. In routine and good news messages, where is the main idea placed?
7. How do the various types of goodwill messages differ?
8. Why is an acknowledgment a goodwill message?

Practical Applications

1. Each of the following is an opening sentence for one of the types of direct order messages discussed in this chapter:

   order
   acknowledgment
   request
   claim
   "yes" response

   Indicate the appropriate category for each sentence.

   a. Would you please replace this faulty lock.
   b. I would like to open a charge account with your company.
   c. Enclosed are the brochures that you ordered.
   d. Your account has been adjusted as you requested.
   e. Please send me the items listed below:
   f. Would you please send me information about your health club.
   g. Here are the prints you ordered.
   h. We are most pleased to open a new charge account for you.
   i. Thank you for your order for 12 two-drawer Ez-Clos file cabinets.
   j. Please credit my account for the cost of one 16-oz. container of Restoration Carpet Cleaner.

2. Charles D. Reneau, your immediate supervisor, has asked you for information on the sales of our heating oil for the past two years. He wants the sales totals for bimonthly periods over the past two years. Compose a memo to Mr. Reneau giving him the requested information.

Year	Bimonthly Period	Sales for Period
	January-February	$12,090,857
	March-April	9,459,371
1986	May-June	6,890,142
	July-August	6,450,006
	September-October	7,584,902
	November-December	10,596,857
	January-February	14,785,544
	March-April	10,897,561
1987	May-June	7,005,365
	July-August	7,060,899
	September-October	8,114,353
	November-December	11,253,894

3. Last week you bought a personal computer, monitor, printer, and word-processing package entitled Wordeze from Haynesville Electronic Company in Cleveland, Ohio. After setting up your computer and printer, you discovered that the Wordeze disk was faulty. Write Mr. Delbert C. Huffstikle, the manager, requesting him to replace your faulty Wordeze disk. You are enclosing the faulty disk with this letter. Mr. Huffstikle's address is Haynesville Electronic Company, 8941 Parklane Drive, Cleveland, OH 44134-2761.

4. In the Unison Construction Company, the Purchasing Department buys supplies for all departments. As head of the Department of Sales and Communication, you need to order 24 printer ribbons for your Model #1489 ZornZac printer, two cases of 25-lb. continuous-feed printer paper, and twenty-four 3½-inch disks. Write a memorandum ordering these materials. The memorandum should be sent to Mr. Frank D. Avenelli, supervisor of the Purchasing Department.

5. You are in the process of opening a sporting goods store—Year Round Sporting Goods. Write to Eurre's Wholesale Sporting Goods, Inc., to apply for a charge account. Indicate that an application form has been filled out and is enclosed. Eurre's address is 15385 Southside Circle, St. George, UT 84770-0361.

6. You, your spouse, and your four children—ages 4, 7, 12, and 16—are planning a trip to San Juan, Puerto Rico. Write Don's Travel

Agency, 501 East Brickhaven, Lodgepole, MT 59524-1420. Ask for brochures on Puerto Rico and for information on the costs of round-trip coach airline tickets to and from San Juan. You plan to leave from Missoula, Montana, the first weekend in March and return after a two-week stay.

7. Assume that you are Mr. Frank D. Avenelli (see item #4), the supervisor of the Purchasing Department of Unison Construction Company. Send Carla Jimeson a memorandum telling her that all the supplies she ordered—24 ribbons for a Model #1489 ZornZac printer, two cases of 25-lb. continuous-feed paper, and twenty-four 3½-inch disks—will be delivered tomorrow. Also tell her that 3 dozen TicToc pens with black ink and 6 three-ring binders from a previous order will be delivered at that same time.

8. Compose a letter congratulating a friend on a recent promotion, anniversary, birthday, or another event. If you cannot identify such a friend, write to a fictitious friend.

9. Assume that you are a loan officer for Rockingham First National Bank of Harrisonburg, Virginia. You have received papers requesting a $15,000 home improvement loan from Mr. and Mrs. Anthony Catinia of 439 White Cobblestone Drive, Bridgewater, VA 22812-3735. Write Mr. and Mrs. Catinia, acknowledging the receipt of their application, and explain that it will take about ten days to process their application.

10. Write Mr. and Mrs. Catinia—address given in #9—and tell them that their loan has been approved. Advise them, however, that the loan will not be available until they come in and sign the loan agreement. The agreement must be signed within 14 days. Because they are such a good credit risk, tell them of other loans—car loans, small investment loans, etc.—which are available to them.

11. A month and a half ago, Ms. Parker Johnson, Rte. 1, Box 369, Kranzburg, SD 57245-1642, purchased a Luster-Clean automatic dishwasher, Model #43769. After a short period of use, it developed a small leak at the side of the door. Upon reading the warranty, she realized that the dishwasher was still under the warranty. As Ms. Johnson, write and request that the Greenville Mercantile and Appliance Shop, 496 Woodward Street, Watertown, SD 57201-1574, repair or replace the dishwasher.

12. As the owner of Greenville Mercantile and Appliance Shop, write Ms. Johnson (address is in #11) and tell her that a service technician will come to her home next Thursday morning at ten to repair her dishwasher. Apologize to her for any inconvenience but reassure her of the high quality of the product she purchased. You tried to call Ms. Johnson but her telephone is out of order.

13. Matthew Klein, a co-worker, has just been elected national president of Gamma Alpha Beta, a professional organization of insurance underwriters. Write Matt a memo congratulating him on his election to such a prestigious office. Also invite him to a small social gathering you are having at your home this weekend. Be sure to give him the necessary information.

14. Tu Lang Chong, a foreign student at Follygate College, has written you, the manager of Penny's Fashions, and asked that a charge account be opened for her. Write Ms. Chong and ask her to complete and return the enclosed credit application. Explain to her that it will take about two weeks to process the application. Ms. Chong lives at 4391 South Appleblossom Avenue, Apartment #6, San Jacinto, CA 92383-0413.

15. Write Ms. Chong (see item #14) and tell her the credit application with Penny's Fashions, 391 East Kamala Lane, San Jacinto, CA 92383-0413, has been approved. Her account will have a $500 limit. The interest rate on the unpaid balance at the end of each billing period—30 days—is 18 percent a year.

16. Assume that you and your spouse are nearing retirement and are investigating the possibility of building a winter home in Country Pond Estates, located at 450 North Estate Drive, Leesville, LA 71446-2408. Write Country Pond Estates. Request a map which will show the location, size, and cost of the lots available. Emphasize that you need this information as soon as possible so that the necessary transactions can take place before your retirement arrangements are made.

17. Write a university of your choice and ask them for admission forms, scholarship information, and on-campus housing information.

18. Two months ago, Martha Medford of 312 Highland Drive, Moberly, MO 65270-0807, ordered 50 graduation announcements and envelopes to be printed on off-white parchment paper. They arrived today. They are on standard paper. Martha does not have time to have them reprinted. The announcements and envelopes on parchment cost $25 more than those printed on standard paper. Playing the part of Martha, write and ask the printer for a $25 refund. The printer is A and J Printing, 3785 West Hadley Circle, Beach Haven, NJ 08008-0021. Enclose with the letter a copy of Martha's agreement of purchase.

19. As the manager of A and J Printing, write Ms. Medford (see item #18 for address). Apologize for the error and enclose the refund, a $25 check. Also enclose a catalogue of the products your company prints and sells. Would a discount on her next purchase encourage her to do business with you again?

20. A year ago, July 1, 19--, your city informed you that the street in front of your house was going to be repaved and that each home-owner would be assessed $150—three monthly payments of $50 each to be paid August 1, September 1, and October 1. You have made these payments. Now it is July of the following year and the street has not yet been repaved. Write Mr. Klyde J. Torbusch, City Engineer, City Government Offices, 4973 South Glen Ellyn Drive, your city and ZIP, and ask for an explanation or for a refund.

CHAPTER 19

Bad News Messages

Objectives

After studying this chapter and completing the chapter exercises, you should be able to:

1. Plan bad news messages.
2. Organize bad news messages.
3. Compose bad news messages.

Letters or memos that convey disappointing or unfavorable news are bad news messages. Messages that deny requests, decline to supply information, refuse credit, or reject a proposal are examples of bad news messages. Such messages require careful planning and organizing if the sender is to convey the disappointing news yet still maintain goodwill.

PLANNING THE BAD NEWS MESSAGE

People do not like to receive unfavorable news. When you send a bad news message, therefore, it must be planned carefully. The tone should reflect a sincere concern for the receiver's interests. It is important to convey that you have thoroughly considered the situation and that the unfavorable decision has not been made without careful thought. Your aim is to present the unfavorable news positively and in a manner that the receiver will view as being fair and in the receiver's best interests.

Begin planning the unfavorable message by asking yourself if the receiver is aware of all the facts. Often the receiver does not have a complete understanding of the situation. Should this be the case, there is little hope that the message will be accepted. Next, determine the logical reasons for the refusal or unfavorable news. Finally, identify how the message will ultimately benefit the receiver.

People are not usually convinced by logic alone, however. Most people must first be convinced emotionally before they fully accept a decision. Therefore, the second step in planning a bad news message is to analyze the receiver and determine what factors the receiver values. Focusing on the receiver will enable you to be more empathetic. Consider how you can best present the reasons so that the receiver will view them as being fair and in his or her best interests.

When planning a bad news message, follow the steps outlined in earlier chapters:

- *Identify the objective:* To convey the unfavorable news and maintain good relations.
- *Identify the main idea:* State the refusal in a positive way that reflects the receiver's best interests. The refusal should be an outcome of the supporting information.
- *Determine the supporting information:* Determine what, if any, additional background information may be needed by the receiver, logical reasons for the refusal, and possible benefits to the receiver.
- *Adjust the content to the receiver:* Determine the receiver's values and concerns. Adjust the supporting information accordingly.

• *Select the channel:* Determine whether the message will be sent by letter, memo, telephone call, or in person.

ORGANIZING THE BAD NEWS MESSAGE

Someone once said that we like people who come right out and say what they think—provided they agree with us. When people don't agree with us, however, we generally appreciate a tactful approach. As you learned in Chapter 16, messages that convey unfavorable news are organized in the indirect order. The indirect order presents the reasons or details that explain the unfavorable news before stating the bad news itself. The reasons are presented first to prepare the reader for the unfavorable news. The direct order is used in bad news messages only when the sender knows that the receiver would prefer this approach.

When organizing a message that conveys unfavorable news, follow these steps:

1. Begin with a neutral opener.
2. Explain the reasons for the bad news.
3. State or imply the bad news.
4. End on a positive note and, if possible, offer an alternative suggestion.

Neutral Opening

The objectives of the opening are to establish rapport and to focus the reader's attention on the topic of the message. To establish rapport, the opening paragraph should be neutral, implying neither a positive response nor a negative response. A neutral opener does not mislead the receiver into thinking the response is going to be positive or discourage the person by revealing the bad news right away.

Assume that the sender of the message is writing to refuse a request to serve on a committee. If the sender starts the message with "Serving on such an important committee would be a real pleasure," or "The Improvements Committee is certainly an important committee on which to serve," the implication is that the sender will accept the offer. Such opening statements are misleading. On the other hand, if the sender begins by saying, "I wish I could serve on the Improvements Committee," the sender would be revealing the negative response.

Maintain a positive tone in the opening by avoiding negative words or phrases such as *we are unable, regret to tell you, problem exists,* or *unfortunately.* Instead, use positive words such as *appreciation, agree with you, thank you.* Be careful, however, not to express too much pleasure or you may mislead the receiver.

As well as establishing rapport, the opening should focus the receiver's attention on the topic of the message. It is inappropriate to begin by discussing some unrelated topic. Compare the following openings responding to an application for a charge account from a person who has just moved into the community:

Inappropriate   How do you like living in Palm City?

Appropriate   Thank you for your application for a charge account.

Avoid beginning the letter by referring to the date of the receiver's request. Openings such as "Thank you for your letter of August 10" are overused and do not introduce the topic of the message. A more sincere and positive opener would be "Your application for a charge account received our immediate attention."

✔ Checkpoint 1   NEUTRAL OPENINGS

After reading the situation below and the neutral openings, determine whether they are *good* or *poor*. If you rate the opening as poor, give the reasons.

The Situation: You are a manager for a company that gives seminars on effective business communication. Dr. Reid Carlisle, a professor at Northern State University, has requested techniques for writing good news memorandums. Since your business depends upon teaching such information, you cannot share the techniques.

1. Writing good news memorandums can be an interesting challenge.
2. We only wish we could send you the techniques you requested.
3. I have been asked to respond to your letter of May 15.
4. We were honored that the author of a business communication textbook would ask us for suggestions.
5. I note from the return address that you teach at Northern State University.
6. Writing effective good news memorandums can be demanding.
7. Your request for techniques for writing good news memorandums must be denied.
8. GoodCom Seminars, Inc., always gives the consumer what he or she wants.

Check your answers in Appendix D.

Reasons for the Bad News

The next section of a bad news message presents the reasons for the unfavorable news. This section may be one or two paragraphs, depending upon the complexity of the message. Present the receiver with a logical explanation of why you are unable to grant the request. Keep the message unified by concentrating on one or two main reasons. If possible, emphasize how the decision will ultimately benefit the receiver. In most cases, good decisions benefit both the sender and the receiver. Note how the following example focuses on the best interests of the customer.

> Providing free repair of telephones out of warranty would add greatly to the retail price of our phones. For example, our improved cordless phone, now selling for $79, would have to be priced at $159. Comparable price increases would be necessary for all our models.

Now analyze the following response to a request for a refund on merchandise that was damaged in shipment.

Weak Reasons If we replaced your sprinkler or refunded your money, we would be doing the work of the shipping company, which is responsible for the damage. Write them and ask them to refund your money. They have insurance to cover their costs.

Such a response is not receiver oriented. It is saying, in effect, "The convenience of the company is more important than the inconvenience to the customer." Such messages damage goodwill between a company and its customers. Compare the following response to the previous response. The refusal is customer oriented because it explains how the company's policy assures the customer that he or she will be treated appropriately by the shipping company.

Improved Reasons The company selected to ship our merchandise was chosen carefully. This shipper guarantees its service yet keeps our costs, and therefore your costs, down. The shipping invoice on your sprinkler indicates that it was in working condition when shipped. Thus, you will need to contact the shipping company to replace the sprinkler or refund your money.

Do not use company policy as a basis for denying a request. Although it may be appropriate in some cases to cite company policy, always explain how this policy benefits the receiver. In the previous example, how would the receiver have reacted if the sender had said, "We would like to refund your money, but company policy forbids it"? The receiver would probably decide not to do business with the company again.

✔ Checkpoint 2   REASONS FOR THE BAD NEWS

Using the situation in Checkpoint 1, rank the following as *good* ways or *poor* ways of presenting the reasons for the bad news when writing Dr. Carlisle.

> **The Situation:** You are a manager for a company that gives seminars on effective business communication. Dr. Reid Carlisle, a professor at Northern State University, has requested techniques for writing good news memorandums. Since your business depends upon teaching such information, you cannot share the techniques.

1. Giving you our techniques would decrease our potential profits.
2. The policy of GoodCom Seminars, Inc., forbids us from sharing our techniques.
3. As you may realize, GoodCom Seminars, Inc., is dedicated to helping our customers improve their communication. They invest in us to increase their efficiency and to gain a competitive edge.
4. We have received many requests for the techniques we use in our seminars. After receiving the first few, we realized that sharing our techniques would lower the attendance at our seminars.
5. Requests for techniques on how to write effectively come to us frequently. Because they have come so often, we conducted a study to determine if sharing these techniques affected the attendance at our seminars. We found that sharing did reduce the attendance. Attendance at the seminars is important because it provides the income by which we pay our employees.

Check your answers in Appendix D.

The Bad News

After learning the reasons for the bad news, the receiver should be prepared to receive the refusal itself. If the reasons are logical, the refusal will evolve almost naturally. Soften the bad news by implying it rather than stating it directly. Convey the message quickly, using positive language.

To imply the bad news and to avoid negative words, (1) use the subjunctive mood, (2) use the passive voice, and (3) focus on what you can do rather than what you cannot do.

Subjunctive Mood   If I could, I would send your order today.

Passive Voice	Your order will be sent just as soon as our shipment is received.
Emphasize What Can Be Done	Your order will be sent just as soon as we receive our shipment from our supplier.

Should negative language be unavoidable, avoid the use of personal pronouns (*I, me, my, mine, we, our, ours, us, you, your, yours*). Personal pronouns combined with negative language can be insulting to the receiver. Saying, "Because of the pressure on the staff, the request will have to be denied," has a better tone than saying, "Because of the pressure on our staff, your request must be denied."

✔ Checkpoint 3   THE BAD NEWS

Using the situation in Checkpoint 1, rate the following sentences as *good* or *poor* in conveying the bad news.

The Situation: You are a manager for a company that gives seminars on effective business communication. Dr. Reid Carlisle, a professor at Northern State University, has requested techniques for writing good news memorandums. Since your business depends upon teaching such information, you cannot share the techniques.

1. Your request cannot be granted.
2. If we felt we could share our techniques, we would.
3. We cannot send you our techniques for writing good news memorandums.
4. If you had requested these techniques prior to our research, we might have been able to share them with you.
5. If you would like to enroll in one of our seminars, you will learn our techniques for writing effective good news memorandums.

Check your answers in Appendix D.

Positive Ending

The ending of a bad news message should be as courteous and as helpful as possible. Its purpose is to maintain or rebuild goodwill with the sender. After refusing the receiver's request, it is time to change the emphasis. The message should end on a positive note.

To maintain a positive tone, do not mention or remind the receiver of the bad news again. Do not apologize simply because you cannot accommodate the receiver. If a mistake has not been made, an apology is not appropriate. Should you have made a mistake, however, bury the apology in the middle paragraphs.

To be as helpful as possible, try to offer the receiver another option. Most problem situations have more than one solution. Presenting another option shifts the emphasis from the bad news to a positive solution.

> Since part No. 1403 is no longer being manufactured, part No. 1402 has been used as a substitute. The substitute is $5 cheaper and seems to function just as well as part No. 1403. If you would like to order No. 1402, just call me at 1-800-284-9021. The day you place your order is the day your order will be sent.

In addition to being helpful and positive, the closing should have a sincere tone. Avoid overused endings such as "If there is anything I can do, please don't hesitate to ask." Avoid conditional words such as *hope, think,* and *maybe.* Analyze the poor endings that follow.

Reminder of the Negative News	Even though we cannot fill your order, we have enclosed our newest catalogue.
Apology	I'm sorry that we cannot fill your order, but we have enclosed our newest catalogue.
Overused Expression	Even though we cannot fill your order, if there is anything I can do, please let me know.

If the receiver is a customer, it is often appropriate to end the message with a soft sale by mentioning a related product, a discount available, or some other relevant item that would be of interest to the receiver. A better ending than those in the previous examples would be, "Enclosed is our newest catalogue. Note that some of our materials are reduced by as much as 50 percent."

✔ Checkpoint 4   ENDINGS

Determine whether the following ending paragraphs are *good* or *poor.* If the ranking is poor, indicate the reason.

The Situation: You are a manager for a company that gives seminars on effective business communication. Dr. Reid Carlisle, a professor at Northern State University, has requested techniques for writing good news memorandums. Since your business depends upon teaching such information, you cannot share the techniques.

1. Dr. Carlisle, would you like to enroll in one of our effective communication seminars? A listing of the times and places of the seminars in your area is enclosed.

2. I hope this response meets with your satisfaction.

3. I am sorry we will not be able to respond to your request as you would have liked.

4. Dr. Carlisle, several companies might share the techniques they use. Have you tried SITCOM Co. or LITCOM, Inc.? Their addresses are enclosed.

5. As you may know, our seminars are very effective. Enroll in one of these and you not only will learn the techniques but will also gain insights into the techniques themselves. Enclosed is an enrollment card and a coupon for a 20 percent discount when you enroll.

Check your answers in Appendix D.

WRITING BAD NEWS MESSAGES

Following are examples of typical bad news messages: declining a request and refusing credit.

Declining a Request

The reasons for declining the request are the most important aspect of the message. The success of the message depends upon whether the receiver judges these reasons to be valid. Based on the situation explained in earlier checkpoints, the following letter is an example of an effective message denying a request.

Neutral Beginning	Writing effective good news memorandums can be demanding.
Reasons for the Bad News	Requests for techniques on writing effectively are frequently sent to us. Therefore, we conducted a study to determine if sharing these techniques with the public affected attendance at our seminars. We found that it did. Attendance at the seminars is important because it provides the income by which we pay
The Bad News	our employees. If you had requested these techniques prior to our research, we might have been able to share them with you.

Ending (Soft Sale)	Dr. Carlisle, as you may know, our seminars are very effective. Enroll in one of them and you not only will learn the techniques themselves but will also gain insights into how to use them. Enclosed is an enrollment card and a coupon for a 20 percent discount when you enroll.

While the above letter says "No" to Dr. Carlisle, it would not damage the goodwill between Dr. Carlisle and the company. Contrast the following poor example of a bad news message. If you were Dr. Carlisle, how would this letter affect you?

Overused, Trite Opening	Thank you for your letter of April 19, 19--. It was most welcome.
Reasons for the Bad News	It has taken us years to develop our techniques for the teaching of skillful writing. The work has been long and hard, but we were willing to pay the price. Other companies may give out their techniques; however, we do not.
Weak Ending	You may wish to contact other companies. Perhaps they will give you a positive response to your request. If they do not, maybe you would be interested in one of our seminars. We will be in your area on June 29. Hope to hear from you soon.

To most of us, this letter would be offensive. The reasons given for the rejection are not receiver oriented and are stated in a negative way. Consequently, the letter is not likely to achieve its objective—that of maintaining Dr. Carlisle's goodwill or of motivating him to enroll in a seminar.

Refusing Credit

Credit may be refused for one of several reasons. The credit application may contain incomplete information or insufficient credit references. The references may not be verifiable or they may be negative. The employment record may not be strong enough or verifiable. The person may have excessive debt obligations, delinquent credit obligations, or insufficient income.

If credit must be refused, the receiver has a right to know why. It is the sender's responsibility to explain the reason(s) tactfully. If the message is written carelessly, the potential customer may be lost. The goal is to refuse credit but to maintain the person as a cash customer. Study the following example.

Neutral Beginning	Thank you for your order for Stonecut Flooring. You have certainly selected a quality product that is extremely durable.

Reasons for the Bad News the Bad News, and an Alternative	Your credit application has been reviewed. As you know, financial experts suggest that individuals maintain an income-to-debt ratio of about 3 to 1. Because your obligations extend beyond one third of your income, we suggest making a cash purchase.
Helpful Ending	Please let us know whether you wish to place a cash order now. In addition to flooring, we have many other quality products for your home at low, discounted prices. As a cash customer, you will receive the same quality merchandise, courtesy, and low prices.

The following rejection of a request for credit could be offensive.

Neutral Beginning	Your application for credit has been considered.
Reasons for the Bad News	Upon examining your credit situation, we found that you have extended your credit to the limit. Therefore, we must reject your application. To give you credit at this time would be unwise.
Ending	I'm sorry we have to refuse your request, but we must. Enclosed is our most recent catalogue. Maybe you would like to purchase some of these products with cash.

While the beginning of this letter is neutral, the reasons for the bad news are not tactfully presented. Negative language (the words *reject* and *unwise*) is used when saying "No." The ending should not include an apology, and even though it does offer an alternative, its tone is harsh.

The checklist in Figure 19-1 on page 282 will help you to compose effective bad news messages. The planning stage, the writing stage, and the editing stage are emphasized. The planning stage will help you to identify the appropriate content of the message. The writing stage will help you select effective language for the message and place the content in an appropriate order. The editing stage will help you to detect errors that may have been made when writing.

SUMMARY

Effective bad news messages convey disappointing news without losing the receiver's goodwill. These messages are written in the indirect order. The opening paragraph introduces the topic of the message in a neutral manner. The next part of the message gives the reasons for the bad news and prepares the receiver for the coming bad news. The bad news itself should be presented using positive language, if possible. The closing of a bad news message should be helpful and friendly, aiming to rebuild or maintain goodwill.

FIGURE 19-1   Checklist for Bad News Messages

	Planning Stage	**Yes**	**No**
1.	Have I identified the objective of the message?	____	____
2.	Have I identified the main idea of the message?	____	____
3.	Have I identified the supporting details needed by the receiver?	____	____
4.	Have I adjusted the main idea and supporting details to the receiver?	____	____

	Writing Stage		
5.	Is the beginning neutral and does it introduce the topic of the message?	____	____
6.	Does the supporting information focus on one or two "you" oriented reasons for the bad news?	____	____
7.	When giving the bad news, have I used positive language?	____	____
8.	When giving the bad news, have I used the subjunctive mood or the passive voice (if possible)?	____	____
9.	When giving the bad news, have I told the receiver what could be done rather than what couldn't?	____	____
10.	Is the ending helpful and courteous? (Including a soft sale is appropriate in a letter to a customer.)	____	____
11.	Does the ending offer an alternative if possible, contain no apology, and avoid reminders of the bad news?	____	____

	Editing Stage		
12.	Is the language clear and concise? Is the tone positive?	____	____
13.	Are the format, grammar, punctuation, and spelling correct?	____	____

Discussion Questions

1. What should a sender do in order to plan an effective bad news message?
2. Why should the beginning of a bad news message be neutral?
3. What are the purposes of the first paragraph of the bad news message?
4. What are the purposes of the supporting information in a bad news message?
5. Is company policy a good reason for saying "No"? Justify your answer.
6. How should the sender state the bad news itself?
7. Name three techniques that can be used to soften the bad news.
8. When should an apology be included in a bad news message, and where should it be placed?

Practical Applications

1. Indicate whether the following beginnings are *good* or *poor*.
   a. Rather than return the form you sent with the request to participate in the study, I am writing to tell you why we will not participate.
   b. Thank you for your letter of August 15, 19--.
   c. Thank you for the letter about your charge account.
   d. Your letter of March 31 is sincerely appreciated.
   e. If your latest payment had been sent on time, we would not have had to write you about it.
2. Rate the following reasons for bad news as *good* or *poor*. If the reason is poorly presented, indicate why.
   a. At the fair, we had to charge you for the booth *because we had to pay the extra help we had to hire in the custodial department.*
   b. *To keep your booth at the fair clean,* it was necessary to hire extra help in the custodial department.
   c. I wish we could send a replacement or a refund, *but company policy forbids it.*
   d. *To provide you with a one-day turnaround,* it was necessary to charge you for the alterations.
   e. *Since your reservations were not cancelled within the set amount of time,* we cannot give you a refund.

3. Rewrite the following to soften the bad news by using the technique listed.

Using the Subjunctive Mood

a. I can't attend the sales meeting because I will be in Chicago at a conference on computer development.

b. Because of budget costs in our department, I cannot let you purchase new furniture for your office.

c. Since your scores on the aptitude tests were so low, we cannot let you into our graduate programs.

Using the Passive Voice

a. Because of the large enrollment, we are unable to reserve a room for you at the hotel where the conference is being held; we have reserved a room for you at the Salter Hotel instead.

b. Because of the amount of art work to be done, we won't have the advertising campaign ready on schedule. It won't be ready until May 19.

c. Because the bid of Toby's Marine Company, Inc., was better than ours, we lost the contract.

Indicating What You Can Do

a. I'm sorry we won't be able to send your personal computer until June 15.

b. I can't start studying for the exam at two o'clock as originally planned. I won't be able to start until eight that evening.

c. I won't arrive in New Orleans until 7 p.m. Thursday because of scheduling difficulties.

4. Indicate the strengths and weaknesses of the following letter:

April 4, 19--

Ms. Tonya J. Leppard
4986 North Magnolia Street
Hampton, SC 29924-0274

Dear Ms. Leppard

Thank you for your letter concerning the warranty on your tape recorder. You are right; the warranty is for six months.

Because you purchased the tape recorder over a year ago, the warranty has expired and the cost of repair will not be covered by the warranty. Generally, however, repairs of this nature are not costly.

To have your tape recorder repaired, please send it to our Repair Department, Attention Mr. Dickerson. We will send an estimate to you within two weeks after the recorder reaches us.

Sincerely yours

Derek Parker
Manager

5. Mr. Cleveland White of 4489 East Prospect Street, Sierra Vista, AZ 85635-0095, has written you to order a book entitled *Working with a Suspect Personal Computer*. He has enclosed a check for $15.95. Unfortunately, the book is out of stock. Write the customer and tell him that the book is out of stock until your next shipment arrives on July 14. You will hold his check until you ship the book.

6. One of your salespeople, Mrs. Torina Hayes, has asked for permission to miss the annual sales meeting in St. Paul this summer. Because many new products are being introduced at this meeting and you do not want to set a precedent of representatives missing such conferences, write to tell her that she cannot be excused from attending the meeting. She works in the Hanford Branch Office in the Sales Department, Hanford, CA 93230-8703.

7. Yesterday you received a request from Mr. Tony Pasqual for spare parts for a 1960 22-inch lawn mower. Unfortunately, you no longer make spare parts for this mower—you stock spare parts up to 19 years. To stock spare parts for all lawn mowers would mean raising the retail prices of your mowers and parts. Write a letter to Mr. Pasqual, 825 Northern Boulevard, Logan, UT 84321-9998, explaining your position.

8. Mr. T. J. Sarter, 6894 North Alexia Avenue, Mount Vernon, WA 98273-9998, bought a pair of slacks from your department at Goldson Clothiers. All of the slacks are unhemmed and are altered to fit the customer. After Mr. Sarter had the slacks altered, he decided they were the wrong color. He has sent back the slacks and asked for a refund. As manager of the Men's Clothing Department, write and refuse his request.

9. As the person responsible for reserving meeting rooms, you often receive requests for their use. The head of the Department of Research, Dr. Gary Orr, has sent you a memo requesting to use Conference Room 215 on the second floor for a meeting of 30 people on May 5 from 8:30 a.m. until 4:30 p.m. The conference room is not available; however, Conference Room 415 on the fourth floor and

Conference Room 515 on the fifth floor are currently available. Both of these rooms seat about 30 people. Write Dr. Orr a memo telling him that Conference Room 215 is already reserved and suggest the alternative rooms.

10. John Hammond, the head of the Accounting Department, has requested ten boxes of 3½-inch disks and other items. Unfortunately, your supply of 3½-inch disks is depleted, but you have the other supplies he ordered. Write John and tell him that you have sent the other items but will not have any 3½-inch disks until Monday, when a new shipment is due.

11. As credit manager for Wentworth Foods, Inc., write Mrs. Tobias DeVille, 3781 Birch Lane, New Haven, CT 06513-1413, and refuse her request for credit. At present, she has many charge accounts and has charged them to their limits. It is questionable whether she would be able to make the payments if you allowed her additional credit.

12. While attending your school, Brad Oakley used the placement office in an effort to obtain a job. When he filled out the forms to request references, he indicated on each form that the reference would be kept confidential. This would be evident to anyone who completed a reference form for Brad. Now Brad has written the placement office asking for a complete copy of his file, including the completed reference forms. As director of the placement office, write Brad and tell him that you will send him a copy of all the material in his file except the reference forms. Releasing the completed forms to Brad would be disclosing information that respondents had been told would be kept confidential. Brad lives at 1396 Turion Drive, Mill City, OR 97360-0442.

13. Mr. Tink Anderson, vice president of Human Resources, has sent you a copy of a proposal for a new company policy. The proposal strongly discourages employees from working overtime. After discussing the proposal with the leaders of your department, you are against the proposal. It would have a very negative impact on the wage earners in the department, who are currently earning less than average for the region. Send Mr. Anderson a memo informing him of your position.

14. Mrs. Suzanne Callings, president of the local chapter of the American Rose Association, has asked you to speak to the chapter at the next meeting, Tuesday, April 19, at 6:30 p.m. in the Golden Room of the Medias Hotel in Robbinsdale. Unfortunately, you already have a commitment that evening and will not be able to speak. Write to Mrs. Callings at 592 East Briarhill Drive, Robbinsdale, MN 55422-0001, and tell her that you won't be able to speak. Sug-

gest, however, that you might be able to speak at the May or June meetings.

15. Dr. Clyde Hester, a researcher at the Utopia Research Institution, 935 West Bengal Junction, Yankton, SD 57078-0135, has asked for the names and addresses of 250 of our stockholders. Company policy forbids giving others the names and addresses of our stockholders. The company has the policy because revealing such information could result in a lawsuit against the company. Write Dr. Hester and refuse his request.

16. Ashad Moshua of 218 East Park Avenue, Aurora, IL 60505-6131, a recent immigrant to this country, has sent you a credit application. Write Mr. Moshua and refuse his request because of his lack of credit references.

17. Mr. Alex Travino of 1704 Londonerry Drive, San Lorenzo, PR 00754-0001, has written asking that his shares of common stock in your company be converted to preferred stock. The conversion basis would be 2 to 1—two shares of common stock for one of preferred. Even though the conversion would be financially advantageous for the company, write Mr. Travino explaining that the company cannot convert the shares. To do this is against the policy of the Securities and Exchange Commission. Suggest that he contact his local stockbroker and make the conversion in the market.

18. Mr. Tony Dunhill had us prepare and print a resume for him. The resume was printed exactly as he gave it to us. When asked to proofread it, he failed to correct a mistake in the address of a past employer, and the resume was printed with the mistake. Now he has asked for a refund. As manager of A & J Printing, write Mr. Dunhill, 701 South 15th Avenue, Red Bank, TN 37415-0551, and refuse his request.

19. Eight months ago, Ms. Sally Rodgers, Rte. 3, Box 121, Rock Springs, WY 82901-0021, purchased a SilverMaster toaster. Now she has written you, the manager of the store at which she made the purchase, to say that the toaster is not working properly and to ask for a replacement. Unfortunately, the toaster is out of warranty, so you cannot grant her request. Write her and refuse her request. Suggest that she send the toaster in for repairs.

CHAPTER 20

Persuasive Messages

Objectives

After studying this chapter and completing the chapter exercises, you should be able to:

1. Plan a persuasive message.
2. Organize a persuasive message.
3. Compose a persuasive message.

288

Persuasive messages are designed to motivate the receiver to act in a certain way. Persuasive messages may attempt to convince the receiver to buy a product or a service, to do a favor, or to change an opinion. Sales letters, requests for special favors, and collection letters are examples of persuasive messages. When developing such a message, use the psychology of persuasion to plan and organize it.

PLANNING PERSUASIVE MESSAGES

Some experts estimate that selling consists of 90 percent planning and only 10 percent presentation. Constructing persuasive messages is similar to selling. Careful planning is required if the receiver is to act on your idea or buy your product.

At the planning stage, it is best to assume that the receiver will be uninterested in or resistant to the persuasive message. Why? Because most business people are extremely busy. Managers and executives typically work many more than 40 hours a week. Their resources of time, money, and energy are limited. The challenge of a persuasive letter is to overcome the barriers caused by lack of resources, resistance to change, or satisfaction with present conditions. To overcome these barriers, you must understand the psychology of persuasion.

People are not persuaded to buy a product or accept an idea just because it has several good features. People are persuaded because they feel a real or perceived need for the product or idea. Although needs vary somewhat among individuals, they often are linked to achievement, recognition, or money.

To successfully persuade the receiver, the sender must first analyze the receiver to determine the person's needs or viewpoints. Keeping the receiver in mind, the sender then determines the main feature of the product or idea that will appeal to the receiver. Finally, and most important, the sender must then convert this main idea into benefits for the receiver. A benefit to one person, however, may not be a benefit to another. Apply the psychology of selling as you follow the steps in planning a persuasive message.

Identify the Objective

The sender's objective in writing a persuasive message is generally very easy to identify. For example, the objective may be to motivate the receiver to buy a product or a service, to share information, to assist with a project, to contribute money, or to cooperate with a decision.

Analyze the Receiver

People are motivated to make a purchase or accept an idea when they are convinced that the product, service, or idea meets one or more of their needs. If these needs are of a monetary nature, saving money may be of prime importance to the receiver. On the other hand, recognition, prestige, comfort, convenience, or physical well-being may be more important.

To discover the receiver's specific needs and the benefits the receiver hopes to obtain from your idea or product requires being empathetic. You must be sincerely concerned about the interests and needs of the receiver.

Analyze the receiver and determine as best you can the characteristics or values that are important to the receiver. Is the receiver interested in status? comfort? convenience? What benefits will appeal to the receiver— price? quality? speed? Is the receiver concerned about income? education? security? The more you can discover about the receiver, the better you can translate the features of the product or idea into benefits for the receiver.

Select the Primary Appeal

Identify the main idea by determining what will most appeal to the receiver. Although several appeals could be used, determine the one that will both attract the receiver's attention and motivate the receiver to act. In a sales letter the primary appeal is often referred to as the main selling point. The primary appeal, like the main idea of a good news message, is the focus of a persuasive message.

If the objective of the letter is to convince the receiver to pay an overdue account, the primary appeal might be maintaining the person's excellent credit rating. If you know that the receiver always waits until the last minute to re-order merchandise, the primary appeal could be fast delivery.

Identify the Supporting Information

Once you have established the primary appeal (main idea), brainstorm the idea to determine what information is necessary to effectively explain or reinforce it. Determine how the features can be expressed as benefits to the receiver. For example, if the primary appeal is the receiver's interest in quality merchandise, the supporting information should provide convincing details that will influence the receiver to buy the product because of its high quality. By developing the main idea through supporting information, the sender creates an interest in and a desire for the product or idea.

ORGANIZING PERSUASIVE MESSAGES

Persuasive messages use the indirect order—the supporting information is followed by the action you want the receiver to take. By using the indirect approach, we prepare the receiver for the main message before presenting it. Though you may not have thought about it, we normally use this approach in our persuasive messages.

For example, if you wanted to borrow $100 from a friend, how would you do it? Most of us would explain the purpose of the loan before we asked for the money. By the time we arrived at the point of asking for the money, our friend would probably be anticipating what we are going to ask.

Follow these steps when presenting persuasive messages:

1. Get the attention of the receiver.
2. Present the supporting information.
3. Present the main idea.
4. End by explaining the desired action.

Attention-getting Openings

The purpose of the opening paragraph is to get the receiver's attention so that the receiver will read or listen to the rest of the communication. The opening paragraph should introduce the topic of the message in a manner that is interesting, original, and relevant to the reader. The tone should be positive, sincere, honest, and "you" oriented.

Gain attention by using one of the following types of openings:
- Propose a solution to the receiver's problem.
- Provide a bargain.
- Present an important fact.
- Quote a famous or respected person.
- Make an analogy.
- Present a "what if" situation.
- List an outstanding feature of the product or service.

Compare the following attention getters for a letter requesting a prominent speaker to address a conference:

WEAK   I am looking for someone to address the Association of Small Businesses next month. I know you are busy, but would you be our speaker?

IMPROVED   The head of the Department of Commerce has said, "Without small businesses, America would be out of work. Nearly half of all new jobs are created by businesses with fewer than 100 employees."

The first opening is weak because it reflects the sender's needs rather than the interests of the receiver, and it has a negative tone. The second opening uses a quote to gain the receiver's attention. It introduces the topic in an interesting, original manner.

This discussion of openings assumes that the persuasive message is unsolicited—that is, the receiver is not expecting the message. If the message is solicited, the interest of the receiver has already been established, so attention-getting techniques are not as critical.

✔ Checkpoint 1   ATTENTION-GETTING OPENINGS

As a recruiter for a university, assume that you are writing a recruit who wants to major in some area in the College of Business. Classify the following attention getters as *good* or *poor*.

1. Fully accredited and highly respected—these two phrases describe the College of Business at Morganton University.

2. Your letter of November 19 is sincerely appreciated.

3. Our business programs at Morganton University are absolutely fantastic.

4. Dr. Harry Trumbull said, "My undergraduate degree in the College of Business at Morganton University prepared me well for my graduate degrees at Harvard."

5. Of the top 30 business colleges in the United States, Morganton University is ranked fourth.

Supporting Information

After gaining the attention of the reader, the next part of the message should create an interest in the main idea. The sender must convince the receiver that the main idea satisfies the receiver's particular needs. The benefits of the main selling point determined during the planning stage become the focus of the message.

Interest and Desire

Persuasion is not possible unless the receiver is first interested in the product or idea. Once interested, the receiver must have a desire for the product or idea. Generally in a business message, little distinction is made between interest and desire. The sender merely attempts to focus on what the receiver considers to be important or what most nearly meets the receiver's needs.

To create interest and desire, explain how the product or idea will be of value to the receiver. Perhaps it will save the receiver money, increase the receiver's self-esteem, gain the approval of the receiver's peers, and so forth. The supporting paragraphs should be "you" oriented and positive. Note how the following letter appeals to the receiver's need for professionalism.

> Each year about 250 professionals from all over the world attend the Conference of Small Businesses. This conference is recognized for its prominent speakers in the areas of small business management, creative financing, and computer technology. Speakers obtain international exposure and have an opportunity to share their knowledge with those who benefit most from it. Because of your expertise in the use of computer applications for the small business, we would like you to be one of our speakers.

One way to create desire is to involve the receiver's senses. For example, real estate agents may suggest to clients who are selling their houses that they bake an apple pie, toast bread, or warm some vanilla extract and water in the oven just before a prospective buyer is expected. These pleasant aromas appeal to a buyer's desire for a homey atmosphere. In written persuasive messages, writers must depend upon words to excite the senses. Active verbs, specific details, and descriptive modifiers excite the senses and show enthusiasm, as illustrated in the following example.

> As you walk into the store, you'll see signs telling you of discounts ranging from 50 to 75 percent off all spring and summer suits. Imagine yourself in that cool, comfortable summer suit with that complementary tie—the only way to go to work on these hot summer days. Both can easily be yours for 90 cents per summer day.

To create interest and desire, the sender must remove obstacles or objections that the receiver may have. This principle is often applied when stating amounts of money. Research shows that people are more likely to buy a product if its price is stated as pennies a day rather than a dollar a week, a dollar a day rather than $30 a month, and $30 a month rather than $365 a year. Why? The lesser amounts sound easier to manage. Note the previous example; the summer suit and matching tie sell for about $81, but "90 cents per summer day" makes payment sound easy.

Conviction

Often an explanation of the benefits is enough to convince the receiver to act. In other situations, however, it may be advantageous to actually provide proof that your idea or product is of value. Such proofs add credibility. Findings of research, statements of satisfaction from customers, names of prominent persons or institutions that use the product, and free samples are examples of proofs. To add credibility, proofs must be specific and as concrete as possible.

Checkpoint 2 SUPPORTING INFORMATION

Below are some paragraphs which attempt to create desire for action. Rank them as *good* or *poor*. If you rated a paragraph as poor, indicate why.

1. Free and young, as the wind blows through your hair—what a great feeling! And it can be you driving that Nimco convertible sports car. All this can be yours for under $10 a day.

2. Because of your wide and varied experience as an administrator in secondary schools, we would like you to address the district's annual meeting of school principals.

3. Because of the tremendous experiences you had on your first and only tour of Russia, we would like to invite you, a real, up-to-date expert, to speak to our social studies class at Hillburn High School.

4. Daytona Beach is the place to be during your spring break. Even while in your room you'll hear the ocean waves breaking on the beach. Yes, you and your friends can stay in rooms next to the beach. For pennies a night you stay in luxury yet can be within steps of the beach.

5. The cost of your subscription to *The Top of the World* is now lower than ever before. This wonderful magazine is pure reading excitement. Order your subscription today for only $36 a year.

Action Endings

After convincing the receiver of the value of your idea or product, the next step is to get action. The ending should reinforce the main idea (or benefit) and indicate the action to be taken.

The action requested should be simple and easy to accomplish. The most common ways to request action are to ask the receiver to telephone or to return a form. Figure 20-1 shows a form that could be enclosed with the letter. If the receiver is to telephone, be sure to include the correct number and area code.

To order your Label Quality all-leather shoes for only $24.75 a pair, just call our toll-free number:

1-800-247-7356

You'll be wearing your new shoes in less than a week.

FIGURE 20-1   Order Form

NAME _____ DATE _____

ADDRESS _____

CITY _____ STATE _____ ZIP _____

SHOE SIZE: 6   6½   7   7½
              8   8½   9   9½
             10   10½   11   11½
             12   12½   13   13½

SHOE WIDTH: A   B   C   D   E   EE   EEE   EEEE

STYLE NUMBER: 127-45   127-57   127-69   134-45   134-57   134-69

COLOR: Brown _____   Tan _____   Burgundy _____

PAYMENT   ☐ AEC   ☐ Century   ☐ Check/Money Order
          ☐ Bill me

ACCOUNT # _____ EXPIRATION DATE _____

SIGNATURE _____

If the receiver is to return a form, it should be accessible and easy to fill out. The form should be attached to or enclosed with the message. A form that folds into an envelope, already addressed with return postage prepaid, or a separate envelope should be provided if possible. The following message provides the receiver with a choice—telephoning or returning the order form.

> To order your Label Quality all-leather shoes for only $24.75 a pair, either call our toll-free number:
>
> 1-800-247-7356
>
> or fill in and return the enclosed form. After we receive your order, you'll be wearing your new shoes in less than a week.

✔Checkpoint 3   ACTION ENDINGS

Below are some endings for persuasive messages. Rate each of them *good* or *poor*. If you rate an ending as poor, indicate why you gave it such a rating.

1. Just send us a self-addressed envelope with the total payment, and we'll send your order as soon as possible.
2. Fill out the enclosed, addressed, postage-paid form, and your order will be sent to you the same day we receive it.
3. Take advantage of this great sale. We hope to receive your order soon.
4. Call 1-800-254-9063 to give us the size and color you want, and we'll ship your blouse(s) to you today.
5. Jim, we would love to have you address our annual banquet, but we know that you are very busy.

WRITING PERSUASIVE MESSAGES

Examples of persuasive messages are sales messages, special requests, and collection letters.

Sales Messages

The objective of a sales message is to motivate the receiver to buy a product or a service. Follow the steps in organizing a persuasive message discussed previously:

- Gain attention in the opener.
- Create interest and desire and convince the receiver with supporting details.
- Provide incentive for the receiver to act.

The objective of the following persuasive message is to motivate the receiver to purchase shoes. The main idea or primary benefit emphasized is comfort. Findings from research are included to convince the receiver of the value of these shoes. The ending makes it easy for the receiver to order the shoes.

Attention-getting Opening	On your feet for eight hours but not foot-weary...what a great way to end the day!!! This can describe you at the end of your day's work.
Supporting Information	Through research and exacting development, a shoe with shock-absorbing features has been developed and tested. Surveys were conducted with doctors and nurses who were continually on their feet during their workdays.
	Over 80 percent of those doctors and nurses surveyed stated that, at the end of their workdays, they were not foot-weary.
Action Ending	As an introductory offer, these Quality Label all-leather shoes are priced at only $24.95 a pair. To order your shoes, just call this toll-free number

1-800-247-7653

or fill in the enclosed self-addressed, postage-prepaid form. You'll be wearing your new shoes within the week and enjoying new freedom from tired feet.

Special Requests

In special requests, the sender is asking the receiver to do something beyond what would normally be expected. Examples of special requests include requests for donations, requests to serve on a committee which will take a lot of time, and special claims letters. Following is a well-written request for a claim. Notice that the sender builds a case through supporting information.

Attention-getting Opening	*Stay Well Medicine* is an excellent magazine that provides practical tips on preventive medicine.
Supporting Information	After reading *Stay Well Medicine* at our library, I realized that I wanted my own copy and immediately subscribed. Because the advertising literature stated that two months should be allowed for the subscription to start, I purchased the May and June issues locally. Needless to say, I was surprised when the May and June issues arrived with the July issue.

Action Ending	Enclosed are the May and June issues you sent. Would you please adjust the time period of my subscription to cover July through June of next year.

Following is a special claims letter that is not well written. It is not "you" oriented, and its tone is harsh and condescending.

> I just started my subscription to *Stay Well Medicine* and already there is a problem.
>
> I filed my subscription with you on May 5. After learning from your ads that I should allow two months for delivery, I immediately purchased the May and June issues. Now you have sent me the May and June issues with my July issue. My subscription starts with the July issue.
>
> Enclosed are the May and June issues you sent. Adjust the time period of my subscription to cover July through June of next year. Thank you.

Collection Letters

Most people pay their bills when they are due. However, a few don't. The purpose of a collection letter is to get the receiver to pay a past-due bill. To collect overdue payments, a four-stage process is generally used. The stages are (1) the reminder stage, (2) the strong reminder stage, (3) the discussion stage, and (4) the urgency stage.

The purpose of the reminder stage is to jog the receiver's memory. This stage assumes that the receiver has just forgotten to make a payment. A message is sent as a reminder. This letter is assumed to be a routine request, so it is written using the direct order. The following is a good reminder-stage collection letter:

Opening	Your prompt payments for all of 19-- are greatly appreciated.
Main Idea	Enclosed is a copy of your January statement. Did you overlook your February 10 payment?
Helpful Ending	A self-addressed, postage-paid envelope is enclosed for your convenience in sending in your payment.

A strong reminder is sent when the customer has, for some reason, failed to respond to the first reminder. The tone of this collection message is direct and firm—send the payment due right away.

Main Idea	Enclosed is a copy of your January statement. Your February 10 payment is overdue.
Supporting Information	By sending us a check for $350, you will bring your account up to date, and you will preserve your credit rating.
Helpful Ending	A postage-paid, return envelope is enclosed. Please use it and clear your account today.

The purpose of the discussion-stage collection message is to obtain full payment, partial payment as a temporary measure, or an explanation of why the customer has not made the appropriate payments.

Attention-getting Opening	Your home loan with First Western Bank has been beneficial to both of us. In the past, your payments have been prompt and consistent. In fact, you have been one of our best customers.
Supporting Information	Two months have passed, however, since your last payment. Although you have received two reminders, we have not received a reply. Is there some reason why you are unable to make a payment?
Action Ending	Preserve your credit rating by following one of these steps.

1. Make your past-due payments totaling $700 within ten days.
2. Send us one payment ($350) immediately and the other payment by March 30.
3. Let us know why you have not made your last two payments, and explain your plans for correcting the situation.

Please let me have your response within one week.

The purpose of the urgency-stage collection message is to obtain payment and advise the receiver of the consequences if payment is not made. The tone of this message should be strong and firm.

Attention-getting Opening	I wish this letter were not necessary, but it is. Previous messages and efforts to obtain past-due payments have failed.
Supporting Information	The enclosed statement explains the exact amount due. Unless full payment is received by April 30, your account will be turned over to the Edwards Credit Agency, a collection company.
Action Ending	To prevent this negative situation, send us your full payment immediately.

See Figure 20-2 for a checklist for persuasive messages. It emphasizes the planning, writing, and editing stages of the message. Use it to create effective persuasive messages.

SUMMARY

Messages designed to motivate the receiver to act in a certain way are known as persuasive messages. To motivate the reader to take the desired action, persuasive messages are organized in the indirect order. Examples of persuasive messages include sales messages, special requests, and collection messages.

FIGURE 20-2 Checklist for Persuasive Messages

Planning Stage	Yes	No
1. Have I identified the objective of the message?	____	____
2. Have I identified the primary appeal (main idea) of the message?	____	____
3. Have I identified the supporting information?	____	____
4. Have I adjusted the main idea and supporting information to the receiver?	____	____

Writing Stage

	Yes	No
5. Is the opener		
a. sincere?	____	____
b. relevant to the receiver?	____	____
c. original?	____	____
d. pertinent to the message?	____	____
e. positive?	____	____
6. Is the supporting information based on the needs of the receiver? "you" oriented? Does the supporting information motivate the receiver?	____	____
7. If action is required, does the ending explain that action clearly? Is it simple to execute?	____	____

Editing Stage

	Yes	No
8. Is the language clear and concise, and is the letter positive and "you" oriented?	____	____
9. Are the format, grammar, punctuation, and spelling correct?	____	____
10. Does the message have unity, coherence, and proper emphasis?	____	____

A persuasive message consists of three parts: (a) an attention-getting opening, (b) the supporting information, and (c) an action ending. The objective of the opener is to gain the interest of the receiver. The next section of the message attempts to create desire and convince the receiver that the product or idea has value. The action ending should reinforce the main idea and request action from the receiver. The action to be taken by the receiver should be easy to understand and execute.

 **Communication Activities**

Discussion Questions

1. Summarize the four steps in planning a persuasive message.
2. Why is the indirect order used in persuasive messages?
3. What does the opening of a persuasive message attempt to do?
4. What are some of the techniques that can be used to develop effective openings?
5. What is the purpose of the supporting information in a persuasive message? How is the supporting information related to the main idea?
6. If a persuasive message requires action on the part of the receiver, how can the sender enhance the possibility that the receiver will do what is asked?
7. Give three examples of persuasive messages.
8. What are the four stages generally used in collection messages? What is the purpose of each stage?

Practical Applications

1. Below are some attention getters for persuasive messages. Rate them as *good* or *poor*. If you rate them as poor, indicate why.

   The Situation: As vice president of sales, you are forming a team of fellow workers to identify strategies which will improve sales. You want to persuade Mike Seal, a young, talented new employee in the production department, to become part of the team.

   a. Thank you for your memorandum of October 15.
   b. If I were you, I would take advantage of this fantastic offer. It is the chance of a lifetime.
   c. Mike, your expertise and fresh ideas would be very helpful for improving our sales techniques.
   d. Fresh ideas and enthusiasm are important ingredients when trying to improve the company's sales.

2. The goal of the following paragraphs is to create desire. Analyze and rate them as *good* or *poor*. If you rate them as poor, indicate why you have given them such a rating.

The Situation: A local company wants to computerize its accounting system. They have narrowed the choices of systems down to the one you are attempting to sell them — the EZE System — and a competitor's system — the Accounting Club.

a. When you sit down to store your records, you won't have to get out a manual to determine how the system stores your records. The EZE System is user friendly. To store accounts receivable data, simply strike the accounts receivable function key, key the name of the account, and enter the data for each entry.

b. The EZE System for record keeping is very user friendly. It will make your record keeping easy and simple. This fantastic system is sweeping the country, and firm after firm is adopting it for its record keeping activities.

c. Sit down at your computer, put in the EZE System, strike the appropriate function key, and enter the account name and data for each transaction — you have just recorded accounts receivable entries. Yes, this system is just that user friendly. Even if you are not a heavy computer user, you will find this system ideal for keeping your accounts.

3. Analyze the following endings designed to attain action. Rate them as *good* or *poor*. If you rate them as poor, indicate why.

The Situation: As sales manager for the Elegant Figurine Company, you are writing a sales letter to be enclosed with a brochure showing three porcelain figurines.

a. To order your figurines, just write or call us today.

b. To receive your figurines, call us at 1-800-318-8937 or fill out the form below and mail it to us today. You'll have your figurines within days.

c. Yes, for just $240, you can have three beautiful, hand-tooled figurines. Order yours today by calling 1-800-318-8937 or by returning the postage-paid, self-addressed envelope.

4. You are managing a team of co-workers who will be responsible for examining the system used to produce tubing for space vehicles. The company has just hired a new engineer in the design department, and you want to get her on the team. To do so, you must get the permission of Beverly Grant, head of the design department. Write Beverly a memorandum seeking permission to ask the new engineer, Ann Sprang, to join the team.

5. As sales manager of Tritic Electronic Games, Inc., write a sales letter to the superintendent of Clarmont County Schools to pro-

mote software packages for elementary school children to enhance spelling ability and vocabulary. These packages were developed to provide elementary school children with the basics of reading and writing. They are for DataSpeed or SST microcomputers. Write Dr. Larry Anderson, Superintendent; Clarmont County Offices; 4592 South Hundred Oaks; Henderson, TX 75652-0931.

6. On May 15, 1986, you bought a one-gallon Save-all garden sprayer. You used the sprayer only twice last spring and summer and once this spring. You have really benefited from its use when fertilizing your garden and spraying for insects. Last Thursday when you tried to spray fertilizer on your garden, however, the sprayer would not work. The guarantee on the sprayer is for one year from date of purchase. Write the manufacturer of the sprayer—Great Garden Products, 983 West Haven Avenue, Clearfield, UT 84015-5920—and ask them to replace or repair the sprayer even though the warranty has expired.

7. You work in the Accounting Department of Harrison & Son, Inc. The accounting system in this department is part manual and part computerized. After talking with friends who work for other companies, you are convinced that Harrison's could save money and time by computerizing the entire accounting system. Write your supervisor, Rosemary Bourgois, and suggest setting up a committee to look into the possibility of computerizing the accounting system. Tell her that you would like to be on the committee and, with her permission, would like to be its chairperson.

8. As a freshman at Westland University, you are trying to work your way through college. So far you have been unable to secure a job. As you have walked around the city where the university is located, you have noticed that many lawns of homes and businesses are not well kept. Thus, you have decided to start a total lawn care service, including mowing, trimming, weeding, fertilizing, and grooming lawns. Compose a message to distribute to prospective customers.

9. Your company has been having trouble with its copying machines— they always seem to be down. The committee that studied the problem is set to buy a Copyrite copier, model J-104. You feel, however, that a J-104 is not big enough to handle the volume of the company's duplicating. Though the J-104 has the same features as your present copier, its monthly capacity is estimated to be 25,000 a month. According to your figures, the new copier will need to produce about 35,000 copies a month. Write Jane Welch, the head of your department and a member of the committee which studied the copying needs of the company, and tell her of your concerns.

10. As credit manager for Clyde's Feed and Seed Company, write Jeff Harrison, Rte. 3, Box 217, Scott City, MO 63780-1039. Remind him that his payment on his account was due March 5. The amount of payment is $249.36. This is the first reminder of the overdue account.

11. Jeff Harrison (see item #10) still has not made his March payment. It has been three weeks since you sent him the reminder, and now the April payment is due. Send him a stronger reminder.

12. It has been six weeks since you sent Jeff Harrison (see item #10) his first reminder and three weeks since you sent him the second reminder. Now, both the March and April payments are due, and in two days another payment will be due. Write Jeff another collection letter — the discussion-stage message.

13. It has been three months since you first wrote Jeff Harrison (see item #10) and reminded him that his March payment was overdue. He has not responded to any of the three letters sent to him. Now the full amount of the account is overdue. Write him an urgency-stage collection letter. Tell him that if you do not hear from him by June 15, you'll turn his account over to Tolbert's Agency, a collection company.

14. Recently, Janet Washington purchased a swim suit which was discounted 25 percent. The tag on the suit indicated that the suit was guaranteed for one year. After Janet had worn the suit for a month, the seams started to split. When she returned it to the store, the clerk explained to her that the suit was a model sold the summer before. Because of this fact, it was discounted 25 percent and no refund or exchange was possible. Janet decided to write the manufacturer and ask for a replacement or a refund. The manufacturer is Sun and Fun Clothing, Inc., 7049 Industrial Drive, Commerce City, CO 80022-0001. Write Janet's letter.

15. Assume that you work for Sunshine Travel Agency, 502 East Woodhaven, Winchester, NV 89101-1205. Select a foreign country you would like to visit. Develop a one-week tour package. Write a sales letter for the tour that would be sent to customers of the agency. The letter cannot exceed one page.

16. Assume that you are in charge of recruiting for the college you are attending. Write a recruitment letter (a sales letter) for your college which would be sent to all graduating high school students.

CHAPTER 21

Planning Informal Reports

Objectives

After studying this chapter and completing the chapter exercises, you should be able to:

1. Explain the purposes of reports.
2. Identify the various types of reports.
3. Understand the steps in planning a report.
4. Prepare for writing a report.

NATURE OF REPORTS

A report is a document that presents the facts about a specific situation or problem. Unlike a letter or a memorandum, which is typically prepared for one person, a report is generally prepared for a specific group of people. The way information is gathered and presented in a report can have an important effect upon decision making and problem solving. In this chapter you will learn how to plan effective reports.

Purposes of Reports

Reports are a business tool that enable management to make decisions or solve problems. Aiding in these two functions, decision making and problem solving, is the most important purpose of reports. Other purposes of reports include providing a permanent record and providing information to others.

Types of Reports

Reports can be classified in various ways: by their style, by their purpose, and by their format. For example, if an organization were conducting a feasibility study to determine the possibility of expanding its markets, the resulting report might be considered a formal analytical report.

Style

Formal reports generally are long, analytical, and impersonal in style. A formal report often contains supplemental parts, such as a table of contents, synopsis, appendix, or bibliography. An example of a formal report is a company's annual report to stockholders or a report to a government regulatory agency. While formal reports are important, informal reports are more common in business.

Informal reports are generally shorter than formal reports and are written in a more personal style. A **sales report** is one example of an informal report. In a sales report, the writer provides a summary of the sales over a specific period of time. Another type of informal report, a justification report, is used to persuade management to approve a proposal or project; for example, to buy new equipment. Because informal reports are the backbone of business, they will be discussed in detail in this chapter.

Purpose

Reports can be classified as informational or analytical. **Informational reports** present information (facts) and include very little analysis. The components of an informational report are the subtopics or areas to be investigated. **Analytical reports** include analysis, interpretation, conclusions, and recommendations. The components of an analytical report are the probable causes of the problem.

Format

Informal reports can be written in several different formats, or arrangements, including *memo, letter,* and *short report* formats. Formal reports, because of their greater length and complexity, are generally written in *manuscript* format.

STEPS IN PLANNING A REPORT

Before writing a report, you must do some preliminary work. Even if you are simply reporting facts, you must first gather those facts and then organize them in a format that is easy to follow. Presented next are the steps in writing a report.

Identify the Problem

The first step in planning a report is to determine the main problem to be investigated and the objective of the study. As in planning letters and memos, determine why you are writing the report and what you hope to accomplish.

When the problem is complex, identifying the problem involves determining the scope of the problem. **Scope** refers to the boundaries of the report—what will be included in the study and what will be eliminated. For example, if an organization were planning to conduct a feasibility study for purchasing new computers, someone would need to determine the scope of the study. Will the study cover the use of computers throughout all departments of the company, or will it be narrowed to one or a few functions, such as accounting, administrative support, or sales? Will productivity be the main concern, or will overall cost of the proposed project be more important?

After identifying the problem, prepare a written statement of the problem. This statement may be expressed in one of three ways: as an infinitive phrase, as a question, or as a statement.

Infinitive Phrase   The purpose of this report is to determine the feasibility of purchasing new computers for the accounting department.

Question	This report answers the question, Is it feasible to purchase new computers for the accounting department?
Statement	This report will determine whether it is feasible to purchase new computers for the accounting department.

Identify Areas to Be Investigated

After identifying the scope of the problem and the purpose of the report, the next step is to develop a comprehensive study plan. The study plan will define the limits of the study, determine the specific issues to be studied, outline the necessary activities, and develop a schedule with breakpoints and reviews. These areas of investigation are the specific issues that are important in the study.

Informational Reports

Assume that you have been given the assignment to determine an effective word-processing software package to be used in your office. The components of this informational report might include the following areas to be investigated: length of documents produced, frequency and extensiveness of revisions, type of printer required, need for special printing effects, and special features needed (such as mailmerge, hyphenation, headers and footers).

Analytical Reports

Let's say that the problem is to determine why your company has a high turnover rate among the support staff. The components of this problem-solving report might include the following possible causes of the problem: low salaries, limited career path for advancement, unattractive fringe benefits, unsafe work environment.

Develop a Preliminary Outline

After you have identified the issues to be studied, organize those issues into a preliminary outline that will help you collect information for your report. This preliminary outline is very likely to differ from the final outline you will develop to present your report. The preliminary outline is simply a means for organizing the areas to be investigated. It will help you gather data and conduct research for the report.

Outlining Informational Reports

In outlining informational reports, you can arrange the subtopics of your study in one of the following ways:

Chronological Order. Organize the material in relation to time; that is, what happened first, next, and so on.

Order of Importance. Organize the material in order of importance, from the most to the least important, or vice versa.

In Sequence. Organize according to steps—first, second, third, and so on.

By Category. Break down the different categories into topics, such as stocks, bonds, and certificates of deposit.

Geographical Order. If appropriate, organize by location.

Outlining Analytical Reports

In outlining analytical reports, organize the issues in one of two ways:

Hypotheses. When you're trying to solve a problem, you will speculate on the possible causes. Each of these causes could be phrased as a hypothetical statement in your outline. The following example outlines the possible causes for a drop in sales of autos.

    I. Our prices are too high.
      A. What are our prices?
      B. What are our competitors' prices?
      C. How important is price to the consumer?

    II. The quality of our product is low.
      A. What are our frequency-of-repair records?
      B. How do our frequency-of-repair records compare with those of our competitors?
      C. What are the results of product evaluation?

    III. Our advertising is not effective.
      A. What type of advertising do we use?
      B. How large an audience do we reach?

Alternatives. When you are evaluating different alternatives to solving a problem, you could arrange your preliminary outline according to the relative merits of each alternative. For example, you might be trying to determine where to establish a new computer lab in your school. You could outline the alternatives as shown in the following example.

    I. Number of Classes Taught Using Computers
      A. School of Arts and Sciences
      B. School of Business
      C. School of Technology

    II. Number of Students Affected
      A. School of Arts and Sciences
      B. School of Business
      C. School of Technology

Figure 21-1 illustrates two frequently used outline formats, the alphanumeric system and the decimal system. Either is appropriate; use the style best suited to the problem and preferred by your organization.

Wording the Outline

You may word the preliminary outline in one of two ways — the *topic* format or the *discussion* format. A topical outline uses just a few words to identify a division of the outline; a discussion outline provides more information about the division. The discussion outline takes longer to write but is more helpful to the report writer. Both formats are illustrated in the following examples.

TOPICAL OUTLINE

I. Characteristics of Voice Mail
   A. Speed
   B. Cost
   C. Equipment

DISCUSSION OUTLINE

I. Voice mail offers the latest technology in sending messages.
   A. It offers rapid speed.
   B. It costs no more than a phone call.
   C. Special wiring and equipment are needed.

FIGURE 21-1 Outline Formats

Alphanumeric

I. xxxxxx
   A. xxxxxx
   B. xxxxxx
      1. xxxxxx
      2. xxxxxx
         a. xxxxxx
         b. xxxxxx
            (1) xxxxxx
            (2) xxxxxx

II. xxxxxx
   A. xxxxxx
   B. xxxxxx
   C. xxxxxx
      1. xxxxxx
      2. xxxxxx

Decimal

1.0 xxxxxx
   1.1 xxxxxx
   1.2 xxxxxx
      1.21 xxxxxx
      1.22 xxxxxx
         1.221 xxxxxx
         1.222 xxxxxx
            1.2221 xxxxxx
            1.2222 xxxxxx

2.0 xxxxxx
   2.1 xxxxxx
   2.2 xxxxxx
   2.3 xxxxxx
      2.31 xxxxxx
      2.32 xxxxxx

Collect the Data

The next step in preparing to write a report is to do the *research* by collecting appropriate information. Two sources of information are available — primary and secondary. **Primary research** involves gathering fresh information, whereas **secondary research** involves locating information that has already been gathered and reported.

Primary Research

The main types of primary research are surveys, interviews with experts, observations, and experiments.

Surveys.   Surveys involve obtaining people's opinions through a series of carefully constructed questions. The value of surveys lies in learning what people think about something at a particular time. An example of a survey would be surveying customers for feedback about a product they have used, such as toothpaste. Surveys can be conducted using printed questionnaires, the phone, or face-to-face interviews.

In collecting your survey data, make sure that it is *reliable* (that is, if the same study were repeated, the results would be the same) and *valid* (the survey measures what it is supposed to measure). Sampling methods and questionnaire design will have a profound impact on the reliability and validity of your research.

When conducting a survey, you will usually question a small portion of the entire population available. Surveying the entire American population would be unrealistic in conducting a presidential opinion poll. Instead, a cross-section of the population is selected for the survey. Their opinions are considered representative of the entire population. To make sure that you have a reliable sample, you must survey enough people and survey only those people who are representative of the group from which you desire an opinion.

Random (probability) sampling is usually considered the most reliable method because participants are selected from a population by chance, giving everyone an equal opportunity to be represented. For example, owners of a certain make of car could be surveyed at random concerning their opinion of the product. **Nonprobability sampling** is less reliable but may still be effective. This method involves selecting the subjects to be studied in the population. An example of nonprobability sampling would be surveying those who are most easily approached, such as shoppers in a mall.

The two means of collecting data for surveys are **mail surveys** and **interviews.** If a large number of people are to be contacted, mail surveys are usually preferred. They involve less cost and time; however, the response is generally low. Interviews conducted in person or by telephone are more costly but the response is better. Surveys often rely on a combination of mail surveys and interviews. Subjects are contacted initially by mail and followed up by telephone.

Whether the survey is conducted by telephone or by mail, questionnaires are generally developed to obtain the information. To make your questionnaire as valid as possible, you must compose the questions carefully. Make sure that the questions are relevant to the study and are not biased in any way. The following guidelines will help you in forming survey questions:

- Make the questionnaire easy to complete. Provide simple, clear directions and construct questions that ask for short answers. Keep the form as short as possible since most people will avoid lengthy questionnaires.

- Avoid questions that influence the reader's response. The question "Do you think loyalty and dependability are two of the most important traits employees should have?" would probably receive a "Yes" response. A more objective way to word the question—and therefore receive the reader's unbiased response—would be to provide a list of desirable traits and ask the reader to rank them in order of preference.

- Avoid vague terms that may be interpreted in different ways. For example, "Are you late to work often?" might be answered differently according to a person's interpretation of "often." A better question would be "How many times have you been late to work during the past year?"

- Ask only one question at a time. The question "Do you enjoy plays and movies?" does not allow for enjoying one but not the other.
- Design a format that will make tabulating responses easier, whether for computer input or manual tabulation. Notice how the questionnaire in Figure 21-2 makes tabulating simple.
- Provide a cover letter and a stamped, addressed reply envelope if the survey is mailed.

Various types of questions can be constructed; mixing the different types makes for a better questionnaire. Figure 21-2 illustrates the different types of questions which can be asked. Notice that all the questions ex-

---

FIGURE 21-2 Sample Questionnaire

SURVEY OF HIGHER EDUCATION PLANS OF HIGH SCHOOL SENIORS

Please check the appropriate space for each of the following items. Do you plan to continue your education after high school?

_____ Yes
_____ No

Indicate the importance of a higher education to you by checking one.

_____ Very important
_____ Important
_____ No opinion
_____ Not very important
_____ Unimportant

What career field are you most interested in? _____

Which of the following certificates or degrees do you plan to obtain? (Choose only one.)

_____ Certificate (one-year)
_____ Associate Degree (two-year)
_____ Bachelor's Degree (four-year)
_____ Master's Degree
_____ Doctor's Degree

(continued)

FIGURE 22-2 (Continued)

Rank the following types of schools in order of your preference in attending, from 1 (most preferred) to 4 (least preferred).

_____ College or university (private)
_____ College or university (public)
_____ Vocational or technical school (public)
_____ Proprietary school (independent)

What features are you looking for in a school? (Check all that apply).

_____ Financial aid
_____ Scholarships
_____ Fraternities and sororities
_____ Co-op work program
_____ Credit by examination
_____ Spectator sports (football, etc.)
_____ Student clubs and organizations

Why is higher education important to you?

cept for the last one are structured and provide for easy tabulation and analysis. The last question is open-ended; you should probably limit or avoid use of this type of question.

Interviews with Experts. Instead of conducting a large-scale survey, you may select experts in a particular area and interview them on the phone, by mail, or in person. Since these people are selected for their expertise, your results should be valid. An example of this type of research might be asking attorneys about the type and number of court cases they handle.

Observations. Another method of doing primary research is to observe certain occurrences and record what has been observed. For example, if you wanted to know how many smokers and nonsmokers frequent a restaurant, you could observe people for a certain period of time and record the numbers. This method of research lends itself to studies of the environment, physical activities, or people.

Experiments. You can also conduct experiments to gather information for a study. Let's say that you want to find out whether people learn to key faster on a typewriter keyboard or on a computer keyboard. You would set up two groups of students receiving the same instruction, with the only variable being the type of keyboard. For the results to be valid, the two groups would need to be the same except for the variable you are measuring.

Secondary Research

Research completed by others can be useful to the report writer. A review of the existing literature on a subject can provide a basis for designing primary research. Consult books, periodicals, and other reports to gather information. Computer data banks, often available at libraries, also offer a more thorough search of the literature than may be available in printed form in a library.

Some references you may find useful are the *Business Periodicals Index*, the *Reader's Guide to Periodical Literature*, and *The Wall Street Journal Index*. Librarians can assist you in locating sources of information. Some of the most useful references are those found within a company, including reports, memos, annual reports to stockholders, and newsletters.

You should record the information that you gather on note cards for use as you write your report. Two basic types of cards should be prepared: bibliography cards and note cards.

Bibliography Cards.   For each separate secondary source that you use, prepare a bibliography card similar to the one shown in Figure 21-3. On the card list the author's full name, the title of the reference, the date of publication, and the name and location of the publisher. These cards can be used in preparing a bibliography for a formal report.

Note Cards.   After reviewing each reference, prepare a separate note card for each point from the reference that you want to refer to in your report. In most cases you will summarize the information you locate in a reference; occasionally you may find it helpful to quote directly from the source. Copyright laws require that you give credit to the author of the original work, but you do not need to document information that is of general knowledge. Be extremely cautious in your use of references. Using another person's words as your own is unethical and illegal.

On each note card, write the number and title of the reference, the page numbers where you located information, and the general subject of the material, as shown in Figure 21-3.

Analyze Data, Draw Conclusions, and Make Recommendations

Unless you have been asked to provide an informational report only, the last step in preparing to write a report is to analyze the results, draw reasonable conclusions, and make recommendations if appropriate.

FIGURE 21-3　Sample Bibliography Card and Note Card

BIBLIOGRAPHY CARD

8

John Naisbitt. Megatrends. New York: Warner Books, 1984.

NOTE CARD

8

Naisbitt　　　　　　　　　Labor unions

Megatrends

Between 1971 and 1981 there were 35 mergers of labor

unions; however, a decrease in labor unions is

projected for the future. P. 107.

Analyze Data

After conducting the research for your report, you must organize the information in a way that will be understandable and helpful to the reader. For example, research on the high turnover rate of support personnel might yield the following data that you would need to present: salaries of different secretarial jobs within the company, salaries of competing organizations, the number and kinds of promotions secretaries have received, and results of questionnaires completed by secretaries.

Draw Conclusions

After analyzing the data through mathematical interpretation and logical thought, you may arrive at conclusions. If you have been working with others on a report, it may be helpful to discuss the conclusions with them and perhaps arrive at a consensus. An example of a conclusion for the study of high turnover among company secretaries might be:

> I conclude that secretaries in our company have a limited number of advancement opportunities.

Make Recommendations

Recommendations should be provided in a report if they have been authorized. A **conclusion** is an opinion based on interpretation of the data; a **recommendation** offers suggestions of what should be done. Recommendations should be directly related to conclusions, as is the following one for the secretarial study:

> I recommend that secretarial positions within our company be reorganized to provide opportunities for career advancement.

Checkpoint 2 COLLECTING DATA

Indicate whether each of the following statements is true or false.

1. Primary research is more helpful to the report writer than secondary research.
2. Primary research methods include surveys, interviews with experts, experiments, and observations.
3. Surveys should be either reliable or valid.
4. A random sample is the most reliable sampling method.
5. A survey questionnaire should be easy to complete.
6. The questions asked on a questionnaire should all be of the same type.
7. Information from secondary research should be recorded on note cards.
8. The conclusions of a report are based on the recommendations the author believes should be made.

SUMMARY

Business reports are written to assist management in making decisions and solving problems. Reports can be classified as formal or informal; most business reports are informal.

In preparing to write a report, first identify the problem by writing a clear statement of the purpose of the report. Next identify areas to be investigated, developing a preliminary outline to help you conduct research. Primary research is carried out through surveys, interviews with experts, observations, and experiments. Secondary research involves a review of information already written on the subject. Finally, analyze the data, draw conclusions, and make recommendations.

● ● ● ● ● ● ● ● ● **Communication Activities**

Discussion Questions

1. Define formal and informal business reports and give characteristics of each.
2. How do informational and analytical reports differ?
3. Describe the first step in planning a report—identifying the problem.
4. Explain how to develop a comprehensive study plan for informational and analytical reports.
5. What are the different ways to outline informational reports? analytical reports?
6. Explain ways of collecting data for primary research.
7. How are data collected for secondary research?
8. Identify and explain the last step in planning a report.

Practical Applications

1. Select a topic in which you are interested in writing a short informal report. Identify the problem (writing the statement of the problem) and develop a preliminary outline for conducting the research.

2. Develop a survey questionnaire for the topic you selected in #1 or one of the following topics:

    Employment of students in your school
    Extracurricular activities of students in your school
    Use of automated equipment in your company
    Educational and career goals of students on campus

3. Conduct secondary research for the topic in #1, using no fewer than five sources. Prepare bibliography and note cards.

4. After conducting research for the problem in #1, analyze the data, draw conclusions, and make recommendations if appropriate.

5. Write a memo report to your instructor on one of the following topics:

    Student clubs and organizations on campus
    Justification for a new school computer lab

6. Assume that you are employed as a market researcher and have been assigned a report on the market outlook for a chain of sporting goods stores. Write a letter report to the president of the company providing information on the progress of the report.

CHAPTER 22

Writing the Report

Objectives

After studying this chapter and completing the chapter exercises, you should be able to:

1. Develop the appropriate parts of a short informal and a formal report.
2. Decide how to organize the report.
3. Write the report.
4. Use visual aids in the report.

After gathering all the information needed and planning your report, you are now ready to organize, write, and format the report. Reports may be prepared as either informal or formal documents. The organization of the report depends upon the nature of the message. Visual aids help the reader interpret the data and, therefore, are appropriate for either informal or formal reports. Reports written to persuade the receiver are also organized in the indirect order.

INFORMAL REPORTS

Most reports written in business are informal reports that either present information that has been requested or analyze a problem and report the findings. The organization and format of informal reports vary depending upon the nature of the message and who will receive it.

Organization

Like business letters and memos, informal reports are organized around a main idea and supporting information. If the report is an informational report, the main idea is the information that has been requested. If the report is an analytical report, the main idea is a summary of the conclusions and recommendations. The supporting information of either an informational report or an analytical report explains or details the main idea.

Reports may be organized in either the direct order or the indirect order. The arrangement of the main idea and supporting information depends upon how receptive the reader is expected to be.

Direct Order

If you expect the reader to be receptive to what you are writing, use the direct order, starting with the main idea. Busy managers prefer reading reports written in direct order because the main ideas are presented at the beginning of the report.

Informational reports such as progress reports and guidelines are commonly written in the direct order. The results (or main ideas) appear at the beginning of the report. Analytical reports that are expected to have a favorable response are also organized in the direct order. The main idea (conclusions and recommendations) comes first, followed by the supporting information.

Indirect Order

Use the indirect order when you do not expect a favorable response or when the receiver may have to be persuaded to accept the main idea. In effect, the main ideas, which are not expected to please the reader, are buffered by presenting the details and rationale first.

The indirect style might be used for justification reports when you expect management to be negative about approving a proposed project or investment of funds. You might also use the indirect style for troubleshooting reports, in which you investigate a problem and propose a solution. If, for example, your recommendation is to close a company operation and you don't expect management to approve the idea, then you would use the indirect order, placing the recommendation—to close the operation—at the end of the report.

Outline

Before beginning to write the report, take a look at the preliminary outline you developed to guide your research. More than likely, the outline will need some revision to be useful in writing the report. This revised outline will become the organizational plan for writing the final report.

The following three figures are organizational plans (outlines) for informal reports in direct or indirect style. Most informal reports can be written using one of these organizational plans.

Figure 22-1 is an outline for an informational report written in the direct style. Notice that the introduction and main idea come first, followed by the findings.

Figure 22-2 is an outline for an analytical report written in the direct style. The main idea consists of conclusions and recommendations followed by the findings and supporting details.

Figure 22-3 is an outline for an analytical report written in the indirect style. The main idea (including the conclusions and recommendations) is placed at the end of the report following the findings and supporting details.

Writing Style

Informal reports are usually written in a personal style, using the personal pronouns *I* and *you*. If, however, a degree of formality is desired, the short report can be written in an impersonal style, avoiding all personal pronouns. The impersonal style is considered more objective.

You also need to decide whether to write in the present or past tense. Avoid switching back and forth between tenses.

FIGURE 22-1 Outline of an Informational Report in Direct Style

 I. Introduction

 II. Main Idea: Unisoft, Preferred Word Processing Software

 III. Findings: Word Processing Needs for Our Office

   A. Lengthy document production
   B. Frequent revisions
   C. Special features needed (mailmerge, hyphenation, headers, footers)
   D. High-speed, letter-quality print (laser printer)

 IV. Findings: Comparison of Four Word Processing Packages

   A. Word processing software package A
   B. Word processing software package B
   C. Word processing software package C
   D. Unisoft word processing software package D

FIGURE 22-2 Outline of an Analytical Report in Direct Style

 I. Introduction

 II. Main Idea

   A. Conclusion: Secretaries in our company have a limited number of advancement opportunities.
   B. Recommendation: Secretarial positions should be revamped to provide opportunities for career advancement.

 III. Findings and Supporting Details

   A. Secretarial salaries compare favorably with those of competing organizations.
   B. Fringe benefits are satisfactory.
   C. Opportunities for advancement are limited.

FIGURE 22-3 Outline of an Analytical Report in Indirect Style

I.   Introduction

II. Findings and Supporting Details

   A. Third- and fourth-quarter sales down
   B. Inventory stockpile up
   C. Union contract demands high

III. Main Idea

   A. Conclusion: We are overproducing cars in our Lakeview plant.
   B. Recommendation: Close Lakeview plant and lay off workers indefinitely.

Format

Informal reports may be formatted like letters, memos, or manuscripts. The format depends upon who the receiver is and the length of the report.

Whatever format is used, informal reports have three main parts:

● Opening (the introduction)
● Body (findings and supporting details)
● Ending

The length of the introduction will vary according to the purpose of the report. For a brief memo report, the only introduction needed might be the subject line. For other informal short reports, the opening may include the following information: the subject of the report, the purpose of the report (why the subject is important), and a preview of the main ideas to be presented in the report. If you are writing in direct order, include the summary of findings or conclusions and recommendations in the opening.

The body of a report includes the findings and supporting details which resulted from the research conducted. Your revised outline will provide the main organizational plan for this section. This section is usually the most lengthy and must be well organized so that the report will be easy to understand.

The ending of a report is important because it leaves a final impression upon the reader. In a report written in direct order, this ending section should reemphasize the main ideas. If you are using indirect order, this is where you will first present the summary of findings (informational reports) or conclusions and recommendations (analytical reports). Make sure that any conclusions or recommendations follow from a logical presentation of the data in the body of the report. If there are several conclusions or recommendations, use a list format for simplicity.

Letter Report

External reports, those written to people outside the organization, are often written in letter format. (Refer to Chapter 17 for details on formatting letters.) In general, a report written in letter format should be no longer than five pages.

The opening may refer to the authorization for the report, including the date of authorization and the person who authorized the report. The report body is the report itself. This middle section includes findings and supporting details and may include an analysis of the situation being studied and recommendations or suggestions. The ending is similar to the closing in any letter. If possible, the closing should refer to expected action on the part of the reader or writer. Figure 22-4 presents an example of a letter report.

Memo Report

Many short business reports are written in memo format, especially internal reports, which are reports sent to others within the organization. These reports are informal primarily because of their format, not necessarily because of their content. Use memo reports for routine internal reports up to five pages. Chapter 17 presents detailed information on formatting memos. An example of a memo report is shown in Figure 22-5.

Manuscript Report

Short reports written in manuscript format are usually longer than memo or letter reports but not as long as formal reports. The manuscript report is often used instead of the letter report for external reports longer than five pages. The opening may include the following information: the subject of the report, the purpose of the report (why the subject is important), and a preview of the main ideas to be presented in the report. If you are writing in direct order, include the summary of findings or conclusions and recommendations in the opening. An example of a manuscript report is shown in Figure 22-6.

Stevens Consulting Group

281 Polaris Avenue
Mountain View, CA 94043-2316

January 14, 19--

Ms. Maria Silva
Director of Office Automation
Haybrook, Sills and Associates
153 Fairmont Street
Linconshire, IL   60069

Dear Ms. Silva

Opening Here is the report you requested on recommended electronic message systems for your organization. After surveying the number
and types of messages your company sends, I recommend that you
consider adding electronic mail and facsimile machines. A breakdown of benefits and features of each is provided below.

Electronic Mail

Body Because your organization sends frequent interoffice memos among
branch offices, electronic mail would speed up communication.
Since you have existing computers, E-mail service would be inexpensive and convenient for your company. A description of the
steps required to implement electronic mail is attached.

Facsimile

Your offices have a need to send illustrations and graphics to
each other. Facsimile machines would speed up the process, provide high quality imaging, yet keep costs low. A list of recommended brands, features, and costs is attached.

Ending If your organization decides to incorporate either of these
recommendations, the Stevens Consulting Group is ready to assist
you in implementing the new systems. Thank you for giving us the
opportunity to work with you.

Sincerely

Ms. Doris A. Stevens
President

xx

Attachments

FIGURE 22-4 Letter Report

Interoffice Memo

Office Systems Technology

TO: Gerald L. Thomas

FROM: Carol Weaver

DATE: June 28, 19--

SUBJECT: High School Visitations

During the previous school year, Greenville Chapter OST members visited the following high schools to make presentations on word processing/information systems.

Because of the increased demand from high school business education classes for OST speakers, I recommend that we encourage additional members to participate in the Speakers Bureau.

Members	Schools
Adair, Joan	Mays High School Palmetto High School Riverdale High School
Cochran, George	Avondale High School McIntosh High School
Davis, Brenda	Jonesboro High School Morrow High School
Gomez, Isabel	Forest Park High School Russell High School
James, Anita	Henry County Senior High School North Clayton High School
Maroni, Carla	Campbell High School East Coweta High School
Sogo, Rinji	Fayette County High School

FIGURE 22-5   Memo Report

SPECIFICATIONS FOR NEW OFFICE SIMULATION LAB

Opening   The Office Administration and Technology Department proposes that an office simulation lab be constructed in the new Technology Building to accommodate 24 workstations plus one teaching assistant/receptionist workstation. The specifications for the work areas and environmental factors are outlined in this report.

Work Area Specifications

Body   The proposed work area and workstations should meet the following specifications:

<u>Space</u>. An open lab area of a minimum of 1,700 square feet (with 120 square feet set aside for a separate storage center) should be provided.

Space should also be provided for instructor's station, aisles (30" to 3'), teaching assistant/receptionist station, conference space, and a reception area.

<u>Furniture and equipment</u>. Modular ergonomic student office workstations should be provided with adjustable seating. No more than four workstations should be grouped together.

Student workstations should measure a minimum of 5' x 6'. Acoustical energy-based panels (approximately 42 inches high) with storage facilities should separate each workstation.

Each workstation should include the following equipment: microcomputer, dictation/transcription machine, electronic calculator, and telephone. Two laser printers should be provided, and computers should be networked.

<u>Storage center</u>. A self-contained storage center measuring at least 120 square feet (with walls and a door with lock) should provide storage for reprographics and audiovisual equipment and instructional resources, materials, and supplies. A sink should be provided for clean-up in the reprographics area.

<u>Teaching assistant workstation</u>. A modular teaching assistant/receptionist workstation with counter and storage space and a telephone should be provided adjacent to the storage area. The workstation should be separated from the rest of the lab by acoustical panels, and it should be visible to the entire lab.

FIGURE 22-6 **Manuscript Report**

<u>Wiring</u>. Appropriate wiring should be provided for the following equipment:

    Microcomputers and printers
    Typewriters (electronic)
    Calculators
    Reprographics equipment
    Telecommunications equipment
    Dictation/transcription equipment

Wired acoustical panels for student workstations should be provided. It is recommended that power poles and in-floor electrical outlets not be used.

Provisions should be provided for networking microcomputers. Master cut-off switches should be placed in protected areas to control all electrical outlets.

Environmental Factors

The proposed work area should meet these specifications for other environmental factors.

<u>Acoustics</u>. Acoustical walls, ceilings, floors, and partitions should be provided to block and absorb noise generated by office equipment. White noise is recommended to mask noise.

<u>Climate</u>. The heating, ventilation, and air conditioning system should be designed to accommodate the extra heat generated by video display terminals and other equipment. Temperature ranges should be between 68-78 degrees Fahrenheit (20-26 degrees Centigrade), and humidity should be at 40-60 percent (noncondensing).

<u>Flooring</u>. Nonstatic carpeted flooring should be provided. There should be a minimum of physical obstructions.

<u>Lighting</u>. Optimum lighting for working at video display terminals should be provided. Indirect, nonglare lighting supplemented by task lighting where needed should be provided.

Summary

Ending The specifications mentioned throughout this report provide information concerning a proposed new office simulation. In summary, the lab should meet the following specifications:

1. The lab area should contain a minimum of 1700 square feet.

2. The lab should have a width of at least 30-35 feet.

3. Modular ergonomic workstations with adjustable seating should be provided.

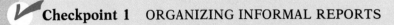

FORMAL REPORTS

Formal reports generally are more complex and longer than informal reports. As a result, there are usually more parts in a formal report than in an informal report.

Parts of a Formal Report

A formal report has three major divisions: the preliminary parts, the body or text of the report, and the supplementary parts. Table 22-1 illustrates the parts of a formal report.

TABLE 22-1 Parts of a Formal Report

Preliminary Parts	Report Body	Supplemental Parts
Letter of transmittal	Introduction	Bibliography
Title page	Findings and	Appendix
Table of contents	analysis	
Synopsis or abstract	Ending	

Preliminary Parts

The preliminary parts come before the actual report and provide the reader with information about the report body.

The **letter of transmittal** transmits the report to the reader. This letter conveys what you would say if you were giving the report directly to the reader; therefore, it is usually less formal than the report itself. Use the direct order for the transmittal letter. Begin the letter with a statement such as "Here is the report you asked me to prepare on..." Include a brief statement of the report objective, followed by a short summary or recap of the report. End the letter courteously, thanking the person who requested the report and offering assistance if needed.

The **title page** includes the title of the report; the name with title and organization of the person for whom the report was written; the writer's name, title, and organization; and the date of the report.

The **table of contents** is an outline of the entire contents of the report. Often the first- and second-level headings in the body of the report are the basis for the table of contents.

The **abstract** is a brief summary of the report. The purpose of the abstract is to convey the key points of the report to the reader. See Figures 22-7 and 22-8 (pages 333 and 334) for an example of these parts.

The Body of the Report

Formal reports are usually organized in the indirect order with the main idea at the end. The body contains three parts: the introduction, the findings and analysis, and the ending. See Figures 22-9 and 22-10 (pages 335 and 336) for an example.

The **introduction** states the purpose of the report. Several topics are generally discussed in the introduction, including any or all of the following:

- *Authorization:* Who authorized the report, when, and how.
- *Statement of the Problem:* The reason(s) the report is being written and what is to be accomplished.
- *Scope:* What the report will cover and what it will not cover. The scope defines the length and complexity of the report.
- *Limitations:* Factors that affect the scope of the report, such as a limited amount of time or a limited budget.
- *Definitions:* List of unfamiliar terms and definitions.

The **findings and analysis** present the findings and the supporting details and analyze them. The **ending** summarizes the findings, draws conclusions, and makes recommendations. The ending contains the main idea.

As you write your report, keep these key points in mind:

- Keep sentences short.
- Avoid wordiness.
- Use familiar terms.
- Start each paragraph with a topic sentence.
- Link ideas with transitional elements.
- Avoid unnecessary details.

Supplementary Parts

The **bibliography** is an alphabetical list of sources used in preparing the report. An **appendix** contains material related to the report but too bulky or lengthy to be included in the body of the report. Examples of appendix items might be questionnaires or a glossary of terms. See Figure 22-11 (page 337) for an example of supplementary parts.

Format

Formal reports generally follow specific formatting guidelines. A style manual will help the report writer in planning margins, spacing, and headings.

Margins

Usually 1-inch side and bottom margins are recommended. For a left-bound report, however, use a 1 1/2-inch left margin. For preliminary and supplementary pages and the first page of the body, generally use a 2-inch top margin. For all other pages, use a 1-inch top margin.

Spacing

The formal report has traditionally been double-spaced; however, some organizations prefer single spacing. If a report is double-spaced, indent for paragraphs. If the report is single-spaced, double-space between paragraphs; paragraph indentions are not required.

Headings

Use headings to help you organize and present data. Headings are like signposts, helping the reader follow your line of thought as you move to your next point. Always include at least two headings at the same level. The same-level headings within a section should be parallel in form. If one heading begins with a noun, for example, then all headings at that

THE IMPACT WORD PROCESSING HAS MADE IN SELECTED

LEGAL OFFICES AND NABTE INSTITUTIONS

Prepared for

Samuel Chandler
Senior Vice President
Meade Legal Services

Prepared by

Benita Harris
Manager of Office Services
Meade Legal Services

May 19--

TABLE OF CONTENTS

Preliminary Part

Abstract iii

Body

Introduction 1
    Statement of the Problem 1
    Scope 1
    Limitations of the Study 2
    Definition of Terms 2
    Summary 3

Findings and Analysis 4
    Responses from Business Educators 5
    Responses from Legal Office Participants . . . 7
    Summary of the Findings 9

Summary 10

Recommendations 10

Supple-mentary Parts

Bibliography 11

Appendices 12
    Appendix A: Questionnaire to Participants . . 12
    Appendix B: Letter to Participants 13

ii

FIGURE 22-7 Title Page and Contents

ABSTRACT

The purpose of the study was to determine the impact that word processing has made in selected legal offices in the United States. Further, the study sought to ascertain the impact that word processing has made on business education curricula offered by selected NABTE institutions.

Methods and Procedures

The participants for the study were secretaries/word processors who were employed in legal offices throughout the United States and NABTE representatives who were from selected collegiate institutions. The legal participants were randomly selected from the Martindale-Hubbell Law Directory, 1983. The NABTE representatives were randomly selected from NABTE institutions located in or near the capital city in each state.

Each legal participant completed a legal questionnaire and each NABTE representative completed a business education questionnaire. The t-test, McNemar test, and Stuart-Maxwell test were used to analyze the data.

Results and Conclusions

The results of the study revealed that attorneys hired high school graduates or two-year secretarial graduates who knew how to answer the telephone, operate a word processing

iii

machine, program a microcomputer, take shorthand, file documents electronically, use various software packages, and key straight copy at speeds of 60 to 80 words per minute. The data also revealed that, in general, the firms had not established evaluation standards for secretaries/word processors and had not increased the number of secretaries/word processors since purchasing word processing equipment. Neither had they increased the salaries of secretaries/word processors. Further, the findings revealed that the cost of processing information in the legal offices had decreased since the implementation of word processing equipment.

The responses received from the NABTE representatives revealed that business educators trained office administration and comprehensive business education majors to operate word processing equipment, use software packages, and key documents at production rates. No changes were noted for teaching basic business or basic English skills. It is worthy to note that most of the legal firms and NABTE institutions purchased IET equipment.

iv

FIGURE 22-8 Abstract (Preliminary Report Part)

334

INTRODUCTION

Advanced technology has caused many changes in the twentieth century. Typewriting and data processing equipment have changed from manual to electric and, in the eighties, from electric to electronic. Information processing and communication methods have progressed to an extremely high level of sophistication (Simcoe, 1980). Some legal offices have become fully automated while others strive for a similar setting. According to Moody (1978), office automation is an extension of the technologies refined and developed to electronically process data and words.

Statement of the Problem

The problem of this study was to determine the impact word processing has made in selected legal offices in the United States. Further, the study sought to ascertain the impact that word processing has made on business education curricula offered by selected National Association of Business Teacher Educators (NABTE) institutions.

Specifically, the study seeks to determine the training and entry-level skills needed for employment, the functions and operations performed, and the equipment and software utilized by secretaries in legal offices before and after word processing operations were implemented.

Scope

The report will study the impact that word processing has had on the legal office but will not include the impact

of other automation technologies on the legal office. Participants identified in the study were from large cities; therefore, the impact of word processing on legal firms in small cities will not be addressed in this study.

The study will also determine any changes in secretarial tasks performed before word processing was implemented and after word processing was implemented.

Limitations of the Study

The limitations of the study are as follows:

Legal Firms. The legal office participants invited to participate in this study were randomly selected from Martindale-Hubbell Law Directory, 1983. Also, the legal firms had to be located in the capital cities in the United States or the largest city in the state where a NABTE institution was located.

NABTE Representatives. The business educators invited to participate in the study were selected from the NABTE Directory. One NABTE institution located in the capital city or a city near the capital per state was identified for the study.

Definitions

These definitions were listed to assist the reader.

1. After word processing means after the implementation of word processing operations (concepts, equipment, procedures).

2. Before word processing means before the implementation of word processing operations.

FIGURE 22-9 Introductory Parts of the Report

10

SUMMARY

This study was designed to determine the impact word processing has made in selected legal offices in the United States. Further, the study sought to ascertain the impact that word processing has made on business education curricula offered by selected NABTE institutions.

RECOMMENDATIONS

The investigation and findings of this study provide the basis for the following recommendations:

1. The NABTE institution representatives participating in this research study and their business education department chairpersons need to carefully study the skills, functions, and operations performed by secretaries in legal offices to determine whether or not the skills, functions, and operations that are being taught in business education programs are meeting the needs of the secretaries employed by legal offices in the local area.

2. The NABTE institution representatives participating in this study and their business education department chairpersons need to analyze the current business education curricula to determine a procedure to eliminate voids in the legal curricula.

4

FINDINGS AND ANALYSIS

The responses received from legal office participants relating to the cost of processing information since the implementation of word processing are shown in Table 4. The data presented are classified by NBEA regions. Fifty percent of the legal office respondents indicated a decrease in the cost of processing information, while 28 percent reported no change had occurred in this area.

A summary of the data supplied by legal respondents reported an increase in the number of secretaries employed in 21 percent of the legal offices since implementing word processing, while 23 percent revealed a decrease. Fifty-six percent of the office respondents reported no change in this area.

Table 4

PERCENTAGE OF LEGAL RESPONDENTS REPORTING THE COST OF
PROCESSING INFORMATION SINCE WORD PROCESSING
OPERATIONS WERE IMPLEMENTED
IN LEGAL OFFICES

Legal Offices by Regions	Increase In Cost	Decrease In Cost	No Change	Total Percent
Eastern	29%	42%	29%	100%
Mountain Plains	19%	39%	42%	100%
North-Central	25%	63%	12%	100%
Southern	21%	49%	30%	100%
Western	19%	55%	26%	100%
Mean	22%	50%	28%	100%

FIGURE 22-10 Findings/Analysis and Ending of the Report

11

BIBLIOGRAPHY

Anderson, R. I. "Word Processing." National Business Education Yearbook. Reston, Virginia: National Business
Education Association, 1980, 55-56.

Brostrom, Gail C. "The Importance of Communication Skills in
the Business World." National Business Education Yearbook. Reston, Virginia: National Business Education
Association, 1988, 1-12.

Bragg, S. M. "A Comparative Study of Major Task Requirements of Word Processing Administrative Support Personnel and the Traditional Secretary." Diss. University
of Georgia, 1979.

Breslow, N. E. and Day, N. E. Statistical Methods in Cancer
Research. Volume I The Analysis of Case-Control Studies.
Lyon: International Agency for Research on Cancer,
1980.

Chaney, Lillian H. and Otto, Joseph Clair. "Are Schools
Meeting Needs of the Business Community?" Business Education Forum (February 1988): 23-24.

U. S. Department of Commerce. Statistical Abstract of the
United States, 1982-1983. Washington, D.C.: U. S. Government Printing Office, 1982.

APPENDIX A

Functions And Operations Performed by Secretaries/
Word Processors In Legal Offices

Please place check marks in the appropriate columns to indicate
functions and operations secretaries/word processors in your
legal office perform BEFORE WP and AFTER WP.

R = Rarely
O = Occasionally
F = Frequently

	BEFORE WP			AFTER WP		
	R	O	F	R	O	F
1. Answering the telephone						
2. Transcribing handwritten copy						
3. Transcribing rough-draft						
4. Taking & transcribing shorthand						
5. Transcribing from machine dictation						
6. Transcribing from telephone						
7. Receiving oral directions						
8. Composing correspondence						
9. Transcribing material received from an attorney						
10. Transcribing material received from a paralegal						
11. Proofreading others' work						
12. Operating a word processor						
13. Using word processing software						
14. Using software other than word processing						
15. Filing manually						
16. Filing electronically						
17. Performing other functions on a word processor						
18. Operating a photocopier						
19. Operating a microfiche reader/printer						
20. Other _____						

12

FIGURE 22-11 Bibliography and Appendix (Supplementary Parts)

level should begin with a noun. If one begins with a verb, then all others should begin with a verb. See the following example.

PARALLEL HEADINGS	UNPARALLEL HEADINGS
I. Steps in Planning	I. Planning the Study
A. Defining the Objective	A. Defining the Objective
B. Presenting the Plan to Management	B. Presentation to Management
C. Determining Project Leader	C. Determine Project Leader
1. Vendor	1. Vendor
2. Outside consultant	2. Hiring an outside consultant
II. The Feasibility Study	II. The Feasibility Study

Figure 22-12 presents an acceptable format for headings. Each heading is illustrated as it is discussed.

Documentation

Documentation provides information about the sources used in writing the report. Footnotes, reference citations, and endnotes are all ways of documenting sources. Refer to a style manual for mechanics on documenting sources.

 Checkpoint 2 WRITING INFORMAL AND FORMAL REPORTS

Indicate whether each of the following statements is true or false.

1. Informal reports have three main parts: the opening, the body, and the ending.
2. The opening in a direct order report would include the summary of findings or conclusions and recommendations.
3. Use headings within the body of the report to assist the reader in following the material.
4. One effective writing technique is to write long sentences.
5. The ending of a report written in indirect order should reemphasize the main ideas.

Check your answers in Appendix D.

FIGURE 22-12 **Format for Headings**

FIRST-LEVEL HEADINGS

The title of a report is centered in all capital letters at the top of the short, informal report. The title may be printed in bold. In a memo or letter report, the title might be in the subject line. If a secondary heading is used, center and capitalize only important words.

<u>Second-Level Heading</u>

Place the second-level heading at the left margin of the report, capitalize all important words, and underline it or print it in bold. The second-level heading should indicate what the following sections are about, perhaps by listing the subdivisions.

<u>Third-level heading</u>. Indent the third-level heading, capitalize the first word, underline the heading, and follow the heading with a period.

<u>Fourth-level headings</u> might be needed in your report. If so, capitalize only the first word, underline, and run the heading into the text of the paragraph. If you need a further breakdown of material, consider using enumerated items. Format enumerated items as follows:

1. Indent enumerated items five spaces from the left margin.

2. Single-space the items; double-space between items.

3. Always include at least two items.

VISUAL AIDS

Visual aids can help the reader understand and interpret the information presented in a report. Tables, charts, and illustrations are graphics that can support and more clearly explain the text of a report. They cannot stand alone, however, and must be introduced and explained.

The outline of your report will help you plan visual aids that will enhance your report. Each major section of the outline probably represents a key point of your report. Decide whether a visual aid would help the reader understand the data you are presenting.

Begin with the data you collected during the research stage of the report. After analyzing the data, you will probably be able to put it in some sort of tabular form. Present the information in an attractive visual aid.

Types of Visual Aids

Among the most often used graphic aids are tables, bar charts, line charts, pie charts, and drawings or photographs.

Tables

Tables are useful for presenting detailed information. Complex numerical information that is presented in tabular form is easier to comprehend than such information presented as textual copy.

Use an attractive layout and keep tables consistent within the report. Headings are particularly important so that the reader can quickly and easily understand the information in the table. Figure 22-13 presents information in a table format.

Bar Charts

Bar charts are useful for comparing the size of items and for showing changes in items over time. The bar chart presents numerical values through use of vertical or horizontal bars of varying length.

Bar charts are very versatile: You can stack the bars to show different components making up the bar; you can double the bars to show comparisons; and you can show positive and negative amounts. The bar chart is most useful for comparing four or five items. Figure 22-14 illustrates two variations of the bar chart.

Line Charts

Line charts are most useful for showing changes in a quantity or value over time. This type of chart is often used to show fluctuations in sales, costs, or production over a period of months or years. The line chart is

FIGURE 22-13 Table Format

SALES OF PC PRINTERS
First and Second Quarter 19--

Type of Printer	First Quarter		Second Quarter	
	Units	Sales (Thous.)	Units	Sales (Thous.)
Daisywheel	280	269.2	265	241.8
Dot-Matrix	476	280.8	521	416.8
Laser	115	690.0	128	765.4
Thermal	30	9.1	46	13.8
Ink-Jet	110	109.2	142	136.2

FIGURE 22-14 Vertical and Horizontal Bar Charts

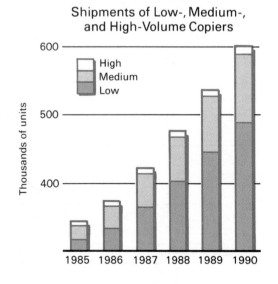

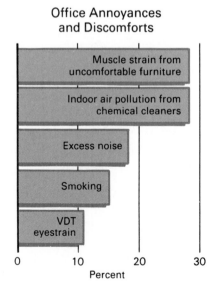

therefore good for illustrating trends. In charts depicting trends, the horizontal axis is used for time or quantity being measured; the vertical axis is used for amounts.

Line charts can be misleading if the scales are not planned carefully. To avoid distorting the facts, choose a realistic scale and use the same scale in similar line charts on the subject. Figure 22-15 provides an illustration of a line chart.

Pie Charts

Pie charts are most useful for showing the parts that make up a whole. Generally, the parts (which should be limited to no more than seven) are represented by percentages. Such statistics as a breakdown of family income into various expense categories or the percentage of the work force employed in major industries are ideally suited to presentation as a pie chart.

In constructing the pie chart, place the largest portion in the twelve o'clock position and place decreasing amounts clockwise from there. A pie chart is illustrated in Figure 22-16.

FIGURE 22-15 Line Chart

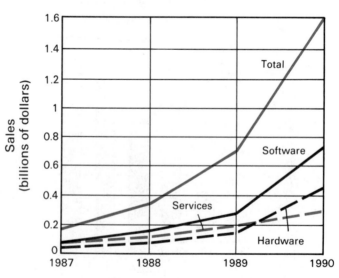

Illustrations

Drawings and photographs can be very effective but are less frequently used than other visual aids because they are more difficult and expensive to produce. In technical reports a drawing or diagram could be used to show how something operates. In annual reports photographs provide visual impact.

Placement of Visual Aids

To make visual aids work for you in a report, position the visual as close to the text reference as possible. Ideally, the visual aid should go on the page where it is referred to in the text. Unless you have access to layout services or computer software that will integrate text and visual aids, however, you may have to place your visual aids on separate pages.

Introduce the visual aid in the text of the report before presenting the visual aid. The visual aid should appear after the reference to it so that the reader will be able to locate it easily.

FIGURE 22-16   Pie Chart

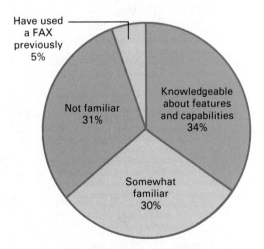

Computer-produced Graphics

Computers have made the production of graphics much easier and less costly. With the appropriate computer software and hardware, you could produce practically all the visual aids described in this chapter. You need a computer with graphics capability, the appropriate software package for producing graphics, an input device (if the keyboard is not sufficient, you may need a light pen, stylus, or graphics tablet), and a printer or plotter (output device). Most plotters produce multiple colors. Today's laser printers produce a great number of type styles.

Checkpoint 3 VISUAL AIDS

Indicate whether each of the following statements is true or false.

1. Visual aids can help the reader understand the text of the report.
2. Tables are useful for presenting complex numerical data.
3. Bar charts show changes and trends over time.
4. Place visual aids at the end of the report.
5. Computers can be used to produce graphics easily and cheaply.

Check your answers in Appendix D.

SUMMARY

Informal reports can be written in memo, letter, or manuscript format. Organizational structure can be in direct order, placing the main idea first when a favorable response from the reader is expected. Write in indirect order, placing the main idea last, when an unfavorable response is expected. From the preliminary report outline, develop an appropriate organizational plan for both informational and analytical reports.

Formal reports are usually longer and more complex than informal reports and may be divided into three main parts: preliminary parts (including letter of transmittal, title page, table of contents, and synopsis or abstract), report body (including introduction, findings and analysis, and ending), and supplementary parts (including bibliography and appendix). Use style manuals to format and document formal reports.

Visual aids can help you illustrate more easily what your report is about. Tables, charts, and illustrations should be introduced in the text and placed as closely as possible to the points being illustrated. Computer graphics programs can create many types of visual aids, including bar charts, line charts, and pie charts.

Discussion Questions

1. Describe the organizational structure (direct order and indirect order) in which reports can be written.
2. How are letter reports formatted?
3. When should memo reports be used?
4. Describe manuscript reports.
5. What are the three major divisions of a formal report?
6. List and describe the preliminary parts of a formal report.
7. List and describe the report body of a formal report.
8. Identify and describe visual aids that can be used to help the reader understand and interpret information presented in a report.

Practical Applications

1. Write a memo report to your instructor on one of the following topics:

    Student clubs and organizations on campus
    Justification for a new computer
    Cafeteria problems
    Parking on campus
    Registration and scheduling procedures

2. Assume that you are employed as a market researcher and have been assigned a report on the market outlook for a chain of sporting goods stores. Write a letter report to the president of the company providing information on the progress of the report.

3. Complete the following steps.
    a. Using the report topic you selected in Chapter 21, Practical Applications, #1, revise the preliminary outline for the report topic to arrive at an organizational plan for writing the report.
    b. Using the organizational plan you have just developed, write the report opening.
    c. Write the body of the report, using headings and effective writing techniques.
    d. Write the report ending.
    e. Develop at least two different graphics to illustrate major points in your report.

Nonverbal and Oral Communication

PART 6

● ●

While much of the business day is spent in producing written documents, other forms of communication are widely used in business, too. When we communicate through body language, tone of voice, or appearance, we are using nonverbal communication. No matter what words we use, the nonverbal signals we send to others often speak louder than our words. Therefore, we should learn to send effective nonverbal signals in both our written and spoken messages.

Listening is a skill often neglected. Since almost half of our communication time is spent in listening, we need to become better listeners. Listening problems can be identified and corrected.

Oral communication comprises about a third of the time we spend communicating. Whether we are talking to one other person, a small group, or a large audience, our speaking skills can be improved so that others will receive the message we are trying to send.

CHAPTER 23

Nonverbal Communication

Objectives

After studying this chapter and completing the chapter exercises, you should:

1. Understand the importance of nonverbal communication.
2. Be able to explain the roles of nonverbal communication.
3. Understand the use of nonverbal symbols in written messages.
4. Understand the use of nonverbal symbols in spoken messages.
5. Understand the use of nonverbal symbols in the environment.

"Your actions speak so loudly that I can't hear a word you are saying" expresses the impact of nonverbal communication. Regardless of what the words convey, the nonverbal symbols usually convey what the sender really feels. Nonverbal symbols convey the degree of importance the sender attaches to the message and to the receiver.

As you learned in Chapter 1, messages consist of two parts—verbal and nonverbal. Words (either spoken or written) make up the verbal part, and the unspoken or unwritten portions of the message make up the nonverbal part. Nonverbal symbols include such things as body language, tone of voice, environment, and appearance. Nonverbal symbols are present in both written and oral communication as well as in the environment.

Nonverbal symbols help the receiver to interpret the words. Receivers interpret nonverbal symbols by using their senses: sight, hearing, touch, taste, and smell. If a receiver hears a secretary say, "This is great," and sees the secretary smile and lean back contentedly while the computer merges a list of addresses with a letter, the receiver will conclude that the secretary is pleased. The receiver interprets the message based on *sight* (the secretary's smile and body language) and *hearing* (the tone of the secretary's voice). A firm handshake, a delicately seasoned sauce, the beep of a computer, or the stale smell of a creek also conveys a message without a word being spoken.

Most of our opinions are based on the nonverbal symbols we observe and how we interpret them. Studies have found that we judge the attitudes of others 93 percent of the time on nonverbal symbols. As we observe others, we simultaneously evaluate their intelligence and thought processes, judge their level of confidence, appraise their appearance, and predict their actions. Understanding the roles of nonverbal communication and the various types of nonverbal symbols will help you to communicate more effectively in both your personal and your business life.

THE ROLES OF NONVERBAL COMMUNICATION

The verbal and nonverbal symbols that make up communication are not separate entities. Rather, both types of symbols should be interpreted in relation to each other. Understanding how nonverbal symbols are used will help you to communicate clearly and accurately. Nonverbal symbols may reinforce, contradict, substitute for, or regulate the verbal portion of the message.

Reinforcing the Verbal Message

Nonverbal symbols usually reinforce the verbal message. Pointing to the door as you state, "The office is the second door on the left," reinforces the verbal message. Patting someone on the back as you tell the person he or she has done a good job reinforces the message. The secretary's words of satisfaction in the earlier example were reinforced by a smile and the secretary's posture. Pounding the table while making a statement, however, not only reinforces the verbal message but emphasizes it as well.

Contradicting the Verbal Message

Sometimes the verbal and nonverbal symbols do not agree. For example, we may say, "That's fine," but if our voice is strained and our eyes are turned away, which symbol will the receiver believe—the verbal or the nonverbal? Research indicates that when verbal and nonverbal symbols conflict, the receiver generally believes the nonverbal message.

Nonverbal symbols differ among cultures. In some cultures, for example, being late for a social or business engagement is polite, while in others it is considered rude. Belching after a meal may be a compliment to the cook in some cultures but a rude response in others.

Substituting for the Verbal Message

Nonverbal symbols commonly act as substitutes for verbal messages. A hitchhiker thumbing a ride is using a nonverbal symbol to send a message. Likewise, gritting your teeth or throwing your hands in the air indicates frustration; clenching your fists, anger; tapping your foot or a pencil, impatience; and nodding or smiling, agreement. When nonverbal symbols act as substitutes, not a word is spoken.

Regulating the Verbal Message

Nonverbal symbols are commonly used to regulate or control communication between the sender and receiver. In oral communication these regulators may signal when you want to speak, when you want others to continue speaking, or when you want to withdraw from a conversation. For example, reestablishing eye contact with the receiver indicates that you will be concluding your remarks shortly. The nonverbal symbol, eye contact, is telling the receiver to get ready to take over the conversation.

Nodding in agreement encourages the other person to continue; however, checking your watch or closing a portfolio means you are through listening. Should several persons wish to respond in a meeting, the chairperson can regulate who will speak by looking directly at an individual. The direct eye contact of the chairperson conveys authority to this individual.

NONVERBAL SYMBOLS IN WRITTEN MESSAGES

Business people strive to convey a professional attitude in all written documents, especially external documents. It is critical, therefore, that careful attention be given to the appearance and correctness of a written document as well as to the timeliness of the response.

The appearance of a document is affected by the quality of paper on which a message is prepared. Documents should be printed on high-quality bond stationery. The letterhead stationery, plain sheets, and envelopes should be of the same color and quality. The typefaces and the design of the letterhead and logo should convey a professional image. Drawings, photographs, charts, and graphs should be appropriate to the content and enhance the document. The print should be dark, crisp, and of a size that is easy to read. Likewise, documents should be prepared in an attractive, easy-to-read format.

Even more important than appearance is correctness. Documents should be free of errors in capitalization, grammar, number expression, punctuation, spelling, and word usage. Accuracy of content, including accuracy of amounts, addresses, dates, and other factual information, is essential. Documents that are correct send a nonverbal message that the sender is reliable and considers quality and the needs of the receiver to be of utmost importance.

NONVERBAL SYMBOLS IN SPOKEN MESSAGES

Several nonverbal symbols have an impact upon oral messages—body language, touching, use of space and time, voice, and paralanguage.

Body Language

Body language includes the messages transmitted by facial expressions, gestures, and appearance. The study of communication through body language is called **kinesics.** A word of caution is necessary when discussing body language. It is surprisingly complex; a single motion can have many different meanings. To assume that someone is sending a clear message because of certain body motions is a dangerous assumption.

Facial Expressions

Facial expressions reveal how a person feels. A frown usually indicates negative feelings; a smile usually indicates happy feelings. Yet there are many different kinds of smiles. Genuine smiles that radiate openness and sincerity portray the person as someone nice to be around. Smiles without eye contact and with lips closed can have the opposite effect. Nervous smiles convey weakness or insecurity.

Eyes are the most revealing part of our expression, and thus they are often called "the windows of the soul." Eyes reveal internal feelings such as excitement, boredom, energy, tiredness, surprise or shock, intensity or concentration, and sadness. Eyebrows also send various messages. Raised eyebrows may mean nervousness, surprise, or questioning; pinched together they may imply confusion or indecision.

FIGURE 23-1 **Feelings of warmth, hesitation, sincerity, or skepticism are visible in one's facial expression.**

Eye contact is an extremely revealing nonverbal symbol. Direct eye contact may convey interest, friendship, or confidence; a lack of eye contact may mean disinterest or boredom. In business, the amount of eye contact varies depending on one's status. Generally subordinates make more eye contact with persons of higher rank than vice versa.

Gestures

Gestures include the use of one's arms and hands to express an idea or feeling. Crossed arms may indicate concentration or withdrawal; a hand placed against the side of the head can imply forgetfulness; trembling or fidgeting hands sometimes indicate nervousness.

Leaning toward a person who is speaking conveys an open attitude. Nodding confirms listening and sometimes agreement. On the other hand, folding your arms or shaking your head from side to side indicates a closed attitude or disagreement.

FIGURE 23-2   Gestures usually reinforce the spoken message.

Appearance

Appearance sends a strong nonverbal message to those we meet. To be viewed as acceptable, competent, and professional, we must project an appearance that is appropriate for the situation and attractive. According to research, people generally believe that attractive people, regardless of sex, possess more socially desirable personality traits than do unattractive people. In fact, people try harder to please attractive people than they do people they consider unattractive.

To be attractive, we must keep our bodies strong and in good shape. Proper diet, rest, and consistent exercise are the keys to maintaining an attractive body. In addition, our clothing must be appropriate to our work and to the organization. In most businesses, appropriate clothes are conservative in fabric, color, and fit. For men, suits are usually appropriate. For women, suits or dresses with jackets are always in good taste.

Posture conveys a person's level of confidence. Poor posture may be a sign of timidity, nervousness, or laziness. To project a strong self-image, sit and stand straight and tall—no slumping, slouching, or pitching forward. To project confidence, project yourself as if you believe you have a right to be where you are.

FIGURE 23-3   Appearance in the business world counts.

Touching

The most acceptable form of touching in a business environment is the handshake. Appropriate for both men and women, the handshake is a gesture used to greet another or sometimes to close a discussion. To refuse another's handshake is extremely rude. We lay down books and papers or stop whatever we're doing in order to respond appropriately to an offer of a handshake.

Some people claim that a handshake reveals everything about a person from the quality of the person's work to the person's honesty. A person who extends a firm handshake (and simultaneously establishes eye contact) projects a cordial, confident image. On the other hand, a weak, soft handshake (the "dead fish" handshake) suggests listlessness or mental dullness. A cold, wet handshake indicates nervousness and possibly a feeling of inferiority.

Other forms of touching, such as hugging or backslapping, are generally not acceptable in business. Persons of higher rank, however, may put their hand on a subordinate's shoulder as a sign of encouragement or support. Care must be taken, however, that the touch is not interpreted as being condescending or paternalistic.

FIGURE 23-4 A firm and direct yet friendly handshake sets the tone for a cordial meeting.

Space

Space as a nonverbal symbol refers to the physical distance between individuals. In general, we stand relatively close to those we like and leave a lot of space between ourselves and those we are afraid of or don't like. When unable to arrange space comfortably, we adjust other nonverbal symbols. In a crowded elevator, for example, we may pretend others are not there by avoiding eye contact, by staring at the numbers indicating which floor is passing, or by remaining silent. People react in such ways even though they may have been conversing before entering the elevator.

The reason that people avoid speaking or making eye contact in such situations is that each of us has our own territory—our own space zone. The size of this space depends upon our activity and our relation with the other person(s) involved. For Americans these space zones are as follows:

1. *Intimate zone* —0 to 18 inches. To be comfortable at this close range, individuals must have an intimate relationship—close friends sharing confidences, a parent reassuring or scolding a child, a husband and wife having a disagreement. Touch and smell are the senses most used. Verbal communication is usually soft or even murmured.

2. *Personal zone* — 18 inches to 4 feet. To stand this close, participants must be well acquainted. Words are spoken softly.

3. *Social zone* —4 to 12 feet. The social zone is common for most business meetings or social gatherings. When persons converse in their social zone, they have some reason for speaking. Should a stranger enter our social zone, we usually break eye contact or turn away. For example, if we notice a stranger as we're walking down the sidewalk, generally we will watch him or her from a distance of about 20 feet. As the stranger gets nearer, however, we break eye contact. If we should speak to a stranger who is within our social zone, it will be in a formal, businesslike voice.

4. *Public zone* —more than 12 feet. From a distance of more than 12 feet, people may look at each other, but they do not maintain eye contact. Interaction is avoided. Communication between a speaker and an audience is within the public zone.

In an office environment, the size and use of space may be a sign of one's status. In general, the more spacious an office the higher the individual's status. Meetings are usually held in the office of the person with the higher status. Persons of higher status also have the freedom to enter a subordinate's space unannounced.

Time

The way you use your time is another aspect of nonverbal communication. Certainly a job applicant who wishes to make a good impression would never be late for an interview. If your boss requests information from you "as soon as possible," you will feel some urgency in getting the information. If your boss asks for the information immediately, you will probably stop what you are doing and get it. Being on time for appointments and responding promptly to requests communicate your sense of responsibility and your respect for other people's time as well as your own.

The use of time also shows status. As mentioned earlier, persons of higher status have the freedom to interrupt subordinates. Higher-status persons generally determine the length of a meeting. On the other hand, executives often work longer hours than do lower-status persons.

Voice and Paralanguage

Maybe you have heard the saying, "It's not what you say, but how you say it that counts." Nonverbal symbols called **paralanguage** account for the difference between the "what" and the "how." Paralanguage includes stress, pitch, rate, volume, inflection, rhythm, and pronunciation. It also includes laughing, crying, sighing, grunting, yawning, belching, and coughing. Even silence, pauses, and hesitations are part of paralanguage.

To see the effect of paralanguage, repeat this sentence to yourself four times. Each time stress the word underlined. Note how the meaning of the sentence changes.

<u>I</u> cannot do this.

I <u>cannot</u> do this.

I cannot <u>do</u> this.

I cannot do <u>this</u>.

Paralanguage can be critical to the correct interpretation of a message.

NONVERBAL SYMBOLS IN THE ENVIRONMENT

The kind of environment in which business is conducted also serves as a form of nonverbal communication. The choice of furnishings and decor; the arrangement of tables, chairs, etc.; the level of lighting, temperature, and sound; and the use of color all contribute to the way we feel in the setting. Let's examine two of these elements—furnishings and color.

Furnishings

Have you ever walked into a room and immediately formed a favorable opinion of the occupant because of the room's attractive appearance? More than likely it was the furniture, paintings, or photographs that impressed you. Elements such as these communicate nonverbal messages.

The choice of furnishings and decor is often a part of business strategy. For example, think of the typical fast-food outlet. The tables are close together, the lighting is bright, the seats are molded plastic. The environment is carefully planned to encourage fast turnover of customers. In contrast, a fine dinner house may have a more spacious environment, dim lighting, padded armchairs, and the table set with fine china, a tablecloth, and fresh flowers.

Color

Color establishes a mood within an environment. Generally the walls of an office should be a soothing color such as beige or light yellow. Such colors are especially suitable in an office where people perform stressful or tedious work. On the other hand, excessive use of light blue can have a dulling effect, tending to make workers feel sluggish. Red and orange are stimulating colors, appropriate for areas where people spend a short period of time (a cafeteria, for example) or perform creative work.

SUMMARY

All messages consist of both verbal and nonverbal symbols. Nonverbal symbols help the receiver to interpret the verbal symbols. Nonverbal symbols may reinforce, contradict, substitute for, or regulate a verbal message.

Nonverbal symbols are present in both written and oral communication as well as in the environment. In written messages the nonverbal symbols of appearance, correctness, and timeliness reflect the sender's attitude and abilities. Nonverbal symbols used in spoken messages include body language, touching, space, time, voice, and paralanguage. Nonverbal symbols used extensively in business environments are choice and arrangement of furnishings and choice of color.

 **Communication Activities**

Discussion Questions

1. Explain the difference between verbal and nonverbal communication.
2. Why is nonverbal communication important in our personal and business life?
3. What types of nonverbal symbols accompany written messages? Explain their importance.
4. Name four ways nonverbal messages are used. Give an example of each.
5. Define kinesics. Why is it important?
6. What type of nonverbal symbol is a handshake? Explain the importance and implications of the handshake.
7. Define paralanguage. Explain its significance as a nonverbal symbol.
8. Of what significance are furnishings in the strategies of a business?

Practical Applications

1. Identify the nonverbal symbols in each of the following situations:

Type of Nonverbal Symbol
furnishings
body language
space
touching
voice and paralanguage

   a. a hand gently touching the cheek
   b. a frown
   c. a bald head
   d. a young girl slumping over to avoid appearing too tall
   e. a vase of flowers
   f. the distance between two people who are conversing
   g. a grunt instead of a "yes"
   h. a hairdo
   i. the sound of a pencil tapping in an examination room
   j. a Louis XIV, hand-carved couch

2. Read each of the following situations and indicate the role of the nonverbal symbol.

Roles of Nonverbal Symbols
contradict
regulate
reinforce
substitute

a. As you talk with a friend, your friend nods his head, confirming what you are saying.
b. While scolding your child, you grip her elbow firmly.
c. You have just returned from a meeting that consumed much more time than was necessary. An associate walks into your office and asks, "How was the meeting?" You scowl while you say, "Great!"
d. A subordinate asks you a question. Instead of saying, "I have to think about the question," you respond by folding your hands together and placing them behind your head.
e. You've had an exhausting day. When you arrive home, you drop down into your favorite chair and say, "What a day!"
f. You're having a discussion with one of your peers. As you finish what you want to say, you glance at your peer.

3. Conduct an experiment with nonverbal communication by doing something that is abnormal. For example, sit too close to someone you don't know; offer to shake hands with someone and as the person extends his or her hand withdraw your hand; put your hand on the shoulder of someone you don't know too well; stare at a stranger; sit down at a table with someone you do not know in the library and spread your books and papers into his or her work area. Note the person's responses to your atypical nonverbal actions. Write a short report describing what you did and the reactions you received.

4. For a period of about ten minutes, observe two or more people conversing. As you observe them, make a list of the nonverbal symbols they use. Then divide the nonverbal symbols by their roles. Develop a short memo report addressed to your instructor describing how each symbol was used and the role it played in communicating the message.

5. Visit a business establishment such as an office, a store, or a restaurant. Observe the environmental factors and determine the image created by the environment. Then write a short report describing the effect of the environmental factors.

CHAPTER 24

Listening

Objectives

After studying this chapter and completing the chapter exercises, you should be able to:

1. Understand the importance of listening.
2. Explain the process of listening.
3. Identify factors that cause listening problems.
4. Practice good listening techniques.

Although we may be born with the ability to hear, we are not born with the ability to listen. Good listening is a skill that is learned by practicing good listening habits. Such habits can be developed by becoming aware of the importance and nature of listening, understanding the barriers to listening, and practicing good listening techniques.

THE IMPORTANCE OF LISTENING

What is the most frequent form of communication—reading, writing, speaking, or listening? If you said listening, you are correct. About 70 to 80 percent of our awake time is spent communicating. Of this time, nearly half (45 percent) consists of listening. In contrast, we spend about 30 percent speaking, 16 percent reading, and 9 percent writing.[1] Administrative positions require even more listening time. Managers spend approximately 60 percent of their workday listening. The higher one climbs in the corporate hierarchy, the more time one spends listening to others.

FIGURE 24-1 Managers spend a large part of their day listening to gather information.

[1]Edward Wakin, "The Business of Listening," *Today's Office*, February 1984, p. 46.

Why We Listen

We listen to relax, to obtain information, to express interest, and to discover attitudes. When we listen to good music and watch television, we listen to relax. Listening to the sounds of summer or the rhythm of the tides helps us clear our minds of worry and relieves stress.

We listen to gather information. Estimates are that 90 percent of the information adults acquire is gained by listening. Gathering information for an assignment, participating in an interview, and obtaining feedback from a customer are examples of listening for information.

We listen to let people know that we are interested in what they have to say. Listening and responding as friends or associates chat over lunch is not only enjoyable but conveys the message that what they think and feel is important to us. Such informal conversations establish a bond between people that makes communication in formal situations easier.

Finally, we listen to discover attitudes. Attitudes are often expressed in the nonverbal cues of the message. Alert listeners are aware of these cues and are thus able to identify the real feelings of the speaker.

The Benefits of Listening

Because listening plays such an important role in communication, listening greatly affects the quality of our relations with others. Through listening we can better understand our own feelings, attitudes, and beliefs as well as those of others. Friendships thrive when people take the time to share and understand each other's feelings. Family members build strong bonds through responding to each other's needs. Likewise, good listening helps businesses develop their most important resource — their employees. Employees who feel their opinions count develop greater self-esteem and contribute more to the organization.

Listening is important because it affects the quality of our decisions. In order to make good decisions, we must gather information that is both meaningful and accurate. To gather accurate information requires being alert and asking the right questions. Those who can listen to persons up and down the chain of command will be able to make the best use of the information available to them.

Good listening skills are essential for success in business. Subordinates who receive and interpret instructions and information correctly win the respect of their supervisors. Successful supervisors listen to both their subordinates and their superiors. Similarly, effective salespersons listen

FIGURE 24-2 Effective salespersons listen actively to understand the customer's needs.

in order to gather meaningful feedback from customers and relay it to appropriate decision makers in the firm. Good listeners at all levels are prime candidates for promotion.

THE NATURE OF LISTENING

Some of us assume we are good listeners because we have been listening all our lives. Yet research by Nichols indicates that we remember only about half of what we hear; and after a few weeks, we remember only one fourth of what we originally heard.[2] Remembering takes effective listening. To become a good listener, it is helpful to be aware of factors that

---

[2]Bertha Collins, "Are You Listening?" *Journal of Business Education*, December 1982, p. 103.

make listening difficult, to understand the listening process, and to appreciate the kinds of listening.

Common Problems of Poor Listeners

Missing an important appointment, discounting a valuable suggestion, overlooking the feeling behind the words, and interpreting a situation incorrectly are just a few examples of problems that occur because of poor listening. Researchers have identified various barriers to good listening. As you read about these problems, evaluate yourself as a listener. Do any of these problems sound familiar?

Attitudes Toward the Speaker

"My, he looks as if he didn't get enough sleep last night." "She speaks so slowly; doesn't she know I've got work to do?" "Oh! I wish he hadn't said that; I'm sure he's educated, but you would never know it from his language." When listeners have private conversations such as these with themselves, they are missing what the speaker is saying.

A speaker's appearance, mannerisms, tone of voice, and body language can distract the listener. Poor grammar or choice of words can also cause persons to stop listening and begin mentally criticizing the speaker.

Attitudes Toward the Topic

"I can't program using BASIC; programming is too complex." "Oh, insurance! Don't talk to me about that dull subject." "I couldn't stand to hear one more detail." Have you ever found yourself thinking such thoughts while you listened to a speaker? Messages that sound technical often intimidate listeners. Messages that sound uninteresting or boring cause people to tune out the speaker. In a similar manner, listeners often lose their patience with messages that are too detailed.

Environmental Distractions

Have you ever been at a luncheon at which the speaker began his or her presentation while the desserts or beverages were being served? Have you ever tried to finish a conversation with the telephone ringing? If so, you know how unrelated activities and noise can interfere with your ability to listen. Likewise, excessive heat or coolness and noise are distracting.

Personal Barriers

An obvious barrier to listening is deafness or partial loss of hearing. A headache or some other temporary physical discomfort also inhibits listening. Aside from these personal barriers, each of us tends to block out messages for various psychological reasons.

Prejudices or Differing Opinions. Most of us have preconceived ideas about certain topics. It is difficult to be objective about important personal beliefs that we hold or have even defended at one time. If a speaker challenges one of these strongly held beliefs, the listener may simply turn off what the speaker has to say. Often the listener begins preparing a rebuttal even before the speaker has finished.

Assumptions. People often tend to disregard messages when they think they already know the information. Perhaps you can remember a time when you did not bother to listen to directions to a certain location because you assumed you already knew how to get there. It has been estimated that assumptions made in advance can account for a 75 percent decline in listening.[3]

Lack of Attention. Mind wandering is another deterrent to effective listening. Worrying about some personal problem or daydreaming about more interesting ideas causes our minds to wander. Sometimes people retain a facial expression that says, "I'm listening," but in reality their minds are somewhere else.

Notetaking

"Today I am not going to miss anything; I am going to take notes on everything that is said." Such is the ambition of a poor listener. In the effort to outline everything that is said, the poor listener hears only about one third of what is presented. Conversely, some listeners write down only the main ideas and fail to record enough of the supporting information to make the main ideas meaningful or clear.

The Listening Process

The listening process consists of four steps: hearing, focusing attention, understanding, and remembering. Hearing is a function of the ears. In the office we may hear people talking, telephones ringing, doors being closed or opened, or other environmental sounds. Hearing is the first step in listening.

Second, listening requires focusing attention on the speaker and concentrating on what is being said. In order to focus our attention, we must ignore the unrelated sounds, the background noise, and other distractors such as people moving about.

Third, listening requires understanding what the speaker has said. A person may hear and focus on someone speaking in an unfamiliar foreign

---

[3]Ibid.

language, but the message is meaningless. For understanding to occur, the listener must be able to attach meaning to the message.

Finally, remembering is the last step in the listening process. If you cannot repeat accurately something you have just heard, you have not really listened. Figure 24-3 illustrates the listening process.

FIGURE 24-3 **The Listening Process**

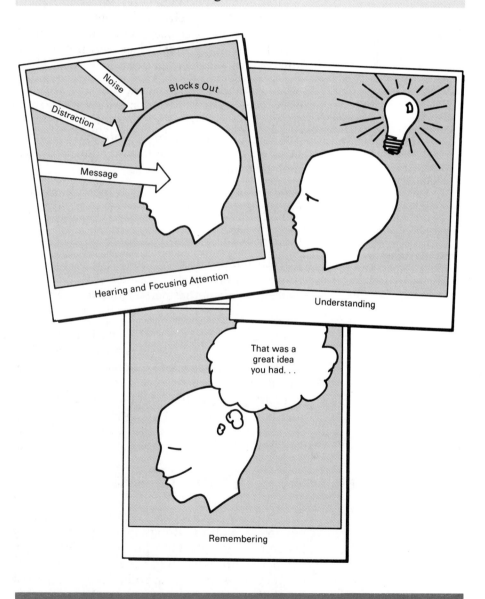

Types of Listening

There are two types of listening—casual and active. Both have different uses. **Casual listening** is what we do most frequently. Casual listening is associated with conversation and entertainment. Watching a movie or making small talk between classes or at lunch are examples of casual listening. The casual listener expends little energy or effort. Although the listener may comprehend the message, remembering it is not critical. Casual listening is relaxed. When we are engaged in informal conversations, however, we must be careful not to listen so casually that others think we are not paying attention.

Active listening, on the other hand, is purposeful listening. Doctors actively listen to their patients; interviewers actively listen to what the applicant is saying. To understand the difference between casual and active listening, try to remember a time that you listened very intently because you had something to gain from what was said—you were motivated to listen by your own self-interest.

When we actively listen, our minds are alert and absorbed in what the speaker is saying. We empathize with the speaker by trying to understand the speaker's perspective, attitudes, and emotions. Empathetic listeners also realize that it is more important to listen than to talk.

Active listening, however, involves an element of risk. The listener risks seeing the world as the speaker sees it. When a listener actually senses the feelings of another person and appreciates what the other person's experiences mean to that person, it may mean changing one's beliefs.

Active listening also requires noticing and interpreting the nonverbal cues of the message. Attitudes are expressed by speakers in various ways: pauses, tone of voice, the emphasis given or not given to words, the nervous habits such as using too many "okay's" and "ahhh's," fidgeting with pointers, grasping the podium too tightly, and so forth. Table 24-1 provides an example of active listening.

EFFECTIVE LISTENING TECHNIQUES

Everyone needs to become an effective listener. Understanding the listening process and the things that cause people not to listen is not enough. Listening is a skill that requires continuous practice. To become a good listener requires knowing one's own personal weaknesses and practicing good listening habits. Follow these suggestions to improve your listening skills.

TABLE 24-1 Active Listening

Step	Action
1	Bob sends a message.
2	Tisha listens to the words and to the way they are used. She also watches the nonverbal cues sent by Bob's face, hands, etc.
3	Tisha analyzes the verbal and nonverbal messages received and decides what she thinks Bob is saying.
4	Tisha summarizes to Bob what she thinks was the intended message.
5	Bob decides whether Tisha's summary is a correct interpretation of what he originally sent. If Tisha's summary is correct, Bob agrees with the summary. If Tisha's summary is incorrect, Bob says "No, it is...." At this point, Tisha returns to step 2, and steps 2 through 5 are repeated until Bob agrees with Tisha's summary.

Share the Responsibility

Although the responsibility for conveying meaning is largely that of the speaker, effective listeners realize that they play a vital role in the communication process. Listeners must be able to attach meaning to what has been said.

People talk at about 100 to 150 words per minute and think at a rate of about 300 to 500 words per minute. Therefore the listener has spare time available. Rather than letting their minds wander, effective listeners use this spare time in ways that will benefit comprehension. To increase comprehension, use your time effectively by focusing on the main idea, evaluating the message, and providing feedback.

Focus on the Main Idea

Some speakers develop their points in a rather disorganized way, mixing the unimportant with the important. Therefore, to be a good listener, you must be willing to wait for the main idea and not be distracted by unimportant details. Separate what is fact from what is opinion. If you are taking notes, record the main ideas and enough of the supporting information to make the main ideas meaningful. Concentrate on the message, not on the speaker's delivery or appearance.

Evaluate the Message

Compare the message of the speaker with what you already know or believe about the topic. When you have some knowledge of the topic, don't turn the speaker off by assuming you already know what will be said. Instead, relate what you already know to what the speaker is saying.

Observe the speaker's nonverbal symbols. A natural, relaxed style and good eye contact show that the speaker feels confident about the message. On the other hand, nervous mannerisms may cause you to question the validity of the message.

Provide Feedback

When you understand the message, smile or nod your head to let the speaker know. Feedback is supportive to the speaker. To assure understanding, ask questions for clarification, paraphrase, or restate the message as you understand it. Statements such as "If I understand you correctly, you mean that..." provide valuable feedback and aid understanding.

Overcome Poor Listening Habits

As discussed earlier, listening is a skill that requires practice. To become an effective listener requires changing attitudes toward speakers, attitudes toward topics, and personal habits that result in poor listening. Figure 24-4 gives suggestions for becoming a better listener.

FIGURE 24-4 Keys to Effective Listening

- Find common interests.
- Judge content, not delivery.
- Delay judgment until the speaker is finished.
- Listen for the main idea of the message.
- Take notes on only the important points.
- Concentrate on listening; be alert.
- Avoid physical and environmental distractors.
- Listen with an open mind; don't let prejudices or assumptions cause you to miss the message.
- Use your spare listening time to analyze and evaluate the message.
- Talk less; listen more.

SUMMARY

Listening is an extremely important communication skill. We spend more time listening than writing, reading, or speaking. Our listening skills affect the quality of our relationships with others, the quality of our decisions, and our ability to succeed on the job.

Most of us assume that we are good listeners, but the reality is that we are not. We listen to only half of what we hear and forget much of that. As a result we miss appointments, take wrong turns, fail to respond to valuable suggestions, and misinterpret what has been said. Factors such as a critical attitude toward the speaker or the topic, environmental distractions, and poor listening habits cause us problems with listening.

The listening process includes hearing, focusing our attention on the speaker and ignoring distractors, understanding the message, and remembering it. Comprehension can be improved by (1) focusing on the main idea, (2) evaluating the message by comparing it with what is already known, and (3) providing feedback. To become an effective listener, share the responsibility for communication and overcome personal habits that inhibit good listening.

● ● ● ● ● ● ● ● ● **Communication Activities**

Discussion Questions

1. Identify four reasons for listening, and give four reasons why listening is important.
2. Explain how the speaker, the topic, the environment, and notetaking can result in poor listening.
3. Identify three personal barriers to listening and give an example of a time when each was a personal barrier for you.
4. Explain the difference between casual and active listening.
5. Describe the four steps in the listening process.
6. Describe three ways the time differential between speaking rate and comprehension rate can be used to improve listening.

Practical Applications

1. Copy this chart. Complete a self-analysis of your listening skills by ranking yourself in each problem area as good, fair, or poor. Indicate ways to improve on each problem.

Listening Problem	Ranking	How to Improve
1. Deciding in advance that subject is uninteresting and unimportant		
2. Mentally criticizing speaker's delivery		
3. Becoming overstimulated when opposing an idea		
4. Listening only for factual data		
5. Trying to outline everything you hear		
6. Not letting speaker know that it's hard to hear him or her		
7. Failing to question speaker when something is unclear or incomplete		
8. Turning off technical messages		
9. Reacting to emotional words or phrases		
10. Letting your mind wander		

2. Engage a friend or acquaintance in a social listening experience. Then develop the conversation into a serious discussion. Try to maintain the serious discussion for three minutes. Write a one-page report to your instructor addressing your feelings about the conversations. Answer the following questions in your report.

a. Were you able to maintain the conversation at the appropriate level? If so, how did you do it? If not, what prevented you from doing it?
b. Of the two types of listening, which was the easier to maintain, casual or active?
c. Which type of listening was easier for you?

3. Compose a letter to your instructor explaining how the common listening problems relate to you. In the letter identify your most serious problem and give some examples. Using the suggestions in this chapter, develop a plan for overcoming this problem.

4. Write a memorandum to your teacher containing the following:
a. a list of the clues that tell the speaker you are not listening
b. a list of the clues that tell the speaker you are listening
c. conclusions about the importance of nonverbal communication in the listening process

5. Observe someone's listening skills for about 15 minutes. Indicate whether the listener was involved in casual and/or active listening. Rate the listener as good, fair, or poor. Justify your answers by using the keys to effective listening and the characteristics of poor and good listening.

CHAPTER 25

Oral Communication

Objectives

After studying this chapter and completing the chapter exercises, you should be able to:

1. Give a short oral presentation.
2. Prepare a formal presentation.
3. Deliver a formal presentation.

374

Oral communication is a common activity in today's business world. The types of speeches and oral presentations you will give will depend upon the career path you take. If you supervise others, you will probably conduct training programs. If you work in personnel, you may be responsible for presenting orientation programs for new employees. If you become a high-level executive, you will be called upon to make presentations to the board of directors, the media, and civic and professional organizations.

If you have never given speeches, you may find that you are nervous and fearful when having to make a presentation. The fear of speaking before a group is universal. People lessen this fear, however, with practice and preparation. This chapter will help you to become more self-confident when making oral presentations.

SHORT ORAL COMMUNICATION

Most of the oral presentations you will give will be short. Typical short speeches are introductions and briefings in meetings or conferences. You will also communicate orally on the telephone, face-to-face, and in meetings.

Short Speeches

Short speeches usually last 15 minutes or less. Because of limited time for these presentations, the subject matter is generally simple and straightforward.

The structure of a short presentation resembles that of a letter or memo. Begin with an opening that arouses the audience's interest and prepares them for what is to follow. Provide the details in the body of your speech. In the closing, summarize the main points of your presentation briefly.

Introductions

When called upon to introduce someone (usually a speaker), find out first if there is a specific format that should be followed. Many organizations provide guidelines for introductions in order to keep them short and uniform. If there are no formal guidelines, consider adapting the following suggestions to the situation.

First, obtain information about the person you are to introduce. Usually you will be given a resume or biographical sketch. If possible, find out what the speaker would like you to mention. Your basic purpose is to prepare the audience to accept the speaker and the speech. Don't provide too much information—this will simply make the audience restless. (After all, they are there to hear the speaker, not the introducer.)

Give the speaker's name and title in your presentation. Try to mention things about the speaker or the speech that the audience can relate to and that will arouse their interest in the speaker and the speech.

Briefings

Briefings are talks usually given at meetings or conferences to bring people up-to-date on business activities, projects, programs, or procedures. Since briefings are short, provide key points with only a few details to illustrate your points.

Telephone Calls

The telephone is still the mainstay of business. Every day you will communicate with others orally over the telephone. Here are some pointers to make your telephone communication more effective.

- Identify yourself and your organization when calling or when placing a call. Don't expect others to guess who you are.
- Use a pleasant, low tone of voice. Remember, others cannot see your face; your voice conveys your personality.
- Be helpful when answering the phone. Offer to take a message or to locate information or even other departments or people for the caller.
- Take messages accurately. Message pads are usually available. Fill them out completely, including the name (and organization, if possible) of the caller, name of person being called, telephone number and extension, message, date and time of the call, and name or initials of the person taking the message.
- When transferring a call, tell the caller whom you are transferring the call to, the reason for the transfer, and the phone number you are transferring to.
- Plan your calls. Before calling, have all available information in front of you, including documents you need to discuss, names of people, telephone numbers, and possibly even a brief outline of points to discuss.
- Be courteous. "Please" and "thank you" are not outdated terms.
- Speak clearly and distinctly into the mouthpiece. Enunciate words carefully.
- Close telephone conversations cordially. Usually the caller is expected to end the conversation.

Face-to-Face Communication

Face-to-face communication is usually informal. You are simply sharing information or discussing some matter with one other person or perhaps a small group of people. Even though this type of communication does not require the extensive preparation of a formal speech, you should be prepared. Have all available material with you. Speak clearly and distinctly and look at others directly. Use a conversational, pleasant tone of voice. And be sure to listen to what others are saying.

Meetings

During meetings and conferences, people communicate orally to share information and discuss business matters. If you are called upon to conduct a meeting, be sure to follow certain accepted meeting procedures which will assure you of a successful experience.

FIGURE 25-2 Meetings are a common form of oral communication in business.

FIGURE 25-2 Meetings are a common form of oral communication in business.

- Prepare a meeting agenda, which lists the matters to be discussed at the meeting. If possible, send the agenda to meeting participants prior to the meeting so that they will be prepared to discuss the items.

- Start and end the meeting on time. Much time is frequently wasted waiting for latecomers to arrive at meetings. If you make a habit of starting your meetings on time, people will usually start arriving at your meetings on time.

- Follow the agenda. As meeting leader, you must move the meeting along, keeping others on target. In informal meetings, people can begin a discussion which leads away from the subject at hand or prolongs the meeting. While you usually do want open discussion at meetings, you as the leader are responsible for keeping the meeting on track.

- Give everyone the opportunity to participate. In meetings of no more than 20 participants, you might even have others report or share by going around the table. Or you could draw out quieter participants by asking their opinion about an issue. For those who are overly talkative, be tactful as you say that time is limited and others need to be heard from.

- At the end of the meeting, summarize key points discussed and any conclusions or recommendations arrived at. This activity will give you the opportunity to clear up any misunderstandings that may have occurred. Make sure everyone knows who has agreed to do what by what date.

✔ **Checkpoint 1**   SHORT ORAL COMMUNICATION

Indicate whether each of the following statements is true or false.

1. The purpose of an introduction is to prepare the audience to accept the speaker and the speech.
2. Briefings should provide many details to bring the audience up-to-date on business.
3. Always identify yourself and your organization when making a telephone call.
4. There is no need to prepare for face-to-face communication since it does not require the extensive preparation of a formal speech.
5. Meetings should begin on time, but it is better to wait until everyone arrives so that you won't have to repeat information.

Check your answers in Appendix D.

FORMAL ORAL PRESENTATIONS

Preparing formal oral presentations is much more involved than preparing short oral presentations. When preparing a long speech, which could last from 20 minutes to over an hour, you have much more information to present than in a shorter presentation. The participants will be *listening* to your presentation rather than reading a written report. Moreover, the audience will have many opportunities to become distracted or bored. Most audiences have an attention span of about 20 minutes—an obvious problem if you have an hour's presentation.

Planning the Presentation

Planning an oral presentation is like planning a written report. Plan an introduction, a body, and an ending. You may also use visual aids, such as tables, charts, and graphs.

Determine Your Objective

Decide what the major theme or objective of your presentation is. What is it that you want to get across to an audience? How do you want your audience to react to your presentation? How much does your audience already know about the topic?

As you consider the answers to these questions, you will be able to state the objective of your presentation. You should write out this objective in statement form, as in the following examples.

- Marketing managers should learn about new products being developed and sales goals.
- Business education teachers should implement business computer software courses in their schools to prepare students for employment.
- A customer should place an order with us because we have a quality product and fast delivery.

Analyze Your Audience

After determining the objective of your presentation, analyze your expected audience in terms of size, knowledge level, and demographics.

The *size* of your audience will determine the approach you take in delivery. If the audience is small (20 or fewer people), you may be able to have more audience interaction. If the audience is large (several hundred), you will need to have a good sound system, and any visual aids you use must be visible to the entire audience.

The *knowledge level* of your audience is important. Try to find out what people already know about your subject and their attitude toward the subject. If you are approaching an audience that has little knowledge of the subject, you will need to provide the necessary background information. If the audience is already familiar with the topic, you might go directly into your subject with little introduction.

The *demographics* of your audience can help you as you are preparing your speech. What are the age ranges? How many are men and how many are women? What is their educational level? What are their occupations? Where do these people live or come from? What socioeconomic and ethnic groups are represented?

Determine Time Available

Often speakers are given a specified amount of time to make a presentation and must work within that limitation. You will be fortunate if you are given an opportunity to set your own limits.

Most speakers can deliver one paragraph, consisting of 125–150 words, in a minute. If you have two main points in your presentation and 30 minutes in which to make the presentation, you could spend 3–5 minutes on opening remarks and an introduction, 15–20 minutes developing your main points, and 5–10 minutes on your conclusions, summary, and responding to questions.

Gather Information

Information for an oral presentation is gathered in much the same way as for a formal written report. In fact, you may be making your presentation based on a report previously prepared. Refer to Chapter 21 for information on gathering data for reports.

Determine Mode of Delivery

Several delivery options are available to a speaker—impromptu (also known as extemporaneous), textual (reading or speaking from notes), and memorizing.

When you are asked to speak without any advance notice, you will be speaking **impromptu.** Perhaps you are asked during a meeting to describe the computer options available in your company. Take a few moments to gather your thoughts before speaking and try not to ramble in your remarks.

When making a **textual presentation,** you will be reading from a written copy of your speech or from an outline or note cards. Reading a speech is not a recommended practice unless your material is highly technical. Even then, be sure to maintain eye contact with your audience. Speaking from an outline or notes is one of the best methods of delivery. You can maintain a good deal of eye contact while having the notes to refer to for major points.

Memorizing an entire speech is not recommended because of the chances of forgetting lines and becoming flustered. Also, a memorized speech often sounds stilted and formal. Memorizing a quotation or opening or closing remarks, however, can be effective in delivery.

Organizing the Presentation

All presentations, whether formal or informal, should have three main parts: an introduction, the body, and an ending.

Introduction

At the beginning of your speech, tell the audience what your topic is and what points you will cover in your presentation. You may want to begin by using some proven attention-getters to gain the audience's attention.

Attention-getters hold the audience's attention during a long presentation. Use some time-tested attention-getters not only at the beginning of your speech but throughout it.

- *Quotes* — Use a quotation to illustrate a point. If you can, memorize the quotation and give the source.

- *Anecdote* — Tell a story related to the audience or the topic. People enjoy hearing a story and will usually perk up and pay attention. They will often get a point better through an anecdote.

- *Humor* — Use humor in your speech. Although most business presentations are serious, a little humor lightens up the atmosphere and makes audiences more receptive to the presentation. If you tell jokes well, then incorporate them into your speech. Many speakers warm up an audience with jokes and then proceed to a totally serious topic. If you can, tell a few jokes (preferably related to the topic), and then don't forget to intersperse some humor later on in your speech.

● *Statistics* —Cite an interesting or unusual statistic when appropriate. People like details, but not too many!

The *preview* of your introduction simply prepares the audience for the body of your presentation. For example, if you are using three points to persuade someone to buy a product, your preview would reveal to your audience the order of presentation of the three points.

Body

The middle part, or body, of your presentation should present the main points you want to make to the audience. While you can use organizational plans similar to those used in writing letters, memos, and reports (direct or indirect), you want to keep your presentation as simple as possible so that the audience will understand your topic and remember the important points.

Try to limit your main points to no more than three, and arrange those points in a logical sequence. As you move along in your speech, summarize previous points made and preview things to come. As you shift topics, provide a transition from one idea to the next. You might say, "Now that we've looked at the problems with our old computer system, let's look at some possible solutions."

Use variety to hold the audience's attention. You can vary the pace of the presentation by using visual aids, asking questions of the audience, and using examples to illustrate your key points.

Ending

Close your presentation by reviewing or summarizing the main points of the speech. Your objective is to have the audience understand the topic and possibly take some recommended action as a result of your presentation.

Outline

An outline can be invaluable as you plan your speech. If you decide to deliver your speech from notes, the outline could end up being your final speech. If you plan to use the outline as your notes, you should consider writing complete statements rather than one- or two-word topic headings.

The outline should be developed according to the organizational plan you are using for your speech—direct or indirect. Remember that direct order (main idea first) is used when the audience is expected to be receptive, while indirect order (main idea later) is used when the audience is expected to be skeptical or nonreceptive.

Suppose that you are the campaign manager for a political candidate. It is the day before the election, and you must make a speech on your candidate's chances of winning the election. If the polls indicate that your candidate has a good chance of winning, you would use the direct order in developing your outline. See Figure 25-4.

FIGURE 25-4   Outline Using Direct Order

I. Introduction

    A. Attention-getter—You are going to win!
    B. Objective—to explain why you are going to win
    C. Preview—order the presentation by districts: District 1, District 2, District 3

II. Body

    A. District 1
        1. Home district of opponent
        2. About 12,000 voters
        3. Opponent to get 58% of the votes—7,000
        4. You will get 42%—5,000 votes
        5. Opponent will carry District 1
    B. District 2
        1. Neutral district
        2. About 15,000 voters
        3. Opponent to get 53%—8,000 votes
        4. You will get 47%—7,000 votes
        5. Opponent will carry District 2
    C. District 3
        1. Your home district
        2. About 15,000 voters
        3. Opponent to get 27%—4,000 votes
        4. You will get 73%—11,000 votes
        5. You will carry District 3 by wide margin

III. Ending (Summary)

    A. Main message—You will win!
    B. Objective—to predict the outcome of the election
    C. Preview paraphrased
    D. Summary of data and conclusions

Suppose, however, that the election is too close to know whether your candidate will win or not. You will develop the outline and give the speech using the indirect order, placing the main idea later in the speech. See Figure 25-5.

FIGURE 25-5 Outline Using Indirect Order

I. Introduction

 A. Attention-getter
 B. Objective — to explain the anticipated results of tomorrow's election
 C. Preview — order the presentation by districts: District 1, District 2, District 3

II. Body

 A. District 1
  1. Home district of opponent
  2. About 12,000 voters
  3. Opponent to get 58% of the votes — 7,000
  4. You will get 42% — 5,000 votes
  5. Opponent will carry District 1
 B. District 2
  1. Neutral district
  2. About 15,000 voters
  3. Opponent to get 53% — 8,000 votes
  4. You will get 47% — 7,000 votes
  5. Opponent will carry District 2
 C. District 3
  1. Your home district
  2. About 15,000 voters
  3. Opponent claims 40% — 6,000 votes
  4. Your remaining share is 60% — 9,000 votes
  5. You need one more vote to win the election

III. Ending (Summary)

 A. Objective — paraphrase objective
 B. Preview — paraphrase preview of the election
 C. Summary — summarize data and conclusions
 D. Main message — election is too close to call. Let's really push to get voters out in District 3.

Checkpoint 2 PREPARING FORMAL ORAL PRESENTATIONS

Indicate whether each of the following statements is true or false.

1. Gathering information for a formal oral presentation is very different from gathering information for a formal written report.
2. Memorizing an entire speech is not an effective delivery method.
3. Opening your speech with an attention-getter is gimmicky and not recommended.
4. Most formal presentations should have no more than three main points.
5. Develop the outline of your speech using direct or indirect order.

Check your answers in Appendix D.

DELIVERY

The delivery of your presentation is just as important as the content. Voice qualities, nonverbal symbols, and visual aids can enhance or inhibit your delivery. Audience feedback can let you know whether your audience has understood and accepted your message. Figure 25-6 provides some suggestions for delivery which will make your presentation more effective.

Voice Qualities

Try to develop vocal qualities that will make an audience sit up and listen. Record your voice to find out what you need to do to improve it.

Pronounce words distinctly, enunciating words carefully. Avoid slang, such as "yeah" and "you guys." Most people have some sort of regional accent that can present a problem in communicating with others who don't have that accent. Try to minimize your accent by pronouncing words as close to "standard" pronunciation as possible. Avoid cutting off word endings, such as saying "buyin'" instead of "buying." You don't want to lose credibility with your audience simply because of your diction. Speak clearly and articulate well—above all, don't mumble!

Speak loudly enough so that everyone can hear you. However, don't speak so loudly that your voice sounds unnatural. To achieve appropriate vol-

FIGURE 25-6 Tips for Effective Delivery of Oral Presentations

Follow these suggestions for effective delivery.

- Know your subject! No matter what delivery mode you are using (impromptu, reading speech or using notes, or memorizing), be familiar with your subject.

- Practice your speech until you become comfortable with presenting it. Consider taping it, either audio or video, to provide feedback for improving your delivery.

- Dress appropriately and use good grooming.

- Maintain your enthusiasm. Keep your energy level high.

- Start and finish your speech on time.

- Use your voice effectively. Speak clearly; project your voice; vary your tone; use correct grammar.

- Use nonverbal gestures effectively.

- Maintain eye contact with the audience.

---

ume, look at the person farthest away from you and project your voice as though you were speaking to that person.

Don't talk too fast. Although you are familiar with your subject matter, the audience is not. If you talk too fast, the audience may not have time to consider all your points and may become confused. Speak at a moderate pace.

Speak with enthusiasm and conviction. If you are excited about your topic and convey belief in it, you will be better able to convince skeptical audiences.

Nonverbal Symbols

Nonverbal symbols used during an oral presentation add to or detract from the presentation. They indicate how the speaker feels about the situation—relaxed, nervous, or confident. Four nonverbal symbols important to making oral presentations are eye contact, facial expression, gestures, and posture.

Maintain eye contact with your audience. When you do, you will keep them personally involved in your speech. Let your eyes move around the audience to let them know you are interested in communicating with them and to read the feedback they are giving you. This feedback can be vital to your success as a speaker.

Use appropriate facial expressions to communicate with your audience. A smile, a frown, a look of concern or surprise can all convey a message to your audience.

Use gestures effectively to emphasize important points in your speech. Gestures also tell the audience whether you are nervous or calm. Studies indicate that nervousness is generally expressed nonverbally by the upper half of the body. Actions such as playing with a pointer used for visual aids, using "ah's" or "um's," tapping fingers, looking at visual aids unnecessarily, clutching the sides of a rostrum, putting your hands in your pockets during the whole presentation, folding your arms across your chest and not moving them—all indicate that the speaker is nervous.

But be aware of the rest of your body as well. Avoid toe tapping, placing the toe of the shoe on the floor and wiggling it about, or slipping a shoe on and off while speaking. Be natural in using gestures. Let your audience see your personality in your presentation.

You may be nervous about giving a speech because of your fear of public speaking. The fear of public speaking is a common and very powerful fear which can be overcome in time by doing the very thing you're afraid of—speaking in public. Figure 25-7 offers tips used by professional speakers to overcome stage fright.

Maintain good posture throughout your presentation. Good posture indicates that you are self-confident, feel good, and are interested in your topic and the audience. A slouch indicates poor self-esteem, lack of interest in the topic, or lack of respect for the audience.

Tips for Using Visual Aids

Visual aids can enhance your ability to communicate when delivering an oral presentation and should be used to emphasize or explain points of your speech or to illustrate your presentation. The following visual aids are commonly used.

Transparencies can be projected onto a screen with an overhead projector. One big advantage is that you don't have to dim the lights; therefore, you don't lose eye contact with the audience. Use transparencies effectively to emphasize major points of your speech.

Flip charts are large sheets of paper bound at the top. You can write on sheets as you speak to illustrate points or use previously prepared sheets

FIGURE 25-7 Tips for Overcoming Stage Fright

Follow these suggestions to overcome stage fright.

- Prepare your speech well.

- Rehearse the presentation thoroughly in advance.

- Realize that your audience is there to learn from you.

- Psych yourself up just before your speech by thinking positive thoughts about your speech and about the audience.

- Take several deep breaths before beginning.

- Drink some water if your throat is dry.

- Establish eye contact with several responsive people in the audience. Their positive feedback will encourage and motivate you.

- Don't panic if you feel that the audience is losing interest. Keep going and try to revive their interest with your enthusiasm and with visual aids if appropriate.

and simply flip the pages during your speech. Felt-tip markers in different colors can be used effectively on flip charts.

Chalkboards or **whiteboards** can be used with small audiences to list major points of the speech or ideas from the audience. Colored pens are used to write on whiteboards.

Slides of photographs or drawings can be very effective to illustrate a topic. You will need to coordinate the slides with your speech and may need to have someone operate the slide projector for you. Slides need to be shown in a darkened room, however, causing you to lose eye contact with your audience.

When using any visual aids, keep these points in mind:

1. Make sure the printing or writing on the visual aid is large enough for everyone to read.

2. Keep your visual aids simple and easy to understand.

3. If you are using equipment, check it beforehand to make sure it works.

4. Use color for emphasis and contrast.

5. Make sure your visual aids look professionally prepared.

Develop your visual aids during the planning stage of the oral presentation. You will then be able to practice using the visual aids when you practice giving the speech.

Feedback

Oral presentations allow immediate feedback to the speaker in the form of questions from the audience. When planning a speech, try to allow time at the end for questions and answers. If the group is very small, you might even encourage comments or questions during the presentation.

By having a question-and-answer period, you can find out what the audience's reaction is to your speech. You also have the opportunity to clarify points that were not clear to the audience and to reemphasize the major points of your presentation.

✔ Checkpoint 3 DELIVERY

Indicate whether each of the following statements is true or false.

1. The delivery of your speech is just as important as the content.
2. To make your presentation sound natural, do not try to minimize a regional accent you may have.
3. Nervousness is usually expressed through body movements such as toe tapping or clutching the sides of the rostrum.
4. To overcome a fear of speaking, avoid practicing your speech because doing so will make you more nervous.
5. Visual aids may be used to emphasize or explain points of your speech.

Check your answers in Appendix D.

SUMMARY

Giving oral presentations is a common activity in the business world. You may give short presentations, such as introductions and briefings, or formal speeches. Almost everyone communicates orally on the telephone, face-to-face, and in meetings.

In preparing for a formal oral presentation, determine the objective of your speech, analyze your audience, find out how much time you have for the speech, and gather information as you would in preparing a formal written report.

Organize the formal speech into three parts—the introduction, the body, and the ending. Develop an outline which may be used in the delivery of your speech.

Use effective voice quality, nonverbal communication, and visual aids to enhance the delivery of your oral presentation. Allow time for audience feedback through a question-and-answer period.

 **Communication Activities**

Discussion Questions

1. Describe the types of short oral communication frequently used in business situations.
2. What steps are involved in planning formal oral presentations?
3. Identify and explain three methods of delivering oral presentations.
4. How can attention-getters be used to hold the audience's attention during a long presentation?
5. What is presented in each of the three main parts of a speech (introduction, body, ending)?
6. What voice characteristics should be avoided in speechmaking?
7. How can you overcome the fear of public speaking?
8. What visual aids can be effectively used and how can they be used for oral presentations?

Practical Applications

1. Prepare a five- to ten-minute oral presentation on a short written report you have prepared.
2. Deliver the oral presentation prepared in #1 to classmates.
3. Listen to a speech and prepare a written evaluation of the speaker's effectiveness in delivering the speech.
4. Assume that you work for the chamber of commerce in your city or town. As a new employee, one of your responsibilities is to recruit new citizens and businesses. Outline a presentation which you could use for recruitment. Visit your chamber of commerce or some other organization to locate the necessary data for the presentation. Develop an outline and appropriate visual aids.
5. Develop and deliver the oral presentation described in #4.

Career Communication

PART 7

· ·

Now that you have effective communication skills, you want to put them to work for you in getting the job you want. In the development of your resume, you will analyze career goals, job qualifications, and the job market. The end result of this process will be the development of a resume that communicates your qualifications to prospective employers.

Along with the resume, the application letter should be carefully written. Both types of application letters, solicited and unsolicited, should gain the reader's attention, present your qualifications, and close with a request for an interview.

The result of the career communication process is to gain an employment interview which will result in a job offer. The final chapter prepares you for the interview and explains follow-up procedures.

CHAPTER 26

The Resume

Objectives

After studying this chapter and completing the chapter exercises, you should be able to:

1. Analyze your career goals.
2. Analyze your job qualifications.
3. Analyze the job market.
4. Prepare a marketable resume.

One of your most exciting and important challenges in life will be the job search. Most of us spend a major portion of our lives at work. We should, therefore, make certain that we carefully consider our choice of career. You will want to select a career that is enjoyable, challenging, interesting, and fulfilling.

Whether you are just starting out in a career or are reentering the job market, obtaining employment requires a good deal of preparation and planning. You should begin this process at least three months before you want to start working. In this chapter we will discuss the job search and writing your resume, which is a summary of your qualifications.

PREPARING FOR THE JOB SEARCH

One of the goals of our education is to prepare us for getting a job. You may now be studying in a specialized area so that you will have the abilities to perform in a particular career field. Perhaps you have not made a final decision about the type of work you would like to do. You may enjoy a variety of activities, including leisure and work activities, but are confused about a career objective. Whether or not you have decided on a career field, this chapter should help you to focus upon your own particular goals and qualifications and to analyze the job market.

Analyze Your Goals

The first step in any job search is to analyze your own goals. Try to answer the following questions (on paper!) so that you will have a clearer picture of your goals:

What do I want to be doing next year? a year from now? five years from now?

Do I want to work independently or as part of a team?

Do I want to work mainly with people? with machines? with ideas?

Where do I want to work? in a large or small community? indoors or outdoors? Do I want to travel?

What type of organization do I want to work for? What type of facility — high-rise? branch office? corporate office?

How much do I want to earn? How far do I want to advance? How fast do I want to progress? How much responsibility do I want to assume?

How much education will I need for my career?

If I should marry, what effect will a spouse or children have on my career?

After answering these questions about your goals, continue your job search by analyzing your particular qualifications and the job market to locate jobs which meet both your needs and your qualifications.

Analyze Your Qualifications

All of us have unique qualifications to offer an employer. Most people, however, do not realize their own abilities and qualifications. In effect, they shortchange themselves.

Before you can prepare an effective resume or prepare for a job interview, you must know your own job qualifications. Analyzing your job qualifications thoroughly is not a 30-minute or even a 2-hour task — you should be prepared to spend longer to do the job right. Begin by creating a special file containing information about you and your qualifications. Here are some items to include in your file:

Academic transcripts

Letters of recommendation and commendation (school, work, or organizations)

Old resumes

Copies of job applications

Awards

Test scores

Certificates or diplomas of coursework completed

Next, write down on paper at least ten skills, abilities, and talents that have given you the most satisfaction and that make you marketable. Include those achievements that reflect your creativity, your initiative, and your ability to work well with others. Perhaps you won a scholarship to attend technical school or college. Maybe you enjoy or excel in an athletic activity, such as tennis, football, or jogging. You can begin building your resume from this list.

After listing your achievements, look for a pattern to emerge from your list. You may find that you most enjoy creative activities, such as art or writing, or that you have leadership abilities, exhibited by serving as an officer in student organizations. Consider how these abilities can be applied on the job and how you can represent yourself honestly, fairly, and in the most positive manner.

Because we often overlook our own achievements, you may also want to ask a friend or relative to assist you with this task. People who know you best can tell you what they think your particular strengths and abilities are. Then compare the other person's answers with your own assessment of yourself, adding important parts you overlooked.

Your file is now starting to grow. Organizing this information about yourself in one place will help you to remember important facts as you write your resume. In addition to the activities above, you should begin to analyze specific employment qualifications, such as work experience, educational preparation, and achievements/activities.

Work Experience

To begin, list on a separate sheet all work experience you have had, even if it has been temporary or part-time. (Perhaps you have a record of this work experience on a previous job application or old resume.) Include the name, address, and phone number of the employer; the full name of your supervisor; salary earned; dates of employment; and, most important, the major tasks and responsibilities you had on the job.

If you have had little work experience, then your first resume may list jobs unrelated to your immediate job goal. For example, you might list a job as cashier at a fast-food chain even though you are applying for a job as a receptionist. As you gain more work experience, you will include those jobs on your resume which are related to your job goal. Military experience may be included in this section.

If you have had no previous work experience, then consider including unpaid volunteer activities such as teaching vacation bible school or working as a fund raiser. Prospective employers are looking for ambitious people who can assume responsibility.

Education

More than likely, you are currently enrolled in a post-secondary program and are working toward an educational certificate or degree. Your education, in fact, may be one of your most important qualifications. Prospective employers are very interested in your educational preparation. Because many companies require technical school or college preparation for employment, always include your educational background.

Include the names of schools you attended (after high school), the city and state, certificates and degrees earned and dates (or expected graduation dates). If space is available, include specific courses or skills acquired that relate to your career objective and any special courses or programs you have completed. Include high school information if you don't have post-secondary educational preparation; otherwise, facts about your high school education do not need to be included. In addition to academic information, include statements regarding work you did while attending school or scholarships that you may have received.

Achievements/Activities

As you analyze your achievements and qualifications, you will develop a list of activities that may be unrelated to work experience or educational preparation. For example, you may have been treasurer of your local Phi Beta Lambda student business organization. You may be an experienced photographer or fluent in another language. Activities and skills of this sort should be included on your resume if they are related to your career goal.

Analyze the Job Market

After analyzing your job qualifications, spend time analyzing the job market before sending your resume to prospective employers or scheduling interviews. Analyzing the job market includes determining actual job openings and gathering information about specific companies to which you are applying. Both types of research are important to your success in getting the job best suited for you. Interviewers are more likely to hire someone who knows something about their company than someone who has not taken time to do basic research. Most people don't take the time to research the job market properly.

Locate Employment Opportunities

Locate as much information about job openings and requirements as you can. The following sources should be of help:

School Placement Offices. Many schools have placement services, such as a job placement office. Placement offices assist both employers and student applicants by providing opportunities for both to meet. Employers frequently inform the placement office about job openings. They may also recruit applicants by visiting campuses and conducting screening interviews or by participating in job fairs on campus. Some schools allow applicants to leave their credentials (resume, recommendation letters) with the placement bureau to be distributed to prospective employers. One advantage of a school placement office is that employers and applicants can be screened by knowledgeable faculty and placement personnel, providing a better opportunity for a good job match between employer and employee.

Newspapers and Professional Publications. The classified sections of newspapers and publications of professional organizations provide help-wanted ads. Respond to these ads as quickly as possible and follow any instructions in the announcement.

Employment Agencies.   Both public and private employment agencies are available to serve job seekers. Employment counselors at the agencies interview and sometimes test job applicants in order to match them with jobs listed with them by employers.

State employment agencies frequently have listings of jobs. To contact them, refer to the government section of your telephone directory under your state's name.

Private employment agencies charge a fee either to the employer or to the applicant. Before signing an agreement, find out who pays the fee and the amount or percentage of the fee. Above all, don't bind yourself to an agreement you may not wish to keep, such as agreeing to work for the employer for a specified amount of time.

Libraries.   Many publications are also available to the job seeker. The following resources, probably available in your library, can reveal much factual and insightful information about a particular industry:

> Best-selling books about business, such as *The 100 Best Companies to Work For in America* by Moskowitz, Levering, and Katz
>
> Million Dollar Directory (Dun's Marketing Service)
>
> Moody's Manuals
>
> MacRae's State Industrial Directories
>
> Directory of Directories
>
> Poor's Register of Corporations

For information about job requirements, refer to the *Dictionary of Occupational Titles* and the *Occupational Outlook Handbook,* published by the U.S. Employment Service. Your school's placement office will also have resources such as career computer programs and publications like the *College Placement Annual.*

Acquaintances.   An informal but often effective way to locate employment opportunities is simply to talk with your friends and professional contacts. Some of the best jobs are never advertised but are filled through personal referral or acquaintanceship.

Research Specific Companies

For information about a particular company, use the publications mentioned above as well as company annual reports, *The Wall Street Journal* (locate articles through *The Wall Street Journal Index*), and *Business Periodical Index*.

Talk with people who are familiar with the company, such as company employees and customers. Figure 26-1 lists data that every job hunter should know about a company:

FIGURE 26-1 Company Information	
Company Identification	Name, city, and state of home office. Local address and phone number. Name of person (if possible) responsible for department with which you will interview. Name of person with whom you will interview.
Company Classification	Public, private, profit, or nonprofit organization?
What the Company Does	Production, sales, or service oriented or a combination of all three. Brand names that are associated with the company?
Size of the Company	Number of employees, which gives you an idea of the size and scope of the organization.

If you have thoughts of career advancement with a company, you may also want to investigate it further. Find out the financial situation (profit or loss?), stated goals for the future, any plans for expansion, company history, stated philosophy, and information about who owns and runs the company (parent organization, board of directors, top officers, and others).

 Checkpoint 1 ANALYZING SELF AND JOB MARKET

Indicate whether the following statements are true or false.

1. To analyze your career goals, ask yourself questions such as: What do I want to do in the future? Where do I want to work? and How much do I want to earn?

2. When analyzing your qualifications, it is not necessary to include special talents and abilities not related to employment or education.

3. In the work experience section of your personal job file, include the following information for all employers: name, address, phone number, name of supervisor, salary earned, dates of employment, and job duties.

4. Most people research the job market thoroughly before looking for a job.

5. Before going on a job interview, know the following facts about a company: company ID, company classification, what the company does, and size of company.

Check your answers in Appendix D.

WRITING YOUR RESUME

After you have analyzed your goals and abilities and the job market, you are ready to move ahead with writing your resume. A **resume** is a summary of an applicant's qualifications for employment. An example is given in Figure 26-2. A resume is sometimes referred to as a **data sheet** or **vita.**

Every potential employee should prepare a resume! It can open doors with prospective employers simply because the applicant took the time to analyze his or her qualifications and put them on paper. While a resume cannot guarantee a job, it can highlight certain abilities that may not show up on a job application. An attractive, well-written resume can lead to your being invited for a job interview. A poorly written or messy resume, however, could hurt your chances for getting a job.

Appearance

Your resume will have only seconds to make a good impression, since employment representatives receive many resumes and must scan them quickly. Based on the resume's appearance, the reader will form a first impression. The resume should be easy to read, attractive, crisp, and clean.

To format a resume, leave adequate margins (at least one inch on all sides) and make sure there are no noticeable corrections. Use quality bond paper (white or off-white) and make sure copies are clear and sharp. Use of a copier, an offset duplicator, or a word processor is recom-

ALICIA HERNADES

147 Crabapple Road
Richmond, IN 47374-2187

Day phone: 317/935-2948
Night phone: 317/935-9382

Career Goal: To become a legal secretary with a large law firm with opportunity for advancement

Qualifications

Operate personal computer	Key 70 words a minute
Take shorthand at 100 wpm	Operate transcriber
Excellent communication skills	Accounting experience

Experience

<u>Legal Secretary</u>. Charles S. Ballard, Attorney-at-Law, Richmond, Indiana, August 1988 to present.

Utilize a computer and word processing software to format and edit legal documents, file documents with the courts, post to client accounts, make bank deposits, answer telephone, greet clients, set up appointments, transcribe from machine dictation, distribute incoming mail, and file correspondence.

<u>Salesperson</u>. Carson's Department Store, Richmond, Indiana, May 1985 to August 1988.

Operated computer terminal, handled transactions with customers, set up displays, stocked department.

Education

<u>Waynesboro Junior College, Waynesboro, Indiana</u>
A.A.S. degree with major in Office Administration. Will graduate with honors in June 1990, 3.5 GPA. Worked full time while attending college. Received Rotary scholarship.

Took elective college courses in business law, business computer software (IBM PC), and business management.

Honors and Activities

Phi Beta Lambda business organization, president, 1987-88
First place PBL district winner in Information Management
Phi Theta Kappa member, Dean's list for four quarters.

References

References will be provided upon request.

FIGURE 26-2 Sample Resume

mended. To emphasize certain words, use boldface, underlining, or capitalization. Use white space around headings to set them off. Graphic symbols such as bullets or asterisks serve to unify listings.

Generally, resumes should be limited to one or two pages. Employers don't have time to read long resumes. If you are applying for a professional position and have years of work experience, however, your resume may have to be longer. Provide complete information, but don't be wordy. Don't use whole sentences; rather, use sentence fragments, as illustrated in the examples on page 402.

Make sure that your resume is grammatically and mechanically correct. Use parallel structure in headings and listings (see examples) and check for correct spelling, grammar, and punctuation. Even one error is unacceptable.

Organization and Content

Most resumes today are written in *functional* order. The functional order lists the most important qualifications first and progresses to the least important. For example, if you do not have much relevant work experience but have attended college or taken several courses beyond the high school level, education is your most important qualification. Position the education section before the experience section. Likewise, within each major category, such as education or experience, list the most important achievements or jobs first (functional order) or, if all work experience is relevant, begin with the most recent job first (reverse chronological order).

Resumes may also be either general or specific in content. A general resume may be used if you are applying for a variety of jobs; a specific resume is written with one particular job or type of job in mind. Later in the chapter you will learn how to tailor your resume for a specific organization or job.

While analyzing your qualifications, you have gathered certain personal and employment data about yourself. Now it is time to go through the file you created and organize that data within certain categories or sections. Most good resumes will have the following sections:

1. Heading
2. Job objective
3. Special qualifications
4. Education
5. Work experience
6. Activities/interests/achievements
7. References

Heading

The heading or beginning section should include your name, address, and a telephone number where you may be reached during the day, in the evening, or both. You may also use the title "Resume" or something related in your heading. Following is an example of a heading appropriate for a general resume.

MARIE C. HAROLD

5333 Carriage Way	Home Phone 203/853-3829
Norwalk, CT 06854-9989	Work Phone 203/853-2911

You could also change the first line as shown in the following two examples:

QUALIFICATIONS OF MARIE C. HAROLD

RESUME OF MARIE C. HAROLD

If you are applying for a specific position, your heading might look like this (followed by address and phone numbers):

CELINE MASON'S PREPARATION

for the Position of Account Executive

with Hargrove and Webster, Inc.

Job Objective

The job objective (or career goal) is a brief statement that indicates the type of position for which you are applying. The job objective is important because it lets prospective employers know immediately whether your interests match their needs. If you omit this section, then the employer must search through your resume to find qualifications which fit job openings. If you are interested in and qualified for different career fields, change this section as needed on your resume. List only positions available within the organization to which you are applying. For example, don't apply for a word processing operator position if the firm does not have word processing positions. Be very brief in this section; use sentence fragments, not complete sentences.

Career Objective

> To secure a position as a word processing specialist with opportunity for advancement into a supervisory position

You might personalize the job objective in this way:

Job Objective

> Position as entry-level computer programmer trainee with Donovan Bros. with potential to become a systems analyst

It is also appropriate to break out short- and long-term career goals:

Career Objective

> Short-Term: Management Trainee in Operations
> Long-Term: District/Regional Manager

Special Qualifications

A condensed statement of your main qualifications may be placed at the beginning of your resume so that a prospective employer will not overlook them. This section should be very strong and achievement oriented. You may also include your date of availability somewhere in this section. Following are examples of how to list your special qualifications:

Special Qualifications

> Programming experience in BASIC, FORTRAN, and COBOL (emphasis in COBOL). Used flow-charting techniques for logic information. Constructed new programs according to specification outlines.

Special Qualifications

> Three years' experience as a legal secretary. Promoted to administrative assistant to senior partner. Excellent word processing, type 80 words per minute, litigation experience, strong organization skills, transcribe from machine dictation, and take shorthand at 120 words per minute.

Education

If you are still in school, your education may be your strongest qualification. Beginning with the most recent post-secondary school you have attended, list for each school the degree or certificate earned, major area of study, and completion dates (month and year). Include credit and non-credit workshops, seminars, and classes you have taken related to the job objective.

If you have excelled academically, include any scholarships, educational awards, and academic honors. If your grade point average is good (at least 3.0 on a 4.0 = A scale), then be sure to include it. Include high school, the military, and course grade information only if pertinent and if space permits. An example of a good education section follows:

Education

B.S. degree in Business Administration with major in Management, May, 1987, Clayton State College, Morrow, Georgia. Additional course work in management information systems and business communication. Overall grade point average: 3.5 (4.0 = A). Worked full time while attending college.

Work Experience

The section on work experience should describe, in the order that makes you look best, all work experience you have had that relates to your job objective. For each job, list the name of the company or organization you worked for, the city and state, dates of employment (optional), job title, and a comprehensive description of your duties and responsibilities.

In this section you have the opportunity to describe your qualifications fully through a thorough listing of job duties. Emphasize your achievements, responsibilities, and initiative. Use action verbs, such as those listed below:

calculated	ordered	set up	verified
typed	recommended	organized	produced
operated	trained	advanced	supervised
designed	supplied	provided	administered
increased	initiated	completed	revised

Work experience may be presented by date, by job title, by employer, or by achievements or skills attained. Figures 26-3 through 26-6 show each of these formats.

It is not necessary to list all your work experience; your application will provide a complete work history. If you include dates, employers will look for any gaps in your employment history. If you are returning to the work force after being out for a period of time, you should account for those years you were not at work.

In general, include all relevant full-time or part-time work experience; list military experience if it is pertinent to the job you are seeking. There is no need to tell why you left a job; this information will go on your application. If you have had any negative work experiences (fired from a job, for example), you will probably not include that listing, particularly if you don't want a previous employer contacted. We will discuss ways to handle negative work experiences in Chapter 27.

FIGURE 26-3 Work Experience Listed by Date

September 1984 to Present
Assistant to buyer of computers.
Business Systems, Inc., Atlanta, Georgia. Assist in purchasing for seven computer stores, deal with vendors, return merchandise, compute price changes, and mark down journals. Set up classes for in-house and vendor computer training. Make arrangements for auto rental, flight schedules, and hotel reservations. Supervise support staff of four.

June 1982 to September 1984
Secretary, Airtime Corp., Morrow, Georgia.
Typed proposals, correspondence, purchase orders, and invoices. Ordered office supplies, kept purchase order book, prepared payroll time sheets, and checked expense reports. Assisted clients on the phone and dispatched technicians or programmers as needed. Made travel arrangements for employees. Designed several forms which simplified office systems. Supervised part-time secretary.

March 1980 to June 1982
Receptionist, Dakota Homes, Atlanta, Georgia.
Operated switchboard, received visitors, processed and distributed incoming mail, made travel reservations, and maintained petty cash.

Activities, Interests, Achievements

Employers are searching for applicants who are willing to work hard and get the job done, who demonstrate creativity and initiative, who can work well with others, and who have leadership qualities. If the information you have presented in the sections on work experience and education does not demonstrate any of these qualities, you may have had other experiences that do. For example, you may have been president of a school or civic organization, coach of a soccer team, or a reporter or photographer for a school newspaper or yearbook. These activities could reflect skills and qualities such as leadership, public speaking or organizational ability, and positive attitude. This section may also show that you are a well-rounded person with varied activities and interests in addition to work. Refer to your self-analysis for relevant information to include in this

FIGURE 26-4 Work Experience Listed by Job Title

Assistant to buyer of computers, Business Systems, Atlanta, Georgia, September 1984 to present.

Assist in purchasing for seven computer stores, deal with vendors, return merchandise, compute price changes, mark down journals. Set up classes for in-house and vendor computer training. Make arrangements for auto rental, flight schedules, and hotel reservations. Supervise clerical staff of four.

Secretary, Airtime Corp., Morrow, Georgia, June 1982 to September 1984.

Typed proposals, correspondence, purchase orders, and invoices. Ordered office supplies, kept purchase order book, prepared payroll time sheets, and checked expense reports. Assisted clients on the phone and dispatched technicians or programmers as needed. Made travel arrangements for employees. Designed several forms which simplified office systems. Supervised part-time secretary.

Receptionist, Dakota Homes Inc., Atlanta, Georgia, March 1980 to June 1982

Operated switchboard, received visitors, processed and distributed incoming mail, made travel reservations, and maintained petty cash.

FIGURE 26-5 Work Experience Listed by Employer

Business Systems, Atlanta, Georgia, Assistant to buyer of computers, September 1984 to present.

Assist in purchasing for seven computer stores, deal with vendors, return merchandise, compute price changes, mark down journals. Set up classes for in-house and vendor computer training. Make arrangements for auto rental, flight schedules, and hotel reservations. Supervise clerical staff of four.

Airtime Corp., Morrow, Georgia, Secretary, June 1982 to September 1984.

Typed proposals, correspondence, purchase orders, and invoices. Ordered office supplies, kept purchase order book, prepared payroll time sheets, and checked expense reports. Assisted clients on the phone and dispatched technicians or programmers as needed. Made travel arrangements for employees. Designed several forms which simplified office systems. Supervised part-time secretary.

Dakota Homes Inc., Atlanta, Georgia, Receptionist, March 1980 to June 1982.

Operated switchboard, received visitors, processed and distributed incoming mail, made travel reservations, and maintained petty cash.

FIGURE 26-6   Work Experience Listed by Achievements or Skills Attained

Supervisory Skills	As assistant to buyer of computers (1984 to present) at Business Systems Inc., Atlanta, Ga., and as a secretary (1982 to 1984) at Airtime Corp., Morrow, Georgia, developed employee supervisory abilities through supervising four full-time clerical employees and one part-time secretary.
Communication Skills	In my position at Business Systems assist in purchasing for seven computer stores, deal with vendors, and return merchandise. At Airtime Corp. assisted clients on the phone and dispatched technicians or programmers as needed and made travel arrangements for employees. In an earlier position as receptionist (1980 to 1982) with Dakota Homes Inc., Atlanta, Georgia, operated the switchboard, received visitors, and made travel reservations.
Creative Skills	At Business Systems, set up classes for in-house and vendor computer training; at Airtime, designed several forms which simplified office systems.
Secretarial Skills	At Business Systems compute price changes and mark down journals. Also make arrangements for auto rental, flight schedules, and hotel reservations. In earlier jobs typed proposals, correspondence, purchase orders, and invoices; ordered office supplies, kept purchase order records, prepared payroll time sheets, and checked expense reports; processed and distributed the mail and maintained petty cash.

section. The following are possible headings for this section, according to the particular information you are including:

> Achievements, Awards, and Honors
>
> Interests
>
> Activities and Achievements
>
> Added Interests and Qualifications
>
> Honors and Activities

Personal Data

Information such as height, weight, state of health, marital status, number of children, or any other *personal* information which has no bearing on your professional performance on the job should not be included.

Much of this data cannot be legally asked of job applicants because of federal legislation preventing discrimination on the basis of such characteristics. Handling personal questions during a job interview will be discussed in Chapter 28 on "Interview and Follow-Up." Include personal information cautiously, *only* if it is relevant and will help you get the job. Don't waste valuable space on your resume including irrelevant, and possibly harmful, information. Do not include a picture of yourself unless physical appearance is a listed job qualification (for example, for a model).

References

To save valuable space on your resume, place your references on a separate page and type a notation such as "References Available Upon Request" at the end of your resume. Many employers are interested only in work-related references, so this section has become less important. Figure 26-7 illustrates an acceptable format for references when listing them on a separate sheet.

FIGURE 26-7 Sample Format for References

REFERENCES FOR SANDY GREEN

Mr. David Rice	Ms. Cindy Lane	Dr. Frances Bowers
Harris Corp.	Bandy Enterprises	Clayton State College
33 Mitchell Street	65 Zion Boulevard	5900 Lee Street
Atlanta, GA 30334	Morrow, GA 30260	Morrow, GA 30260
404/555-4523	404/555-3259	404/555-3578
(Employer)	(Former employer)	(College professor)

 Checkpoint 2 WRITING THE RESUME

Answer the following questions.

1. List five qualities your resume should have to make a good impression.
2. Name the seven sections that should be included in a good resume.
3. How does a general resume differ from a specific resume?
4. Which formats may be used for listing your work experience?
5. Why are personal data (age, marital status, weight, etc.) no longer recommended for resumes?

Check your answers in Appendix D.

SUMMARY

An important step in the process of searching for a job is preparing a resume, which is a record of your qualifications for employment. Before preparing the resume, take the following steps:

1. Analyze your career goals. Determine the answers to such questions as where you want to work and what you want to do.

2. Analyze your qualifications. Create a special file and include in it a list of your employment qualifications and supporting documents such as transcripts, letters of recommendation, awards, and copies of resumes and job applications.

3. Analyze the job market. Through print and people resources, gather information about job openings and requirements as well as specific information about companies to which you are applying.

After analyzing yourself and the job market, begin to write your resume. Include the following sections: heading, job objective, special qualifications, education, work experience, activities/interests/achievements, and references. Present your most important qualifications first (functional order). Keep your resume concise. It should be attractive, on white or off-white bond paper, with sharp print and no errors. A good resume may enhance your chances of getting a job, while a poor resume may hurt them.

 Communication Activities

Discussion Questions

1. What questions should you ask yourself as you analyze your employment goals?
2. What items should be included in your job file?
3. What are different sources for locating employment opportunities?
4. What information should every job hunter know about a targeted company (a company the person is interested in)?
5. Discuss the proper appearance of a job resume.
6. What major sections should be included in a resume?
7. What should the content of each major section of a resume include?
8. What role does personal data have in a resume?

Practical Applications

1. Analyze your own career goals by answering the questions in the section headed "Analyze Your Goals" (see page 395).

2. Analyze your employment qualifications by creating a special file and including in it the items and information described in this chapter.

3. Select two career fields you are interested in and assess the job market for job openings and job requirements. Use at least three print sources (see listing in chapter) and two personal sources.

4. Select two companies you are interested in working for and locate the following information:

   > Name, city, and state of home office
   > Local address and phone number
   > Name of interviewer or department head
   > Company classification (public, private, or nonprofit)
   > What the company does (products, services, etc.)
   > Size of company (number of employees)

5. Select one company you are interested in working for and locate the following information:

   > Financial situation (profit or loss)
   > Stated goals and philosophy
   > Company history
   > Information about who owns and runs the company
   > Other pertinent information you can locate

6. Prepare a resume for yourself using all the guidelines covered in this chapter. Type the resume in an appropriate style.

CHAPTER 27

Application Letter and Application

Objectives

After studying this chapter and completing the chapter exercises, you should be able to:

1. Identify two types of application letters.
2. Write and edit an effective application letter.
3. Fill out an application blank correctly.

When job-seeking, you will frequently need to write a letter of application. When you answer a help-wanted ad in the newspaper, for example, you are usually asked to send a letter of application. In addition, you may want to contact prospective employers who have *not* advertised positions. Since your primary purpose in sending the letter is to get the employer to consider your qualifications and to give you a job interview, you should include your resume with the letter.

Some prospective employers ask for an application letter in order to see your communication skills in action. If you are then called in for an interview, you will probably be asked to complete an employment application blank. It is important, therefore, that you learn to write an effective letter of application and to fill out an application blank fully and correctly.

APPLICATION LETTER

Application letters may be either solicited or unsolicited. You write a **solicited** letter of application when you apply for a specific job opening for which an application letter is requested. For example, you may be applying for a position advertised in the newspaper or which you learned about from a current employee. You write an **unsolicited** application letter to apply for positions that have not been advertised or that may or may not be available. Although you should approach each letter a little differently, there are three basic parts to any letter of application:

1. An opening which states that you are applying for a position and which gets the reader's attention.
2. A middle section which summarizes your main qualifications for the job.
3. A closing which asks for an interview.

Opening Paragraph

In the opening paragraph, you must get the reader's attention so that your letter will be read. While getting the reader's attention, be sure to include the following information in your opening paragraph:

- Indicate that you are applying for a position.
- Name the position for which you are applying.
- Tell how you learned of the opening (solicited letter).

If you were a prospective employer, would you want to read further after reading the following opening paragraph?

> I am applying for the position of sales associate which I recently heard was available in your company.

This is a rather weak opening which will certainly not get anyone's attention. This opening also is "I-centered," not written with the reader in mind—the "you" approach. Applying the "you" approach in an application letter means indicating how the applicant can benefit or be of service to the employer, as in the following example:

> Peggy Gardner, job placement counselor at Newark College, has told me about an opening for a sales associate with your company. In June I will graduate with a B.B.A. degree with a major in marketing. My education and my three years of experience in sales qualify me for such a position. Please consider me an applicant.

Solicited Letter

If you are writing in response to an advertisement, you might open your letter as follows:

> In the July 21 edition of the *Sun-Times*, you advertise for a management trainee. My degree in management and work experience as an assistant manager qualify me for this position.

Often, an employee will tell you about an opening with his or her company. You might write an opening paragraph in the following way:

> When Sam Burke, vice president of your bank, spoke to me about applying for a position as customer service representative, I became enthusiastic about the possibility of working with Second State Bank. My business administration degree and three years of customer service experience qualify me for the position.

Unsolicited Letter

Focus on your abilities in the opening paragraph of an unsolicited letter of application. You might open your letter in the following way:

> If you have an opening for a secretary with strong communication and word processing skills, then consider me an applicant.

If appropriate, demonstrate your knowledge of the company's needs in an unsolicited letter:

> According to the February issue of *Changing Times*, positions for accountants exist in many major companies. If your fast-growing company has a need for accountants, I would like to be considered an applicant. I believe that my bachelor's degree in accounting, work experience in a CPA firm, and strong desire to succeed make me a qualified applicant.

Middle Paragraphs

After gaining the reader's attention in the opening paragraph, you need to convince the employer that you are qualified for the job. Instead of just repeating the facts presented in the resume you are enclosing with the letter, interpret these facts. The second—and possibly third—paragraph should demonstrate that your educational preparation, work experience, or special qualifications are relevant to the job requirements. Be specific, providing concrete evidence of your qualifications and achievements. If you are responding to a published job opening, be sure to include qualifications asked for in the job notice or advertisement.

Make this section interesting and lively to hold the reader's attention. You might mention some special knowledge you have about the firm or the reader, if it is relevant, or your understanding of the job requirements. Your goal is to get the reader to want to meet you in person to interview you.

Here is an example of a way *not* to write the middle section of a letter of application:

> I completed the associate degree in office administration, which included taking courses in office management, business communications, and word processing. I have also worked for the past year at Aircond Corporation.

This paragraph does not make the most of the applicant's qualifications. Instead, you might write this section in the following manner, emphasizing accomplishments:

> The skills I gained from my associate degree in office administration (including courses in office management, business communication, and word processing) enabled me to assume responsible tasks at Aircond Corporation. I designed forms for the payroll department, decreasing the amount of paperwork 30 percent while increasing productivity in that department by 5 percent.

Here is another example of an effective middle section, focusing upon the applicant's work experience:

> As a quality control inspector, I worked closely with the plant manager to improve quality and reduce costs; in fact, during my year at this position, my department was rated Number 1 in quality while costs went down by 8 percent.

Even if you can't point to particular statistics on the job, you can still provide specifics which emphasize your qualifications:

> While working toward my word processing certificate, I worked part time at a parochial school, where I answered the phone and took messages for 12 people. I also maintained school attendance reports and produced correspondence and reports on a microcomputer. When I left the position, five of my supervisors offered to be references for me and three wrote me letters of recommendation.

If you have not had much work experience, then concentrate on other qualifications, such as education, related activities and honors, the ability to learn quickly, and the desire to work. Note the wording of the following section:

> During my second year of college, I was awarded a Rotary scholarship. While working toward my associate of science degree in data processing, I was vice president of the school's Phi Beta Lambda chapter. As vice president, I led the organization to a first-place state award in Most Outstanding Service Project, which involved organizing and hosting a dance-a-thon for muscular dystrophy.
>
> As a computer programmer for Datacorp, I will offer these same qualities of involvement and commitment that I demonstrated while in school.

The applicant in the next example has had little work experience but concentrates on qualities important in employees:

While working toward a degree in accounting, I maintained a 3.4 grade point average. This diligence in completing my courses will be brought to my work as an accountant with your company. In addition, I have extensive experience with several computerized accounting programs and with computer spreadsheets.

I am people-oriented and a team member, as demonstrated by my participation in the school organizations listed on the enclosed resume.

In the middle paragraphs, you should also explain any information in your resume that may raise questions or cause a negative reaction. For example, if you have an interrupted work history, provide an explanation in your letter. (Chapter 26 also advises you to account for employment gaps in your resume.) If you took an especially long time to complete your degree, explain why in your letter. Here is an example:

While attending college, I worked full time to support myself and pay for all school expenses. Since I could take only two courses each quarter, it took longer than usual for me to complete my degree.

Closing Paragraph

The closing paragraph should ask for an interview. In order to make it easy for the employer to contact you for an interview, provide your telephone number. Avoid the overused wording, "May I have an interview at your convenience?"

The following closing paragraph is not effective because it is too brief and abrupt:

> Please call me at 289-1285 for an interview.

Instead, lead up to requesting an interview:

> You will see from the enclosed resume that my education and experience qualify me for this position. May I have an interview with you to discuss my qualifications for the job? You may reach me at 390-1284 between 8:30 a.m. and 4:30 p.m. any weekday.

If it would be difficult for a prospective employer to reach you or if you prefer to take the initiative for the interview, consider the following closing:

> I would appreciate the opportunity to discuss my qualifications with you. Since it is difficult to reach me at school, I will call your office early next week to see when we can arrange an interview.

If you are writing to an out-of-town company, mention if and when you will be in the area for an interview.

✔ Checkpoint 3   CLOSING PARAGRAPH

Indicate whether each of the following closing paragraphs is effective or weak.

1. Since my qualifications are best described in person, I would appreciate an interview with you. Please telephone me between 2 and 5 p.m. any weekday at 962-2810 to let me know a day and time convenient for you to talk with me about this position.

2. Any information about your company and an application for the job opening will be appreciated. Please contact me at 452-8329 both day and night.

3. May I come for an interview within the next two weeks? You can reach me at 281-1922 or at the above address. I look forward to discussing the possibility of my joining your staff.

General Guidelines for Application Letters

You can make your letter of application work for you by following these general guidelines:

- Address the letter to an individual. If you don't know the name of the person in charge of employment, call the company to obtain the name.
- Use a simple, concise writing style and the "you" approach. Don't be wordy or use worn-out expressions. Be original in your writing. While you may refer to sample letters for ideas, don't use the same sentences!
- Enclose a resume with your letter and refer your reader to it, preferably in the middle paragraphs when you discuss your qualifications.
- Key your letter on good-quality white or off-white bond paper. Print should be sharp and clear. Use appropriate letter format.

Figure 27-1 provides an example of an effective solicited letter of application. Figure 27-2 illustrates an unsolicited letter of application.

APPLICATION BLANK

Most companies require you to complete an application blank when you apply for a job. The application blank is a standardized type of data sheet which the company uses to compare qualifications of different job applicants. When companies have job openings, they frequently refer to applications already on file. Employers usually refer to the application during a job interview.

The application blank is an important part of the job process—don't neglect it. Some people erroneously assume that, because they have a well-written, attractive resume, the application is not important. In fact, some people even decline to complete application blanks! Don't make

```
                1758 River Park Drive
                Hartford, WI  53027-1093
                December 3, 19--


                Ms. Sarah Richmond
                Director of Employment
                Oriole Industries
                561 State Street
                Hartford, WI  53027-1093

                Dear Ms. Richmond

                Oriole Industries has an excellent reputation as a major industry
                in Richland.  I would very much like to become a part of your
                organization as the assistant manager you advertised for in the
                Times December 2.

                Earning the associate degree in marketing, which I will complete
                in June from Nashua College, has given me valuable skills in
                marketing and management.  Putting these skills into action, I
                developed a marketing project, which was awarded first place in
                a state competition.

                While attending college full time, I worked part time as a sales
                associate at Warner's Department Store during summers and Christ-
                mas vacation and received the Sales Associate of the Month award
                last December.

                I assume responsibility willingly, work well with others, and
                possess excellent communication skills.  These abilities, along
                with my education and experience, would enable me to assume the
                responsibilities of assistant manager with your company.

                After you have reviewed the enclosed resume, could we discuss my
                qualifications for the position?  After 3 p.m., you may reach me
                at 815/555-1985.

                Sincerely yours


                Mr. Lee Klieman

                Enclosure
```

FIGURE 27-1 Solicited Letter of Application

```
261 Simpson Avenue
Northbrook, IL  60062-1987
December 2, 19--


Mr. Francis Byrne
Corporate Recruiter
Atlantic Company
555 Commercial Way
Northbrook, IL  60062-1987

Dear Mr. Byrne

As one of the leading manufacturing corporations in the city, the
Atlantic Company has a reputation for excellent office adminis-
tration.  I would like to bring my abilities as a highly skilled
secretary to your organization.

While obtaining an associate degree in office administration from
Piedmont College, I have developed my secretarial skills to a
high level.  A specialized course in business computer software
taught me to use spreadsheet, database, and graphics software.
Courses in word processing, business communication, and office
management developed additional specialized abilities.

Two years of part-time secretarial experience have given me
the opportunity to apply these skills on the job and improve my
decision-making and communication skills.  In my position with
McMann and Ellman, I have major responsibility for payroll, files
management, and word processing.

My education and work experience, along with the desire to meet
new challenges, would make me an asset to your company.  May I
come for an interview at your convenience?  Please contact me
between 1 and 5 p.m. at 632-2931.

Sincerely yours


Ms. Ann Oliveri
```

FIGURE 27-2 Unsolicited Letter of Application

this mistake. Treat the application blank as though your success in being offered the job hinges upon how well you complete the form. This could well be true.

The following guidelines should help you complete application blanks:

Take a sample application to the interview. Before going job-hunting, fill out a sample application you have obtained from an instructor or have filled out for a previous job. This sample application should include information such as Social Security number, work experience (dates, addresses, supervisor, salary), education (dates, schools, addresses, hours completed, GPA), and references (names, positions, addresses, telephone numbers). If you have certifications or licenses, include date granted and number assigned for each.

Don't depend upon your memory at the job site! You will very likely be nervous if you are anticipating an interview. Also, you don't want to spend too much time completing the application blank.

A copy of your resume will be helpful in completing the form. Make sure that either your resume or sample application includes special qualifications you may have (equipment operated, for example) in case the form has space for additional information.

If you can obtain a copy of the company's application blank in advance, make a copy of it to practice on. Then complete the actual application (typing it, if possible). Don't forget to make a photocopy of the completed form—this may become your sample application! Figure 27-3 illustrates a sample application blank.

Take an erasable-ink ballpoint pen. *And* take a spare pen in the same color, blue or black. A fine-point pen will enable you to write in small spaces. Make sure your pens write clearly and sharply, without smears or smudges. If your pen will not erase, then neatly draw a line through any errors–don't scratch out errors messily.

Skim through the application when you first receive it. Reading through the application quickly will give you an idea of the kinds of information you need to supply and will help you avoid repeating yourself in different sections.

Follow instructions. Read instructions before writing anything on your application. Many applications begin with general instructions, including "Type or print in ink." In the work experience section, you may be instructed to list your experience beginning with the "current or most recent job." You can be sure you will be evaluated on your ability to follow instructions!

STANDARD
APPLICATION FOR EMPLOYMENT

PLEASE FILL IN THIS APPLICATION YOURSELF, GIVING COMPLETE ANSWERS TO THE QUESTIONS WHICH APPLY TO YOU.

Date 4/1/--

Name Alicia Hernades   317/935-9382

Home Phone

Address: 147 Crabapple Rd., Richmond, IN 47374-2187

Social Security Number: 224 - 68 - 4512

How long have you lived at current address?

☒ Position applied for: Legal secretary

OR

☐ Position desired: _____

Yrs. 6   Mos. _____

Date available to start: Immediately

Do you wish to work? ☒ Full time; ☐ Part time? If part time, hours or days: _____ . Have you ever held this position or done this kind of work before? ☒ Yes. ☐ No. (If "No," use the Employment Experience section below to show your experience at the work you like best).

Why did you apply at our company? Advancement opportunities

PLEASE USE SPACE BELOW to provide a summary of your *past employment and your education/training* as these relate to "position applied for". Space for complete details inside.

Employment Experience

Date last worked at this job: Still working

Salary: Most recent at this job: $ 1275
☐ Hourly
☐ Weekly
☒ Monthly

Important job functions: Word processing, posting to client accounts, filing documents

Most recent employer for this work: Charles S. Ballard, atty.

Length of experience (all employers): 5 Yr. _____ Mo.

Special skills or machines operated: Proficiency:

Personal computer

Typing   70 wam

Shorthand   100 wpm

Specialty area (what you do best): Type, word processing

What do you like most about this kind of job? Being involved in the legal environment

What do you like least? Filing

Education or Training Experience

HIGHEST GRADE OR DEGREE IN SCHOOL:

Grade or degree: A.A.S.   Date graduated ☒ Within last 5 yrs. or last attended: ☐ Over 5 yrs. ago

Major course work: Office Administration

School: Waynesboro Junior College, IN

SPECIAL TRAINING (ON THE JOB OR IN SCHOOL):

Description: Word processing, legal documents and terminology

Organization where training received: College
☒ Within last 5 yrs.
☐ Over 5 yrs. ago

Description: _____

Organization where training received: _____
☐ Within last 5 yrs.
☐ Over 5 yrs. ago

Description: _____

Organization where training received: _____
☐ Within last 5 yrs.
☐ Over 5 yrs. ago

Do you plan to continue your education? .... ☐ Yes ☐ No
Do you look for on-the-job training .... ☐ Yes ☐ No

Explain: _____

Other work I have done and/or would like to do: Salesperson

Job title or job description while doing this work: Sales Associate

_____ Date last worked at this: 8/85

WE ARE AN EQUAL OPPORTUNITY EMPLOYER. Federal/state laws, and our own company policy, prohibit discrimination in employment on the basis of age, sex, race or national origin, religion, marital status or handicaps unrelated to job performance. Persons denied employment based on above conditions may file a complaint with our firm and/or with state or federal authorities.

FIGURE 27-3 Sample Application for Employment

Record of Employment

PRESENT (OR MOST RECENT) EMPLOYER: May we contact your present employer about this application? __Yes__

Company __Charles S. Ballard, Attorney__	Type of Business __Law firm__
Address __515 Main St., Richmond, IN 47374__	Phone __317/935-6025__

WHEN YOU STARTED	CURRENTLY OR WHEN YOU LEFT	Name of last Supervisor:
Date __8/85__	Date __4/__	__Charles Ballard__
Salary __$12,000__	Salary __$15,300__	Title __Attorney__
Description of job: __Type legal documents, file court documents__	Description of job: __Same__	Reason for leaving: __Career advancement__

PREVIOUS EMPLOYER

Company __Carson's Department Store__	Type of Business __Retail__
Address __460 Greene Ave., Richmond, IN 47374__	Phone __317/935-4600__

WHEN YOU STARTED	CURRENTLY OR WHEN YOU LEFT	Name of last Supervisor:
Date __5/83__	Date __8/85__	__Ann Sanders__
Salary __$3.50/hr.__	Salary __$4.75/hr.__	Title __Dept. Manager__
Description of job: __Salesperson__	Description of job: __Salesperson__	Reason for leaving: __Legal secretarial position__

PREVIOUS EMPLOYER

Company	Type of Business
Address	Phone

WHEN YOU STARTED	CURRENTLY OR WHEN YOU LEFT	Name of last Supervisor:
Date	Date	
Salary	Salary	Title
Description of job:	Description of job:	Reason for leaving:

IF MORE THAN TWO PREVIOUS EMPLOYERS, LIST OTHERS HERE

Employment Dates From To	Company and City/State	Position or Type of Work	Salary or Wage	Reason Leaving

Have We Missed Something Important?

Please use the space below to note down any special activity, awards, or other information that may help us to understand your skills and abilities that will be helpful on this job:

Phi Beta Lambda business organization - chapter president 87-88

First place PBL winner in Information Management - state of Indiana

Phi Theta Kappa member; Dean's List - 4 quarters

Record of Education

School	Within last 5 yrs? Yes	No	Name of School	City	Major Course or Subject	Did you Graduate? Degree?
Grammar School		x	Richmond Elem.	Richmond		Yes
High School	x		Wayne Co. H.S.	Richmond	Business	Yes
College or University	x		Waynesboro Junior College	Waynes- boro, IN	Office Admin.	A.A.S. 6/89
Other Special Training						
Business College						
Correspondence School						
Night School						

TO THE APPLICANT:

Please answer those questions checked below. The check-mark indicates that the information requested is a bona-fide occupational requirement; a health, safety or security requirement; or otherwise legally permissible. *If the box is not checked, you need not answer that question (but may answer, if you choose).*

☐ EMPLOYMENT Are you legally eligible for employment in the United States? __Yes__

☐ HEALTH Do you have any physical limitations or health conditions (including allergies) which might affect your ability to perform the job applied for? __No__ If yes, please explain _____

☐ MILITARY SERVICE Brancn Served __NA__ Active duty from _____ to _____
Discharge date _____ Discharge rank/grade _____ Reserve Obligation _____
Nature of military duties _____

☐ DRIVER'S LICENSE Do you currently hold a valid driver's license? __Yes__ State __Indiana__
Expiration date __11/92__ License #__224684512__ Restrictions _____

☐ BONDING Have you ever been bonded? __No__ When? _____ For what position? _____
Has bond ever been refused? _____ If yes, please explain _____

References (NOT EMPLOYERS OR RELATIVES—AT LEAST THREE)

Name and Address	Occupation	Phone
Gary Moe, 617 Spring St., Richmond, IN 47374	Attorney	317/935-0421
Amy Volz, Wayne Co. H.S., Richmond, IN 47374	Teacher	317/935-5224
Ann Lee, Waynesboro Jr. College, Waynesboro, IN 47375	Professor	317/935-8221

IN CASE OF EMERGENCY PLEASE NOTIFY:

Name __Florence Hernades__ Relationship __Mother__ Phone __317/935-9382__
Address __147 Crabapple Road__ City State Zip __Richmond, IN 47374__

Please Read Carefully:

I hereby certify that the answers given and statements made are true and correct. I hereby authorize all my previous employers, or references, to furnish any information concerning my personal character, habits or employment records. You may make investigation through credit and other investigating agencies. I hereby release all such persons from liability or damages incurred as a result of inquiry and furnishing this information.

Witness: _____ (Signature of Company Interviewer) Applicant: *Alicia Hernades* (Signature of Applicant)

Don't leave sections blank. If a question or section doesn't apply to you, place N/A (for not applicable) or a dash in the space so that the employer will not think you have overlooked or omitted something. For example, if you've had no military experience, simply place N/A (or a dash) in the first space related to that section. There is no need to continue placing N/A or a dash in each space of a related section; in fact, doing so will make your application look cluttered and messy. In some cases, answering a question might be negative for you. For example, there may not be enough space to explain why you left your last job, or the employer may request personal information which is not to your benefit. (See the section on illegal questions in Chapter 28, "Interview and Follow-Up.") In these situations, it is better to leave the space blank or to indicate that you will discuss the answer during the interview, whichever is better for you.

Be honest. The application, which the applicant generally signs, certifying that all information is correct, becomes a part of the permanent personnel record when a person is hired. Many items are verifiable, including work experience and education record. If an employer finds out later that you provided false information, it could hurt your career or even be grounds for dismissal.

Don't carry honesty to a fault, however. For example, there may be a question related to your health. If the state of your health will not affect your performance on the job, then answer that your health is "excellent," even though you may have a minor health problem that you've learned to live with. While you want to be honest, you also want to make a positive impression.

Decide how to complete "Salary Desired" section. Research the market before you begin job hunting so that you are aware of the salary range possible. While you may put a figure in this space, the best response is to put a salary range or write "open." In this way, you can discuss salary at the appropriate time in the interview.

Provide complete information. For example, in the work experience section, provide all information asked for, such as employer's address (including ZIP Code), supervisor's name (first and last), and phone number (including area code, such as 404/928-3821).

Provide appropriate references. Use as references people who know your qualifications for the job and will give you a good recommendation. If possible, use a variety of references, such as a former employer, a teacher, and a business colleague, instead of using three teachers as references. Include complete names, addresses, and phone numbers.

Sign your application. Don't forget to sign your application verifying that all information is accurate.

If you take time and care in completing the application blank, then you will simply increase your chances of being offered the job.

SUMMARY

As part of the job-hunting process, you may send letters of application. A solicited letter of application is one for which there is a specific job opening; an unsolicited letter is one which you send to companies that haven't advertised positions. Each application letter should have effective opening, middle, and closing paragraphs. The purpose of the opening paragraph is to gain the reader's attention, indicate the position for which you are applying, and state where you learned of the opening. In the middle paragraphs you present your qualifications that are relevant to the job requirements. In the closing paragraph you ask for an interview.

Complete the job application blank carefully and thoroughly. Take a sample completed application blank to the job site, follow instructions, fill in sections completely, and remember to sign your application.

● ● ● ● ● ● ● ● ● Communication Activities

Discussion Questions

1. What is the primary purpose of a letter of application?
2. Explain the difference between a solicited and an unsolicited letter of application.
3. Describe the three basic parts of any application letter.
4. What is the purpose of the opening paragraph of a letter of application? What information should it include?
5. What type of information is included in the middle paragraph of a letter of application?
6. How should you end a letter of application?
7. What are some general guidelines for writing effective application letters?
8. What guidelines should you follow in completing application blanks?

Practical Applications

1. Critique the following letter of application by listing its strengths and weaknesses, using principles of good grammar and suggested chapter guidelines for writing application letters.

   I am applying for the administrative assistant position you advertised in the December 9 edition of the <u>Town Weekly</u>.

   I am enrolled in the Business Technology program at Windmere Technical School and will complete my studies this month. Therefore, I would like to be considered for this position, which I believe I am qualified for.

   While attending school full time, I worked part time as a secretary for Owens and Smith for over a year. While there I had responsibility for payroll and word processing and supervised a clerical employee.

   Please contact me at 331-5495 for an interview at your convenience. I would very much like to work for your company.

2. Critique the following letter of application by listing its strengths and weaknesses, using principles of good grammar and suggested chapter guidelines for writing application letters.

   When Joan Hedman told me about an opening in your company for a management trainee, I became very excited about the possibility of working with Holmes Corporation. My degree in business administration with a major in management makes me a qualified candidate for this position.

   While in college I maintained a 3.5 grade point average overall and a 3.8 grade point average in the six management classes I took. I have experience with several business computer software programs, including database and spreadsheets.

   Throughout high school and college, I worked part time while attending school full time to earn tuition. While working in various fast-food chains, I was promoted to supervisory positions in which I had the opportunity to put my management skills to work. The enclosed resume provides further details of my education and experience.

   May I interview with you at your convenience? Since you may have difficulty reaching me at my part-time jobs, I will call your office by Thursday, June 13, to ask for an appointment. I look forward to discussing my qualifications with you.

3. Write a personal letter of application to an employer you are interested in working for. Provide an effective opening, middle, and closing section according to the guidelines in this chapter.

4. Fill out a sample application blank provided by your instructor. Complete the form with your own personal information.

CHAPTER 28

Job Interview and Follow-up Messages

Objectives

After studying this chapter and completing the chapter exercises, you should be able to:

1. Prepare for a job interview.
2. Present yourself effectively during the interview.
3. Conduct follow-up activities after the interview.

Throughout your working life, you are likely to be interviewed for various jobs and positions. Interviews can be nervewracking experiences unless you are well prepared. In this chapter we will discuss employment interviews and how to conduct yourself effectively during them.

THE PURPOSE OF A JOB INTERVIEW

Employers generally do not hire solely on the basis of a resume or application. They want to talk with job applicants to determine whether the applicants are qualified for the position and to see if there is a good company fit.

As a job applicant, you want to be interviewed to determine whether you want to work for a particular company. During the interview, you have the opportunity to evaluate the company and the position through your observations and questions.

Interviews may last anywhere from 20 minutes to two days or more. During the interview process, you may be interviewed by one person or by several persons. How you present yourself in the interview is crucial — first impressions count. Very often, an interviewer will make a decision *not* to hire during the first 15 seconds of an interview. That is why it is so important for you to be well prepared.

PREPARING FOR A JOB INTERVIEW

Your success in a job interview depends in large part on how well you have prepared for the interview. Preparation includes investigating the company and the position, anticipating questions that will be asked, preparing questions you will ask, and other preliminary activities.

Investigate the Company and the Job

Before the interview, find out pertinent information about the company:

- Full name
- Location
- Products or services

Learn what you can about the particular job for which you will be applying. Talk with current and former employers and check with your placement office for the following information before you go on the job interview:

- Job title and responsibilities
- Qualifications needed
- Salary range and benefits
- Advancement opportunities

During the interview you will learn more about the specific job from the interviewer. Chapter 26 provides tips on how to assess the job market and investigate specific companies.

Anticipate Questions

Before going on a job interview, prepare yourself for probable questions from the interviewer. It is natural to be nervous during an interview, but don't add to your anxiety by not being prepared to answer typical questions. You can expect to be asked about your work experience, education, interests and achievements, feelings toward work and school, and relationships with others. Refer to pages 438–439 for a list of frequently asked questions. Jot down brief but complete answers to these questions, and practice the answers, possibly taping them.

Prepare Questions to Ask

During the interview, generally at the end, you will be asked if you have any questions. Be prepared to ask questions that demonstrate your interest and professionalism. Remember, you are trying to determine whether you want to accept the position if it is offered to you. Keep your questions related to the job. Until you are offered a position, it is best not to ask questions about salary or benefits. As when composing correspondence, concentrate on the interviewer's point of view—what you can offer the company. Here are some questions you might ask:

1. What would my major responsibilities be?
2. What qualities are you seeking in the person for this position?
3. Does your company have training programs?
4. What can you tell me about the person(s) I would be working for? Working with?
5. What would you like to see a person accomplish in this job?
6. What are the major tasks that need to be accomplished now in this job?

7. Does the company have plans for new products? services?

8. What are the company's major markets?

Look Good for the Interview

Your appearance has a lot to do with your success on an interview. Be well groomed and wear appropriate clothes. Here are some pointers:

- Dress conservatively; avoid flamboyant styles or colors.
- For white-collar jobs, wear a business suit if you can. The best colors are navy, gray, or brown. If you don't have a suit, men should wear a sport coat and tie and women should wear a dress and jacket or skirt and jacket.
- Women should avoid heavy fragrances, bright nail polish, flashy jewelry, frilly clothes, and heavy make-up.
- Wear a conservative, attractive hair style.
- Be extra well groomed — good deodorant; clean clothes; polished shoes; trim, clean nails; and freshly brushed teeth.

Be on Time

If you are unfamiliar with the interview route, allow plenty of travel time so that you will arrive a little early. Remember, you may have to park in a garage, locate the correct building, and ride in an elevator. Build in extra time to allow for heavy traffic or any problems that may occur, such as having to drive around the block a few times looking for the right building or a place to park. You will not impress an interviewer if you are late.

Take Appropriate Information

Take an extra copy or two of your resume (including references), a completed sample application (to help you complete a job application quickly and easily), two pens, a small notebook and calendar, and perhaps your portfolio. Your portfolio may be an attractive folder, notebook, or small briefcase containing samples of your work, academic transcripts, letters of recommendation and commendation, and certificates of awards and/or educational achievements. If the interviewer asks questions related to these items, you may indicate that you have brought them with you and offer to show them.

Practice for the Interview

If at all possible, get someone to videotape you during a mock interview. Playing back the interview will help you assess your interview skills, particularly your nonverbal skills (body language), and improve upon them.

✔ Checkpoint 1   PREPARING FOR THE INTERVIEW

Indicate whether each of the following statements is true or false.

1. Before going on a job interview, prepare yourself for probable questions from the interviewer.
2. When the interviewer gives you the opportunity to ask questions, ask about salary and benefits.
3. The best clothing colors for an interview are navy, black, brown, or burgundy.
4. Arrive at the interview a few minutes early.
5. All you need to take to the interview is your resume.

Check your answers in Appendix D.

THE INTERVIEW

At the interview site, you will usually be introduced to the interviewer by a receptionist or secretary. As you wait in the reception area for the interview to begin, conduct yourself in a professional manner. The secretary may very well have an influence on whether you are hired or not. Some points to remember:

- Don't smoke.
- Don't chew gum.
- Greet the secretary cordially.
- Don't bring friends or relatives to the interview.

The Introduction

Greet the interviewer with a smile and direct eye contact. Use the interviewer's name if you can pronounce it correctly. Although a firm handshake is always appropriate and professional, you may feel more comfortable letting the interviewer initiate the handshake. Wait until you're asked to sit down. Then let the interviewer begin the interview and direct the discussion.

Nonverbal Skills

Your nonverbal, or nonspeaking, skills are very important during the interview. From the time you meet, the interviewer will be assessing you for the job. Since the first impression the interviewer has of you is crucial, you must look and act like someone the interviewer would like to hire. Appearance has already been discussed, so let's focus on other nonverbal signals.

Posture. Carry yourself erectly and confidently. Hold your head up and don't slump your shoulders. When you sit, remember to maintain good posture. If you make sure your back is touching the back of the chair, you will usually be able to avoid slumping. Practice good posture daily so that it is a habit rather than something you have to concentrate on.

Facial Expression. Keep a pleasant, interested expression on your face during the interview. A warm smile will send the message that you are someone the company would like to have as part of the team.

Gestures. Try to keep your gestures natural. Since you will probably be nervous, this may be difficult to do. Avoid extremes: Don't sit like a concrete block, making no arm movement at all, and don't wave your hands wildly like a windmill. If you know you have distinctive habits, such as hand twisting or leg shaking, try to minimize these during the interview.

Eye Contact. One of your most important nonverbal communication skills will be maintaining eye contact with the interviewer. Looking at the interviewer when he or she is talking communicates that you are interested.

Listening Skills

The interview will require you to listen effectively so that you will be able to answer questions and gather appropriate information. Here are some tips for effective listening during the interview:

- Concentrate on what the interviewer is saying. Try not to let your mind wander.
- Look at the interviewer. Remember, eye contact will let the interviewer know you are listening.
- Be observant. Notice the interviewer's body language so that you can pick up on nonverbal cues.

FIGURE 28-1 Nonverbal skills play an important part in an interview.

- Listen eagerly. Show that you are interested by providing feedback, such as nodding or smiling and giving verbal cues, such as saying "Yes" and "Uh-huh."
- Listen carefully for the important points so that you can respond to them later.

Interview Questions

From the time the interview begins, you will be expected to answer questions so that the interviewer can get to know you and your abilities. Speak clearly and distinctly as you answer these questions, using good grammar. The way you communicate with the interviewer indicates whether you have good communication skills, an important qualification for most jobs.

Opening Questions

Many interviewers will begin with ice-breaker questions, such as "I see that you're in the school band. What instrument do you play?" These questions are intended to put you at ease and establish rapport. Just answer them naturally, allowing yourself to be yourself. Well-trained interviewers want you to be comfortable and natural so that they can get an accurate impression of your personality.

Main Questions

During the next stage, the interviewer gathers information about you by asking questions such as those in Figure 28-2. If you have anticipated typical interview questions and have thought through possible answers, you will be more relaxed and confident than if you have not. Listen to each question carefully, pause to gather your thoughts before answering, and elaborate on your answers. Don't answer with just a simple "yes" or "no." Convince the interviewer that you are the best person for the job. Don't assume that the interviewer will learn everything about you from your application or resume.

Interviewing for a job is similar to making a sale—except that the product is you. Don't exaggerate or be too modest. Talk about your accomplishments and abilities; employers want to hire people who are sincere, confident, and capable.

Illegal Questions

You may be asked questions of a personal nature which you do not desire to answer. In fact, federal law prohibits employers from discriminating in job hiring on the basis of race, color, religion, age, sex, marital status, national origin, or handicap not related to job performance. You may volunteer any personal information, but only provide information that will be to your advantage.

The best way to handle illegal questions is to deflect them courteously, possibly providing some useful information. For example, if the interviewer asks you how your children will be taken care of while you work, you might answer: "If you're asking whether I will be on time and do a good job, the answer is definitely 'Yes.'" Another way to answer this question is to assure the interviewer that child care is taken care of. You could also refer to a good job and attendance record in a current job.

Do not answer an inappropriate question if your response could hurt your chances of getting the job, but try not to place blame upon the interviewer. Keep your reply lighthearted, offering to provide information if the interviewer can show you that the question is job-related. Figure 28-3 provides some examples of illegal interview questions. Look them over and decide how you would answer these questions if asked.

FIGURE 28-2 Sample Interview Questions

Educational Experiences

1. Why did you major in _____ ?
2. Which courses did you like best? Least? Why?
3. What motivated you to seek a college education?

Work Experiences

4. Why do you want to work for our company?
5. What kind of work did you do in your last job? What were your responsibilities?
6. Describe a typical day on your last (or present) job.
7. What was the most difficult problem you encountered on your last (or present) job and how did you handle it?
8. What did you like best about your previous positions? Least?
9. Why did you leave your last job?
10. What do you know about our company?
11. What aspects of this job appeal to you most?

Human Relations

12. What kind of people do you enjoy working with? Find difficult working with?
13. How do you get along with other students? With instructors? With co-workers or superiors?
14. In your previous jobs, how much of your work did you do on your own? How much did you do as part of a team?

Goals

15. What are your current goals? Your long-term goals?
16. What are your career objectives?
17. Why did you choose your particular field of work?

Self-Concept

18. What are your greatest strengths? Weaknesses?
19. What qualities need to be strengthened?
20. Tell me about yourself.
21. Why do you think you are qualified for this job?

FIGURE 28-2 (Continued)

22. How do you spend your leisure time?

23. What do you consider to be your chief accomplishment in each of the jobs you've held?

24. What have your superiors complimented you for? Criticized you for?

FIGURE 28-3 Illegal Interview Questions

- Are you married? single? divorced? widowed?
- Do you plan to have children?
- What is your birthdate?
- Have you ever been arrested?
- Where were you born?
- Where does your husband (wife, father, mother) work?
- Are you pregnant? Plan to have children?
- Do you belong to a church? Which one?
- Do you rent or own your home?
- What is your maiden name?
- Do you have a girlfriend? (boyfriend?)

Salary Questions

Try to avoid discussing salary until you are offered a position. If you are asked your salary requirements early in the interview, indicate that you require the standard salary for the position in question. By letting the interviewer make a salary offer rather than naming a figure yourself, you will be in a better position to negotiate. You should also always research salaries before interviewing so that you know whether the salary range meets your requirements.

The Closing

The interviewer will provide both verbal and nonverbal signals that the interview is over. Stand up, offer a handshake, and thank the interviewer. Usually a job is not offered at this point. However, it is appropriate to ask the interviewer when a decision will be made.

If you are offered the job, accept it only if you are sure you want it. This decision is important, and it may require some time to consider. If you need more time, tell the interviewer that you need to think it over since you are interviewing for other positions. Then give your answer by the agreed-upon time. Ask for the interviewer's business card before you leave; you will want to write a follow-up message.

FOLLOW-UP MESSAGE

Within two days after the interview, write a brief follow-up letter thanking the interviewer and, if you are interested in the position, indicating your interest and asking for a decision. Not only is this a courteous action but it brings your name before the interviewer again. Organize the letter as a neutral message, as the example below illustrates:

Main Idea	Thank you for giving me the opportunity to interview yesterday for the legal secretarial opening with your firm. After talking with you and seeing first-hand the office operations, I am convinced that I would like to join Powell and Martin's legal secretarial staff.
Supporting Information	During the interview we discussed whether I would be available for the northside office. After further consideration, I am happy to say that I would be able to work in any of the firm's locations in the city.
Helpful Closing	My education and experience make me confident that I would be able to perform the duties of the position well. If you need further information about my credentials, I would be glad to provide it.

✔ Checkpoint 2 THE INTERVIEW AND FOLLOW-UP

Indicate whether each of the following statements is true or false.

1. Maintaining eye contact with the interviewer is an important nonverbal skill.

2. During the main part of the interview, you will be asked questions about your abilities.

3. You should not refuse to answer illegal questions because the interviewer might hold it against you.

4. If you are offered a job, accept it immediately.

5. Write the interviewer a thank-you note within two weeks after the interview.

Check your answers in Appendix D.

SUMMARY

Job interviews provide an opportunity for companies to find suitable employees and job applicants to locate appropriate employment. Be prepared for the interview by investigating the company and job, anticipating interview questions, and preparing questions to ask the interviewer. Make sure that you are well groomed and dressed appropriately for the interview. Take appropriate information, including a resume, with you and be on time.

During the interview, use good nonverbal and listening skills. Answer questions completely, presenting yourself and your qualifications well. Be prepared to handle illegal questions and salary questions. After the interview, write the interviewer a short thank-you letter.

 Communication Activities

Discussion Questions

1. What information should you find out about a company and the job being advertised before going on the interview?

2. What are typical questions asked on a job interview?

3. What are questions you might ask during a job interview?

4. What are some do's and don'ts concerning appearance for the job interview?

5. Discuss appropriate nonverbal skills for the interview.

6. How can you use effective listening skills during the interview?

7. What are illegal interview questions, and how should you handle them?

8. How should you respond to salary questions?

Practical Applications

1. Participate in a class project in which you are interviewed for a real or an imaginary job. Have your interview videotaped, if possible, and view the playback to assess your strengths and weaknesses.

2. Make a list of at least five interview strengths and five interview weaknesses you have. For each of the weaknesses, indicate a plan of action for improvement.

3. Prepare your answers to the sample interview questions in Figure 28-2.

4. Prepare your answers to the illegal interview questions in Figure 28-3.

5. Prepare at least five questions you would like to ask during an interview.

6. Write a thank-you letter for the interview conducted in #1.

APPENDIX A

Frequently Misspelled Words
Words Frequently Misused

Frequently Misspelled Words

accommodation
acknowledgment
allocate
analyze
announcement
anxiety
apologize
approximately
argument
attorneys
automation
awkward

bankruptcy
basically
beginning
believe
bookkeeping
brochure
bulletin
business

calendar
cannot
career
census
changeable

client
clientele
commitment
committee
congratulations
conscientious
conscious
consistent
controlling
convenience
corporation
courteous

deficiency
definitely
dependent
discrepancy
discussion

efficient
eligible
enthusiasm
enthusiastic
envelope
environment
equipment
evaluate

excellent
existence
extension
extraordinary

facilities
familiar
February
financial
forcible
foreign
fulfill
fundamental

grievance
guarantee

illegible
immediately
incidentally
innovation
interference
interrupt
institution

judgment
justifiable

knowledge

leisure
liaison
libel
librarian
library

maintenance
manageable
material
mathematics
memorandum
miscellaneous
misspell
morale
mortgage

necessary
ninety
noticeable

obvious
occasionally
occurrence
occurring
offered

omitted
opportunity

pamphlet
parallel
partial
personnel
planning
precede
preferred
prejudice
privilege
procedure
proceed
proprietor

quantity
questionnaire

receipt
receive
recommendation
reference
referred
relevant
responsible
restaurant
ridiculous

salary
schedule

scissors
separate
similar
succeed
successful
sufficient
supersede
synonymous

television
temperament
tragedy

unique
usable

using

vacancies
variable
vein
versus
visibility
volume

waive
warranty
weather
whether
withheld

Words Frequently Misused

Below is an alphabetized list of words that are frequently misused in business communication. Your understanding of these words is tested in some of the activities at the ends of the chapters. To help you understand how to use these words, the definition of each word is given and/or its usage is explained. An example of each of its usages is given.

a lot   *n.* many (Note that *a lot* consists of two words.)

Ex. She has a lot of trophies in her room.

accept   *v.* to agree to; to receive

Ex. I happily accept your suggestion.

addition   *n.* increase; enlargement; part or thing added

Ex. With the addition of the new wing, the hospital will have 142 rooms.

The new addition will add 40 rooms to the hotel.

advice   *n.* counsel

Ex. The lawyer gave him good advice.

advise   *v.* to give advice; to inform

Ex. I advise you to go to the meeting.

affect   *v.* to influence; to make a pretense of

Ex. Will the new policy affect you?

She was very upset by his behavior but affected indifference.

all ready   *adj. phrase* completely prepared

Ex. The scouts were all ready to go to their meeting.

allot   *v.* to give or share in arbitrary amounts; to apportion

Ex. Each speaker was allotted three minutes.

allude   *v.* to refer to something not specifically mentioned

Ex. The report in the paper alluded to his involvement but did not openly state it.

already   *adv.* by or before a specified or implied time

Ex. She had already finished the report.

assure   *v.* to make sure

Ex. Let me assure you that Bob will be there.

choose   *v.* to select based on judgment

Ex. I will choose Tom because of his experience and talent.

chose   past tense of *choose*

Ex. He chose Tony because of her work experience.

cite   *v.* to acknowledge; to quote as a reference

Ex. Dick cited several references in his term paper.

complement   *n.* anything that completes a whole   *v.* to complete or make perfect

Ex. (*n.*) A complement of accountants would bring the staff to full strength.

(*v.*) The color of the trim complements the wallpaper.

compliment   *n.* recognition; praise; flattery   *v.* to praise

Ex. (*n.*) The compliment given to Deborah was very nice.

(*v.*) Terri complimented Doris.

consul   *n.* an official appointed by the government to live in a foreign city to attend to the interests of the official's country

Ex. The consul provided good advice to the tourists.

cooperation   *n.* assistance; help

Ex. The cooperation between the two countries is encouraging.

corporation   *n.* type of business organization

Ex. They organized as a corporation.

council   *n.* group of people called together to provide counsel

Ex. On item B, the vote of the council was divided 3 to 2.

counsel   *n.* advice   *v.* to provide advice

Ex. (*n.*) She thinks we need legal counsel.

(*v.*) Joan was counselled to change occupations.

edition   *n.* an issue of a book or newpaper

Ex. This is the fifth edition of the book.

effect   *n.* the result or outcome   *v.* to bring about

Ex. (*n.*) The effect of the company's new product strategy was a sharp increase in the price of its stock.

(*v.*) The new leader effected many changes in the company.

elude   *v.* to escape notice or detection

Ex. By staying up in the trees, Timmy was able to elude the searchers.

ensure   *v.* to make sure; to guarantee

Ex. Bail is a means of ensuring the appearance of defendants in court.

envelop   *v.* to surround; to cover completely

Ex. The natives enveloped the stranger.

envelope   *n.* container for letters, reports, etc.

Ex. The envelope for the letter costs five cents.

except   *prep.* with the exclusion of; other than

Ex. All received plaques except Charles.

farther   *adj.* more distant

Ex. David lives farther away than Brad.

forth   *adv.* forward; onward

Ex. From that day forth, she never hid again.

fourth   *adj.* any one of four equal parts; the item following the first three in a series

Ex. Here is your fourth of the pie.

Herb's team came in fourth.

further   *adv.* to a greater degree or extent

Ex. Let me state further that I was most upset with the decision.

hear   *v.* perceive by the ear

Ex. Did you hear the explosion?

here   *adv.* in or at this place

Ex. Place your orders here.

insure   *v.* to secure from harm; to guarantee life or property against risk

Ex. The property is insured for $50,000.

its   possessive form of *it*

Ex. Where did you see its paw prints?

it's   contraction for *it is*

Ex. It's very hot this afternoon.

Appendix A   Words Frequently Misused

lay *v.* to place; to put (transitive verb — requires an object)

> Ex. Did you lay the mail down on the book-case?

lie *v.* to recline; to remain (intransitive verb — no object)

> Ex. She lies down for a short nap every day after lunch. (present tense)
>
> He lay on the couch most of the afternoon. (past tense)

loose *adj.* not restrained; not fastened

> Ex. My shoe is loose.

lose *v.* to fail to win; to be deprived of

> Ex. If we lose, we will be eliminated from the tournament.

passed *v.* past tense of *pass*

> Ex. He passed the other cars and now leads the race.

past *adj.* finished; gone by

> Ex. His smoking habit is past.
>
> He finished the project this past week.

principal *n.* the amount of the money borrowed in a loan; the head official in a court proceeding or school *adj.* most important or influential

> Ex. (*n.*) The principal of the loan was $15,000.
>
> (*n.*) Mr. Bigworth is the new principal of West Elementary School.
>
> (*adj.*) Her principal objection was the cost.

principle *n.* a basic belief or truth

> Ex. Moral conduct should be based on one's own set of principles.

quiet *adj.* still; calm

> Ex. The students were very quiet during the exam.

quit *v.* to stop; to discontinue

> Ex. Rita quit her job so that she could persue her painting career at home.

quite *adv.* very or fairly; positively

> Ex. With that tint, the paint will be quite blue.
>
> He is quite a hero to his team.

sight *n.* the ability to see; vision *v.* to see

> Ex. (*n.*) Gwen's sight is excellent.
>
> (*v.*) Several deer have been sighted in the area.

site *n.* a place; a plot of land

> Ex. The site for the new branch has been chosen.

stationary *adj.* fixed; unmovable

> Ex. The machine is stationary.

stationery *n.* paper for letters and envelopes

> Ex. The department's stationery is being printed.

than *conj.* in comparison with *prep.* except; besides

> Ex. (*conj.*) Manuela is taller than Chiquita.
>
> (*prep.*) It was none other than Frank who changed the combination.

their plural possessive form of *they*

> Ex. You should have seen their faces when he announced that they were the winners.

then *adv.* at that time

> Ex. After receiving the data, Phil was then able to finish the graphic aid.

there   *adv.* in or at that place

Ex. The man was sitting there.

they're   contraction for *they are*

Ex. They're going to the concert tonight.

to   *prep.* in the direction of; the first word of an infinitive

Ex. Derrick will take the plane to Shreveport.

Brad wanted to see the pandas at the zoo.

too   *adv.* also; excessively

Ex. He went to the meeting too.

The meeting lasted too long.

two   *adj.* the number *2*

Ex. The two members will attend the conference.

your   possessive form of *you* (may be singular or plural)

Ex. That is your hat. (singular)

Connie and Libby, your coats are hanging in the closet. (plural)

you're   contraction for *you are*

Ex. Do not drive when you're sleepy.

APPENDIX B

Proofreaders' Marks

Symbol		Marked Copy	Corrected Copy
||	Align	|| $298,000 $145,098	$298,000 $145,098
∿∿∿	Bold	tone of the message	**tone** of the message
☰	Capitalize	thomas Johns	Thomas Johns
—	Change copy as shown	criteria ~~was~~ *were*	criteria were
◡	Close up space	hap py	happy
℘	Delete	complete℘	complete
DS	Double-space	to seeing you soon. DS Sincerely yours	to seeing you soon. Sincerely yours
∧	Insert	*the* Send letter.	Send the letter.
#	Insert space	# a∧lot of time	a lot of time
italic —	Italicize or underline	The Boston Globe	*The Boston Globe* **or** The Boston Globe
stet...	Ignore correction	~~effective~~ individual	effective individual
lc /	Lowercase	Yours T̸ruly,	Yours truly,
[ ] ⊔ ⊓	Move in direction of bracket	Mr. Tony Smith [747 Oak Street [Placerville, CA	Mr. Tony Smith 747 Oak Street Placerville, CA

No ¶	No paragraph	no ¶ When expressing	When expressing
¶	Paragraph	¶ In summary,	In summary,
SS	Single-space	Mr. Tommy Jones	Mr. Tommy Jones
		SS	4479 Elm Avenue
		4479 Elm Avenue	
⟨sp⟩	Spell out	449 (No.) Baltic ‾sp	449 North Baltic
∿	Transpose	acheive	achieve

APPENDIX C

Glossary

abstract   A brief summary of a report.

active listening   Purposeful listening; the listener is alert and is absorbed in what the speaker is saying.

active voice   The form of a verb that shows the subject acting.

adjective   A word that describes a noun or pronoun.

adjective clause   A dependent clause used as an adjective.

adjective phrase   See *phrase.*

adjustment   A positive settlement to a receiver's claim.

adverb   A word that describes a verb, adjective, or other adverb.

adverb phrase   See *phrase.*

analytical report   A problem-solving report that includes analysis, interpretation, conclusions, and recommendations.

anecdote   A story that a speaker uses to illustrate a point or spark the audience's interest in the topic.

antecedent   The word a pronoun replaces.

appendix   A supplemental part of a report which is placed after the body of the report.

applications software   Program that provides instruction to the computer on how to carry out a particular application such as word processing or database management.

appositives   Words or phrases that describe preceding nouns or pronouns by renaming them.

attention line   A letter part that directs the correspondence to a particular individual within an organization.

bibliography   An alphabetic list of sources used in preparing a report.

casual listening   The type of listening commonly associated with conversation and entertainment; little energy or effort is required.

central processing unit (CPU)   The part of a computer that controls its operating functions.

channel   The means the sender selects to send a message.

claim letter   A special type of message that requests an adjustment.

clarity   The use of clear words and logical organization to convey meaning accurately and effectively.

clause   A group of related words containing a subject and a verb.

coherence   A clear, logical relationship among the ideas presented in a communication.

collective noun   Noun that identifies a group.

command/request   A statement that makes a command or a request and ends with a period.

communication   The process used to send and interpret messages so that they are understood.

communication barriers Factors that interfere with or interrupt the communication process.

comparative degree The degree of adjectives or adverbs used to compare two things or persons; formed by adding *er* to simple adjectives or adverbs or *more* or *less* to long adjectives or adverbs.

complex sentence A sentence that contains one independent clause and one or more dependent clauses.

compound sentence A sentence that contains two or more related independent clauses.

compound-complex sentence A sentence containing two or more independent clauses and at least one dependent clause.

computer-based message system (CBMS) A form of electronic mail sent between two or more computers.

conciseness A characteristic of effective communication requiring a message to be as short as possible yet still achieve its objective.

conjunction A word that joins two or more parts of a sentence.

connotation A meaning suggested beyond the literal meaning of a word.

consideration The characteristic of effective communication that involves showing empathy for the receiver; it requires being sensitive to the attitudes, feelings, needs, and emotional state of a receiver.

coordinate conjunction A word used to connect sentence elements that are grammatically and logically equal.

correlative conjunctions Conjunctions used in pairs to join two or more elements of equal rank; e.g., *either/or, neither/nor.*

courtesy The characteristic of effective communication that involves being polite, kind, and respectful to others.

dangling modifier A modifier (usually a phrase or a clause) incorrectly placed by a word that it does not modify.

dependent clause A clause that does not form a complete thought and cannot stand alone as a sentence.

desktop dictation equipment Dictation equipment that is designed to be placed on the originator's desk.

direct object A noun or pronoun that receives the action of the verb.

direct order The organizational structure of a message that presents the main message first and then the supporting information.

direct question A statement that asks a question and is followed by a question mark.

direct-indirect order The organizational structure of a message that presents the good news first in direct order and then presents the bad news in indirect order.

distribution/transmission stage The stage in the document cycle wherein the document is sent to its destination.

document cycle The flow of a document from the time it is created until it is distributed and stored.

editing The process of making corrections and revisions in a document.

effective communication Communication that is interpreted as the sender intended and that achieves the objective of the sender.

electronic mail Communication that is sent from one machine to another by electronic means.

enumeration A listing.

exclamation A word or phrase that shows strong emotion and is followed by an exclamation point.

external barriers Factors that exist outside the sender/receiver and that interfere with or detract from the communication process. Examples include environmental factors such as comfort and noise.

external communication Messages that originate within an organization and are sent to receivers outside the organization.

feedback The response the receiver gives to a message.

flexible diskette A removable storage medium that is used by word processors and computers.

formal communication Messages that are sent through the established lines of authority within an organization.

formal report A long, analytical, and impersonal report; often contains supplemental parts.

formatting Arranging a written message in an acceptable style.

gender-neutral language Language free of sexual stereotyping.

gerund Verb form with an *ing* ending that is used as a noun.

goodwill The favorable reputation that a business has with its customers.

goodwill message A message designed to build interpersonal relationships.

hard disk A storage medium used by computers and word processors.

helping verb An auxiliary verb that indicates timing.

imperative mood The mood of a verb used to command or to give orders.

impromptu speech A speech given without any advance notice.

indefinite pronoun A pronoun that does not refer to a specific noun.

independent clause A clause that can stand alone as a complete sentence.

indicative mood The mood of a verb used to make statements or ask questions.

indirect object A noun or pronoun that indicates to whom or for whom something is done.

indirect order The organizational structure of a message that presents the supporting information before the main idea.

indirect question A statement that includes someone else's question but does not use the person's exact words; this type of sentence should be followed by a period.

informal communication Messages within an organization that do not follow established lines of authority.

informal reports Reports that are shorter than formal reports and are written in a personal style; usually informal reports do not include supplemental parts.

informational report   A report designed primarily to present facts rather than analyze them.

interjections   Exclamatory words or phrases used to express emotion; e.g., *Oh! My goodness!*

internal barriers   Factors within individuals such as education, personality, culture, and experience that affect the sender's and receiver's ability to communicate.

internal communication   Messages that originate within an organization and are sent to receivers within the organization.

intervening modifier   A set of descriptive words positioned between the subject and the verb.

interview   A means of collecting information by talking with a person face-to-face or over the telephone.

intransitive verb   A verb that does not need an object to complete its meaning.

keyboard   The part of an electronic workstation that contains the traditional alphabetic and numeric keys and additional keys that perform various functions such as formatting and editing.

kinesics   The study of communication through body language.

letter of transmittal   A cover letter for a report.

linking verb   A verb that joins a noun, pronoun, or adjective to the subject.

local area network (LAN)   A connection of various workstations within a building or nearby buildings.

mail survey   A means of collecting data by sending questionnaires through the mail system; often used when a large number of people are to be contacted.

main idea   The focal point of a message.

main verb   A verb that expresses action or state of being.

memorandum   An internal document used to communicate with one or more co-workers.

message   A set of verbal or nonverbal symbols that represent meaning.

microform   A reduced image of a paper document stored on film.

minutes   The official report of a meeting.

mixed punctuation   The punctuation style that uses a colon after the salutation and a comma after the complimentary closing of a letter.

modifier   A word, phrase, or dependent clause that describes a noun, pronoun, verb, adjective, or adverb.

news releases   Brief announcements prepared for distribution to newspapers and magazines.

nominative case pronoun   A pronoun that acts as the subject of the verb or the complement of the linking verb; also referred to as a *subjective case pronoun.*

nonprobability sampling   A sampling technique which involves selecting the subjects to be studied in the population; compare *probability sampling.*

nonrestrictive clause   An adjective clause that is not required to identify the word being modified.

nonverbal symbols   Symbols such as gestures, posture, facial expression, appearance, time, tone of voice, eye contact, and space used to communicate. Nonverbal symbols convey attitudes.

noun phrase   See *phrase.*

object of the preposition   A pronoun or noun that follows a preposition and answers the question "what" or "whom."

objective case pronoun   A pronoun that acts as an object to complete the thought expressed by the subject and verb.

open punctuation   A punctuation style that uses no punctuation after the salutation or complimentary closing in a letter.

origination stage   The first stage of the document cycle; the point at which ideas are created.

paralanguage   Nonverbal symbols such as pitch, stress, volume, inflection, rhythm, and pronunciation.

parallel adjectives   Adjectives that are of equal importance to the noun they modify.

parallel construction   A grammatical concept that requires each part of a series to be of the same grammatical construction.

passive voice   The form of a verb that shows the subject being acted upon.

personal pronoun   A pronoun that takes the place of a person's name.

phrase   A group of related words used as a single part of speech. A phrase does not contain a subject and a verb.

positive degree   The simple form of an adjective used when no comparison is being made.

possessive case pronoun   The form of a pronoun used to show ownership.

predicate adjective   An adjective that follows a linking verb and describes the subject.

predicate nominative   A pronoun or noun that renames the subject and follows a form of the verb "to be."

predicate noun   A noun following a linking verb that renames the subject.

predicate pronoun   A pronoun that follows a linking verb and renames the subject.

preposition   A word used to show the relationship between a noun, a pronoun, or a phrase or clause used as a noun and another word in the sentence.

printer   A device used for printing the final copy of a document.

probability sampling   A sampling technique in which every member of the group to be sampled has an equal chance of being selected as a participant in the study; considered the most reliable survey method for this reason.

production stage   The second stage of the document cycle; the point at which the document is prepared in its final form.

random sampling   See *probability sampling.*

receiver   The person or machine to whom a message is sent.

relative pronoun   A pronoun such as *who, which,* or *that* used to introduce a dependent clause.

report   A document that provides meaningful information to a group of people.

reproduction stage   The stage of the document cycle that includes making copies of a document.

reprographics   The process of reproducing copies using photocopiers or duplicating equipment.

restrictive clause An adjective clause that is necessary to identify the person, place, or thing being described.

resume A document that summarizes an applicant's qualifications for employment; sometimes referred to as a data sheet or vita.

run-on sentence A sentence that contains two or more independent clauses joined without the correct punctuation or without the appropriate conjunction.

sales report A report in which the writer provides a summary of the sales over a specific period of time.

scanner A machine that converts typewritten text into digital form.

screen The part of an electronic workstation that displays a document as it is keyed.

sender A person or machine that originates a message or initiates the communication process.

simple sentence A sentence that contains one independent clause.

soft sale An attempt to sell a product or service using a relaxed approach.

solicited letter of application A letter of application written for a specific job opening.

storage device The part of a computer that records and stores information; the storage device may be internal (hard disk drive) or external (floppy disks).

storage/retrieval stage The last stage in the document cycle; a copy of the document is filed for reference or for further distribution.

subject A noun or pronoun that indicates what the sentence is about.

subject complement A noun, pronoun, or adjective that follows a linking verb and complements or describes the subject.

subjunctive mood The mood of a verb used to express an idea contrary to fact or to express a demand, desire, or recommendation.

subordinate conjunction A conjunction used to join a dependent clause to an independent clause.

superlative degree The form of an adjective or adverb used to compare three or more things; formed by adding *est*, *least*, or *most* to the positive form.

supporting information Facts, examples, or reasons that support the main idea of a message.

survey A means of obtaining people's opinions on a subject through a series of carefully constructed questions.

table of contents An outline of the sections of a report and their corresponding page numbers.

teleconferencing A meeting of two or more people in different locations by means of telephone or other electronic media.

tense The form of a verb that shows time of the action or state expressed by the verb.

textual presentation A presentation in which the presenter reads from a written copy.

title page A prefatory part of a formal report that contains the title of the report; the name, title, and organization of the person for whom the report was written; the name, title, and organization of the writer; and the date of the report.

tone   The manner of expression that reflects the writer's attitude toward the subject and/or the receiver.

transitive verb   A verb that passes its action along to an object.

unsolicited letter of application   A letter of application for a position that has not been advertised and that may or may not be available.

verb phrase   See *phrase*.

verbal symbols   The words used when writing or speaking.

vita   Another term for resume.

voice mail   A mail system in which the sender dictates the message into a telephone and the message is stored in a computer system until the receiver retrieves it.

"you" oriented   An approach to writing that focuses on the needs and wants of the receiver.

APPENDIX D

Answers to Checkpoints

CHAPTER 2

 Checkpoint 1 ORIGINATION AND PRODUCTION

1. h
2. e
3. d
4. a

5. b
6. c
7. f
8. g

Checkpoint 2 REPRODUCTION, DISTRIBUTION, AND STORAGE

1. e
2. h
3. g
4. f
5. a

6. d
7. i
8. c
9. b
10. j

CHAPTER 3

 Checkpoint 1 FORMING PLURALS

1. volumes
2. wishes
3. cities
4. commandos
5. cafes
6. halves
7. criteria
8. trademarks
9. sons-in-law
10. news
11. hives

12. audiences
13. businesses
14. raspberries
15. trios
16. knives
17. thieves
18. moose
19. data
20. icebergs
21. fathers-in-law
22. tables

23. classes
24. dramas
25. heroes
26. moneys
27. tornadoes
28. wives
29. calves

30. children
31. bases
32. mothers-in-law
33. post offices
34. councils
35. mice

Checkpoint 2 FORMING POSSESSIVES

Singular Possessive
1. Johnson's
2. city's
3. alto's
4. datum's
5. mouse's
6. executive's
7. brother-in-law's
8. dictionary's
9. deer's
10. knife's

Plural Possessive
1. Johnsons'
2. cities'
3. altos'
4. data's
5. mice's
6. executives'
7. brothers-in-law's
8. dictionaries'
9. deer's
10. knives'

CHAPTER 4

 Checkpoint 1 VERB TENSES

Corrections are in bold.

1. She slammed down the receiver and then **stormed** out of the office. (Avoid unnecessary changing of tenses.)

2. Don Wright **had been** with Temp four years when he was promoted to office manager. (Here it is necessary to change tenses; use the past perfect to show an

action completed before another past action.)

3. C

4. C

5. By 5 p.m. Friday, Johnson **will have completed** a full 40 hours of work. (Use future perfect to indicate an action that will be finished by a certain time in the future.)

Checkpoint 2   ACTIVE AND PASSIVE VOICE

1. To reduce stress, employees should take vacations.

2. C

3. The accountant helped Mr. Carson with his problem.

4. C

5. Dr. Paulson gave the speech.

Checkpoint 3   MISUSED VERBS

1. set

2. lie

3. raised

4. May

5. would

CHAPTER 5

Checkpoint 1   SINGULAR AND PLURAL SUBJECTS

Subject	Verb Choices
1. memorandum	indicates
2. cafes	are
3. fathers-in-law	neither
4. class	either
5. moose	either
6. criterion	restricts
7. tenor	has sung
8. wishes	come
9. executive	works
10. knife	is

Checkpoint 2   COMPOUND SUBJECTS

Corrections are in bold.

1. Alisa and William **are** to be at the sales meeting.

2. C

3. Every executive and secretary **is** to attend the conference.

4. Neither Jean nor the other managers **are** happy about the decision.

5. C

6. When they **were** asking for the data, Juan and Neil **were** checking the content of the report.

7. Either the men or Margaret **was** to complete the form.

8. C

Checkpoint 3   COLLECTIVE NOUNS AND INTERVENING MODIFIERS

1. likes

2. neither

3. are

4. was

5. either

CHAPTER 6

Checkpoint 1   SELECTING PRONOUN CASES

1. I   6. Your, our

2. he   7. he

3. your   8. her, my

4. It's; theirs   9. her, their

5. I; he   10. It's, whose

Checkpoint 2   SELECTING CORRECT PRONOUNS

1. him   3. himself

2. me   4. whom

5. who
6. whom
7. me
8. whoever
9. him
10. whom

10. The administrator **who** [or **that**] presided over the meeting was an eloquent speaker.

CHAPTER 7

 Checkpoint 1 PRONOUN-ANTECEDENT AGREEMENT

1. she — executive
2. they — William Wilson, Mrs. Phillips
3. they — managers
4. I — Jeff Clark
5. his or her — engineer
6. their — workers
7. his or her — Each
8. their — Others
9. their — Some ... players
10. its — faculty

Checkpoint 2 PRONOUN REFERENCE

Corrections are in bold.

1. C
2. Listening to Mr. Callens speak was inspiring. That **speech** made everyone feel much better.
3. Tanya told Clarise that **Clarise** should attend class.
4. The statement was issued last week. This **action** satisfied everyone.
5. Mrs. Ruiz told Miss Gray, "I will be able to travel to Europe this summer."
6. Because of the lack of equipment, neither John nor the men will have **their** jobs completed on schedule.
7. C
8. Even though you may not approve of the time set for the presentation, **you have** to be happy with the opportunity to give it.
9. When one has to do a job, seldom is **one** happy about it.

CHAPTER 8

 Checkpoint 1 IDENTIFYING MODIFIERS

In the following sentences, each adjective is italicized and each adverb appears in bold.

1. *The secretarial* field presents *a* **tremendously** *complex* challenge for *the 21st* century.
2. If *a* word is **mistakenly** typed, *the spelling* checker will highlight *the* error.
3. It is **extremely** *rare* to find *two* individuals in *any* office who are **exactly** *the same* height, weight, and proportion.
4. We **recently** bought *a new computer* system for *our* office.
5. Place *the 30 ergonomic* chairs **there**.

Checkpoint 2 SELECTING MODIFIERS

1. cheerful
2. quickly
3. Five
4. surprisingly
5. efficient

Checkpoint 3 PLACING MODIFIERS

Corrections are in bold.

1. Any business package **under 70 pounds** shipped during the normal business hours will arrive the same day.
2. **Only** the new Syntax 500 office copier gives you the same features as a more expensive copier.
3. C
4. C
5. Stepping into the new office, **you see** 50 electronic typewriters.

Checkpoint 4 COMPARING
MODIFIERS

1. better
2. more economical
3. fastest
4. most intelligent
5. most efficiently

Checkpoint 5 USING MODIFIERS

1. surely, well
2. Those, those kinds
3. almost, fewer
4. bad, badly
5. really good, well

CHAPTER 9

 Checkpoint 1 PREPOSITIONAL
PHRASES

In each of the following sentences, the prepositional phrases are italicized and the words modified appear in bold.

1. The phone **is ringing** *with that important call* and you **have** just **gone** *on break.*
2. **Select** a planning calendar *from our catalog* **located** *in the stock room.*
3. **Happily** *for our stockholders,* we made a profit this quarter.
4. **One** *of my favorite cartoons* shows a secretary **suggesting** *to her boss* that they throw out old files.
5. **Write** *for the free booklet* "How to Maintain **Records** *for Government Offices.*"

Checkpoint 2 PROBLEM
PREPOSITIONS

1. Like, as
2. into, in
3. Besides, beside

4. among, between
5. from

Checkpoint 3 CONJUNCTIONS

Solutions are in bold.

1. We have a wide variety of word processors **and** computers in our organization.
2. I will not be able to go to the circus **because** [or **since**] I have to work late.
3. We plan **not only** to go to dinner **but also** to see a movie.
4. **When** the paint dries, we will move the furniture back into the office.
5. Dr. Cortez plans to attend the conference, **but** Dr. James will not be able to attend.

Checkpoint 4 INTERJECTIONS

1. Help!
2. Well
3. Gee
4. Yes
5. Ouch!

CHAPTER 10

 Checkpoint 1 PHRASES

1. Adjective
2. Noun
3. Verb
4. Adverb
5. Noun

Checkpoint 2 PHRASES AND
CLAUSES

1. Independent clause
2. Phrase
3. Dependent clause
4. Dependent clause
5. Phrase

Checkpoint 3 DEPENDENT CLAUSES

The dependent clauses are in bold.

1. Adverb **When you use the new Alpha filing system,** you reduce misfiles.
2. Noun Tough performance is **what you demand** from office copiers.
3. Adj./R Eisen's Office Supply provides business forms **that meet our needs.**
4. Noun Everyone knows **that inflation is decreasing.**
5. Adj./N My Siamese cat, **which is three years old,** likes to chase birds.

Checkpoint 4 SENTENCES AND PUNCTUATION

The end punctuation appears in bold.

1. Command/request Mail the coupon or call our toll-free number**.**
2. Statement You can print one document while you work on another**.**
3. Statement The first plain paper copier that doesn't come at a premium is sold by Excel**.**
4. Exclamation Wonderful news — Pat won first place in the state Phi Beta Lambda competition**!**
5. Command/request Will you please order supplies for your department**.**
6. Question What supplies did you order for your department**?**

Checkpoint 5 SENTENCE STRUCTURE

The dependent clauses are italicized.

1. Compound Her approach is colorful, and she has made all of us think about the importance of organization.
2. Simple Combining a number of special conveniences, these grills are designed to cook steaks, chops, and burgers.

3. Complex *Since companies try to put their best foot forward in their annual reports,* you have to search through the glossy photos to find important information.
4. Compound-complex *When she started her flower-importing business,* she had no marketing strategy, but she quickly put one together.
5. Compound Hawaii has many treasures, but its greatest one is its beaches.

Checkpoint 6 COHERENT CONSTRUCTION

Corrections are in bold.

1. If you're dissatisfied with the lower rates currently available on many investments, **you should shop around among financial institutions.**
2. At 26, she's already exactly where she wants to be, professionally and **personally**.
3. This performance **is** made possible by Autolife.
4. Kazuko spent most of his vacation in England; **however**, he returned to the United States for a family reunion on July 4.
5. Appleby says many companies are requesting these names and **using them** to send invitations to the annual meeting.

CHAPTER 11

 ### Checkpoint 1 SERIES AND INTRODUCTORY ELEMENTS

Corrections are in bold.

1. Stocks, bonds, and T-bills were among the investment options discussed at the financial planning seminar.

2. While waiting for the bus, she spoke with Kelli about the vacant position.

3. To obtain the information, it was necessary to recall the document file.

4. C

5. Incidentally, there will be a large Christmas bonus this year.

6. C

7. C

8. Applications software will be made available for word processing, desktop publishing, spreadsheets, and database management.

Checkpoint 2 NONESSENTIAL ELEMENTS

Corrections are in bold.

1. Jeanne indicated, nevertheless, that she will run in the track meet.

2. The bill, as you can well imagine, is now overdue.

3. When visiting the Information Management Department, see Ms. Hopkins, the department's supervisor.

4. Mr. Eli Johnson, the new secretary/treasurer, will attend the meeting and represent us.

5. Dale Murphy, who plays for the Atlanta Braves, was the National League's Most Valuable Player in 1983.

6. C

7. C

8. Postage prices are being driven up by the Postal Service's labor costs, which account for 85 percent of its expenditures.

Checkpoint 3 ADDITIONAL COMMAS

Corrections are in bold.

1. The hard-working, contented subordinate complimented her supervisor by telling him that he was competent.

2. The bank gives low-cost, low-interest loans.

3. We went to the movies last night, and we saw an outstanding film.

4. C

5. C

6. Julie Johnson, M.D., is the floor supervisor on the fifth floor of the hospital.

7. Please review my analysis by Monday, August 10; send your revisions directly to me.

8. Turk now lives at 4592 Yearly Drive, Visalia, California, a garden spot in the state.

CHAPTER 12

 ## Checkpoint 1 SEMICOLONS AND COLONS

Corrections are in bold.

1. Art collectors might rejoice at this news: A computer data bank now lists all major works.

2. We have scheduled regional meetings on the following dates: October 8, 1988, in Charleston, South Carolina; October 15, 1988, in Atlanta, Georgia; and October 20, 1988, in Knoxville, Tennessee.

3. She gets up at 5:30 a.m.; she has to be at work by 7:00.

4. Everyone who drives should have automobile insurance; furthermore, every driver should have adequate liability coverage.

5. Our office now has a great deal of automated equipment: for instance, electronic typewriters, microcomputers, and word processors.

6. In the article on real estate, the author stated: "Middle-class, single-family homes are the best investment."

Checkpoint 2 THE UNDERSCORE
AND QUOTATION
MARKS

Corrections are in bold.

1. Some of the respondents answered no to several questions in the survey entitled "Computer Skills for the Future."

2. The July issue of <u>Changing Times</u> describes new kinds of mortgages, including "stripped" mortgages.

3. Writers sometimes confuse the words <u>accept</u> and <u>except</u>.

4. "When buying a new house," she said, "be sure to shop around for a mortgage."

5. Chapter 28, " Job Interview and Follow-up Messages," from the text <u>Fundamentals of Business Communication</u>, helped prepare me for job interviews.

Checkpoint 3 APOSTROPHES AND
HYPHENS

Corrections are in bold.

1. Our company's mailroom staff uses up-to-date equipment.

2. One-third of the executives don't need to attend seminars on self-motivation.

3. Twenty-five students plan to run for student-council offices.

4. His application letter shouldn't contain so many I's.

5. Chris has applied for a high-level position with the firm.

Checkpoint 4 DASHES AND
PARENTHESES

Corrections are in bold.

1. One of the first—and often the only—contacts the public has with an organization is by telephone.

2. Results of the survey indicate that more than half (67 percent) of the people interviewed—and that is a large percentage—favored Lynn for school superintendent.

3. Frequent overtime is one of the drawbacks to this job—but you would rather talk about benefits, I'm sure.

4. Be sure you know the components of a computer system—the monitor, keyboard, CPU (central processing unit), and disk drives.

5. In the telephone directory (the white pages) you can locate information by (1) company names, (2) government listings, and (3) individuals' names.

CHAPTER 13

 Checkpoint 1 ABBREVIATIONS

Corrections are in bold.

1. **Dr.** Stanley White visits his patients on **Tuesday** and **Wednesday** mornings beginning at 8 a.m.

2. The meeting was held at the Dexter **Street YMCA** on **November** 4.

3. Send my mail to the following address:

   Mr. Fred Blum **Jr.** [or comma before **Jr.**]
   Blum & Smith, Inc.
   522 State **Street** NW
   Boulder, **CO** 80322-3621

4. He was driving 80 **miles per hour** when stopped by the **state** patrol last Friday in Cleveland, **Ohio**.

Checkpoint 2 CAPITALIZATION

Corrections are in bold.

1. **S**am, **D**r. **P**arker, and **I** drove south to reach **C**ape **C**od, located in eastern **M**assachusetts.

2. **T**he **O**ffice **A**dministration **D**epartment of **B**ridgeport **J**unior **C**ollege purchased ten new **B**rother typewriters, **M**odel No. **EM**-811.

3. **A**s a member of the **A**ssociation of **I**nformation **S**ystems **P**rofessionals, **G**wen **C**lark (president of the **M**iami chapter) receives *Words* magazine.

4. During fall quarter **G**overnor **A**ndrews will visit the **N**orth **C**ampus of our school; he was unable to visit last spring.

5. **B**oth of my parents believe in **G**od; however, my father is a **B**aptist, while **M**other is a member of the **P**resbyterian **C**hurch.

6. **T**he author of *Traveling Through America* stated: "**T**he **A**rkansas and **M**issouri rivers both flow into the **M**ississippi **R**iver."

Checkpoint 3   NUMBER EXPRESSION

Corrections are in bold.

1. The new **five**-story building, which houses **120,000** square feet of office space, was first planned **20** years ago.

2. In our **Seventh Avenue** office, approximately **thirty** dictation machines are available for work groups of **2** to 15 managers.

3. **Seventeen** people from our office, located at **62** Mason Street, caught the 5:50 p.m. train to Washington.

4. Over **two-thirds** of the staff will attend the luncheon on April **3** at a cost of **$350** to the company.

5. According to page **6** of the annual report, in our **twelfth** year of operation, profits are down by **4** percent in the second quarter.

6. Anna Powers, 42, will move **60** miles to her new job, which begins on the 5th of November.

7. At our **41st** Street office, our staff is housed in 14 **twelve-room** suites.

CHAPTER 14

Checkpoint 1   "YOU" ORIENTED

This memorandum is offensive to Mrs. Powell for these reasons:

1. It has taken Mr. Wessels over a month to write this very short, simple memorandum. Such a delay says to Mrs. Powell that she is unimportant.

2. The clause "I give you my permission" is offensive because it implies that Mr. Wessels views himself as more important than Mrs. Powell.

3. "Your claim" has a negative impact because it implies that the sender questions Mrs. Powell's description of the chair.

4. The instruction to buy a "cheap" chair is inconsiderate and offensive. It implies that the receiver's comfort is not as important as money.

5. "Boy! What a family!" is insensitive to people with large families.

6. The comment about the Powells' household budget is also inappropriate.

Checkpoint 2   POSITIVE, PROMPT, AND GENDER-FREE LANGUAGE

Revisions may vary.

1. Of the 75 items on the test, Marian had 65 of them correct.

2. To renew your policy, please send us a check for the amount of the premium.

3. When our supply of item #3895-a is replenished, your order for two dozen ribbons will be sent.

4. The sales representatives [or salespersons] will meet at the home office next week.

5. If you will send us the sizes you need, we will send your jeans and shirt.

CHAPTER 15

Checkpoint 1   CONCISE MESSAGES

1. Customers who place their orders by November 30 will receive a gift.
2. Please send me additional information about the new employee benefit package.
3. Dr. Jansen presented only relevant information. He omitted the extraneous.
4. The report is too short.
5. Many people have become workaholics.

Checkpoint 2   CLEAR SYMBOLS

1. Topek motor scooters get 95 miles to the gallon.
2. Even though it has several new lights on it, the front of the old building has disintegrated badly.
3. As you requested, I was able to complete the report on the microcomputer.
4. The diskette will be sent to you in a separate package.
5. He is slender but strong.

Checkpoint 3   CORRECT GRAMMAR AND PARALLEL STRUCTURE

Corrections are in bold.

1. To get a good job, **one should present** a crisp, well-polished image.
2. Anyone can enter **his or her** paintings in the contest.
3. Because he was out of town last week, **he had lots of unopened mail.**
4. The new employee is efficient, accurate, and **hard-working.**

5. The meeting will be held in the first floor conference room, **in** the company library, or in Mr. Fletcher's office.

or

The meeting will be held in the first floor conference room, the company library, or Mr. Fletcher's office.

Checkpoint 4   COMPLETE MESSAGES

Changes are in bold.

>   TO: Matthew Avenel
>   FROM: Project Team
>   DATE: March 29, 19--
> SUBJECT: System Selection Meeting

On Tuesday, **May 5,** we will have a meeting **in Conference Room D on the third floor at 10:00 a.m. The purpose of the meeting is** to refine policies for selecting our new computer system and software for text processing and electronic mail. Be sure to have everyone in your department complete the survey forms prior to the meeting. **Bring the survey forms to the meeting so that they can be tabulated.**

By adding "May 5" and "in Conference Room D on the third floor at 10:00 a.m." the when and where are answered. A last sentence may be added to clarify what the team is to do with the survey forms.

CHAPTER 16

Checkpoint 1   PLANNING THE MESSAGE

1. Yes, I am available to speak at your meeting on the 23rd; thank you for the invitation.
2. For each new item, please provide the release date, the packaging requirements, and the units available.
3. I will be most happy to pick you up at the airport at 5:30 on the 16th.

Checkpoint 2   ORGANIZING THE
MESSAGE

1. Direct
2. Indirect
3. Direct
4. Direct

Checkpoint 3   COHERENCE

Corrections are in bold.

1. He saw the information in an article in
   America Today; so as soon as he got to
   work he **called** his supervisor.
2. Upon seeing the opportunity, the investor sold her 500 shares of common stock
   and **made** $50,000.
3. Dick was unhappy with his sales for
   the month, **but** his supervisor thought
   Dick had done well.
4. **Because** Alex's sales totaled 300 percent of his monthly sales quota, he
   received the Salesperson of the Month
   award.
5. The university has an excellent academic reputation, but **we must raise**
   thousands of dollars of private funds
   each year to support it.

Checkpoint 4   EMPHASIS AND
VARIETY

Revisions will vary.

Our spring sale illustrates a problem we
often have during large sales—getting
behind in alterations. During sales, our
suits are marked down 40 to 60 percent;
thus, demand increases greatly. The customers, however, still want their suits
altered in the normal turnaround time,
which is two days. The solution to this
problem is twofold: During a sale, (1) hire
additional help for the Alterations Department and (2) charge for alterations to help
pay for the additional help.

CHAPTER 17

 Checkpoint 1   FORMATTING
MEMOS

1. Correct
2. Incorrect
3. Correct
4. Correct
5. Incorrect

Checkpoint 2   FORMATTING
LETTERS

1. a. Complimentary close
   b. Dateline
   c. Enclosure notation
   d. Salutation
   e. Copy notation
2. All lines begin at the left margin.
3. The dateline, complimentary close,
   and typed signature line begin at the
   center.
   All other lines begin at the left margin.
4. The dateline is placed on line 12.
   The letter address may be keyed using
   the U.S. Postal Service guidelines.
   The salutation and complimentary
   close are omitted.
   A subject line is included, beginning
   a double space below the letter
   address.
   All lines begin at the left margin.
   The writer's name and signature line
   may be typed in all capital letters or
   uppercase and lowercase, whichever
   is preferred.
   Standard margins are used.

CHAPTER 18

 Checkpoint 1   MAIN IDEA

1. Poor. Does not tell the receiver that the
   requested information is enclosed.

2. Poor. Does not tell the receiver that the requested information is enclosed.

3. Good

4. Poor. Does not tell the receiver that the requested information is enclosed.

5. Good

Checkpoint 2   GOODWILL CLOSING

1. Poor. Is not helpful to the receiver.

2. Good

3. Good

4. Poor. Typical, overused ending. Does nothing to build or maintain goodwill.

5. Poor. Does nothing to build or maintain goodwill.

CHAPTER 19

Checkpoint 1   NEUTRAL OPENINGS

1. Good

2. Poor. Reveals the negative answer.

3. Poor. Does not reveal the topic of the letter.

4. Poor. Might mislead the receiver into thinking he or she will receive what he or she requested.

5. Poor. Does not reveal the topic of the letter.

6. Good

7. Poor. Reveals the negative answer.

8. Poor. Could mislead the receiver into thinking that the response will be positive when it is going to be negative.

Checkpoint 2   REASONS FOR THE BAD NEWS

1. Poor. Is sender oriented rather than receiver oriented.

2. Poor. Hides behind company policy and reveals the answer to the request.

3. Good

4. Poor. Not receiver oriented and reveals the answer to the request.

5. Good

Checkpoint 3   THE BAD NEWS

1. Poor. Uses negative language.

2. Good

3. Poor. Uses negative language.

4. Good

5. Good

Checkpoint 4   ENDINGS

1. Good

2. Poor. Using the word "hope" is weak and insincere in this context.

3. Poor. Should not contain an apology.

4. Good

5. Good

CHAPTER 20

Checkpoint 1   ATTENTION-GETTING OPENINGS

1. Good

2. Poor. Does not introduce the main idea.

3. Poor. Insincere.

4. Good

5. Good

Checkpoint 2   SUPPORTING INFORMATION

1. Good

2. Good

3. Poor. Insincere tone.

4. Good
5. Poor. Insincere tone—exaggerates benefits.

Checkpoint 3   ACTION ENDINGS

1. Poor. Sender is making it difficult for the receiver.
2. Good
3. Poor. Insincere tone.
4. Good
5. Poor. Exaggerates and has a negative tone.

CHAPTER 21

Checkpoint 1   DEVELOPING A REPORT

1.	False	4.	False
2.	True	5.	True
3.	True	6.	False

Checkpoint 2   COLLECTING DATA

1.	False	5.	True
2.	True	6.	False
3.	False	7.	True
4.	True	8.	False

CHAPTER 22

Checkpoint 1   ORGANIZING INFORMAL REPORTS

1. False
2. True
3. True
4. True
5. False

Checkpoint 2   WRITING INFORMAL AND FORMAL REPORTS

1. True
2. True
3. True
4. False
5. False

Checkpoint 3   VISUAL AIDS

1. True
2. True
3. False
4. False
5. True

CHAPTER 25

Checkpoint 1   SHORT ORAL COMMUNICATION

1. True
2. False
3. True
4. False
5. False

Checkpoint 2   PREPARING FORMAL ORAL PRESENTATIONS

1. False
2. True
3. False
4. True
5. True

Checkpoint 3   DELIVERY

1. True
2. False

3. True
4. False
5. True

CHAPTER 26

 Checkpoint 1 ANALYZING SELF
AND JOB MARKET

1. True
2. False. Your special talents and abilities may not show up in the education or work experience section of your resume.
3. True
4. False
5. True

Checkpoint 2 WRITING THE
RESUME

1. One page in length (no more than two)
Complete but not wordy
Sentence fragments rather than complete sentences
Clear, sharp type
Adequate margins (1-inch minimum)
Boldface, underlining, or capitalizing used for emphasis
Error-free (correct spelling, punctuation, and grammar) with no noticeable corrections
2. Heading
Job objective
Special qualifications
Education
Work experience
Activities/interests/achievements
References
3. A general resume stays the same for all prospective employers. A specific resume is written for a specific employer (usually the heading, job objective, and work experience sections are changed).

4. By date, by employer name, by job title, and by achievements or skills attained.
5. Not only is it illegal for employers to ask for this information, but this information is also not usually relevant to your qualifications and takes up valuable space you could use for more important items.

CHAPTER 27

 Checkpoint 1 OPENING
PARAGRAPH

1. Weak
2. Weak
3. Effective
4. Weak
5. Effective

Checkpoint 2 MIDDLE
PARAGRAPHS

1. Weak
2. Effective
3. Effective
4. Weak
5. Effective

Checkpoint 3 CLOSING
PARAGRAPH

1. Effective
2. Weak
3. Effective
4. Effective
5. Weak

CHAPTER 28

 Checkpoint 1 PREPARING FOR
THE INTERVIEW

1. True
2. False
3. False
4. True
5. False

Checkpoint 2 THE INTERVIEW
AND FOLLOW-UP

1. True
2. True
3. False
4. False
5. False

INDEX

dash, 160–161
at end of sentence, 129–130
hyphen, 159
mixed, in letters, 240
open, in letters, 240
parentheses, 161–162
quotation marks, 156–157
semicolon, 153–154
underscore, 156
Purchase order, 261–262

Q

Qualifications, analysis of, in job
search, 396–398
achievements, 398
education, 397–398
work experience, 397
Question, 130
Questions, for job interview,
432–433, 436–439
illegal, 437, 439
preparing, 432–433
on salary, 439
Quotation marks, 156–157

R

Reasons for bad news, in bad
news message, 275
Receiver, of message, 7
analysis of, 290
Recommendation, in report, 317
Redundant expressions, 200–201
Relative pronoun, 93–94
Remembering, in listening
process, 366–367
Repetition of key words, 222–223
Reports, 12, 306–318, 321–344
analytical. *See* Analytical
reports
external, 325
formal. *See* Formal reports
formats of, 307, 324–329,
332–339
informal. *See* Informal reports
informational. *See*
Informational reports
internal, 325
nature of, 306–307
purpose of, 306
sales, 306

scope of, 307
types of, 306–307
visual aids used in. *See* Visual
aids, used in reports
Reports, steps in planning,
307–317
analyzing data, 316
collecting data, 311–315
developing preliminary outline,
308–310
drawing conclusions, 317
identifying areas to be
investigated, 308
identifying problems, 307–308
making recommendations, 317
Reproduction stage, of document
cycle, 17, 32
Reprographics, 32
Requests
declining, 279–280
special, 297–298
Restrictive clause, 128, 145–146
Resume, 395–411
activities, interests,
achievements, 407–408
appearance of, 401–403
defined, 401
education, 405–406
heading, 404
job objective, 404
personal data, 409
references, 410
special qualifications, 405
work experience, 406, 407–409
Routine message, 258–260
checklist for, 265
claim, 260
request, 258–260
Run-on sentence, 134

S

Sales messages, 296–297
Scanners, 23
Scope, of report, 307
Screen, in electronic
workstation, 24
Secondary research, for report,
315
bibliography cards, 315, 316
note cards, 315, 316
Semicolon, 153–154
Sender, of message, 5–6

Sentence, 70, 125–136, 221–222
coherent, 133
complete, 133–134, 206
complex, 132
compound, 132
compound-complex, 132–133
run-on, 134
simple, 132
structures of. *See* Sentence
structures
topic, 221
types of, 130–131
unity of, 221–222
Sentence fragment, 133–134
use of, in resume, 403
Sentence structures, 125–136
clauses, 126–129
coherent construction in,
133–135
phrases, 125–126
Series, use of comma with, 143
Simple sentence, 132
Sincerity, 189
Singular subject, 70
Soft sale, 257
Software, applications. *See*
Applications software
Spacing, in formal reports, 332
Speaker, attitudes toward, 365
Special requests, 297–298
Spelling and usage of common
business terms, 443–448
Spreadsheets, 28
Statement, 130
States, abbreviations of, 168–169
Storage device, in electronic
workstation, 24
Storage/retrieval stage, of
document cycle, 17, 37–38
Subject
compound. *See* Compound
subject
defined, 70
plural, 71
singular, 70
Subject, and verb, agreement
of, 70–75
forms of *to be* and *to have*,
71–72
Subject complement, 57
Subjunctive mood, 62
used to soften negative
response, 192

PHOTO CREDITS

FRONT COLOR SECTION

Title Page   p. ii: Photographed with cooperation of Northern Kentucky University.

Preface   p. vi: IBM Corporation; p. vii: (left) IBM Corporation, (right) Xerox Corporation.

Contents   p. viii: IBM Corporation; p. xi: (left) Honeywell, Inc., (right) © Don Johnson, 1987/THE STOCK MARKET; p. xii: (right) Courtesy of Hawaii Visitors Bureau; p. xiii: (left) IBM Corporation, (right) HUD photo.

MAIN TEXT

Chapter 1   p. 2: © 1988 Arnold Zann/Black Star.

Chapter 2   p. 16: © Pierre Kopp/WEST LIGHT; p. 19: Photo Courtesy of NCR Corporation; pp. 20, 21, 22: Dictaphone Corporation, Rye, New York; p. 23: DEST Corporation; pp. 30, 34: Xerox Corporation; p. 35: Western Union Corporation; p. 36: NEC Showroom (C & C Plaza) in Tokyo, Japan.

Chapter 3   p. 44: University of Cincinnati.

Chapter 5   p. 69: © Janice Fullman/THE PICTURE CUBE.

Chapter 7   p. 89: University of Cincinnati.

Chapter 9   p. 113: Jean L. Eggers/University of Cincinnati.

Chapter 10   p. 124: Printed with permission of Safeway Stores, Inc., © 1986.

Chapter 11   p. 142: © Susan Lapides, 1986/DESIGN CONCEPTIONS.

Chapter 12   p. 152: H. Armstrong Roberts.

Photo Credits